GENDER
IN THE THERAPY
HOUR

The Routledge Series on Counseling and Psychotherapy With Boys and Men

SERIES EDITOR
Mark S. Kiselica
The College of New Jersey

ADVISORY BOARD

Deryl Bailey
University of Georgia

Chris Blazina
Tennessee State University

J. Manuel Casas
University of California–Santa Barbara

Matt Englar-Carlson
California State University–Fullerton

Ann Fischer
Southern Illinois University–Carbondale

David Lisak
University of Massachusetts–Boston

William M. Liu
University of Iowa

James O'Neil
University of Connecticut

Steve Wester
University of Wisconsin–Milwaukee

VOLUMES IN THIS SERIES

FORTHCOMING

GENDER
IN THE THERAPY
HOUR

Voices of Female Clinicians
Working with Men

Edited by
Holly Barlow Sweet

Routledge
Taylor & Francis Group
New York   London

Routledge
Taylor & Francis Group
711 Third Avenue
New York, NY 10017

Routledge
Taylor & Francis Group
27 Church Road
Hove, East Sussex BN3 2FA

© 2012 by Taylor & Francis Group, LLC
Routledge is an imprint of Taylor & Francis Group, an Informa business

Printed in the United States of America on acid-free paper
Version Date: 20120120

International Standard Book Number: 978-0-415-88551-5 (Hardback) 978-0-415-88552-2 (Paperback)

Library of Congress Cataloging-in-Publication Data

Gender in the therapy hour : voices of female clinicians working with men /
   [edited by] Holly Barlow Sweet.
      p. cm.
   Includes bibliographical references and index.
   ISBN 978-0-415-88551-5 (hardback) -- ISBN 978-0-415-88552-2 (paperback)
   1. Women psychiatrists. 2. Men--Mental health. 3. Psychotherapist and patient. I. Sweet, Holly Barlow.

   RC440.82.G46 2012
   616.89--dc23   2011038059

Visit the Taylor & Francis Web site at
http://www.taylorandfrancis.com

and the Routledge Web site at
http://www.routledgementalhealth.com

Contents

Series Editor's Foreword

Throughout my career, numerous women colleagues have told me they are mystified about how to work with boys and men in therapy, finding males to be either unwilling to participate in therapy or difficult to engage in a therapeutic process. This has been an especially common concern among the women graduate students in counseling I have taught since I became an academician 21 years ago. Time and time again, my women students have reported to me that they have experienced difficulty relating to male clients, were frightened by men's anger, and were unsure about how to help men address their reluctance to seek help when they are in distress.

Partially in response to these concerns, I developed a graduate course, Counseling Boys and Men, which I have taught once a year since Spring 2007 at The College of New Jersey. When I designed the course, I decided to include a wonderful book chapter as a required reading for the class because it was focused on a woman's perspective about working with men in therapy. Written by Dr. Holly Sweet (2006), the chapter is titled, "Finding the Person Behind the Persona: Engaging Men as a Female Therapist." It was featured in *In the Room with Men: A Casebook of Therapeutic Change*, which was edited by Matt Englar-Carlson and Mark Stevens and is one of the finest books ever published about men in therapy. I wanted the students in my course, which typically has an enrollment of mostly or entirely women, to read Dr. Sweet's compassionate insights about the difficulties men can experience if they are subjected to a socialization process in which they are taught that men must be tough, hide their vulnerabilities, dominate others, work till they drop, and avoid any overt expressions of affection toward other men. I also felt that my students would benefit from reading Dr. Sweet's description of a variety of transference and countertransference issues that can occur when women therapists work with male clients, and her practical suggestions for how female clinicians can manage these issues and establish rapport with men, while empathizing with men's struggles. And my hunch that my students would value Dr. Sweet's chapter were correct: They loved it!

Because my students found the chapter to be very helpful to them in their work with male clients, I realized that Dr. Sweet's understanding of men and their troubles and her ideas for how to help them would be useful for other women, including women graduate students and professional practitioners, who work with men. I also felt that all mental health professionals, including those of us who are men, could benefit from hearing Dr. Sweet's voice and the voices of other women therapists who have worked successfully with men. So, I encouraged Dr. Sweet, a long-time colleague and friend whom I know through our mutual participation in the Society for the Psychological Study of Men and Masculinity: Division 51 of the American Psychological Association, to tap her extensive network of women colleagues to develop an edited book on women counseling men. Fortunately for all of us, Dr. Sweet agreed with my suggestion, reached out to her network, and received commitments from a team of fellow women professionals to produce *Gender in the Therapy Hour: Voices of Female Clinicians Working with Men*, an outstanding collaboration that is the latest addition to the *Routledge Series on Counseling and Psychotherapy with Boys and Men*.

Dr. Sweet and her colleagues have produced a very special book. The chapters contained in this volume cover a wide range of topics, including core treatment issues, modalities of treatment, and different populations and problems of men, each of which is explored through a gender-sensitive lens. Expressing a high degree of connected knowing— that is, knowledge gained by empathically understanding someone else's point of view (Belenky, Clinchy, Goldberger & Tarule, 1986/1997)— the authors describe their very personal experiences with boys and men and then explain how, as women mental health professionals, they have come to understand and help men through counseling and psychotherapy. Their stories are gripping and informative for any female therapist who wants to know more about what it is like to work with male clients and how to empathize, connect, and intervene with men in an effective manner. Although the book is geared toward an audience of women professionals and students, the authors' experiences are also instructive for both novice and veteran male practitioners who want a better understanding of the challenges their women colleagues face when working with men. Male clinicians will also benefit from the authors' practical suggestions for doing male-friendly therapy with men. Thus, this book offers valuable lessons for every mental health professional who works with men or wants to learn more about doing so.

Two other features of this book should be noted. First, toward the end of this book, the authors demonstrate a strong collaborative approach to teaching and learning by "joining with other voices in dialogue" (Tarule, 1996, p. 275) regarding their ideas about men's psyches and gender-aware therapy with men. Second, the book concludes with the voice of Dr. Fred Rabinowitz, a feminist man and national authority on psychotherapy with men, whose Afterword reflects on his experiences as a male in therapy with women practitioners, offers his thoughts about when it might be good for a male client to have a male therapist, and suggests ways that women therapists can help male clients.

I am grateful to Dr. Sweet and her colleagues for providing us and this series with *Gender in the Therapy Hour: Voices of Female Clinicians Working with Men*. All of us can learn a great deal from their empathy for men's experiences and the gender-sensitive manner in which they relate to men in therapy.

Mark S. Kiselica, Series Editor
*The Routledge Series on Counseling and Psychotherapy
with Boys and Men
The College of New Jersey*

REFERENCES

Belenky, M. F., Clinchy, B. M., Goldberger, N. R., & Tarule, J. M. (1986/1997). *Women's ways of knowing: the development of self, voice, and mind*. New York, NY: Basic Books.

Sweet, H. (2006). Finding the person behind the persona: Engaging men as a female therapist. In M. Englar-Carlson & M. Stevens (Eds.). *In the room with men: A casebook of therapeutic change* (pp. 69–90). Washington, DC: American Psychological Association.

Tarule, J. M. (1996). Voices in dialogue: Collaborative ways of knowing. In N. R. Goldberger, Tarule, J. M., Clinchy, B. M. & Belenky, M. F. (Eds.). *Knowledge, difference, and power: Essays inspired by Women's Ways of Knowing* (pp. 274–304). New York, NY: Basic Books.

Preface

WHY WAS THIS BOOK WRITTEN?

The idea for this book was a result of discussion among male and female psychologists in Division 51 of the American Psychological Association (APA), a division dedicated to studying the psychology of men and masculinity. These clinicians felt there was a need for more education about how to work best with male clients. In particular, they were interested in a book geared to female clinicians who were working, or would be working, with male clients yet felt that they did not have enough experience or knowledge to do so effectively. I was curious about the literature on this subject and searched for books written by women therapists for women therapists. I found almost nothing, except for Beth Erickson's book on *Helping Men Change* (1983). Almost all of the books that deal with counseling men were written by men. Like so many things in life, the most obvious is sometimes the most hidden. Since many clinicians are women and a growing number of clients are men, we thought there was a need to have a book written by women about counseling men.

In my own conversations with female graduate counseling students, I have been struck with how much they were interested in a book of this kind—one that would directly address the concerns of the female students about what it is like to work with men and what more experienced female clinicians have to say about the subject.

I knew what kinds of books have been useful to me in my training as a therapist. These were books that not only addressed the core topic but also discussed personal experience and how this had an impact on the author's professional development. I was interested in writing a book that I would like to read—one that contained autobiographical information, personal and professional experiences with men, and practical ideas from the author's own experience working with male clients. I also thought that it would be useful to end such a book sharing our experiences about what it is like to work with men, with women's voices together.

As the idea for this book grew, there was growing interest among the authors of the book in meeting in person for a retreat and having a conversation about our experiences before we actually started writing our chapters. It would be three things in one: a jump start to writing our chapters, a working vacation, and a chance to get to know each other on a personal level. We had several retreats during the course of creating this book. At each retreat, we talked about how we grew up, why we were interested in men's issues (especially for those us of who came of age in the 1970s when feminism was a compelling topic with great impact on both our personal and professional lives), and how we viewed doing therapy with men. It occurred to us that we were writing a book in a woman's way—collaborative and personal—and taking time to really get to know each other.

When some of us got together to wrap up our chapters, we realized we were onto something quite exciting, which we began to call *fourth-wave feminism*. This kind of feminism was about being inclusive of men and taking a compassionate approach to both genders. We were feminists, women who had reaped the benefits of the first three waves of feminism, but were also interested in true gender equality: Men and women who could strive to lead lives beyond the restrictions of their respective gender role norms.

WHO ARE WE?

The authors of this book range from those with a psychoanalytical approach to those who do coaching. No single approach is inherently better than others, although some approaches may work better for specific male clients. What is important, however, is the complex duality of not only believing in your approach, but also being open to trying new approaches so that the approach can be tailored to fit the client's needs. We gravitate to certain approaches because they have worked for us when we were clients, they fit our particular style of relating, we were trained in that approach, or we had mentors or supervisors who influenced us in a certain direction. Whatever style in which we have been trained, it is important to be open to learning about other styles of therapeutic techniques and approaches. This will not only give us an expanded repertoire of skills but also allows us to work with a greater variety of clients. This is particularly true in the case of male clients, who may respond differently to therapy than women would.

The authors' basic demographics such as age, race, sexual orientation, and ethnicity varied. Included are women in their 40s, 50s, and 60s. Some work in rural mental health settings, some in college settings; others are in private practice. Some authors are married, some are divorced, and some have never married. Some authors are straight; some are lesbians. Some have children; some do not. Some are Anglo-Americans; some are Hispanic. Some come from working-class backgrounds; some were born into wealthy families. Some come from traditional backgrounds and were housewives at 25; others were involved in feminist activities while still in high school. Some authors have only been therapists for a few years, some have been doing therapy for well over 40 years, but all are knowledgeable about men's issues as well as compassionate toward men.

Our personalities are also different: Some of us are outgoing, some are more introverted, some are very thorough, while others are more spontaneous. We have had different experiences with our dads: Some of us had fathers we adored who took an interest in us; others had detached or narcissistic fathers. Our experiences with romantic partners also vary considerably. Some have had boyfriends or husbands who were self-centered, even abusive; others are married to their first and only husband, with whom they have an egalitarian relationship. Some are married to or living with a man; some are in a primary relationship with a woman after being married to a man; and others are single. In the long run, none of this seems to matter. The important factor is that we have taken the time to explore how our own experiences with men affect our interactions with male clients.

As female therapists, our own feelings about men are important to explore. The authors of this book have taken the time to do this. We have had difficult male clients who remind us of men we have encountered in our personal lives, men who have put us down when we wanted respect, ignored us when we needed their attention, or abused us physically or emotionally when we needed their care. All of the authors have dealt with men in their lives who have disappointed or hurt them in some way. This is the stuff of real life and is also true of women in our lives who have failed us. All of the authors have grown up in cultures that had sexist overtones in many areas, including in academia and in the workplace. However, we have learned for the most part to view men in general, and our male clients in particular, with compassion and liking. We have learned to genuinely like most men. Our male clients know this and are better able to trust us. If you are reading this and do not really like or trust men, keep reading. It is hoped the authors' personal and professional journeys will resonate with you on some level. These journeys may give you hope that even though you have had various negative perceptions of and experiences with men in your life, you can move beyond those experiences to a genuine appreciation for men and their suffering.

Although the book is about the experiences of women therapists, I felt it was important to include the voice of a male therapist. The afterword is written by Fred Rabinowitz, a male psychologist who has written extensively about men and male-type depression and has been actively involved in Division 51 for many years. As a colleague and friend, I have learned much from Fred both personally and professionally. He represents a man who has gone through his own learning about what it means to be a man in a culture with restrictive gender roles and has gained the trust and respect of male and female colleagues, regardless of differences of opinion on professional issues.

THE STRUCTURE OF THE BOOK

The chapters in this book are divided into three main sections: core treatment issues (Chapters 1–4); different modalities of treatment (Chapters 5–7); and working with different pathologies and populations of men (Chapters 8–13). In Chapter 1, I discuss general treatment issues facing women therapists working with men, including specific challenges that male therapists might not have. In Chapter 2, June Martin examines the ways in which men enter and leave therapy with female clinicians and the lessons the author has learned about how to best handle these crucial aspects of treatment. Judith Logue looks at the practice of psychodynamic/psychoanalytic therapy in Chapter 3, with special attention paid to how transference and countertransference play out in male/female therapy dyads. Chapter 4 is written by Melba Vasquez, who is a leader in the field of ethics. She reviews ethical principles in general, as well as those that apply to women working with men.

Section 2 covers a range of different treatment modalities, including coaching, gender-aware therapy, couples counseling, and psychodynamic therapy. Roberta Nutt explores couples counseling from a gender-sensitive perspective in Chapter 5, including finding ways to avoid some of the pitfalls that female therapists may encounter. In Chapter 6, Terri Morse examines her experiences as a relatively new clinician about how she conducts gender-aware therapy with men, particularly with men with serious issues, such as substance abuse and sex offenses. Chapter 7 focuses on coaching, an alternative therapeutic modality that the author, Carolyn Steigmeier, believes may be easier for some men to utilize because it carries less stigma than "psychotherapy" and speaks in a language familiar to many men.

Section 3 examines doing therapy with different populations of men as well as helping men with different pathologies. Chapter 8, written by Cynthia de las Fuentes, explores working with men in the minority, including African American men, Latino men, and gay men. In Chapter 9, I examine the hidden nature of depression in men and how to work effectively with depressed men from a multimodality perspective. Dora Chase Oren focuses in Chapter 10 on how to work with men who are fathers and may not feel like "good dads" and discusses the value of a strength-based approach in working with men. Chapter 11, written by Michèle Harway, an expert in the field of domestic violence, explores how to take a more empathic approach in assessing men who may be abusive with their partners, working to protect their partners and also to get the men the help they need. Chapter 12 is written by Jeri Newlin (a clinician who has spent five years in the Marines) and explores how to work with men in the military who have trauma histories. In the final chapter of this section, Karen Wilbur addresses the special issues that older men may face, in particular how developmental issues for older men may differ from those of older women.

Chapter 14 consists of authors' responses to a set of questions that may not have been covered in their own chapters, as well as feedback on how authors view other authors' styles and chapters. This chapter also includes some responses by female therapists who are not authors in the book but are actively involved with men's studies.

For Chapters 2–13, each author was asked not only to discuss her core topic and case studies related to that topic but also to write about her own personal and professional journeys leading up to her interest in working with men. These journeys are as varied as our personalities and backgrounds, yet a common theme emerges: that of overcoming stereotypes and struggles to work successfully as a therapist. It is hoped these stories will inspire you, the reader, and reassure you that if you struggle at times, you are not alone.

ONE FINAL THOUGHT

We live in interesting times in which gender roles are shifting and changing. Women work and support their families; men stay home and are househusbands. Women serve in the military; men are nurses and elementary school teachers. Women can make the first move sexually; men can wait to be pursued. Yet, many of us still struggle with old notions of what it means to be male or female, and those notions are brought into our therapy offices, by both ourselves and our clients. It is important that we pay attention to those stereotypes because they may affect us more than we realize, and not always in helpful ways. As therapists, we have a responsibility to our male clients to be well informed about the pressures on them to be "manly" men. We also have a responsibility to be conscious of the ways in which we, as women, were socialized that might help or hinder the therapy process with men. It is my hope that this book will serve to help all therapists, but especially female therapists, understand more about what it is like to work with men and to appreciate men's struggles as they strive to lead more fulfilling and connected lives.

Holly Barlow Sweet

REFERENCE

Erickson, B. (1983). *Helping men change: The role of the female therapist.* Newbury Park, CA: Sage Publications.

About the Editor

Holly Barlow Sweet, PhD, is a psychologist in private practice in Brookline, Massachusetts, and holds a doctorate in counseling psychology from Boston College. She has over 20 years experience working with adolescents and adults. She is the co-founder of the Cambridge Center for Gender Relations, a consulting firm specializing in improving personal and professional relationships between women and men. She has presented on gender issues at national and international conferences. In 2005, she won the Practitioner of the Year award from Division 51 (Society for the Psychological Study of Men and Masculinity) of the American Psychological Association (APA) for her work in helping women understand more about men's issues. Dr. Sweet also teaches at the Massachusetts Institute of Technology and has offered a number of experientially focused seminars on psychology and gender issues over the past 30 years, including an award-winning seminar and peer training program in Sex Roles and Relationships.

About the Contributors

Cynthia de las Fuentes, PhD, is a psychologist in full-time private practice in Austin, Texas, where she enjoys applying theory and research with her clients. Dozens of presentations and publications are included in her areas of scholarship such as ethics in psychology, feminist psychology, and multicultural psychology. She is active in governance of the American Psychological Association (APA), for which she has served as president of Division 35 (Psychology of Women), been on the Board of Education Affairs, and is currently on the Committee for Women in Psychology. She also serves on the Board of Trustees of the Texas Psychological Association and advocates for issues related to psychology and social justice in the Texas legislature.

Michèle Harway, PhD, ABPP, is on the faculty of the School of Psychology at Fielding Graduate University. She was the founding chair of the Clinical Psychology Doctoral program at Antioch University in Santa Barbara, California. She also maintains a small private practice in Westlake Village, California, where she specializes in couples and family therapy and working with trauma survivors. She is board certified in couples and family psychology (American Board of Professional Psychology). Dr. Harway has authored or edited eleven books and many book chapters and journal articles and has presented at numerous professional conferences on couples therapy, cultural issues, domestic violence, trauma survival, and gender and family issues. Active in several divisions of APA, she is a fellow of four divisions, a former president of Division 43 (Family Psychology), former treasurer of Division 51 (Society for the Study of Men and Masculinity), and current representative to its Council of Representatives from Division 43.

Judith Felton Logue, PhD, is a practicing psychotherapist; supervising, training, and teaching psychoanalyst; licensed clinical social worker; and certified professional life and business coach in Princeton, New Jersey. Her practice is eclectic and integrative, emphasizing psychoanalytic psychotherapy, and including solution-focused and cognitive-behavioral (CBT) techniques, for individuals and couples. In addition to diplomates in forensic medicine and psychological specialties, she is on the board of the *Journal of the American College of Forensic Medicine*, Division 39 (Psychoanalysis) of APA, past president of Section III (Women and Gender) of APA Division 39, and on several committees and task forces of the American Psychoanalytic Association (APsaA). Dr. Logue has led numerous presentations and workshops and published book reviews and papers in psychology, social work, and psychoanalytic journals and newsletters on gender issues, narcissism, anxiety, sexual exclusivity, and family dynamics. She belongs to Divisions 35, 46 (Media Psychology), 39, and 51 of APA.

June Martin, PhD, is a licensed clinical psychologist; a licensed marriage and family therapist with a PhD in human sexuality; is board certified by the American Association of Sexuality Educators, Counselors, and Therapists; and has a neuropsychology certification from Fielding Graduate University. She has more than 22 years of clinical experience in sex therapy and psychotherapy, working with men, women, and children—individually, in couples, and in groups. She has worked in a variety of settings, including a psychiatric hospital, county outpatient clinics, outpatient drug and alcohol treatment centers, and a juvenile detention center, but most of her clinical interests and work with men continues to be in her private practice.

Terri Morse, LHMC, works at a community mental health agency in Essex County, New York. She also teaches groups at St. Joseph's Addiction Treatment and Recovery Center on a part-time basis and is working toward a credential in substance abuse counseling. Terri completed a master's degree in liberal studies (administration and leadership) at Plattsburgh State University in 2000 and a master's degree in clinical mental health counseling from Union Institute and University in 2008. She serves on the board of directors for the Mental Health Association in Essex County, for which she previously served as president. Terri is a member of Division 51 of APA.

Jeri Newlin is a doctoral candidate in counseling psychology at the University of Illinois at Urbana-Champaign. She is currently working at her predoctoral internship at Colorado State University Health Network's Counseling Services. She spent four years serving her country in the U.S. Marine Corps. During her graduate training, she provided therapy for the college population, community members of Champaign, and veterans. She is a member of Divisions 17 (Counseling Psychology) and 51 of APA.

Roberta L. Nutt, PhD, ABPP, is the training director of the counseling psychology doctoral program at the University of Houston. She is the former director of the counseling psychology program at Texas Woman's University and the former director of professional affairs of the Association of State and Provincial Psychology Boards. She has served as president of Division 17 of APA and Division 43 as well as on a variety of APA and APA-affiliated boards and committees. Her scholarship has focused on gender issues, feminist therapy/counseling, and training issues. She is a Fellow of APA, seven APA divisions, ASPPB, and a Diplomate of the American Board of Professional Psychology.

Dora Chase Oren, PhD, is a psychologist in private practice in Westlake Village, California. Dr. Oren received a PhD in clinical psychology from the California School of Professional Psychology–Los Angeles and a master's degree in developmental psychology from Columbia University. She has experience working in university counseling centers, community mental health, and private practice. She presents nationally and locally on issues concerning men and fathers. Dr. Oren coedited *Counseling Fathers* (Routledge, 2009), a book designed to bridge the gap between fathers and professional helpers. Currently, she is conducting a national exploratory survey about fathers and therapy. She also is a full-time mother and coparent of four amazing children.

Fredric E. Rabinowitz, PhD, is professor of psychology and the associate dean at the University of Redlands in California. Since 1984, his private psychology practice in Redlands has specialized in individual and group psychotherapy with men. Dr. Rabinowitz has coauthored numerous articles and books, including *Deepening Psychotherapy With Men* (APA, 2002), *Men and Depression: Clinical and Empirical Approaches* (Academic Press, 1999), and *Man Alive: A Primer of Men's Issues* (Brooks Cole, 1994). He is a past president of Division 51 of APA.

Carolyn Steigmeier, PhD, is an executive coach and organizational consultant with a PhD in human and organizational systems from Fielding Graduate University, with a concentration in organizational change and adult learning. She also has a master of science in human development. She held marketing and product management positions in the corporate world for over 10 years before returning as a consultant to help others succeed, which is what she has been doing for over 15 years. Having worked in male-dominated industries, and then focusing her research on men, she designs workshops and programs for men and coaches both men and women. Dr. Steigmeier is a member of Division 51 of APA.

Melba J. T. Vasquez, PhD, ABPP, is a psychologist in private practice in Austin, Texas. She was the 2011 president of APA. She has served as president of the Texas Psychological Association and APA Divisions 35 and 17. A cofounder of APA Division 45 (Psychological Study of Ethnic Minority Issues), and of the National Multicultural Conference and Summit, she has published extensively in the areas of ethics, multicultural psychology, counseling and psychotherapy, and psychology of women. She is a Fellow of ten APA divisions, and a Diplomate of the American Board of Professional Psychology.

Karen Wilbur, PhD, has been a psychologist since 1988. She was director of training at the University of New Mexico Student Health Center, where she worked from 1986 through 1992. She has served as clinical or adjunct faculty at the University of New Mexico School of Medicine, Emerson College, and the Union Institute and has provided clinical supervision for graduate students at the University of New Mexico, Smith School of Social Work, and Boston College. Dr. Wilbur has been in private practice since 1992, treating children, adolescents, and adults. She is currently in private practice in Dallas, Texas.

Core Treatment Issues

1

Women Working With Men

Challenges and Opportunities

HOLLY BARLOW SWEET

WHY SHOULD FEMALE THERAPISTS CARE ABOUT MEN'S ISSUES?

Projections made on future enrollments in counseling and clinical psychology noted the fact that fewer and fewer men have been entering clinical fields. Oren and Oren (2009) found that men currently make up only 21% of graduate students in psychology, whereas 25 years ago they used to constitute 50% of that population. In a survey done by *Psychology Today* and a major health maintenance organization in 2004 on the gender of people in psychological treatment (*Psychology Today*, 2004), 37% of the total number of patients surveyed were male. When those sets of statistics are combined, it seems plausible that future clinicians are likely to be female rather than male and working with populations that will include a substantial number of men.

Although there has been a significant increase in interest in men's studies since the early 1990s, there has been a lag in the incorporation of materials about men's issues in counseling programs. Few academic programs currently incorporate classes on the psychology of men into their curriculum. In a survey of 52 doctoral programs in counseling psychology (Mellinger & Liu, 2006), only 17% of these programs had any classes in the psychology of men available to students. The books that do exist in reading lists on the psychology of men are almost exclusively written by male authors and do not address the needs or experiences of female clinicians who are working or will be working with men. As a result, most women go through an education in psychology without ever having studied men's issues from either a theoretical or a clinical perspective, yet many will end up working with men in their counseling careers.

The result of this lack of knowledge may have negative consequences for both female and male clinicians and their male clients. Traditional talk therapy in general is a more female-oriented activity because of its focus on interpersonal connection, vulnerability, and emotional expression (Sweet, 2006). This focus can conflict with traditional male norms of autonomy, toughness, and emotional restriction. Male clinicians may understand those norms more directly from their own socialization and may be better able to relate to a style that might focus more on action, structure, and clear goals. Female clinicians, on the other hand, may not directly understand how powerful those norms may be because their own socialization and life experience may be quite different. Women are typically socialized to be connected and emotionally expressive. Therapy is also an intimate activity in which the client talks about personal and often emotional matters in secret behind a closed door. Such intimacy can have erotic overtones on the part of the male client as well as the female therapist.

Erickson (1993) noted the importance of female therapists taking a look at their own histories to make sure that they are not operating out of negative countertransference and to examine the value of having more information about men's issues to better understand the male experience. For female therapists not familiar with the literature on covert depression in men, depression in their male clients may go undetected and hence untreated. Untreated depressed men may then start or continue self-medicating themselves with alcohol, drugs, or overwork or harming themselves or others (Cochran & Rabinowitz, 2000; Real, 1997). For those who do not understand the dynamics of male socialization, in which sadness may be expressed as anger or irritability, working with angry men can be challenging. It can create countertransference reactions and projections in the therapist that inhibit both positive regard for the client and the ability to create a safe place for the man to express his feelings (Erickson, 1993). Female therapists who do not understand the ways men have learned to inhibit themselves verbally and emotionally to live up to "being a man" may be impatient with men who have difficulty accessing and articulating their feelings in therapy.

Female clinicians who are informed about the range of issues facing them in treating male clients and are more knowledgeable about how other female clinicians have approached their work with men will be better able to help their male clients. In addition, knowledge of men's issues can aid therapists in helping their female clients understand the motivations and behavior of the men they care about, including fathers, husbands, brothers, sons, friends, and colleagues. This is the "trickle-down" effect of therapy: What clients learn in therapy can potentially benefit those with whom the clients are in contact. For example, if Jane understands more about how her husband's behavior (social withdrawal, anger, or workaholism) may indicate an underlying untreated depression, she may be better able to deal with her husband in a less-defensive, more empathic way and support him in getting help. If Susan has a highly critical father, helping her learn about rigid male norms of achievement might aid her in not internalizing his negative assessments as much.

A BRIEF REVIEW OF MALE AND FEMALE NORMS IN AMERICAN CULTURE

Levant and Kopecky (1995) identified seven key norms in their book *Masculinity Reconstructed*: restricted emotionality, emphasis on the importance of strength and aggression, sex disconnected from intimacy (nonrelational sex), self-reliance, avoidance of femininity, pursuit of achievement and status, and homophobia. David and Brannon (1976), some of the first authors to explore men's roles, came up with one meta-norm for men that they called "no sissy stuff." In other words, above all, men should never act, think, dress, feel, talk, or look like women. Pollack (1998) talked about the boy code and how these roles, especially the role of no sissy stuff, are socialized in boys from early on in formidable ways. Men growing up in our culture are trained to see male role models as tough, independent, sexually active, successful professionally, and never expressing vulnerable feelings. Without perspective or alternatives in sight, many men come to see themselves as weak, wimpy, or a sissy if they do not follow normative male behavior.

Traditional male norms are not necessarily bad, especially in the workplace. Certainly, strength, self-control, self-reliance, and the pursuit of achievement and status can be positive traits that both women and men might wish to cultivate. However, rigid adherence to these roles can be problematic, especially in interpersonal relationships in which another set of skills is needed, such as the ability to be connected, nurturing, receptive, interdependent, and emotionally expressive. Other norms can be directly damaging in and of themselves. These norms include restricted emotionality, avoidance of femininity, homophobia, and nonrelational sex. What compounds the problem is the excessive emphasis on the positive sides of these norms while not seeing their drawbacks. It then becomes even harder for men to engage in behavior that counters male norms, especially in the area of showing need for others and expressing vulnerable feelings. For a man, even talking about one's problems can be seen as a sign of weakness and lack of masculinity.

In contrast, traditional female norms are centered on being emotionally open and connected to others. In a textbook on the psychology of women (Hyde, 2007), mention is made of a survey done by Spence and Buckner (2000) in which a sample of Americans believed that female characteristics include being warm, gentle, understanding, devoted to others, helpful to others, aware of others' feelings, and emotional (p. 87). Hyde discusses the strong and persistent socialization influences behind these traits and says that "gender socialization shapes emotions, beginning with parental socialization from infancy...girls and women are more facially expressive of emotion and talk about emotions more than boys and men do" (p. 190). In another updated textbook on the psychology of women (Matlin, 2012), a summary of research on women's communication patterns shows that women are more likely than men to gaze more at their conversational partners, smile more than men, and are generally more accurate than men in decoding nonverbal messages that other people send (pp. 186–187). Girls are also more likely than boys to self-disclose to their friends (p. 196).

Being open, connected, and self-disclosing as a therapist is probably beneficial to many male clients for whom this style might help establish a strong therapeutic alliance and make them feel more cared for in the therapy hour. However, this style can also lead to miscommunication and confused expectations for men who adhere more rigidly to traditional male norms. The "traditional" male client may misinterpret a female's style of connectedness (smiling, gazing directly at him, etc,) as sexual in nature. Too much openness and emphasis on emotions might be unsettling for a man who has been taught that his emotions are to be kept inside at all costs. Asking a man to speak intimately about his life in weekly sessions with a person who is there to help him might make him uneasy since it goes against the stereotype of the independent "Marlboro Man" who relies on himself and doesn't really need others. Given the difference in gender norms and in the experience of growing up male or female in American culture, it is important that female clinicians learn about the socialization of men and how male norms might affect their male clients. In addition, female therapists need to learn about their own expectations and biases about what a "good" client should do in therapy and how therapy should be conducted. If therapy is practiced according to norms that are largely female, then therapy can end up feeling unfamiliar (or even threatening) to many men. It is no wonder, therefore, that the average man might not be inclined to think of therapy as his first line of defense against anxiety, depression, or other mental health issues.

MAKING THERAPY MORE MALE FRIENDLY

Increasing attention has been paid since the beginning of the twenty-first century to the consequences of male norms for how men perceive and utilize psychotherapy. Prominent researchers in the field of men and psychotherapy (Addis & Mahalik, 2003; Good, Thomson, & Braithwaite, 2005; Mahalik, Good, & Englar-Carlson, 2003; Rochlen & Hoyer, 2005) have written about the restrictions caused by male norms to men's help-seeking behavior. These norms include (a) being stoic in the face of personal difficulties; (b) not showing feelings; (c) striving to be independent; and (d) not relying on others. These norms have generally been seen in our culture as positive traits for a "real" man: an independent, action-oriented person with a stiff upper lip who does not have to rely on anyone and never asks for (or even appears to need) help. How often have you heard the expression "man up" as a way of saying, tough it out, or "crying is for sissies"? An ad appeared recently on television that showed a male therapist making fun of a male client who is trying to express his tender feelings. "You're in namby-pamby land," says the therapist, "What a wimp you are!" It is supposed to be funny since it was a take-off on a drill sergeant as therapist. However, it represents a commonly held view that real men do not cry, and that men should take care of their personal problems by themselves. If they cry or ask for help, they are seen as wimps or wusses, "girlie" men, men who are not to be respected or valued.

Where does this leave the average guy who needs some help in dealing with his emotions or situations that are difficult for him? Many men probably do not even go to therapy when they have issues. Instead, they may withdraw from others, get angry or irritable, turn to substances such as alcohol or drugs for relief, act out sexually, become workaholics, or turn violent with themselves or others. For those who try therapy (often at the insistence of a spouse or boss), it means confronting those barriers to therapy and still being able to see themselves as manly. If therapy is not male user friendly (i.e., done by a therapist who is not sensitive to men's issues or someone who does not really like men or is angry with or afraid of men), it can actually do more harm than good. Men who are shamed, blamed, or not listened to in therapy are not likely to come back. They may even share their negative experiences of therapy, discouraging others from seeking help.

Mark Kiselica (2011) suggests that we make therapy more accessible to boys and men by changing the focus of how we view male clients as well as the style of therapy we use with them. He appreciates the new psychology of men that looks at the social construction of masculinity and has raised awareness among both professionals and the general public about the influence of masculinity on male attitudes and behavior. However, he has concerns about viewing masculinity currently in a more negative light and states that the tendency of the new psychology of men to emphasize male pathology has resulted in a comparative neglect of male strengths and the good things that boys and men do. As a result of overlooking these strengths, psychologists have a tendency to view males as being damaged victims of flawed development. . . . Embracing this type of deficit model fosters the mind-set that boys and men are defective and damaged, that they need to be fixed, and that they are at fault for the problems they bring to therapy. (pp. 132–133)

He indicates we need to develop a new focus on the way we counsel boys and men that he calls "male-friendly" therapy (Kiselica, 2005) or "male-sensitive" counseling (Kiselica, 2003). He addresses how to make therapy more user friendly for boys and men, including how to attract males into therapy and how to make the actual therapy process more directly applicable to their specific needs and style.

Other authors in the field of men and therapy have reiterated the value of practicing male-friendly therapy in a variety of counseling approaches. Wexler (*Men in Therapy*, 2009) mentions the roadblocks to men entering therapy, including the stigma of counseling (i.e., you must be sick to see a therapist) and the fear of being changed against one's will, not being understood, and being confused about what the whole process is all about. Wexler gives some excellent practical suggestions in his book about how to work with these roadblocks, including using guy talk, making it clear how a man can benefit from therapy, respecting resistance and the male style of relating, using self-disclosure, giving empathic responses when the client tries new behavior, setting a pace that works for the client, and advertising therapy as having specific skill-based tasks. Brooks (*Beyond the Crisis of Masculinity*, 2010) also focuses on the value of cognitive and behavioral therapy (CBT) for men. He indicates that the key points of CBT (here-and-now focus, action oriented, less emphasis on emotional expression, psychoeducational style, skill building, and control of client over process) may work better with a man, especially with traditional men who tend to be less comfortable in a female-style therapy world of feelings, reliance on others, and intimacy.

Pollack (2005) highlights how psychodynamic therapy can help men acknowledge the issues of grief and loss in an empathic way by highlighting the emotional wounding and trauma common in male development. Rabinowitz and Cochran (2002) use a more active style that goes beyond just talking with their clients and say that "experiential interventions that allow a man active expression of his feelings and behavior enhance the therapy process and work well in combination with traditional psychotherapeutic strategies" (p. 4). There are many other approaches (including feminist therapy, interpersonal therapy, couples counseling, and group therapy) that can be used effectively if the clinicians employing those approaches are sensitive to men's issues and styles.

Despite some of the negative aspects (e.g., emotional restriction) of traditional male norms for a therapeutic relationship, there are also many positive aspects of male norms that should be acknowledged if possible. Kiselica and Englar-Carlson (2010) outline a positive psychology/positive masculinity model of psychotherapy with boys and men. They describe this model as drawing from the emerging literature on the psychology of human strength and see it as

> a model of boys, men and masculinity that accentuates noble aspects of masculinity, including the following: male relational styles; male ways of caring; generative fatherhood, male self-reliance; the worker-provider tradition of men; male courage, daring, and risk-taking; the group orientation of boys and men; fraternal humanitarian service; male forms of humor; and male heroism. (p. 277)

The open acknowledgment of and respect for a man's strengths, in fact, may be the crucial building block of a positive therapeutic alliance between client and clinician. As female clinicians, we must be particularly sensitive to the degree to which these traits need to be openly acknowledged and appreciated since we do not always share or value the same traits or may choose to focus on the negative consequences of those traits for men entering therapy.

In considering working with men, it is important to learn how to meet the male client where he is instead of expecting him to adjust to our way of doing things. This may involve learning new techniques and approaches and moving us out of our comfort zone in terms of how we work. How and why men start therapy, what they find useful in the sessions, and when they decide to leave may be quite different from female clients with whom we have worked. Female clients tend to bring themselves into therapy on their own, whereas many men may come to therapy reluctantly and often at the insistence of others. Female clients are usually more comfortable with the emphasis on feelings and relationships; men may find this threatening or difficult to do. Female clients may better fit the model of the standard therapy flow (i.e., weekly sessions for a prolonged period of time), whereas men may come and go on a more intermittent schedule. Simply put, what we learned in graduate school and subsequent training may not work well for male clients.

Although the focus of this book is on ways to better serve male clients, our female clients can benefit as well. Better understanding the implications of rigid male norms for interpersonal relationships can help women deal more effectively with men in their lives. Men who are in therapy may become less depressed and angry and therefore more available to the women who love them. New approaches and techniques we learn to work more effectively with men can also help our female clients. We ourselves can benefit as we develop a more compassionate and knowledgeable approach to men that may spill over into our personal lives. The once-common belief held by many women that men have all the power and privilege and do not suffer is not only outdated but also shortchanges both men and women. Empathy for men's struggles to be free of restrictive sex role norms helps us all. In a zero-sum game approach to gender, the more attention we pay to men, the less attention we have available to pay to women. In a gender empathy approach, the more attention we pay to men, the more women also benefit. If men can become more nurturing, less constricted, more available emotionally, and less rigid in their approach to their lives and those around them, aren't we all better off?

FEMALE THERAPISTS AND MALE CLIENTS: CHALLENGES AND OPPORTUNITIES

I saw *Hurt Locker* the other day, a film about men trying to fulfill traditional male roles under extraordinarily difficult circumstances. I thought about the phrase *hurt locker* as it applies to the men who come into therapy. Many of them have put their hurt feelings in a locker and hidden the key. My job as a therapist is to make the environment attractive and safe enough for them to explore those hurts and to come to terms with their wounds so that they can lead more productive and emotionally connected lives. My role as a *female* therapist is to understand how my experiences as a woman can help or hinder the creation of that kind of environment and to understand how men's fears of or needs for women can have an impact on that safe place.

Given that women have probably not had the same set of experiences and expectations as men, we have some special challenges to address in doing our clinical work with men. As you read the following list of challenges and ways to deal with them, think about male clients you have now and how this might apply to your work with them. If you do not yet have male clients, you probably will in the future since increasing numbers of men are entering therapy. At the least, all of us have relationships with men in our lives, be they partners, colleagues, relatives, friends, employees, or supervisors. Not everyone will agree with this list. For some, it will seem too short; for others, it will seem too long. You might want to write up your own list or work with others to come up with a different list. The important thing is to think about how you work with men and where you might need to grow or change in how you approach this work.

CHALLENGES FOR WOMEN WORKING WITH MEN

- **Not knowing enough about male norms and their impact on men in therapy.** As women, we have not been socialized to feel unfeminine if we express emotions or ask for help from others. We may not have had firsthand experience of what it feels like to be shamed for doing something that goes against long-held and ubiquitous gender norms. Therefore, we have a special obligation to understand male norms and their impact on how men perceive therapy. Taking a class or workshop on men's issues or doing reading in this area is essential for practicing both ethical and effective therapy with men. One possibility is to start your own "gender-in-the-therapy-hour" book club with other therapists. Sharing ideas with others is a great way of learning.

- **Negative countertransference.** Without solid understanding of our own experiences with men, we may end up reacting to our male clients as we would to men in our personal lives. This could take the form of misinterpreting a man's motives, becoming defensive with a male client, or being cold and distant as a way of protecting ourselves from old wounds that may be activated in our work with men. We may feel detached from men when they do not share feelings or pathologized by men when they put down emotions or therapy in general. If we are doing couples counseling, we may tend to take the side of the female partners. Discussing our reactions with colleagues and supervisors is one way of handling this; personal therapy is another. As we learn more about ourselves, we are likely to be better therapists, more compassionate and less reactive, and more emotionally available to our clients.

- **Making therapy attractive to men.** Because of their upbringing, men are particularly sensitive to being seen as unmanly when they ask for help and may feel shame for needing support. Starting with an upbeat focus such as "I appreciate you coming in today—it shows you care about taking some positive steps" can help bring the man back for future sessions. Reframing therapy as a place for winners, not losers, is important, as is viewing the client as heroic rather than as a victim. In addition, the way we advertise therapy can help bring men in or scare them off. Consider using some action words in your description of what you do and having a more psychoeducational approach to advertising your work, such as "building an action plan," "setting specific goals," or "developing a skill set."

- **Dealing with sexual feelings in the therapy hour.** Men who confuse emotional intimacy with sexual intimacy may become attracted to us in ways that may feel uncomfortable to us or push our boundaries. Many men may only know how to relate to women sexually, which limits their interactions with women. Being nonjudgmental and curious together about sexual transference can lead to growth on the part of your clients. Some of us may experience erotic feelings toward our clients. This can be useful information for us and is nothing to be ashamed of. We may be picking up on the feelings of our clients (projective identification), or we may be responding to our own internal reality. Kenneth Pope (Pope, Sonne, & Holroyd, 1993) stated that we do not talk enough about this topic and therefore limit ourselves and our clients. Reading about how to handle erotic feelings in therapy or discussing them in supervision can be helpful to you in exploring this issue further.

- **Working with judgmental male clients.** We may have a difficult time responding positively to men who are dismissive or conde-scending toward women. If we are working with men who ques-tion our credentials or the value of therapy in general, we can take that as an opportunity to be honest with them (after all, they have a right to know) and then explore why they asked the question and what lies behind it. Rather than feeling threatened or disre-spected, we can see their confrontation as a valuable opportunity to learn about our client's concerns and fears. Sometimes men who challenge us are using that as a smoke screen for fear and sad-ness. What they may be asking is, "Will you really be able to help me?" Respecting their view and being willing to hear more about it is a better way of helping them feel comfortable than resisting and defending.

- **Being afraid of male anger.** We may become afraid of a man's anger in part because it can trigger memories of our own experiences with angry men who might have hurt us emotionally or physically. Even if we have not had angry or violent men in our lives, it is hard not to be affected by examples in the media of men acting violently against women. Anger is a normal and healthy emotion, one of the few emotions that men are able to access without feel-ing unmasculine. Use that anger to see what is really going on for your client. If we can listen to a man's anger, we are likely to find that underneath that anger is a great deal of hurt, wounds that have never healed. If we find that we react negatively to the anger in our male clients, then we should get some help from supervisors, our own therapists, or colleagues to figure out ways to adopt a more detached and compassionate stance.

- **Responding to male clients who think we cannot help them.** Sometimes, male clients say to us, "You can't understand about what I'm going through; you're not a guy." Instead of feeling inad-equate to the task, we can just answer, "Yes, that's quite right, but I'm interested in learning more about your experience." This answer supports their concerns about working with someone of the other gender and opens the door to more dialogue. In addition, it acknowledges they have something to teach us, which can help them feel on a more equal level with us. Therapy is not a one-way street: We have things to learn from our clients as well as vice versa. Learning more about what it is like for our male clients is normal and healthy.

- **Making your office male friendly.** Therapy should be a place where men feel comfortable and where they can be themselves. This includes what your office looks like. Think about what would make a man feel comfortable in your office. For example, consider getting rid of women's magazines and find some neutral ones, such as travel magazines. Be aware of how you decorate your office; it should feel like a place where a man would feel at home. If you are not sure about your decor, have some male friends or colleagues come over and give you feedback.

- **Learning guy talk.** Women do not always know how to use "guy talk" in therapy. This involves everything from a straightforward introduction with a firm handshake, to male metaphors (e.g., going on a fishing trip as a metaphor for doing therapy), to discussing ostensibly nontherapy topics such as sports teams. It also includes using male words for feelings ("I'm feeling down" versus "I'm depressed"). The rule here is to make the man feel like he does not have to check his masculinity at your door.

- **Being impatient with men and their emotions.** Men take time to access, understand, and express emotions (the currency of traditional talk therapy). As women, we have been socialized to express emotions relatively easily. For men, the experience is very different. Some men do not even know what they feel (having been trained to ignore emotions except for anger), have feelings but do not know how to name them (alexithymia), or know what they feel but are afraid to express their emotions for fear of being shamed by others. In research on women's views of men's experiences in heterosexual romantic relationships (Sweet, 1995), the women surveyed underestimated the degree to which men are afraid to show their feelings or did not know how to. Pushing a man to express emotions before he is ready will not help him feel comfortable and may scare him off.

- **Seeing therapy as serious business.** Humor can be a powerful tool for making a man feel at home in the therapy hour. Not only is shared laughter a bonding experience, but also it helps the man develop more of an observing ego and a healthy sense of detachment from his woes. Do not be afraid to share a laugh with your male clients. It can help both of you feel more comfortable with each other.

- **Operating on a male client's timetable.** Men may stop coming to therapy in a different way than the traditional ways taught in graduate school. The recommendation for a proper "termination" (always a strange word to me because it sounds so . . . final, even sinister) was that the client would indicate that he or she was ready to leave therapy because goals had been accomplished. The two of you would spend a few sessions reviewing your work together, gains made by the client, possible unfinished business of the client, ways to handle that, and acknowledgment of the relationship between the two of you. It seems, however, that some men do not follow this model. Some men may come and go, never quite finishing therapy and often leaving before you think they are ready to quit therapy, but coming back months or even years later to review old issues or work on something new. Perhaps they see a therapist much like they see a primary care physician—there when they need them and "on call" when they do not. Brooks (2010) recommended that "therapists must be exceptionally patient with this 'fits-and-starts' type of therapy, realizing that even when therapy starts positively, it will not always result in the preferred smooth and linear unfolding of a long-term therapeutic journey" (p. 91). Men may need control over the process of therapy, including when they leave. It is important to respect their pace and not challenge it as wrong.

- **Using self-disclosure.** Some of us may have been taught that disclosing information about ourselves is unprofessional, so we may be uncomfortable sharing our own views and experiences with our male clients. In fact, opening up about yourself can be a way of making your male clients feel more on an even level with you. Just coming in to therapy can feel like a "one-down" setting for them already. Being "real" in the relationship with your male client can be reassuring to him and make him better able to open up to you down the road.

- **Educating clients about the therapy process.** Some of us assume, based on our experiences with female clients, that men coming in to therapy will be familiar with the process. In fact, many men do not have any idea about what is involved and may only know about therapy from movies and the media. We need to spend time educating them about what is involved in therapy and finding out more about what they want. The first session is an important one with any client, but especially with male clients who may not know what to expect. Consider developing materials to hand to clients that explain the process of therapy. Developing a well-written treatment plan in conjunction with the client is also helpful.

- **New techniques and approaches.** Many of us have been taught to use talk therapy as the primary way in which we work with our clients. Therapy that uses talk as its primary technique might not work as well with men who may not be as comfortable with words. Consider learning some nonverbal techniques, such as those outlined in Rabinowitz and Cochran's book *Deepening Psychotherapy With Men* (2002) or Weiner's book *Beyond Talk Therapy* (1999). Another possibility is to use other modalities in conjunction with your individual work with the man. These might include a referral to a clinician who specializes in EMDR (Shapiro, 2001) or having your client join a men's group. Men's groups can be powerful (Andronico, 1996) and can work well in tandem with individual therapy.

- **Viewing men and masculinity in a positive light.** Female clinicians may have trouble seeing the strengths that men bring in to therapy (such as emotional reserve and independence) since they don't fit the model of traditional therapy (emotional expression and reliance on others). In addition, we may have issues with men in our own lives which may skew our view of men in general in a more negative direction (i.e., detached fathers, emotionally repressed partners, or judgmental or demeaning bosses). We may also consciously or unconsciously view masculinity as inherently flawed and think like a female Henry Higgins—"Why can't a man be more like a woman?" In welcoming men into our offices, we must be able to appreciate men for who they are, regardless of the way in which they engage in therapy. A strength-based approach is useful for establishing any therapeutic alliance, but even more so in working with men who may not feel at home in the therapy hour.

Challenges can turn into positive opportunities for both clinician and client. As female clinicians, we can play a really important and positive role with our male clients. We can serve as a role model for a healthy relationship between a man and a woman. Men who have been afraid of women or angry with them can learn to be comfortable in our presence. We can remother them, giving them the respect and attention that they may not have had. We can help them learn about new ways of relating to women, using the therapy hour as a laboratory for experimentation. Since many men may be more comfortable sharing distress with a woman (who is seen as nurturing) versus a man (who may be seen as threatening or top dog), we have a particularly important role to play in making therapy safe and attractive to them. If a man's distress is caused in part by lack of intimacy, we can provide a safe environment where he can open up to us without being afraid of being seen as weak. We can also learn from our male clients about different ways of relating and being. This knowledge can inform our relationships with men outside a professional setting. The best therapy is a two-way street, with client and clinician learning from each other in an atmosphere of trust and respect.

PERSONAL REFLECTIONS

As you read this book, take a moment to reflect on your personal and professional journeys. Think about your own relationships with men in your life, how you conduct therapy with men, and what you can do to become a more effective therapist with men. If you have not worked with men yet clinically, imagine what you might encounter when you do. The authors of this book, in their own chapters, considered the following questions in their personal and professional journeys. Take some time to think through your own answers and write them down. For a more powerful exercise, get together with some colleagues you like and trust and share your answers with each other. Individuals might have experiences or suggestions that could help everyone in the group.

1. How do you view masculinity? Positively? Negatively? On what do you base your views?
2. What has been your experience with men in your personal life, and how might this color your work with male clients?

3. Have you taken a course, class, or workshop in men's studies or done reading in this area? If not, would you consider doing so in the next six months?
4. Are you willing to learn about new techniques and approaches that might work better for men than some of the traditional approaches you learned in your training? In what ways might you learn about and try out new ideas?
5. Do you genuinely like and trust men? If you cannot answer "yes" wholeheartedly, think about why and imagine how you might find ways to develop more trust and liking for men.

As female therapists, we have an obligation to educate ourselves about the world of men—how men were raised and what it is like being a man in this culture. We need to understand how our socialization as women and our own history with men may interfere with working most effectively with our male clients. We need to investigate different methods of working with men that may challenge our particular preference for doing therapy. Above all, we must continue to strive to be compassionate and nonjudgmental with the men in our offices, particularly with male clients who sexualize us, threaten us, or shut us out. It is by continuing to grow both personally and professionally that we stand the best chance of working effectively with men.

REFERENCES

Addis, M. E., & Mahalik, J. R. (2003). Men, masculinity, and the contexts of help seeking. *American Psychologist, 58*, 5–14.

Andronico, M. (Ed.). (1996). *Men in groups: Insights, interventions, and psychoeducational work*. Washington, DC: American Psychological Association.

Brooks, G. R. (2010). *Beyond the crisis of masculinity: A trans-theoretical model for male-friendly therapy*. Washington, DC: American Psychological Association.

Cochran, S. V., & Rabinowitz, F. E. (2000). *Men and depression: Clinical and empirical perspectives*. San Diego, CA: Academic Press.

David, D. S., & Brannon, R. (1976). *The forty-nine percent majority: The male sex role*. Reading, MA: Addison-Wesley.

Erickson, B. (1993). *Helping men change: The role of the female therapist*. Newbury Park, CA: Sage.

Good, G., Thomson, D., & Braithwaite, A. (2005). Men and therapy: Critical concepts, theoretical frameworks, and research recommendations. *Journal of Clinical Psychology, 61*, 699–711.

Kiselica, M. S. (2005). A male-friendly therapeutic process with school-age boys. In G. R. Brooks & G. E. Good (Eds.), *The new handbook of psychotherapy and counseling with men: A comprehensive guide to settings, problems, and treatment approaches* (pp. 17–28). San Francisco: Jossey-Bass.

Kiselica, M. S. (2003). Male-sensitive counseling with boys. *Counselling in Education*, 16–19.

Kiselica, M. S. (2011). Promoting positive masculinity while addressing gender role conflicts: A balanced theoretical approach to clinical work with boys and men. In C. Blazina & D. Shen-Miller (Eds.), *An international psychology of men: Theoretical advances, case studies, and clinical innovations* (pp. 127–156). New York, NY: Routledge.

Kiselica, M. S., & Englar-Carlson, M. (2010). Identifying, affirming, and building upon male strengths: The positive psychology/positive masculinity model of psychotherapy with boys and men. *Psychotherapy Theory, Research, Practice, Training, 47*, 276–287.

Levant, R. F., & Kopecky, G. (1995). *Masculinity reconstructed: Changing the rules of manhood—At work, in relationships, and in family life.* New York, NY: Dutton.

Mahalik, J., Good, G., & Englar-Carlson, M. (2003). Masculinity scripts, presenting concerns, and help seeking: Implications for practice and training. *Professional Psychology: Research and Practice, 34*, 123–131.

Mellinger, T. N., & Liu, W. M. (2006). Men's issues in doctoral training: A survey of counseling psychology programs. *Professional Psychology: Research and Practice, 37*, 196–204.

Oren, C. Z., & Oren, D. C. (2009). *Male psychology doctoral students.* Symposium presented at the 117th Annual Convention of the American Psychological Association, Toronto, August.

Pollack, W. S. (1998). *Real boys: Rescuing our sons from the myths of boyhood.* New York, NY: Random House.

Pollack, W. S. (2005). Masked men: New psychoanalytically oriented treatment models of adult and young adult men. In G. E. Good & G. R. Brooks (Eds.), *A new handbook of counseling and psychotherapy with men* (pp. 203–216). San Francisco: Jossey Bass.

Pope, K., Sonne, J., & Holroyd, J. (1993). *Sexual feelings in psychotherapy: Explorations for therapists and therapists-in-training.* Washington, DC: American Psychological Association.

Psychology Today. (2004, July).

Rabinowitz, F. E., & Cochran, S. V. (2002). *Deepening psychotherapy with men.* Washington, DC: American Psychological Association.

Real, T. (1997). *I don't want to talk about it: Overcoming the secret legacy of male depression.* New York, NY: Fireside.

Rochlen, A., & Hoyer, W. (2005) Marketing mental health to men: Theoretical and practical considerations. *Journal of Clinical Psychology, 61*, 675–684.

Shapiro, F. (2001). *Eye movement desensitization and reprocessing basic principles, protocols, and procedures.* New York, NY: Guilford Press.

Sweet, H. (1995). *Perceptions of undergraduate male experiences in heterosexual romantic relationships: A sex role norms analysis.* Unpublished doctoral dissertation. Boston College, Chestnut Hill, MA.

Sweet, H. (2006). Finding the person behind the persona: Engaging men as a female therapist. In M. Englar-Carlson & M. Stevens (Eds.), *In the room with men: A casebook of therapeutic change.* Washington, DC: American Psychological Association.

Weiner, D. J. (1999). *Beyond talk therapy: Using movement and expressive techniques in clinical practice.* Washington, DC: American Psychological Association.

Wexler, D. (2009). *Men in therapy: New approaches for effective treatment.* New York, NY: Norton.

RECOMMENDED READING

Brooks, G. R., & Good, G. E. (2005). *The new handbook of psychotherapy and counseling with men: A comprehensive guide to settings, problems, and treatment approaches.* San Francisco: Jossey-Bass.

Englar-Carlson, M., & Stevens, M. (Eds.). (2006). *In the room with men: A casebook of therapeutic change.* Washington, DC: American Psychological Association.

Johnson, N. G. (2005). Women helping men: Strengths and barriers to women therapists working with men clients. In G. R. Brooks & G. E. Good (Eds.), *The new handbook of psychotherapy and counseling with men: A comprehensive guide to settings, problems, and treatment approaches* (pp. 291–307). San Francisco: Jossey-Bass.

Sweet, H. (2010). Women treating men. *Psychotherapy Networker, 54,* 32–35.

2

Starting and Ending Psychotherapy With Men

JUNE MARTIN

INTRODUCTION

When male clients terminated their psychotherapy with me prematurely in the early days of my private practice, I felt that it must somehow have been my fault. I noticed that when I jumped right into interpretive psychotherapy with male clients, they frequently became anxious or defensive and either canceled their next session or simply did not show up for it.

I remember one of my first clients, Leon (not his real name), a 21-year-old single Caucasian man, walking into my office for his first session with an air of confidence and friendliness. He boldly stated that he was fine, not crazy, but just could not get over his anger at his girlfriend, who had left him three weeks before. Leon assured me that he was smart, made good money in his dad's company, and had never been dumped by a woman before. In fact, he said that he had actually been "bored" with his girlfriend after four months. Shaking his head, he told me that he was shocked when she left him because he was planning to "dump her first." Toward the end of the session, as he booked his next appointment, he said that he liked having someone listen to him as he worked out his thoughts.

Ten minutes before the end of his second session, Leon told me that he thought I was nice and pretty, and we should stop therapy so we could date instead. I was unprepared for this comment, but acknowledged his kind words. Aware that I was shifting my posture into a more authoritative pose and raising my voice, I told him, "Therapy is never terminated so that a romance can begin." I also informed him that legal and ethical professional boundaries are enforced for the protection of the client and the therapist, but reassured him that he was safe in my office, and that I respected him.

Sensing that Leon was pulling back into himself, I suggested that being listened to and acknowledged as he explored his thoughts and feelings with me may have reminded him of the intimacy in his relationship with his ex-girlfriend. "Yeah, maybe," Leon responded without much enthusiasm. I added that his request to date me may have been a wish for another woman to comfort and distract him from his frustration over his ex. Although he said that made sense, he was looking increasingly distracted. Since we had already run over the allotted time, I did not ask him what he was feeling. We ended the session with his scheduling his next appointment, but I never saw or heard from Leon again.

This was not the first time a male client had terminated therapy with me prematurely, although not all men who had terminated without warning had done so as abruptly and unexpectedly as Leon. As I sat in my empty office, realizing that Leon was not going to appear for his third appointment, I asked myself what I needed to do to learn from this experience and grow as a female therapist working with men. Put bluntly, what was I doing wrong?

First, I realized that many of these men came in, consciously or not, to vent their anger, and that this emoting was a way for them to deal with their sadness and fear. As a novice therapist, I wanted to quickly explore with them their underlying psychological dynamics, when what I should have done was let them vent.

Second, I assumed that male clients had come to me the way they would go to a car mechanic—in other words, they wanted me to fix their problems for them. What I discovered over time is that male clients usually need to interview me, to test my knowledge and credentials first, before they are ready to start the work. Furthermore, they want me to fix their problems *with* them, rather than *for* them. In other words, they (or most of them, at least) do not simply want me to hand them ready-made solutions; rather, they want me to respect their problem-solving skills and work on their concerns with them.

Third, when male clients vocalized their frustration over their lack of progress in therapy, what they often meant by "progress" was that they wanted me to fix *someone else*—usually a wife or lover—and they were disappointed that I was not giving them tools to do so. Instead of asking those men to focus on their feelings, which only made them more anxious or irritable, I should have given them some techniques to resolve their problem. For example, if a man said that his wife was complaining that he did not pay enough attention to her, I should have worked on helping him to listen to her more attentively. We could get around to dealing with his feelings later.

Fourth, I noticed a difference in *when* the men told me they were discontinuing work with me—if, unlike Leon, they told me at all. Those who announced they were leaving therapy at the *beginning* of a session were frequently willing to express their unmet expectations about problem resolution. For example, Andrew, a 42-year-old Caucasian man who started therapy a week after his wife left him, informed me at the beginning of his fourth session of supportive interpersonal therapy that this was his last appointment. Since he was feeling better now, he said, it was time to end therapy. When I asked him what he felt better *about*, he said that his wife had come back. But then he stated that he was "annoyed and disappointed" that I had not helped him to deal with his wife's yelling. I thanked Andrew for telling me his disappointment with the course of his treatment. I proposed that we work directly on that problem, and together we revised his treatment plan to include assertiveness training, active listening, and appropriate emotional self-disclosure techniques. After completing an additional seven sessions, Andrew told me that he had attained his treatment goals. "I trusted you more," he said in his final session, "when you took my frustration seriously. That's when I decided to stay and work with you."

PERSONAL JOURNEY

Although I am an only child, I had a close extended family. Since my mother worked, I spent my days with my maternal grandmother, with whom I developed a deep connection. When I was three or four, I noticed that the men in my family, unlike the women (with the exception of my mother), went off to work during the day and then, when they came home, addressed various "man" tasks, which often got them dirty. For example, my Dad, Grandpa, uncles, and male cousins would fix things at night. This might include repairing or painting the house or working on the cars. Since my grandparents had a grape farm outside the city, I also learned that men used big machines. But, they also did more delicate work along with the women, such as tilling the soil around the grape roots and harvesting the fruit.

In my family, men demonstrated traditional masculine sex role norms. They were tough and self-reliant, defended themselves through yelling and aggression when threatened, were served by women, and did not talk about their feelings—styles that David and Brannon (1976) respectively called "The Sturdy Oak," "Give 'Em Hell," "The Big Wheel," and "No Sissy Stuff." Fortunately for me, Grandpa did not consistently hold traditional attitudes of female gender roles—what Peck (1981) called female norms of "dependency and achievement inhibitions." Grandpa expected me to deal with the world by being alert and smart. Over the years, he told me repeatedly that I had to get an education because a fire could take away my house and my possessions in a minute, but no one could take away my skills or my knowledge.

Among my peers, I was a tomboy. Although I liked girls' games (jump rope and hopscotch), the boys' games (street hockey and climbing) were much more fun for me because they were more physical, exciting, and competitive. One day in kindergarten, I beat up a boy who stole my colored drawings and passed them in to the teacher as his own. When I came home with a swollen nose and blood all over my dress, Grandma was horrified. "You can't fight with a boy," she admonished. "That's not ladylike." Grandpa, on the other hand, told me privately that I had to be tough in this world, and that even though I got punched in the nose, he was "proud" that I had stood up for myself with a boy who stole my property. "But," he warned, "don't fight boys because they can hurt you or laugh at you for not being a good little girl. So be smart, not strong." I took this warning to mean that men and women have different sources of power, and girls need to rely on their intellect. In other words, once again, I had to get an education to learn how to persuade others, including boys.

The first time I recall that I actually appreciated being a girl was when I was 16. In the late 1960s, boys were still expected to pay for everything on a date, and I liked that a lot. I also liked the fact that they were supposed to pick me up for the date, drive me around town, drop me off, and keep me safe the whole time. But then I learned that this arrangement could not always be counted on, and boys could not always be trusted. When I was 17, my date got drunk and started to let his hands wander, so I had to call my Dad to rescue me. Thus, although I was temporarily lulled into Cinderella Land for a year, I quickly discovered that there are prices to be paid for being a passive princess.

That incident with the drunken boy led me to make a profound decision about my life. From that point, I resolved never again to let myself be so vulnerable, and I became determined to control my own destiny in every way. In the short term, when I went out with guys, I had enough money in my purse to call a cab if I needed one. In the long term, I would pay my own way through life.

By 18, I was living on my own and paying my own tuition. It was in college studying English literature to become a teacher that I started reading works by authors who gave me some perspective on and insight into what I had been feeling all these years. The first seminal author I discovered in this context was Bertrand Russell (1929), who analyzed the social and sexual inequalities between men and women in marriage. That inspired me to read Friedan (1963) and Chesler (1972), deeply immersing myself in the literature of women's liberation and feminism.

Wondering what I could do, politically and socially, to raise my own and others' consciousness of feminism and women's gender roles, I took a job as an assistant program director at a women's center. My work there focused on organizing consciousness-raising groups for women of all socioeconomic backgrounds and ethnicities. When the grant ran out for the job at the women's center, I made the practical decision that I needed to find more reliable work that would give me health insurance and ultimately a pension.

That led me to obtain certification as a high school teacher, with a minor in library science. During my first year as an English teacher and school librarian, I was troubled by the number of girls who were getting pregnant and dropping out of school. This motivated me to request to teach the family life course so that I could inform the girls about contraception and other issues related to their relationships with boys. However, the principal denied my application, citing my lack of formal training in human sexuality.

That led me to enroll in the doctoral program at the Institute for the Advanced Study of Human Sexuality in San Francisco. During that training, I obtained clinical and research experience at the Pacific Center in Berkeley, which provided mental health services for gay, lesbian, bisexual, and transsexual populations. One of my clients, who was a postoperative male-to-female transsexual, asked me, "What do other people like me do sexually, and are they satisfied with their sex lives?" I replied that I did not know, but I would go to the library to find out.

To my surprise, I could find nothing in the literature on the subject. That led me to choose the topic of the reported sexual behaviors of 64 postoperative male-to-female transsexuals for my doctoral dissertation (Martin, 1988). Aside from completing my doctoral with this project, I was immensely gratified by the reaction I received from the client who had inspired the study in the first place for she was relieved to learn that what she was doing was "normal."

PROFESSIONAL JOURNEY

After I earned my PhD and my board certification from the American Association of Sexuality Educators, Counselors, and Therapists, I launched a full-time private practice as a sex therapist with a specialty in gender dysphoria. Because many of my male sex therapy clients were also coming to me with problems other than sexual concerns, I decided that I needed additional training in relationship issues and mental health in general. Therefore, I attended the master of science in counseling program at San Francisco State University and eventually became a licensed marriage and family therapist (LMFT).

When I was practicing as an LMFT, one of my senior clients was a 70-year-old man with Parkinson's disease and early-stage dementia, which impeded his cognitive, behavioral, and sexual functioning. Bill's biopsychosocial sexual problems with his Parkinson-related cognitive/memory deficits, his marital/extramarital relationship distress, and his fear of permanent erectile dysfunction inspired me to learn more about the effects of brain disorders on sexual functioning. His case also made me reflect on the increasing number of individuals and couples over the age of 75 in my practice who were requesting relationship therapy and sex therapy.

Wanting to know more about the assessment of brain dysfunctions, I enrolled in the neuropsychology program at Fielding Graduate University in Santa Barbara, California, from which I received my certificate in neuropsychology. To become a board-certified neuropsychologist, I needed a PhD in clinical psychology; therefore, I entered the PhD program in clinical psychology at Fielding.

When I began my psychology doctoral program, I planned to do a dissertation in the area of neuropsychology and memory. However, I ultimately had to admit that I had a deeper interest in learning how I could improve my clinical skills with male clients since I had observed that more men than women were dropping out of therapy with me within the first three sessions. Therefore, in my dissertation project, I pursued gender research again, attempting to identify the factors that almost 200 adult male clients reported as contributing to their establishing a positive therapeutic alliance with their current therapist. These factors turned out to be: (a) their comfort with the therapist; (b) their own emotional expressiveness; (c) their own openness; (d) their respect for the therapist and their sense of being respected by the therapist; and (e) their trust in the therapist. I also found that emotionally secure men formed higher levels of therapeutic alliance with their therapist than did insecure and avoidant men (Martin, 2007).

Now that I have over three decades of work in the field of gender studies and clinical experience working with male clients, I have repeatedly seen the impact of gender roles on how men start and end therapy. In the early days of my private practice, I wanted guidelines about this issue. I hope this chapter may help you as you start and end your work with male clients.

HOW MEN START AND END PSYCHOTHERAPY

Starting Therapy With Men

Numerous authors have identified unique challenges to starting therapy with male clients who adhere to masculine gender role norms. These challenges include men's reluctance to ask for help and, once they are in therapy, their unwillingness or inability to identify, disclose, and explore their emotions (Brooks, 2010; Englar-Carlson, 2006; Greer, 2005; Levant et al., 1992).

Whereas feminine gender role norms lead female clients to demonstrate relational and expressive character traits in their interactions with therapists, masculine gender role norms lead male clients to demonstrate instrumental (i.e., directive) character traits and behaviors with therapists (Scher & Good, 1990). In other words, men's need to "stay in control" can contribute to avoiding therapists in the first place and, if they do enter therapy, to discontinue it as soon as possible.

Female therapists who have male clients must understand how they have been influenced by their own gender role norms and by the stereotypical messages about femininity that they have received from their own culture (e.g., Brown, 2010; Johnson, 2001; Potash, 1998; Sweet, 2006; Wexler, 2009). Female therapists with male clients must also understand whatever stereotypes of men they may possess, consciously or unconsciously (e.g., Brown, 2010; Johnson, 2001; Potash, 1998; Sweet, 2006; Wexler, 2009).

Before any female therapist starts to work with clients of either gender, she must be thoroughly familiar with the federal and state or provincial laws and the ethics code of her professional association (also see Rappleyea, Harris, White, & Simon, 2009; Vasquez, Bingham, & Barnett, 2008). Female therapists should explain to male clients how therapy works, what they can expect from the therapist and treatment, and what is expected of them. As Potash (1998) noted, men "feel more comfortable knowing the rules and what to expect" (p. 288).

Regardless of one's theoretical orientation, therapy typically includes the assessment/evaluation phase, the middle phase, the pretermination phase, the termination phase, and the posttermination phase (Novick & Novick, 2006; Ward, 1984). During these five phases, clients may be in any one of six stages of change, which Prochaska and Norcross (2002) called precontemplation, contemplation, preparation, action, maintenance, and termination. Thus, therapists must always take into account which stage of which phase a client may be in at a particular time.

In the first session, therapists simultaneously aim to help men feel welcomed, understood, and hopeful as the men reveal their personal history and as the therapist and client jointly develop a treatment plan with goals and tasks. However, therapy with men also includes a prominent organizing principle—namely, understanding men from within the context of their male socialization into masculine gender role norms (Stevens & Englar-Carlson, 2006). To gain a male client's trust and participation in the therapy process, the therapist should identify (a) a man's problem(s) within the context of traditional masculine norms, such as being tough, competitive, status driven, and emotionally stoic; (b) his gender role strain, which includes the pressures on him to be accomplished in every endeavor yet be equally emotionally sensitive, tender, and intimate; and (c) the positive attributes of his masculine gender role, such as providing for others, being assertive, being independent, and being confident to use the new experience of therapy (Good & Mintz, 2001; Levant, 1990, 1998; Stevens & Englar-Carlson, 2006).

Numerous authors maintained that, when working with men, female therapists should examine their own perceptions of men and help them to hold a positive view of their own masculine identity. For example, Johnson (2001), Potash (1998), and Sweet (2006) specifically noted that a female therapist should understand the role of shame that a man brings to therapy, which may prevent his engagement in and use of the therapy process. Johnson (2001) advised female therapists to tell male clients, during the first phone contact and again in writing on the intake forms, what they can expect from the therapy process and what the rules, limits, and boundaries are in therapy. For example, Johnson recommended informing the client about who will participate in family therapy and about the nonnegotiable limit on the physical expression of anger/rage in the therapy room. Sweet (2006) cautioned that female therapists must examine their own countertransference, which may be triggered by men's defenses. This may include the therapist feeling threatened by men's anger or by unprocessed sexual energy in the male/female therapeutic dyad (Hobday, Mellman, & Gabbard, 2008; Sweet, 2006). Such countertransference should be examined without responding to the male client with blame or shame. Female therapists must also anticipate potential ruptures in the therapeutic alliance with their male clients, identify the responses of those clients to the ruptures, and take measures to repair the ruptures (Safran, Muran, Samstag, & Stevens, 2001).

Ending Therapy With Men

Although it is well known that women enter therapy much more readily than men do (e.g., Addis & Mahalik, 2003), no one, to my knowledge, has ever quantified by gender the clients who terminate therapy prematurely. Premature termination, in the words of Hatchett and Park (2003), occurs when "a client has left therapy before obtaining a requisite level of improvement or completing therapy goals" (p. 226). We do know that somewhere between 30% and 60% of all clients terminate prematurely, but we do not know their gender (e.g., Swift, Callahan, & Levine, 2009; Wierzbicki & Pekarik, 1993). In any case, the consensus in the masculine gender role literature is that to prevent male clients from terminating therapy prematurely, therapists must *understand the influence of masculine ideologies or scripts, masculine gender role norms, and gender role conflict in* men's decision to seek therapy in the first place (Englar-Carlson, 2006; Levant & Kopecky, 1995; O'Neil, 1982).

Termination is the time between setting the date for the final session and holding the final session itself. Overall, there is no pantheoretical model in the psychotherapeutic literature that proposes when and how to process a therapeutic termination (Joyce, Piper, Ogrodniczuk, & Klein, 2007b). Termination may be either therapist initiated or client initiated, but the latter is far more common (Rappleyea et al., 2009). Furthermore, termination may be completed or premature (Davis, 2008; O'Donohue & Cucciare, 2008).

Completed therapy can be thought of in terms of a client leaving after he has completed the goals that he and the therapist set for him. Successful termination of therapy can take three forms: (a) *time-limited therapy*, which lasts for a certain number of sessions, after which it stops completely; (b) *spaced therapy*, which allows for time between treatment sessions to be extended for weeks or months, with a gradual approach to the termination; and (c) *intermittent therapy*, which allows for a series of breaks or interruptions in treatment with the same therapist throughout one's lifetime (Salberg, 2010; Ward, 1984).

Authors tend to agree that the termination stage of therapy includes critical tasks and challenges that the client and the therapist must complete as they end their work together and say goodbye to the therapeutic relationship (Davis, 2008; Gabbard, 2009; Rabinowitz & Cochran, 2008; Salberg, 2010). A successful therapeutic termination progresses through three phases of therapy. These consist of

1. The *pretermination phase*, during which the therapist assesses the client's readiness to stop therapy and consolidate his learning. It also includes a review of the client's experience in therapy, which includes a discussion of (a) what has improved; (b) which goals still need to be completed; and (c) which skills will be helpful to use in the future.
2. The *termination phase*, during which the therapist helps the client to resolve his feelings about the therapy and the therapist. As part of saying good-bye to a client and the working relationship, therapists tend to use the last few sessions to (a) review the client's experience of the work they did together; (b) provide a summary of the goals achieved and changes made by the client; (c) suggest use of acquired skills to address possible future challenges to the client; and (d) ask the client to independently do steps (a), (b), and (c). Therapists also tend to share their appreciation of having the opportunity to work with the client. For their part, clients tend to share their appreciation of their therapist and how valuable it was to understand and use therapy.
3. The *posttermination phase*. After therapy has ended, some clients will book a follow-up session to "stay on track" with their therapy gains. Many male clients will use the time after termination as an intermittent period between therapeutic treatments (Davis, 2008; Salberg, 2010).

In addition to the varieties of complete termination, there are two forms of incomplete or premature termination, depending on who initiates it. Abandonment is an inappropriate termination *by the therapist* of a client who continues to need therapy (Behnke, 2009; Younggren & Gottlieb, 2008). Premature termination *by the client* can be thought of in terms of the client dropping out of therapy before he completes the goals that he and the therapist set up for him.

Numerous authors have reported reasons for male client dropout, which include having male alexithymia, which impedes emotional expression; being too anxious about self-disclosure; disagreeing with the therapist on which problems to address or how to address them; feeling criticized or unappreciated by the therapist about the client's masculine gender role socialization or personal experience; perceiving the therapy process as taking too long; lacking motivation to do the work; being in denial; seeing no solution to their problem; experiencing negative transference reactions; and having unrealistic expectations of the therapist or the therapeutic process (e.g., Joyce, Piper, Ogrodniczuk, & Klein, 2007a; Levant & Sherman, 2006; Ogrodniczuk, Joyce, & Piper, 2005; Owen, Wong, & Rodolfa, 2010; Rochlen & Hoyer, 2005).

MY OWN APPROACH TO STARTING AND STOPPING THERAPY WITH MEN

Starting Therapy

When a man first calls me on the phone, I try to determine what his problem is, and if it is something that I can help him with. If I do not believe it is, I will refer him to someone else. If I do believe it is, I ask about his experience with psychotherapy, if any. Then, I ask what he thinks would be a positive outcome of treatment with me. Finally, I tell him that he can come in for one session without making any commitment to longer-term therapy, and in that session, we will set up treatment goals to address his concerns.

Early in the initial phone call, I tell him that I use a multidisciplinary approach to therapy, which is based on short- and long-term psychodynamic, cognitive-behavioral, attachment, feminist, and gender-role theories of men and masculinity. Potential male clients fall into one of several categories after the first call.

Some men book a session and then call to cancel it. A few of these men will disregard my cancellation policy by canceling fewer than 24 hours before the appointment—some as late as 1 minute ahead of time. Other men will book a session with me and then simply fail to appear. A possible explanation for these cancellations and no-shows is the shame they feel about asking for help or about being seen walking into a psychotherapist's office (Wexler, 2009). An alternative explanation might be that the work schedules of these men have changed, and their work takes priority for them over their mental health needs. Since many men struggle with normative male alexithymia, or the inability to label their emotions (Levant, 1998), my last-minute cancellers may have been apprehensive about being emotionally vulnerable in front of a stranger.

Most men who cancel, no matter how late, will ask to reschedule, which I am willing to do if they will pay for the next appointment in advance. In my experience, almost all of these individuals will comply with this request. Interestingly, this cancellation problem almost never occurs with women, at least in relation to the first appointment. Perhaps male clients' perceptions of the therapeutic relationship are not initially as important to them as they are for women, who tend to have established an alliance with me early in the phone conversation.

In my experience, men are far more concerned than women to establish narrowly defined goals from the very beginning. Men want to know that therapy will be meaningful to them and that I will not keep them in therapy "forever." In my experience, they tend to prefer short-term, skill-building sessions versus emotional catharsis and ongoing supportive therapy, which women tend to favor. In fact, most potential male clients request treatment that will require two or three sessions, at most. This conforms to the masculine gender role norm of self-reliance.

I always try to remember that my countertransference can begin on the phone (see also Gelso & Hayes, 2002). When I started my private practice, I quickly learned that I was impatient to get started, but naïve about the business world. For example, when a male caller offered to pay me to fax him *the* technique to resolve his problems with a "demanding" wife, I laughed and said, "You're joking, right?" He said, "Look, I'm a busy professional and don't have time to waste. I said I'd pay you, so just give me the technique." Feeling annoyed at what I considered his sense of entitlement and his dismissal of the whole field of psychology, I snapped back, "I can't do *that!*" He hung up. Afterward, when I consulted with a psychologist about how I might have handled the situation better, she led me to understand how my spontaneous response to my countertransference had driven away a man I otherwise might have been able to help.

There are rare instances when I have decided not to begin therapy with a potential male client. For example, one man who called me told me that he had already worked with five female therapists, who had all disappointed him. Nevertheless, he wanted to stop seeing his current male psychiatrist, who was prescribing medications for depression, which the man did not want to take, despite his suicidal thoughts. If he were to see me, he said, I would have to promise not to insist on referring him to someone for a psychiatric evaluation. I told him that was unethical, but he replied that he did not care, and I would have to follow his instructions. At that point, I was compelled to tell him that I could not be his therapist.

When I schedule the first appointment with clients, I ask them to arrive 20 minutes early to fill out and sign a packet of intake papers for patient-informed consent. The packet includes (a) *a patient information form* to collect his demographics, residential and business addresses and phone numbers, an emergency contact name and phone number, insurance and billing information, and an agreement to pay for missed sessions and bounced checks; (b) *an office policy form*, which includes information on payment, cancellation, office hours, termination, and compensation for additional services, such as writing legal reports or reading a patient's writing, including his articles, books, or transcripts, on my own time outside his therapy hour; (c) *a limits-of-confidentiality form*, which notifies the client about his right to privacy as well as the limits of that right; (d) *a Health Insurance Portability and Accountability Act (HIPAA) Privacy Rule*; (e) *a goal sheet*, which includes questions that ask him to state what he wants to change about his life, how he will know he has changed, how I will know he has changed, what will or might get in the way of his making these changes, and how long he thinks he will be in therapy to make these changes; and (f) *an outpatient services contract*, which includes information about the kind of services I provide, namely, psychological testing and individual, couples, or group psychotherapy. I describe the therapeutic process, my theoretical orientation, what we can both do to facilitate a positive treatment outcome, and what the limitations and boundaries in therapy will be.

My strategy with a new male client is to listen to him identify his presenting problems in *his own* words, without interpretation. Also, I follow the recommendations of various writers who advise therapists to identify a man's problems within the context of traditional masculine norms, such as being self-reliant, competitive, status driven, and emotionally stoic (Kilmartin, 2010; Wexler, 2009). I also try to establish realistic expectations about what the therapy can accomplish and what the client's responsibilities will be to move the therapy forward. Since clients generally bond with their therapists, I discuss termination issues from the beginning of treatment. For example, in the first session, I look for his history and issues with anger, separation, loss, abandonment, and rejection, which may affect how he will bond or terminate with me and how each of us will view his presenting problem. By the end of the first session, I will have assessed his presenting concerns, diagnosed his mental health condition, conceptualized a treatment plan with him, and deepened the therapeutic alliance that I initiated on the phone (Brooks, 2010; Rabinowitz & Cochran, 2002).

Identifying the Man's Real Concern

It is important, especially with male clients, to check that the presenting problem represents the real concern. For example, one day, I got a call from a 39-year-old Filipino man named Carlo, who said that his 28-year-old wife, Rita, had complained that he had a low sex drive and needed to get some help. When he came in, he told me that Rita was six months pregnant with their third child. It wasn't that he found her unattractive because of her pregnancy, he said, and he *did* love her, but for some reason he didn't want to have sex with her most of the time. Rita felt ignored, he said, and wanted him to be more affectionate. In the course of our first session, Carlo and I set up a treatment plan to address his loss of sexual desire for his wife.

It was not until the middle of the second session that Carlo began to admit that he did not really have a low sex drive at all. Behind Rita's back, he said, he would masturbate while looking at men's magazines. "There's nothing wrong with my dick, Doc," he said. "I just feel a sadness in my soul." I realized at that point that it was less shameful for Carlo to admit to his wife that he had a low sex drive than to admit to being depressed. In his world, men *never* get depressed.

It soon became apparent, both to Carlo and to me, that he had a lot of resentment toward Rita because this third child was going to place an extra financial burden on him when he was already stressed by his job. Carlo was a salesman, who was always under pressure to "hit the numbers." As he looked ahead to turning 40 soon, he felt that he should be further along in his career than he was and this undermined his faith in himself as a man. Once he revealed all this, we developed new goals for him and a new treatment plan, this one focused on his unhappiness over his masculine role stress and midlife crisis. Thus, the ostensible presenting problem (in this case, low sexual drive) may only have been a mask for the true one (in this case, feelings of professional inadequacy). This is consistent with the masculine gender role norms discussed above (e.g., extreme self-reliance and primacy of work) and the masculine gender role conflict (e.g., success, power, and competition conflicts between work and family relations), also discussed earlier (Mahalik, Good, & Englar-Carlson, 2003; O'Neil, Helms, Gable, Davis, & Wrightsman, 1986).

The evaluation process in the first session, and beyond, involves, among other things, identifying my male clients' transference reactions to me, including their gender role perceptions of me as a female therapist. Despite my years of clinical experience and continuing education, I occasionally hear myself demonstrating my countertransference with male clients by being impatient, blunt, or condescending. I suspect this comes from my unconscious view of some male clients' disapproval of me for being in a position of authority.

In Leon's case, my defensive reaction to his flirtatious proposal immediately undermined any possibility of creating a therapeutic alliance. My reaction in this instance was not so much to the challenge of my authority as it was to the implicit denigration of my authority as springing from my physical attractiveness. Leon's valuing me for my beauty rather than my intellect momentarily revived my fear of having to defend myself against the stereotypical "power-in-beauty" view of women (Rudman & Glick, 2008).

Today, I am usually able to steer the flirtatious Leons into productive therapy by recognizing and empathizing with their problem, rather than shaming or blaming them. In the process, I have found it important to recognize my own unconscious, unexamined stereotypes about men as well as, if appropriate, openly discuss with them their unconscious, unexamined stereotypes about women.

The literature states that men like to focus on one problem at a time, advising therapists not to discuss issues that are unimportant to their male clients, such as exploring the past, but to focus on specific goals of immediate interest to them (Greer, 2005). This can be tricky because a client (such as Carlo) may choose not to disclose certain information out of a sense of shame or guilt. He may also be in denial about certain aspects of his life that cause him anxiety. I agree with Rabinowitz and Cochran's (2002) observation that male clients may avoid important topics in the first few sessions of therapy and may leave therapy if challenged about their issues or emotions before they are ready to address them.

Ending Therapy

In my experience, men tend to remain in therapy for far fewer sessions than women do. In fact, men can start and end therapy in the *same* session, which women rarely do. Also, I have found that men tend to come to therapy intermittently, seeing me for a while, dropping out, and then coming back—whereas my women clients tend to follow the more traditional route of addressing their problems from the beginning and working through the middle to the end. If certain pitfalls are avoided with male clients, however, both brief and long-term therapy with them can end in mutual termination.

As my skills at practicing what Good, Gilbert, and Scher (1990) called "gender-aware therapy" into whatever theoretical approach I use to treat male clients—that is, viewing a man's problems within the social context of restrictive gender role norms as discussed by the authors—over the years the dropout rate for my male clients has decreased considerably. I also use what Philpot, Brooks, Lusterman, and Nutt (1997) called "gender-sensitive therapy" in my work with heterosexual and gay male couples. When I apply these authors' directives to use what I know and understand about my own gender role journey, as well as what I know and understand about men's socialization processes that may influence how my male clients use therapy, my male client dropout levels have decreased. Because the client and I have discussed the beginning, middle, and end stages of therapy from the first session, he is prepared for when and how termination might proceed.

The Pretermination Phase

In the pretermination phase, which is most often initiated by the client in the case of men (since they usually do not want to participate in long-term therapy), I will suggest that we review their most recent goal sheet to see if they have hit their targets. This phase, which can take weeks or months, presents opportunities for the therapist to use the client's positive transference to work through still unresolved issues. For example, Bill, a 41-year-old single Caucasian male who had been seeing me for 8 months, told me one day that he felt ready to terminate therapy since he had successfully resolved his problems. He added that he trusted me. At that point, I felt confident to suggest something that I had been contemplating for some time.

Bill, who was a big, strong man who did seasonal work as a lumberjack along the Pacific Coast and in Alaska, had originally come to see me with complaints about panic attacks when he tried to make love with his new girlfriend. He had been having similar problems with girlfriends, he said, ever since he had been a teenager. My empathy for his suffering helped to form a therapeutic alliance between us. It was difficult for him to talk about the shame associated with his problem, so I let him stray from that topic whenever he needed to do so.

Bill and I worked on his developing a long-term connection with his current girlfriend, which included his learning how to identify and disclose his emotions to her. Furthermore, to help him negotiate sexual intimacy with his girlfriend, I helped him to learn healthy ways to manage his anger, set boundaries, build trust, and develop nonsexual forms of intimacy. We worked for several months doing a combination of gender role therapy, sex therapy, and cognitive-behavioral therapy.

The gender role therapy involved inviting Bill to discuss his personal experiences of learning how to be a boy and how to become and be a man. For example, he told me that he had been brought up to believe that it was a man's job to have an erection whenever he wanted one because it was a man's responsibility to pleasure a woman and bring her to orgasm. This belief system probably lay behind Bill's feelings of inadequacy.

The sex therapy involved Bill enhancing his sensory awareness. For example, to improve his sense of touch, I taught him sensate focus techniques (Masters & Johnson, 1970). These might involve a homework assignment with his girlfriend during which he attempted not to dissociate or panic while she touched his skin.

The cognitive-behavioral therapy involved Bill's identifying his distorted thinking and belief patterns about himself in particular and about relationships in general. For example, he believed that the only person in this world whom he could totally trust was himself. I told him that intimacy involved trust and self-disclosure and invited him to share with his girlfriend something about himself that made him feel vulnerable. He chose to tell her about an incident in his highly dangerous work as a lumberjack during which he experienced what he called "white knuckle" terror, which literally paralyzed him for several moments. He was reluctant to confess this "weakness" to his girlfriend because he feared she would view him as a coward. In fact, he reported to me afterward that she had been totally understanding, and this had increased their intimacy and his sense of trusting her.

Despite all this therapeutic work, it took eight months for Bill to divulge experiences that were at the core of his problem with sexual intimacy. His disclosure began with his describing a dream that he had had the night before, which was making him extremely anxious. In the dream, he said, he was beating one of his cousins to death—a man named Sam, whom Bill had never mentioned to me before. As we discussed the possible meaning of the dream, Bill revealed to me that, as a child, he had been sexually abused by Sam for two years. Starting when Bill was 8 and Sam was 12, the older boy had forced his smaller, younger cousin to perform oral and anal copulation. This continued until Bill was old enough and big enough to put an end to it. For the past 33 years, Bill said, every time he tried to be sexually intimate with a woman, memories of those painful experiences with Sam would surface, and he

would lose his erection. I suggested to Bill that his having been forced
into a feminine sexual position as a child was interfering with masculine
sexual performance now.

For the next two months, Bill and I discussed the feelings he had
about Sam's abuse of him and how these feelings altered the developmental history he had given me at the beginning of his therapy. Bill realized that he no longer felt as victimized and powerless as he had eight
months earlier. Subsequent to these insights, Bill's sexual problems with
his girlfriend began to fade away. It was then that he suggested he was
ready to terminate therapy, having solved his initial problem.

The suggestion I made, which had been on my mind for a while,
was for Bill to invite his cousin Sam to attend a session with us. That
was possible because Sam lived nearby, and he and Bill were still close
friends. Bill was intrigued by the idea, but at the same time, he was terrified at the prospect. It took two months of working together on Bill's
rage toward Sam for him to be ready to invite his cousin to a session.
I used Levant's (1990) psychoeducational approach in my work with
Bill, which the client said allowed him to feel in control of and back
away from his more overwhelming emotions. I also suggested he read
some books that were relevant to masculinity and sexual abuse, which
formed the core of much of our discussion.

When he finished reading the books, Bill told me he was now ready to
confront his cousin over what had happened between them as children.
First, however, he wanted my assurance that I would in no way attack
Sam, whom he regarded with affection. I gave that assurance without
hesitation and scheduled a two-hour appointment for Bill and Sam so
that there would be enough time to process their feelings about this old
traumatic issue.

I spent the first few minutes thanking Sam for coming to support Bill
in his therapy. Sam said that he cared deeply for Bill, and he would do
anything to help him. "The reason Bill invited you here to his therapy,
Sam," I said, looking to Bill for approval to proceed, "is that he wants
to talk to you about what happened between you when you were children." "Yes," Bill said, "I want to talk to you about how you made me
do sex when we were kids." Sam let out a huge sigh of relief. "I'm glad
you're bringing this up," he said, "because it's been bothering me all
these years. . . . I'm *very* sorry for what happened, Bill. I've never known
how to tell you that." "I've gotta tell you how it's affected *me*, man," Bill
said, "'cause I've hated you for this for years."

They spent the remainder of the two hours talking, hugging, and
crying. My role in all this was to encourage Bill to express his feelings
and to assure Sam that he was safe. Nevertheless, it was important that
Sam take full responsibility for what had happened years before, which
he did. At the end of the session, Sam thanked me for giving him the
opportunity to help Bill. At the door, Bill himself gave me a big hug, for
the first time ever. I never saw Sam again, but Bill and I worked for the
next two months on the feelings that had come up in Bill during that

session. After that, Bill was truly ready to terminate therapy, and on leaving his final session, gave me the second big hug of our time together.

I was glad that I had followed my hunch to bring Bill and his cousin together when we entered the pretermination phase. It is always best, I believe, assuming that the client agrees, to resolve any lingering issues prior to termination.

The Termination Phase

The termination phase is the client's time to review his experience, integrate the work he has done, internalize the supportive regard from the therapy relationship, and say good-bye to me, our work together, and the therapy environment. For example, Venka, a 36-year-old engineer from India, called me to ask if I had ever worked with Indian people. When I confirmed that I had, he told me that he had not been able to consummate his marriage with his 24-year-old wife, Rekha. In our first session, I learned that Rekha had been complaining about this problem to her parents back in India, who in turn had complained to Venka's parents, and now he was thoroughly shamed by his family.

Venka admitted that he and his wife were both virgins. His only sexual experiences were episodes of mutual masturbation with other males in the years from elementary school through college. He explained that neither he nor his culture viewed this activity as sexual. When he attempted to penetrate his wife, however, she would cry out in pain as soon as he came near her hymen, at which point he would lose his erection. He had thought of visiting a prostitute, he said, but had instantly rejected that notion because he feared that if he had a better time with her than with his wife that would ruin his marriage forever.

As Venka told me his story, he was enlightening in many ways about his Indian customs and traditions, to which I had to be culturally sensitive. Nevertheless, I initially made some missteps in this connection. For example, I suggested that he urge his wife to stop complaining to her family, to which he replied, in a very kind and respectful voice, "I cannot do that, Doctor Martin. That's an American way to think about your elders." Taking a bibliotherapy approach, I suggested that he read a few books, articles, and handouts on relationships and intimacy. I also proposed that he get a copy of the *Kama Sutra* and read and discuss with his wife the book's sexual union section on kissing, embracing, and coupling.

When he came back to me to ask about certain details in the book and in his other readings, I was pleased to see that, through our open and explicit discussions of anatomy, sexuality, and his personal sexual history, we had created an atmosphere of trust in which he was not ashamed to ask such questions. Within 10 weeks of cognitive-behavioral and psychosexual therapy, Venka was able to consummate his marriage. On the cognitive side, I addressed his distortions about sexuality, intimacy, and male sexual performance. On the behavioral side, I gave him breathing and muscular techniques to help him relax and taught him communication skills, so that he could connect emotionally with his wife by talking to her, instead of obsessing about performance failure. Psychosexually, I worked on Venka's cultural expectations surrounding sexuality, and then I taught him sensate focus techniques (Masters & Johnson, 1970). Once Venka consummated his marriage, he was pleased to terminate his therapy.

During the termination phase in Venka's case, he was able to review the work he had done in therapy and to integrate the new skills he had learned. He stated that he experienced our therapeutic relationship, which was the only one he had ever participated in, as positive and helpful, despite our gender and cultural differences. He also talked about how hard it always is to say good-bye, which reminded him of how sad he had been when leaving his family in India. After thanking me for our work together, he talked about what he could do if problems arose in the future and what he would keep working on.

For my part during the termination phase with Venka, I tried not to avoid my feelings as I witnessed his sadness over parting. I also strove to avoid denial when he expressed his appreciation of me and my work. Termination can bring up my countertransference feelings and my defenses. For example, I needed to examine my maternal countertransference toward Venka, almost as if I were watching him graduate from college. The feeling was bittersweet. I was happy to see him go, at the same time being sad. I have learned to appreciate the attachment feelings that develop in the therapeutic environment. Separation anxieties and defenses against them include my own feelings of withdrawal and emotional numbness. However, I also experience the pleasure of seeing the client do well in his life. As Venka left my office for the last time, I told him that he was free to call me at any time or to return to therapy with me if he ever wished to do so.

The Posttermination Phase

Six months after my last session with Venka, I got a posttermination call from him, delightedly informing me that Rekha was pregnant. He thanked me once again for our work together, told me he was communicating well with his wife, that their sex life was comforting and satisfying, and that Rekha was no longer complaining to her family about his sexual inadequacy. He ended by saying that he was fine now, but if he should ever need me again, he wanted to know that it was okay to contact me in the future. I assured him again that he was welcome to return any time he wished.

TIPS FOR FEMALE THERAPISTS WHO WORK WITH MALE CLIENTS

Starting Therapy With Men

- Know the legal and ethical considerations of starting therapy with male clients.

- Know the literature on gender-aware and gender-sensitive therapy.
- Examine your own gender myths and stereotypes about men and masculinity.
- Begin the therapeutic alliance during the first phone call.
- Have clients fill out intake forms prior to the first session to gain their informed consent to therapy and to gather information about their previous therapy experiences and treatment outcomes.
- Provide your clients with a goal sheet in their intake packets so they can fill in the form privately in the waiting room before the first session.
- Let new male clients vent their anger, if they wish, before trying to direct them to discussion of the goals of therapy.
- Collaborate with your clients on the goals of treatment in a mutually agreed treatment plan.
- Engage men in therapy by telling them about the process and how they can use it to help themselves.
- Discuss all the phases of therapy, including your termination procedures, during the first session.
- Be prepared to list numerous advantages of therapy if new male clients challenge you about its utility for their problem.
- Fix men's problems *with* them, not *for* them.
- Repair therapeutic ruptures quickly. Apologize if you have been defensive in response to any comments, questions, or concerns about treatment.
- Be aware that the presenting problem may be misleading.
- If you sense that a male client is avoiding his deeper feelings, it may be important for him to "dance around" his problems for a while.
- Be open when a man wants to interview you about your expertise with his problem.
- Do not assume that you share a mutual understanding of male clients' presenting problems and their expectations for treatment outcome.
- Identify and try to resolve ruptures in therapy.
- Listen and respond respectfully when male clients question the utility of therapy.
- Set appropriate boundaries for therapy, which may include starting and stopping times of each therapy session, fee payment terms, and 24-hour notice for cancellations.

Ending Therapy With Men

- Know the legal and ethical requirements for ending therapy with male clients.
- Provide a client sufficient support and referrals if you need, for any reason, to terminate therapy.

- Acknowledge male clients' gender role identity changes regarding their presenting problems and how they currently resolve them.
- Be prepared to do a summary of the therapy work for male clients' last sessions.
- Let your male clients know that you, as a female therapist, have tried to understand their male gender experience and their experience of being therapy clients.
- Acknowledge your male clients' growth and the end of the working relationship.
- Encourage male clients to be prepared to use the skills they learned in therapy to meet their future challenges.
- Acknowledge the cultural understandings, both by gender and by race or ethnicity, that your male clients have given you throughout your work together.
- Allow yourself to be emotionally (as well as rationally) present as you witness your clients' sadness, and possibly your own, as you both say good-bye during the final session.
- Offer your clients the option of continuing or returning to therapy whenever they wish in the future.
- Review the treatment plan and update the therapeutic goals to determine your clients' readiness to enter the termination phase of therapy.
- Do not let male clients terminate on the phone without trying to contact them, by phone or in writing, for a final session.
- Take care of yourself, both physically and mentally. Terminating with clients to whom you have become emotionally attached can be exhausting if you do not have ways to let go. Personal individual psychotherapy may facilitate your development and coping as a new therapist.

REFERENCES

Addis, M. E., & Mahalik, J. R. (2003). Men, masculinity, and the contexts of help–seeking. *American Psychologist, 58*(1), 5–14.

Behnke, S. (2009). Termination and abandonment: A key ethical distinction. *Monitor on Psychology, 40*(8), 70.

Brooks, G. R. (2010). On the doorstep—Engaging men in psychotherapy. In G. R. Brooks, *Beyond the crisis of masculinity: A transtheoretical model for male-friendly therapy* (pp. 68–84). Washington, DC: American Psychological Association.

Brown, L. S. (2010). *Feminist therapy*. In J. Carlson & M. Englar-Carlson (Eds.), *Theories of psychotherapy series* (pp. 1–15). Washington, DC: American Psychological Association.

Chesler, P. (1972). *Women and madness*. Garden City, NY: Doubleday.

David, D. S., & Brannon, R. (Eds.). (1976). *The forty-nine percent majority: The male sex role*. Reading, MA: Addison-Wesley.

Davis, D. D. (2008). *Terminating therapy: A professional guide to ending on a positive note.* New York, NY: Wiley.

Englar-Carlson, M. (2006). Masculine norms and the therapy process. In M. Englar-Carlson & M. A. Stevens (Eds.), *In the room with men: A casebook of therapeutic change* (pp. 13–47). Washington, DC: American Psychological Association.

Friedan, B. (1963). *The feminine mystique.* New York, NY: Norton.

Gabbard, G. O. (2009). What is a "good enough" termination? *Journal of American Psychoanalytic Association, 57,* 575–594.

Gelso, C. J., & Hayes, J. A. (2002). The management of countertransference. In J. Norcross (Ed.), *Psychotherapy relationships that work: Therapist contributions and responsiveness to patients* (pp. 267–283). New York, NY: Oxford University Press.

Good, G. E., Gilbert, L. A., & Scher, M. (1990). Gender aware therapy: A synthesis of feminist therapy and knowledge about gender. *Journal of Counseling and Development, 68,* 376–380.

Good, G. E., & Mintz, L. B. (2001). Integrative therapy for men. In G. R. Brooks & G. E. Good (Eds.), *The new handbook of psychotherapy and counseling with men: A comprehensive guide to settings, problems, and treatment approaches* (rev. & abridged ed., pp. 582–602). San Francisco: Jossey-Bass.

Greer, M. (2005). Keeping them hooked in. *Monitor on Psychology, 36*(6), 60–62.

Hatchett, G. T., & Park, H. L. (2003). Comparison of four operational definitions of premature termination. *Psychotherapy: Theory, Research, Practice, Training, 40,* 226–231.

Hobday, G., Mellman, L., & Gabbard, G. O. (2008). Complex sexualized transferences when the patient is male and the therapist female. *American Journal of Psychiatry, 165*(12), 1525–1530.

Johnson, N. G. (2001). Women helping men: Strengths of and barriers to women therapists working with men clients. In G. R. Brooks & G. E. Good (Eds.), *The new handbook of psychotherapy and counseling with men: A comprehensive guide to settings, problems, and treatment approaches* (rev. & abridged ed., pp. 291–307). San Francisco: Jossey-Bass.

Joyce, A. S., Piper, W. E., Ogrodniczuk, J. S., & Klein, R. H. (2007a). Patient initiated termination. In A. S. Joyce, W. E. Piper, J. S. Ogrodniczuk, & R. H. Klein. *Termination in psychotherapy: A psychodynamic model of processes and outcomes* (pp. 133–156). Washington, DC: American Psychological Association.

Joyce, A. S., Piper, W. E., Ogrodniczuk, J. S., & Klein, R. H. (2007b). The process of termination. In A. S. Joyce, W. E. Piper, J. S. Ogrodniczuk, & R. H. Klein. *Termination in psychotherapy: A psychodynamic model of processes and outcomes* (pp. 9–40). Washington, DC: American Psychological Association.

Kilmartin, C. (2010). *The masculine self* (4th ed.). New York, NY: Sloan.

Levant, R. F. (1990). Psychological services designed for men: Psychoeducational approach. *Psychotherapy, 27,* 309–315.

Levant, R. F. (1998). Desperately seeking language: Understanding, assessing and treating normative male alexithymia. In W. Pollack & R. Levant (Eds.), *New psychotherapy for men* (pp. 35–56). New York, NY: Wiley.

Levant, R. F., Hirsch, L., Celentano, E., Cozza, T., Hill, S., MacEachern, M., et al. (1992). The male role: An investigation of contemporary norms. *Journal of Mental Health Counseling, 14,* 325–337.

Levant, R. F., & Kopecky, G. (1995). *Masculinity reconstructed: Changing the rules of manhood-at work, in relationships, and in family life.* New York, NY: Dutton.

Levant, R. F., & Sherman, C. (2006). *Effective psychotherapy with men—A viewer's manual.* San Francisco: Psychotherapy.net.

Mahalik, J. R., Good, G. E., & Englar-Carlson, M. (2003). Masculinity scripts, presenting concerns, and help seeking: Implications for practice and training. *Professional Psychology: Research and Practice, 34*(2), 123–131.

Martin, J. (1988). *The incidence, frequency, and rate of genital satisfaction of 64 post-operative male-to-female transsexuals reported to be experienced during various sexual behaviors: A descriptive study.* Unpublished doctoral dissertation, Institute for the Advanced Study of Human Sexuality, San Francisco.

Martin, J. (2007). *Male clients' perception of positive therapeutic alliance.* Doctoral dissertation retrieved from ProQuest Dissertations and Theses. (Accession order No. AAT3287691)

Masters, W. H., & Johnson, V. E. (1970). *Human sexual inadequacy.* London: Churchill.

Novick, J., & Novick, K. K. (2006). *Good goodbyes: Knowing how to end in psychotherapy and psychoanalysis.* New York, NY: Aronson.

O'Donohue, W. T., & Cucciare, M. A. (Eds.). (2008). *Terminating psychotherapy: A clinician's guide.* New York, NY: Routledge.

Ogrodniczuk, J. S., Joyce, A. S., & Piper, W. E. (2005). Strategies for reducing patient-initiated premature termination of psychotherapy. *Harvard Review of Psychiatry, 13*(2), 57–70.

O'Neil, J. M. (1982). Gender role conflict and strain in men's lives: Implications for psychiatrists, and other human service providers. In K. Solomon & N. Levy (Eds.), *Men in transition: Theory and therapy* (pp. 5–44). New York, NY: Plenum Press.

O'Neil, J. M., Helms, B. J., Gable, R. K., Davis, L., & Wrightsman, L. S. (1986). Gender role conflict scale: College men's fear of femininity. *Sex Roles, 14*, 335–350.

Owen, J., Wong, Y. J., & Rodolfa, E. (2010). The relationship between clients' conformity to masculine norms and their perceptions of helpful therapist actions. *Journal of Counseling Psychology, 57*(1), 68–78.

Philpot, C. L., Brooks, G. R., Lusterman, D. D., & Nutt, R. L. (1997). Gender-sensitive psychotherapy. In C. L. Philpot, G. R. Brooks, D. D. Lusterman, & R. L. Nutt (Eds.), *Bridging separate gender worlds: Why men and women clash and how therapists can bring them together* (pp. 163–182). Washington, DC: American Psychological Association.

Pleck, J. H. (1981). *The myth of masculinity.* Cambridge, MA: MIT Press.

Potash, M. S. (1998). When women treat men: Female therapists/male patients. In W. S. Pollack & R. F. Levant (Eds.), *New psychotherapy for men* (pp. 282–307). New York, NY: Wiley.

Prochaska, J. O., & Norcross, J. C. (2002). Stages of change. In J. C. Norcross (Ed.), *Psychotherapy relationships that work* (pp. 303–313). New York, NY: Oxford University Press.

Rabinowitz, F. E., & Cochran, S. V. (2002). Working phase through termination of deepening psychotherapy with men. In F. E. Rabinowitz & S. V. Cochran, *Deepening psychotherapy with men* (pp. 137–156). Washington, DC: American Psychological Association.

Rabinowitz, F. E., & Cochran, S. V. (2008). Men and therapy: A case of masked male depression. *Clinical Case Studies, 7*(6), 575–591.

Rappleyea, D. L., Harris, S. M., White, M., & Simon, K. (2009). Termination: Legal and ethical considerations for marriage and family therapists. *American Journal of Family Therapy, 37*(1), 12–27.

Rochlen, A. B., & Hoyer, W. D. (2005). Marketing mental health to men: Theoretical and practical considerations. *Journal of Clinical Psychology, 61*(6), 675–685.

Rudman, L. A., & Glick, P. (2008). *The social psychology of gender: How power and romance shape gender relations.* New York, NY: Guilford Press.

Russell, B. (1929). *Marriage and morals.* Oxford, UK: Liveright.

Safran, J. D., Muran, J. C., Samstag, L. W., & Stevens, C. (2001). Repairing alliance ruptures. *Psychotherapy, 38,* 406–412.

Salberg, J. (2010). *Good enough endings: Breaks, interruptions, and terminations from contemporary relational perspectives* (Relational Perspectives Book Series 44). New York, NY: Routledge.

Scher, M., & Good, G. E. (Eds.). (1990). Special feature: Gender issues in counseling. *Journal of Counseling and Development, 68,* 370–391.

Stevens, M. A., & Englar-Carlson, M. (Eds). (2006). *In the room with men: A casebook of therapeutic change.* Washington, DC: American Psychological Association.

Sweet, H. (2006). Finding the person behind the persona: Engaging men as a female therapist. In M. Englar-Carlson & M. A. Stevens (Eds.), *In the room with men: A casebook of therapeutic change* (pp. 69–90). Washington, DC: American Psychological Association.

Swift, J. K., Callahan, J., & Levine, J. C. (2009). Using clinically significant change to identify premature termination. *Psychotherapy: Theory, Research, Practice, Training, 46,* 328–335.

Vasquez, M. J. T., Bingham, R. P., & Barnett, J. E. (2008). Psychotherapy termination: Clinical and ethical responsibilities. *Journal of Clinical Psychology: In Session, 64*(5), 653–665.

Ward, D. E. (1984). Termination of individual counseling: Concepts and strategies. *Journal of Counseling and Development, 63,* 21–25.

Wexler, D. B. (2009). *Men in therapy: New approaches for effective treatment.* New York, NY: Norton.

Wierzbicki, M., & Pekarik, G. (1993). A meta-analysis of psychotherapy dropout. *Professional Psychology: Research and Practice, 24,* 190–195.

Younggren, J. N., & Gottlieb, M. C. (2008). Termination and abandonment: History, risk, and risk management. *Professional Psychology: Research and Practice, 39,* 498–504.

3

Gender Matters— Transference, Countertransference, and Men

A Psychodynamic/ Psychoanalytic Perspective

JUDITH FELTON LOGUE

INTRODUCTION: BOYS WILL BE BOYS AND MEN WILL BE MEN. WHAT IS A THERAPIST TO DO?

The adage "boys will be boys" implies that the nature of all boys and men is to be destructive or hapless and immature. Take, for example, this remark of an exasperated parent whose son had been caught breaking windows, upending trash cans, throwing snowballs at car windows, and whatever else some boys might do: "That's the way it is; there's no help for it." The expression "boys will be boys" has been around for a long time, as indicated by similar expressions appearing in print as early as 1589 (Deloney, 1903).

The cliché "boys will be boys" has even formally infiltrated contemporary pop culture. "Boys Will Be Boys" is the signature song of the indie rock band The Ordinary Boys. "Boys will be boys" refers to grown men, as well as young boys and male adolescents, with the implication that gender stereotype is a rationalization for unacceptable behavior, physical or interpersonal.

But, to me, "boys will be boys" is not an obvious truth. I do not agree, and it has not been my predominant experience with boys and men. In my opinion, the cliché represents an unconscious devaluation of boys and men; it is as harmful to men as many of the common sexist beliefs about females are to women. It is a negative stereotype and a generally distasteful view of the male gender—that boys behave badly and cause trouble, and that adult men are generally guilty of a broad range of reprehensible behavior. Too often (and more so than women), boys and men are seen as aggressive and violent, narcissistic, cold, unemotional, insensitive, irresponsible, cunning, disloyal, and unfaithful. Ascribing these characteristics to men as a whole implies that they are inferior to women and thus devalues the entire male gender.

So, what does "boys will be boys" have to do with my topic, "Gender Matters—Transference, Countertransference, and Men"? Everything and nothing. Nothing, because in real life the adage implying that men are "bad" does not apply to most adult men, certainly not to men who are at their best. But, it has everything to do with it because it suggests a stereotype and overgeneralization that many patients and clients do accept, either consciously or unconsciously.

The truth lies somewhere in between.

Most clinicians are trained to be careful not to fall for such superficial or oppressive generalizations. From the first day of our education, we know it is imperative that we recognize and understand our own prejudices and preconceived notions about people, and that we refrain from using any techniques that we might associate with these prejudices.

Our countertransferences are our own feelings toward patients, based on experiences in our own lives and our transferences toward all people, including patients. They are defined as *broad* countertransference feelings; they include all feelings toward the patient or client. *Narrow* countertransference feelings are the transference feelings of the therapist to the patient from the therapist's own history and life. When the therapist unconsciously relates to a patient in patterns similar to one's parent or sibling, this is a transference reaction that is called a *narrow countertransference* because it is specific rather than encompassing any and all reactions.

Countertransference feelings—both broad and narrow—have to be understood and integrated into our practices. We must have the self-awareness to discern between times when we retain biases that might affect our perception of a patient or practice situation and times when an offensive and demeaning adage or cliché, like this one, might seem to fit a client or practice situation. We need this insight to know how to use our countertransference to enhance treatment through understanding and insight, rather than allowing our countertransference issues (the therapist's feelings) to interfere with it. However, not all of us, at different times and for different reasons, are always aware that we have incorporated prejudices against men. Increasing our awareness of what we think and feel, both consciously and unconsciously, is essential to good therapeutic technique.

PERSONAL HISTORY: AN OVERVIEW

My personal story reflects my major theme: that our personal experiences affect our professional journey—and that this applies to clinical work with men. Just as "the personal is political" was a famous phrase of feminists in 1970, "the personal is professional" is a relevant phrase for clinicians today.

My own particular background and upbringing included a preponderance of "good boys" and "good men." Thus, I am inclined to be sensitive to comments and actions that I perceive to be unconsciously disdainful of men, and of women, for that matter.

I typically bring a strong positive countertransference when the patient in the treatment room is male. Why? I have always liked men, plain and simple. I liked and loved my father, my grandfather, and the boys of my childhood. For me, it has always been a natural high working with, learning about, and understanding men.

In addition, my life has been filled with excellent men friends and colleagues who are warm, supportive, and kind, and who have been as loyal and as good as my women friends have been. I have a brother-in-law who is a gem. And I have a husband who is the love of my life, with whom I can successfully work out conflicts.

My primary experiences with men have been very positive. That men are sensitive was made even more apparent to me because my father was more empathic than my mother was. Today, my male friends may or may not be typical, but they are good guys—the kind of men I want in my life. Since childhood, I have believed that men are as sensitive as women are, and that they have just as many complicated feelings. Of course, not all the men I have known have been socialized to put their feelings up front. However, in my profession I work with men who are psychotherapists and psychoanalysts and who are in the healing professions; many have learned to express and to articulate their feelings or have come by this naturally.

On the other hand, is there a woman who has not had a negative relationship, experience, or outcome with a man, be it fury or heartbreak? Is there a clinician whose personal story is not related to her professional journey? For sure, this is true in my own life. In 1963, I had a boyfriend who was kind, sensitive, a good friend and lover, but not straightforward. He did not want to marry me, and this became a crisis for me.

For the next year, I lost confidence in myself. I was a mess. I began to see a male psychiatrist and psychoanalyst, with whom I discussed what proved to be a pivotal dream. In the dream, my doctor was working at his desk in the Pennsylvania Railroad station in Philadelphia. My associations to that dream included wanting to be like him and to do his work. I identified with him and wanted to do what he did. In the transference, I was also idealizing him as I had idealized my father. He analyzed my unconscious motivations and wishes, and he supported my goals. He insisted, by consistent encouragement, that I complete my year as a first-grade teacher, despite the fact that I cried daily. I gained 50 pounds and struggled more than ever before in my life.

PROFESSIONAL JOURNEY: THE IMPACT OF GENDER AND CLINICAL CONSIDERATIONS

This chapter, a psychoanalytic perspective on "gender matters," uses my personal professional history and three case studies to illustrate the following:

1. The importance of understanding countertransference
2. The varieties of transference of men to women therapists
3. Issues of theory and technique
4. Challenges and changes in the profession
5. Reflections on my experience
6. Recommendations for women therapists
7. Implications for the future

My involvement with men's issues and working with men began at the start of my 48-year career as a psychotherapist and psychoanalyst. My professional journey began with the "early years" from 1964 to 1980. Two case studies, Mr. M and Mr. R, from the very early years highlight my struggles and learning at the beginning of my professional career.

The "middle years" from 1980 to 1996 and the "later years" from 1996 to 2012 led to new insights. With experience, I gained deeper understanding of the effect of my countertransference in working with men. The case of Dr. D, in my middle and later years, attempts to show that no matter how old or experienced we are, there is always more to discover about the men we treat and about ourselves in relation to them.

After the heartbreak of my broken romance, I pursued a master of social work (1964–1966), so that I could do clinical work and help people to heal and resolve their emotional problems, just as my own psychoanalyst had done with me. I began this clinical work in 1964, when I was a first-year graduate student in Social Work at Rutgers University in New Brunswick, New Jersey.

In 1964–1965, my fieldwork was in medical social work at the Orange Memorial Hospital in Orange, New Jersey. While there, I worked primarily with the psychosomatic and psychosocial aspects of medical conditions, family matters, and relationship problems. It was early in my career, and I was just 22. As a neophyte, I was so excited and eager to begin my life work that it did not matter to me whether I worked with men or women. I had no preferences, no conscious negative transferences as far as I could see, and believed that I was treating both genders alike. In other words, to my mind, I treated each individual as a separate and unique person, and that gender was not a factor in my approach to treatment—at least that is what I thought at the time.

During the first year at Orange Memorial, I was timid and inhibited and at times afraid to ask questions of my patients—both men and women. Sometimes, I simply did not yet have good techniques for asking them in a helpful or therapeutic way. My supervisor was highly critical, and I almost failed fieldwork. I had hardly any money, and I was still recovering from my broken heart. To say that it was a difficult year is an understatement.

My second year, 1965–1966, was at the Veterans Administration (VA) outpatient Mental Hygiene Clinic in Newark, New Jersey, where I worked three days a week as a student and one year on staff. When I first began as a psychotherapist at the VA in 1965, I saw different levels of ego functioning among the men, many of whom were diagnosed with schizophrenia; most of the women I was treating were higher functioning. At the VA clinic, nearly all of the patients were male veterans of World War II and the Korean Conflict. They were suffering horribly, mostly from chronic schizophrenia, anxiety disorders, obsessive-compulsive disorders, and what are now called posttraumatic stress disorders (PTSDs). At that time, medications were transforming psychiatric treatment. The psychiatrists prescribed the phenothiazines and new antipsychotic medications (Thorazine, Stelazine, Mellaril, and similar drugs), which controlled the veterans' delusions and hallucinations. With the attendant improvements in patients' behaviors, hospitals then had greater opportunities and reasons for releasing them from inpatient care and returning them to the community.

I liked working with this population. As a young woman protected from harm by psychopathic or corrupt people, I was inclined to trust men (more so then than today since I now have more life experience). In the more traditional sociocultural milieu of the era, they were a part of a demographic that liked to take care of women. The cultural standard (or bias) was that women needed protection, and that men were superior physically and perhaps morally as well. They took care of me by treating me with respect. They also trusted my authority, despite the fact that I looked like a teenager. In turn, I liked taking care of them.

Moreover, their confidence in my authority was inspiring. Fortunately, my supervisor and the many outside consultants for the VA, who were well-known psychoanalysts in the New York metropolitan area, also demonstrated confidence in my ability—even when I lacked confidence in myself and was without any idea of how to approach a particular case.

The men were suffering, but they were also sufficiently motivated to get help and to understand themselves. Reflection and introspection were as important as action and solutions. I was highly motivated, not only because I was at the beginning of my career and enthusiastic about doing psychotherapy as a professional, but also because I liked learning about World War II firsthand. For me, it was preferable to the formal military history I studied at a women's college, where my undergraduate major was Government. I already had addressed the matter-of-fact history of World War II—strategy, tactics, battles, diplomacy, and politics. But, I was more intrigued by the personal experiences of people who had actually been there, which only intensified my interest in these patients.

As would be expected, psychotic patients talked about bizarre and unrealistic things. Obsessive-compulsive patients talked about the inability to control their thoughts or repetitive actions. Many of my patients with an anxiety disorder diagnosis would be diagnosed today with PTSD, acknowledging the trauma of the war experience. (For an excellent contemporary perspective, Brenner's 2009 work offers a unique casebook of clinical material pertaining to men who have sustained trauma.)

I intentionally encouraged and drew out my patients so that they felt comfortable enough to talk about almost anything. I helped them to be more accepting of their own feelings, whatever they were. I was naturally curious and especially eager to help, which made it easy for me to listen with fascination and without judgment. I wanted to hear about every subject and to avoid none. That interest is still with me today. I cannot think of a fantasy, wish, memory, or thought that I do not want to explore, including the most socially unacceptable things or what Freud called our "unbearable ideas" (1895).

I then moved to Santa Barbara, California, in 1967, for two years, where I saw patients and individuals in two county family mental health clinics. Professional training included workshops at Esalen Institute (led by Fritz Perls and others) and Carl Rogers's Western Behavioral Sciences Institute (WBSI), and supervision with psychoanalysts. I loved my work and my life on the Southern California coast.

I began my psychoanalytic training in 1969, when I left Santa Barbara, California, to move east to New York City. In Santa Barbara, I had been in private supervision with Dr. Ben Weininger, a physician analyst who had worked with Dr. Frieda Fromm-Reichmann at Chestnut Lodge in Washington, D.C., one of the most respected psychoanalytic writers and clinicians in the 1950s (Fromm-Reichmann, 1950). Ben suggested that if I wanted work in New York City, I should look up Dr. Reuben

Fine, who founded and directed five analytic institutes, as well helped found Division 39 (Psychoanalysis) of the American Psychological Association (APA).

I could not know at the time that Dr. Weininger's suggestion would yield so many dividends. Reuben gave me a job in his Fifth Avenue Center for Psychotherapy, along with a fellowship for course work and free supervision in his psychoanalytic institute. My association with Dr. Fine's institute and center proved to be a rewarding professional opportunity. I saw many patients there. Without even realizing it, I was beginning a formal commitment to my current profession of psychoanalysis. Moreover, it was the heyday of psychotherapy. And, at the same time, we were also preoccupied with issues of feminism, gender, sexuality, and the Vietnam War.

Between 1969 and 1980, and before obtaining my PhD in 1983, I completed psychoanalytic training, published articles, and did presentations related to gender, sexuality, transference, and countertransference. I taught courses on these subjects at two analytic institutes, a medical school, and two graduate schools. I also taught courses on supervision, psychopathology, and dreams and unconscious processes. After leaving the Fifth Avenue Center for Psychotherapy in 1970, I started my private practice in New York City.

In 1971, I was fortunate to teach one of the first classes in the psychology of women from a feminist perspective in an undergraduate program in New York City. Vivian Gornick and Barbara Moran had written an excellent text, *Woman in Sexist Society* (1971), which was revolutionary at the time. A colleague called me to suggest a wonderful "postpartum opportunity" and prompted teaching this class. I had just had my daughter. I also had recent experience as a member of a radical feminist conscious-raising group. My colleague thought (correctly) that teaching would be a good way to balance motherhood with a gradual transition back to my career and work.

In 1972, when I moved to New Jersey to take a position as a clinician at Rutgers Medical School, some of my patients continued with me in my part-time private practice. In 1975, I left the outpatient clinic at Rutgers to go into full-time practice (which continues to this day) and to complete my doctoral degree. By then, about two thirds of my patients were women; a third were men in individual and group therapy.

In 1974, doctoral course work, which required two years of study, enhanced my thinking and practice. It was a difficult and intense time because my private practice was supporting a family, child care, and three tuitions (besides my own, one was for my husband's medical college, and the other for preschool). Not surprisingly, as I look back, it took four unsuccessful proposals to settle on a manageable and interesting research project. Like many PhD candidates, there were moments when I was ready to drop out.

My PhD thesis (Felton, 1983) was a psychological attitude study, "Exclusivity in Women: A Research Study of Attitudes Toward

Extrarelationship Involvement," in sexually intimate relationships. I chose this topic for a variety of reasons, but primarily because so many people of my generation were questioning sexual exclusivity.

In my early years, sometimes I simply did not yet have the knowledge or techniques for asking essential and probing questions of my patients in a helpful or therapeutic way. Going back to 1965–1966, in my second year as a student at the VA, I had begun to develop more confidence and courage. However, as I became bolder and courageous, I sometimes "overcorrected."

In the latter part of my early years and in my middle years, I had to learn moderation, frustration tolerance, and patience. I learned about patients' resistances (ego defenses) and increasingly began to understand how to analyze them through interpretations that included memories, history, and psychology.

It was difficult for me to integrate and fully understand such conceptual thinking while doing my best to maintain a kind and empathic style that was probing, but not too intrusive. As all clinicians know, this is a lifelong goal, if not a struggle, no matter the gender of the patient. With more experience, I observed that, in contrast to women, men often brought different vulnerabilities into the consulting room.

BEYOND GENDER: TRANSFERENCE, COUNTERTRANSFERENCE, AND OTHER CHALLENGES FOR FEMALE CLINICIANS WORKING WITH MEN

It is important to note that transference may be beyond actual gender identity and role. That is, frequently a client may have a paternal (male) transference to you, even though you are a female. Conversely, you may have a countertransference to a male client as a female who has patterns and conflicts more similar to a significant female in your life than to a male.

Homosexuality and gender are also critical variables to consider in the female clinician-male patient dyad. They are relevant and helpful to understand (analyze) in terms of transference and countertransference.

All of my case examples are heterosexual men treated by a heterosexual woman. I have treated gay men, although my experience is limited. I suggest that if you are a straight clinician who treats gay clients, it is good to seek consultation from gay colleagues and to learn as much as possible about gay cultural dynamics and the medical and psychological aspects of homosexuality (Goldstone, 1999). If this is a new or first-time experience, you may even want to seek personal therapy to explore and understand more deeply your own emotions and reactions. I am fortunate to have excellent gay and lesbian colleagues who are in independent practice and who teach and publish. They offer perspective and assistance that I would otherwise not have.

When your patient's gender is male and his object orientation (choice) is male (homosexual object orientation), regardless of your own object orientation, it is wise to understand your own history, psychology, and biases (transferences and countertransference feelings). If you are a heterosexual female and your object orientation is male, your counter-transference will differ from when you are a lesbian female and your object orientation is female. In fact, although this may at first seem obvious, the permutations and nuances in the treatment situation might be complex and complicated—and may not be clear or transparent.

We are often called on to do brief treatment, whether in an agency, clinic, or private practice. In addition, sometimes a new patient specifi-cally requests either a female or a male therapist. It is hard to imagine a therapist not discovering on intake and early evaluation the psychol-ogy or experiences leading to such a requirement. Frequently, the time constraints of contemporary counseling or therapy may limit our ability to address transference issues. In these cases of shorter treatment, sup-portive, instructive, cognitive-behavioral, and solution-focused tech-niques may predominate and handicap clarification or confrontation of unconscious issues in a direct way. The therapist then has to settle for unconfirmed hypotheses, with fewer in-depth interpretations.

PSYCHODYNAMIC AND PSYCHOANALYTIC PSYCHOTHERAPY AND MEN

Most psychology textbooks today inaccurately define psychoanalytic psychotherapy and psychoanalysis as we currently practice it (Hansell & Damour, 2005). Popular definitions of psychodynamic therapy suggest that it is more eclectic and short term than psychoanalytic psychother-apy. In fact, however, psychoanalysts today are eclectic and incorporate empirical research from neuroscience, CBT (cognitive-behavioral ther-apy), and medicine. We also frequently see patients for crisis therapy and for short-term counseling.

Psychoanalysis is no longer defined as only three to five times a week on the couch, although this frequency and use of the couch are required for graduate and teaching psychoanalysts. Psychoanalysis, which is tech-nically defined as making the unconscious conscious and the analysis of transference and countertransference in a two-person, couple, or group clinical relationship, is practiced at various frequencies and in a num-ber of settings. Therefore, the rigid distinction between psychodynamic and psychoanalytic is outdated.

How did this happen? Decades of debate related to gender similari-ties and differences (in biology, character, intellect, development, etc.) have led to new ideas and new perspectives (McWilliams, 2004). Also, decades of controversy and questioning have led to solid multidisci-plinary research, especially in gender, transgender, and neuroscience studies about neuroplasticity.

For the most part, such progress has been cumulative, built on a foundation established by earlier knowledge, research, education, and clinical experience. At the same time, many of the terms in the mental health field, which includes psychiatry, psychology, and social work, have evolved or changed with modern and postmodern times. In psychoanalysis, the modern period is from the 1970s to the 1990s. The postmodern period began in the 1990s with relational psychoanalysis.

For example, the feminist second-wave (1960s and 1970s) and third-wave (1990s to the present) revolution/evolution ended the outdated preoccupation with penis envy; added concepts from research and clinical experience with women, such as primary femininity; and advanced new perspectives on gender and on object choice and orientation.

Research has been published on the efficacy of psychoanalytic psychotherapy and its equivalence or superiority to CBT and expressive therapy (Shedler, 2010). Links to contemporary research studies and presentations (PowerPoint reviews) are available and updated at Web sites of the American Psychoanalytic Association (http://www.apsa.org) and Division 39 (http://www.division39.org) (Lowder, Hansell, & McWilliams, 2006). An incorporated research organization, the Psychoanalytic Psychodynamic Research Society (PPRS), currently coordinates and promotes evidence-based treatment results on gender and other issues.

In 1968, Robert J. Stoller in his book, *Sex and Gender,* along with the writings of other psychoanalytic clinicians and researchers, produced critical reviews of Freud's ideas on early female sexuality. Harold Blum was the editor of the *Journal of the American Psychoanalytic Association* (JAPA), and he devoted an entire issue to advancing modern feminist views. He also published a special volume (Blum, 1977) introducing new formulations that changed theories about male and female development.

More recently, as part of postmodern psychoanalysis in the 21st century, Dimen (2003) focused on a contemporary relational psychoanalytic perspective. Dimen's 18-page reference list in her book is among the most comprehensive and useful. Her thorough bibliography lists numerous important publications and research studies from the 1970s through 2003.

Many other researchers and clinicians have had a significant impact on current theory and practice in the field of gender, including masculinity (Reis & Grossmark, 2009). Treatment techniques have evolved from a dyadic two-person and linear framework to a wider perspective, which includes multiplicities and the idea that gender role relations are constructed by societal expectations in addition to biological determinants. The concept of the cocreated therapist-patient dyad emphasizes what analysts call "the third' (the relationship of the therapist and patient) (Dimen, 2003). This is a nonheterosexist approach that takes into account multiple factors, such as culture and interpersonal relationships. The concept integrates traditional drive and defense theory with object relations, attachment, self psychology, and relational theories. It includes constitutional, genetic, developmental, and sociocultural factors with more precision and detail than in the past.

Is there a difference between treating men and women? No, yes, and sometimes:

> No: In traditional classical psychoanalytic thinking, gender is not supposed to make a difference. A long, open-ended analysis of four or five times a week on the couch is supposed to address homosexual and heterosexual wishes, fantasies, and drives, regardless of the sex (gender) of both the analyst and the patient. The belief is that the outcome of the analysis would not, and should not, be affected by the therapist-patient dyad.
>
> Yes: Contemporary thinking is that history, development, personality, and culture influence gender in ways that affect the clinician-patient dyad. In addition, the gestalt often depends as much, if not more so, on the clinician's history, attitudes, and experience (countertransference feelings) than on the rules or requirements of therapy—or even sociocultural factors. (Cultural changes are inevitable for long-term career professionals.) These are all reasons that make it essential for us to understand ourselves and to remain self-aware throughout our careers and to focus on our unconscious functioning with respect to the gender dyad.
>
> Sometimes: In a presentation of my paper (Felton, 1986) at a conference for the Society for Psychoanalytic Training in New York City, I publicly challenged the classical psychoanalytic position. I thought that the sequence, shape, and form of the transference would be different and affected by the four clinical dyads: female clinician-male patient, female clinician-female patient, male clinician-male patient, or male clinician-female patient (Felton, 1986).
>
> However, I agreed with the classical position that, in a long analysis, gender does not matter since ideally (although nothing is ever perfect or ideal), gender makes no difference. All transference issues are analyzed, just in a different sequence, shape, and form. This suggestion looks forward to paying attention to gender (which until then analysts believed was irrelevant), but it is different from the contemporary view, which is clearly a "yes," and based on a sociological and constructionist/constructivist psychological perspective.

In many analytic meetings, we consider some of the classical theories and techniques anachronistic and out of date. At this time, we have evolved and gained much. But, I have concerns that sometimes we might have overcorrected—losing too much by going too far—and minimized sexuality by deemphasizing biology, drive, and gender differences. In our postmodern and current contemporary attempts to be politically correct, we may also be denying the relevance and importance of making conscious what is unconscious and of analyzing the transference and countertransference feelings of our patients and ourselves.

CLINICAL TREATMENT WITH MEN
FROM A PSYCHOANALYTIC AND
PSYCHODYNAMIC PERSPECTIVE

Mr. R: A Case of Anxiety and Phobic Neurosis

My first long-tem patient at the VA in 1965 was Mr. R, a 31-year-old, Protestant, heterosexual, college graduate who had served in the Korean Conflict. Mr. R was diagnosed as obsessive-compulsive and was the most obsessional person I have ever met in my entire 48-year career. He came to me for treatment in a state of upset and anxiety. He feared he would die at 32—the same age that his father had died.

In treating Mr. R, and in my supervision and reading, I learned about the psychodynamics of the obsessive-compulsive character structure. My clinical supervisors diagnosed him as at a neurotic level of ego functioning—not borderline or psychotic. I treated him with psychodynamic psychotherapy. (At that point, behavior therapy had not yet become so popular.) Unlike today, psychoanalysis and psychoanalytic psychotherapy were the preferred forms of treatment. Positive transference and positive countertransference feelings were predominant in this case. In other words, we liked and respected each other. He told me how much he looked forward to his weekly therapy session; he wore a jacket and tie and looked his best.

Mr. R was a slim, handsome, educated man, highly articulate and personable. He was anxious—not disagreeably, but in a way that engendered my wishes to help him. My treatment of him made me feel highly effective, and he also made me look good as a clinician. Every beginning therapist should be so fortunate to get a case like this.

My positive countertransference led me to read as much as possible about the psychodynamics of obsessive-compulsive character patterns and structures. I also requested as much supervision and consultation as was available. I was fortunate when a weekly peer group of more experienced colleagues, which included a staff psychologist, physician, and social worker, invited me to join them. Their insight and support for my work were invaluable. They taught me a lot and enhanced my ability to present initial interpretations and reconstructive hypotheses that were attuned to my patient. This legitimized my authority with Mr. R and added to my confidence when he accepted them.

My inclination to have a positive countertransference to Mr. R, who feared dying within the next year at age 32, proved highly beneficial since it enabled me to gain his trust. Also, because I was presenting him in supervision and in an experienced peer group at the VA, I was beginning to learn how to address his feelings toward me and therapy. Had men filled my past with physical or verbal abuse, I might have been less comfortable with Mr. R's issues around aggression. Specifically, I might have been more reluctant to focus on his obsessive-compulsive ego defenses and security operations as a means of defending himself from knowledge of his own aggressive and hostile wishes and fantasies.

Had I myself had more experiences distrusting men, or been fearful of men, I probably would have had more difficulty. It would most likely have been harder for me to address the (usually unconscious) aggressive aspects of his personality and character patterns.

For example, the rare, and perhaps only, time that Mr. R was late, I was able to help him see that he had some negative feelings about coming to the session. He acknowledged that the previous therapy session had been painful to him, and that he was beginning to be aware that his fear of dying might have to do with his anger about being drafted and "forced to go to war."

Nevertheless, in retrospect, were I more experienced at that time, and if I had worked with Mr. R for more than a year and a half, I believe I would have done more in-depth analysis of his conflicts and personality patterns. As a beginner, I was limited. With hindsight, however, I can see that because I had the advantage of excellent consultation and supervision and high motivation, I may have done better than I thought.

Mr. M: A Case of Chronic Schizophrenia and Psychosis

Mr. R was nothing like another patient, Mr. M, a veteran of World War II. He was Italian American, age 42, short and chunky, and a sweet and kind man. Nevertheless, he was what some would characterize as "crazy as a loon." He talked about the Arabian Nights, which for him were real phenomena, with life figures—knights—inhabiting the streets and the theaters in Newark, New Jersey. There was no reasoning him out of his perceptions and delusions.

Because this kind of problem was new to me, it was interesting and challenging, and I looked forward to our sessions. I wanted to discover how someone with a psychotic mind thought, talked, and expressed himself. After almost 50 years, I still appreciate this kind of challenge. I learned firsthand and in vivo, not just from books, about concrete versus abstract thinking. I learned how to ask the psychiatric evaluation questions for the capacity to abstract, and for orientation of time, place, and person. One day, I asked my patient, "Mr. M, what brought you here today?" His answer was responsive, yet concrete. He said flatly, "The bus." This was a charming, but maddening, example of the type of withdrawal from abstraction and the tangible.

By contrast, Mr. R's answer to the same question was a thorough rendition of his inability to think of little else except his fear of dying. While Mr. M spent much of each session in the "Land of the Arabian (K)Nights," Mr. R lived in the land of depressive reality. Mr. M escaped from worries about reality and his war and hospital traumas. Mr. R not only escaped death in the war but also now replicated his past unconscious fears repeatedly by imagining and expecting death within the next year. Since he escaped death in the external war, he transferred his fears and continued to conduct an internal war.

Transference and Countertransference Analysis in the Cases of Mr. R and Mr. M

Mr. M and I represented the female therapist-male patient dyad for the observation of transference and countertransference themes. Gender mattered, but so did age, level of mental capacity, severity of pathology, and my level of experience.

As mentioned, Mr. M spent much of each session talking about his Arabian knights. With more training and education, I most likely would have been able to help him connect some of his feelings toward me— whether positive, negative, or mixed—with his automatic withdrawal into unrealistic fantasies, which he believed were real. But my experience was limited, and Mr. M's mental state was psychotic. Thus, he did not and could not articulate his transference feelings toward me in sessions. I also did not yet know how to elucidate in the therapy hour the recurrence of themes in our relationship (transference and countertransference), such as the possibility that Mr. M related to me in a way that was similar to the way he related to his sister or mother.

However, from his history and patterns of relating to me, I inferred in peer group and in supervision, with the help of more experienced professionals, a sisterly (older) and maternal transference to me. He had respected and admired his protective and kind sister, who continued to care for him. His mother was also still alive, and he remained close to her. Although I was 20 years younger than Mr. M, my authority as a clinic therapist appeared to evoke respect, if not deference, and a pattern of idealization that was similar to his relationships with his sister and mother.

Again, the therapy with male psychotics was the best education and training for me. I loved it. By jumping into the fire, I learned firsthand just how disturbed the mind can be. In fact, experienced therapists suggest that beginning therapists work with psychotic patients because when we are new, we are not yet discouraged by the challenges and typical intractability of conditions like schizophrenia. Analyzing schizophrenic/psychotic defenses, especially in men who are back from war, is increasingly a lost skill and art. It has saved more than a few men's (and women's) lives.

Now, however, so much later, I find that psychotic processes are as distressing to me as they are fascinating. As an experienced psychotherapist and psychoanalyst, I have seen schizophrenia wreck patients and families. It is a cancer of the mind—debilitating, painful, and harmful, not only to the patient, but also to family members.

The case of Mr. M well illustrates how the combination of psychosis and the trouble with putting feelings into words, typical of men of the World War II era, is a major challenge for treatment (Levant et al., 2006). Ordinarily, my inclination (as described in my introductory comments about "boys will be boys") is to avoid gender-based generalizations, such as the one that men have "trouble putting feelings into words." Nevertheless, empirical research by Levant and his coauthors demonstrated the reliability and validity of this common observation. The research term is *normative alexithymia.*

Today, unfortunately, most psychotic patients of both genders are treated in medical settings with pharmacology and little if any psychotherapy. At times, graduate education and training of physicians and nonmedical clinicians continue to recognize and respect the concepts of transference and countertransference. However, based on my experience, it is my view that relatively few clinicians understand or know how to apply these important concepts to everyday clinical practice. Few programs in psychology, psychiatry, and social work (other than psychoanalytic institutes) today teach in-depth clinical transference and countertransference analytic techniques. Nevertheless, my colleagues and I find profound interest and enthusiasm for learning them because they explain in depth how the mind works, and they suggest specific techniques that lead to successful therapeutic outcomes.

In addition, the transference and countertransference analysis of the gender dyad of female clinician-male patient in these cases includes age as well. I was a young woman treating Mr. M, a single, disturbed older man in his 40s. As I stated, he had close relationships with his mother and sister. He was inclined to trust and respect females. Perhaps the mantle of authority that I had as his treating professional may have contributed to a positive transference from his relationships with his protective, loving, and kind sister and mother.

Mr. M had no known history of abuse, but the war had traumatized him and triggered a schizophrenic break. His father was a hard-working man and not abusive or mean. Whatever negative transferences and feelings from childhood that may have existed were repressed or expressed in his Arabian delusions. But, if I knew then what I know now, as already described, I could have attempted to address and analyze some of Mr. M's delusions in terms of what was going on in the therapy hour—specifically, his thoughts, feelings, and associations prior to lapsing into his delusional Arabian fantasy world. I might have been able to help him connect his feelings toward me, whatever they were, with his need to withdraw into an unrealistic world.

The analysis of transference and countertransference dynamics in the therapy hour can effect the treatment goal of strengthening the patient's ability to tolerate the unbearable pain, feelings, and thoughts associated with living in the real world with appropriate anxiety that is not overdetermined or neurotic (conflicted). The therapist who analyzes transference reactions learns to clarify in detail and in the moment when the patient is suddenly or abruptly withdrawing into his fantasy world or becoming obsessive about his symptoms and conflicts. The therapist can assist the patient when confronting, clarifying, and interpreting immediately following a particular interaction with the therapist.

The goal of this technique is both insight and behavior change. With this method, the patient gains insight that leads to choice for behavior change. The patient can understand affectively and in the connection to the therapist that his delusional fantasies, or his neurotic symptoms, are protective psychological operations and ego defenses to protect him from unbearable ideas and feelings. This understanding through therapeutic discussion should lead to increased strength and ability to tolerate the feelings associated with difficult reality. The patient has less need to live in a delusional world and less need for psychological symptoms—and he increases his ability to see the real external world as it is, with its frequent pain, suffering, unfairness, or cruelty.

In successful analysis of the transference in psychodynamic and psychoanalytic therapy, the patient learns that the benefits of increased tolerance and acceptance of external reality outweigh the cost of living in a delusional world or with conflicts (neuroses and anxiety) that prevent functioning at the highest level.

Looking back, I surmise that there might have been unanalyzed erotic transference issues in the treatments of both Mr. R and Mr. M. I was a reasonably attractive young clinician, and Mr. R was a handsome young man, only about five years older than I. He was generally not involved with women, and he was lonely. He looked forward to the therapy hour, and he even dressed up for the appointment.

Mr. M may also have had unspoken feelings or fantasies about me. For all I know, he might have imagined me as a figure and participant in his Arabian life. Had I the opportunity for long-term analytic treatment and the relevant training, I might also have figured out some of the meaning, as well as why he chose and needed an Arabian diorama to consolidate and maintain his mental functioning.

However, it was not until my analytic training in the 1970s that I learned how to understand, treat, and address erotic and other transference and countertransference issues with comfort.

It is often difficult for women therapists, especially young women therapists, to treat and talk about the erotic transference and countertransference. Sociocultural sexism, professional emphasis on attachment and relational issues, and personal intrapsychic factors may converge to cause avoidance, if not ignorance, about these important clinical phenomena.

To clinically address the erotic feelings and fantasies of a client requires in-depth understanding and acceptance of one's own psychological sexual and erotic fantasies and feelings, including guilt, shame, fears, inhibitions, or the wish to transgress boundaries or go against convention. It also requires confidence and competence to feel and talk about erotic subjects without acting on them or being afraid that anyone in the consulting room (the clinician *or* the patient) will act on them. Our culture and current professional education and training often offer insufficient help for this tall order. Kenneth Pope (Pope, Sonne, & Greene, 2006) is one of the most practical, thoughtful, and helpful practitioners to examine uncomfortable topics sometimes ignored in the professional development of psychotherapists. He has coauthored a number of books that explore the sensitive issues embedded in mental health practice.

Dr. D: A Complicated Case

The case of Dr. D is illustrative of difficult character traits (character pathology) and conflicts (neuroses). I was a mature professional in my late 40s when I first treated him and in my late 50s when he returned for treatment with me a second time. When he first consulted me, Dr. D was in his late 30s, married for 10 years, and the father of several children. He was a successful physician, charming and handsome. He could easily be categorized by some as a "player" or a "cad," depending on his motives, mood, and goals—and on the person who was doing the assessment.

The presenting problem was marital conflict. It took several months, however, to uncover addictive behaviors, including substance abuse (alcohol, marijuana, and cocaine), a severe eating disorder, and extensive and secretive extramarital sexual activity (referred to as a "love addiction" by 12-step programs and by some clinicians). Treatment included both analytic insight therapy and, later, CBT techniques.

Initially, Dr. D responded well to treatment, which continued for three years. His symptoms subsided, and he completed a divorce. Termination went well. However, after several years, Dr. D relapsed and returned for therapy.

Unwilling to accept a "boys will be boys" approach, with disappointment but also with optimism, I reviewed our work and attempted to move forward in the second part of the treatment. The death of his mother had triggered his relapse. Unfortunately, Dr. D not only had returned to his earlier self-destructive behaviors but also had now added high-risk behaviors, including reckless driving, unprotected sex, and abuse of sexual stimulant drugs.

After two more years, treatment was only partially successful. Dr. D was not able to maintain his progress. He relapsed from a second resolution of his addictions, high risk behaviors, and compulsive lying to women. In my worst moments, I felt completely frustrated. It became clear to both of us, especially to me, that I was not sufficiently effective, and that additional and more effective treatment was required. Dr. D refused my frequent attempts to introduce CBT techniques (structured exercises) or referral to 12-step programs. Interpretations began to be used as a resistance to change, rather than to analyze conflicts and to free and direct his substantial energy toward healthier behavior.

I referred Dr. D for a second opinion to one of the most prominent and respected CBT clinician-researchers, Dr. A. I also thought it was important for Dr. D to see a male therapist, especially because of his history of losing his father and his need to identify with a strong man with integrity and good judgment. Dr. A, my first choice of therapist for Dr. D, was an excellent match in terms of gender, experience, and orientation. He understood my frustration and helped me tremendously. Despite my request, however, he did not think he was the best clinician for this case because he was limiting his practice to short-term clients.

Dr. A then referred Dr. D to another clinician-researcher, Dr. T, who agreed to consult with Dr. D. Six months into that treatment, Dr. D called to tell me he was satisfied with new progress reducing his symptoms, and that his relationship with Dr. T was a "match."

Dr. D did well in treatment with Dr. T, an experienced specialist in addictive disorders, particularly difficult eating disorders. He is a cognitive-behavioral researcher who takes a no-nonsense, structured clinical approach. He is firm and directive, yet kind and sensitive. He was interested in the case of Dr. D and wanted to treat him. That Dr. D had been unsuccessful with a psychoanalyst may well have added some spice (and healthy competition) to this situation.

Gender was indeed a factor in this case. Dr. D was the apple of his mother's eye. While still a teenager, the death of his father triggered his eating disorder. He remained extremely close to his sister, jealous of his stepfather, and competitive and sometimes insecure around other men. He was more comfortable talking with a woman, and he instinctively knew how to charm and ingratiate himself with women, including me. He was respectful, likable, personable, intelligent, responsible, and seemed highly motivated in the treatment situation.

It is not hard to see that gender was also a factor in both the transference and the countertransference. Dr. D loved, or appeared to love, women, and he found genuine excitement in the conquest and challenge of getting a woman to fall in love with him. Once he succeeded, however, he was finished, bored, and ready for another conquest. He used exit behaviors to end relationships, rather than voice or work through conflicts or any annoyances and criticisms (of which he had many). These included finding another woman immediately, substance abuse, compulsive eating and purging, dangerous driving, and disappearing.

Dr. D's lovers were usually beautiful, professional, sexy, intelligent, and accomplished businesswomen, physicians, teachers, or entertainers. Despite his repeated claim that he wished to find a permanent intimate life partner, it took them (and me) some time to figure out that he had no real interest, and that his capacity for it was questionable. I began to question Dr. D about his motivation for change and for serious in-depth treatment. I also privately questioned whether he had gotten me to dislike him or his behaviors.

In the transference, Dr. D replicated his pattern with his mother, his lovers, his sister, and with me. I interpreted his patterns of lying and hostility as a defense against underlying feelings of inadequacy, insecurity, sexual inhibitions, and wishes to be special and the best. He seemed to genuinely see and intellectually understand these patterns, yet his repetitive compulsions remained strong, defined, and intractable. These repetitions are clinically defined as the compulsion in some patients to repeat distressing, even painful, situations without recognizing their own participation in bringing about such incidents or the relationship of current situations to past experiences. Although he achieved insight and sustained a faithful relationship with a woman for a year and a half, at times he sounded as if he had been reading Freud (1895/1961) while concurrently continuing to behave in the most destructive ways. I began to feel like a Catholic priest whose congregant does penance but repeatedly returns to the confessional with the same "sins."

Despite my dedication to character analysis of Dr. D's self-defeating and hostile behaviors, and my genuine affection and respect for him, I had reached the limit of my ability to be of use to him.

In retrospect, despite my occasional dislike or criticism, if I had a less-positive countertransference, I would probably have more quickly become direct and firm in addressing Dr. D's character pathology. Although I had sensed that doing this would have led to a negative transference reaction and crisis or a premature termination and aborted treatment, I still second-guess myself and am uncertain whether I was too patient or tolerant regarding his destructive character pathology. It is also possible that Dr. D's history as the son of a dominating and directive mother, and my different temperament, led in part to this stalemate. That is, were I a firmer therapist with a personality more like his mother's, I may have been a better match for treatment success.

DISCUSSION AND SUMMARY

On review and reflection about many of my male cases, besides those discussed in this chapter, it is clear to me that my positive countertransference to men has upsides and downsides.

It is evident that a positive countertransference to my patients sustained me in my second year of training at the VA Mental Hygiene Clinic. I believe it helped my male patients since my trust and respect for men came through to them. It may have even helped me to get an "A" in fieldwork and a well-paying staff job the following year because, according to my supervisors, I was able to do reasonably successful therapy with these men.

Mr. R resolved his panic and his phobia. He gave up his obsessive fear of an early death at age 32. He turned 33 while seeing me for therapy, and he did not die. By the time I was ready to take a position at County Mental Health Services in Santa Barbara, California, he was ready to terminate. At that point, his neurosis appeared to be resolved, temporarily if not permanently.

Mr. M continued a routine life outside the hospital and continued weekly supportive therapy at the VA clinic, possibly for the rest of his ambulatory days. When I left for California in the summer of 1967, he was ready to transfer to another therapist. He continued to maintain himself in an apartment, and his loving relatives visited regularly to oversee his activities of daily living.

However, the case of Dr. D demonstrates a downside to my tendency toward a positive countertransference in treating men. Perhaps if I had been more wary of men and their behaviors, I might have been firmer and more astute, and in less time. I might have been quicker to observe and to confront Dr. D on his pattern of seduction and rejection, exploitation, and hostility toward women—and toward me. That does not necessarily mean that I would have alleviated his symptoms or analyzed them to a successful resolution. However, with review, I now believe that even if being firmer were not effective, I would have referred him much sooner for a second opinion and transfer.

FEMALE THERAPIST, KNOW THYSELF

With regard to the gender and the beyond-gender challenges of being a new female therapist, I realize that in my early years I was in some ways very aware. In other ways, I was clueless. But, hindsight can be highly instructive.

Although not specific to only transference or countertransference issues and men, our own events and feelings (broad factors and experiences) affect how we approach clinical transference and countertransference events (narrow factors and experiences). They also affect our retrospective analyses.

In my later years (1980 to the present), it has been my experience that some men in a female clinician-male patient dyad, especially men over 40, may be more comfortable in the initial sessions talking about work, money, and career problems rather than love, romantic, sexual, or family problems. However, this is not so true when the presenting problem is a marital issue or romantic crisis. Because I encourage free association and ask patients to say what comes to mind, eventually any inclination to focus on action, solutions, or work rather than on feelings or relationship evolves into talking about both.

My experience with women in treatment is often different in the initial sessions. Many women prefer that I be highly empathic with their hurt and angry feelings, as well as with the frustrations of their situation, especially their personal relationships. Conversely, I have sometimes found that a male patient will experience a highly empathic response as patronizing, or that I perceive him as weak or more vulnerable than he believes himself to be. Some of my professional and highly androgynous younger women patients are similar. They want to focus on goals, solutions, and how-to techniques and strategies, rather than reflection, insight, feelings, and resolution of neuroses or conflicts. Most of us would argue that the most important thing is to establish a relationship of trust with a patient, regardless of gender, and to address the client's needs rather than promote our own agenda. I have never forgotten an early analytic training dictum: "You must first make a relationship and engender trust before you can analyze anything" (Fine, 1971).

I think and hope that I have come a long way and learned a lot about treating men since my early years. What has become clear to me is that if I knew in my 20s what I know in my 60s, I would have better understood how my own history and biases affected my work with men. I would also have had more confidence, more competence, and more techniques for my work with men. Most important, I would have had a deeper awareness of men's experiences and states of being.

Today, to the benefit of my patients, I am more astute regarding men's frustrations and anger—not only their legitimate anger or rage but also the defensive anger that shields vulnerability and helplessness. My positive transference and countertransference history with a good father does not limit my attunement to the selfishness, narcissism, and not-so-exemplary character traits of too many men. I believe that because of what both boys and men have taught me, I am somewhat wiser.

I recommend that, as female therapists, regardless of our level of experience, we do our best to remain aware of the negative and positive transference and countertransference and of our sexuality and the particular ways it may affect patients, clients, and ourselves in our role as a therapist and as an individual. It is important to be comfortable with one's own body and with oneself as a sensual and sexual person and to be as aware as we can of how male patients are reacting to us and why—and how we are reacting to them.

Depending on the depth of treatment, one may address the erotic transference, as well as maternal, paternal, and sibling transferences through interpretation, analysis of dreams, and by clarifying patterns of relating and of behavior in the treatment situation. Self-analysis, especially individual consultation and peer group supervision/consultation, is not only useful but also essential to maintain self-awareness and to do your best professional work.

I believe that it is invaluable to be a patient and a client, as well as a therapist and counselor, which a number of experts espouse as critical to becoming a better therapist. While there are some therapists who have never been a client or patient, it is a relatively rare occurrence in my experience. Psychoanalysts and psychoanalytic psychotherapists are required to experience their own personal analysis or psychotherapy. Most psychodynamic psychotherapists, however, regardless of their training and education modality, have some personal psychotherapeutic experience, whether or not it is required for certification from a particular educational or training institution or organization.

However, as therapy training moves more toward manualized CBT treatments and medication, my colleagues report that fewer doctoral students and psychiatry residents appear to be seeking their own therapy. The popularity of shorter-term, more structured, and noninterpersonal or expressive treatment modalities probably affects the current trend of therapists not having gone through personal therapy themselves.

Nevertheless, it is preferable that female clinicians who work with men intuitively understand and agree that, in addition to ongoing consultation and peer supervision, personal therapy is an essential part of knowing oneself. And, it is essential to working at the highest level of competence. If one is eventually able to have the experience as a patient of both a male and female therapist or psychoanalyst, it can be a tremendous advantage in understanding the influence of gender on one's own personal reactions.

GENDER MATTERS

Despite the classical belief that gender does not (or should not) matter, I believe that gender does matter. Sex does make a difference in the female therapist and male patient or client dyad, particularly when treatment is shorter, which today is typical in the practice of psychotherapy and counseling. In my discussion of whether sex makes a difference (Felton, 1986), I suggest that in an open-ended and longer treatment, there is an opportunity for more in-depth analysis of different gender transferences. In those cases, the shape and the form of the transference vary. Understanding both the patient's heterosexual and homosexual transferences is more likely, regardless of the gender of the clinician.

Sexual object orientation, and whether a person is attracted to men, women, or both, also matters (Harkless, 2005). We are at the cutting edge of going beyond current thinking about gender as either constructivist or essentialist or connected to only cultural and other factors, such as biology and genetics or constitution. Complex and in-depth analyses suggest multiple ways to consider gender from an intrapsychic perspective. Reconstructive surgery techniques, research, and in-depth clinical understanding of people with bisexual and transgender issues are changing the way we think and practice.

To summarize, using case illustrations of the treatment of Mr. R, Mr. M, and Dr. D, I demonstrated some of the vicissitudes and complex possibilities that may occur when female clinicians work with male clients. I shared my personal and professional experiences to refute the stereotype and bias implied in the adage "boys will be boys." I added depth and complexity to understand gender in the therapy hour—and to add another voice of women clinicians working with men.

Most important, by connecting my personal history and psychology with my professional journey, I suggested some ways that a female clinician might personally relate her own individual history, unique psychology, and professional journey to her work with her male patients or clients.

I still bring into the treatment room the positive countertransferences that are rooted in my childhood. While this is usually helpful, it can sometimes have a downside. With regard to patients, a blind spot—or what is known as a *scotoma*—to negativity, anger, disappointment, sorrow, resentment, rage, and hostility is a highly undesirable factor that leads to unanalyzed negative transference or destructive character traits. A frequent result is that the patient unconsciously acts out conflicts in his or her life, rather than analyzing and talking about them in therapy. In short, missing negative transferences can lead to unsuccessful and incomplete treatment outcomes.

Similarly, clinicians who bring to the consulting room their own negative countertransferences to men—rooted in the past—are not doomed to failure. Just as I continually monitor my inclination to see the glass as half full, those who tend to see men through the lens of a painful or disappointing past must pay attention to their difficulty with trust or difficulty perceiving the positive. I cannot repeat too often how important it is for all of us—regardless of our level of experience—to have a consultant in the wings, just a phone call away. This backup and support are essential to improving our effectiveness as therapists to the benefit of our patients—regardless of gender.

Finally, there is no substitute for the personal experience of therapy, in addition to excellent education, training, supervision, and consultation—whether ongoing or intermittent—as needed. To do this work we must continuously learn and know our patients and ourselves. Like our patients, we remain a work in progress required to remain open to new possibilities and to know that (as my first analytic supervisor used to say) "everything is temporary."

REFERENCES

Blum, H. P. (Ed.) (1977). *Female psychology, contemporary psychoanalytic views.* New York, NY: International Universities Press.

Brenner, I. (2009). *Injured men—trauma, healing, and the masculine self.* New York, NY: Aronson.

Deloney, T. (1903). *The gentle craft.* London: Palaestra.

Dimen, M. (2003). *Sexuality, intimacy, power.* Hillsdale, NJ: Psychoanalytic Press.

Felton, J. (1983). *Exclusivity in women: A research study of attitudes toward extra relationship involvement.* Rutgers, New Brunswick, NJ.

Felton, J. (1986). Sex makes a difference—How gender affects the therapeutic relationship. *Clinical Social Work Journal, 14*(2), 127–138.

Fine, R. (1971). *The healing of the mind.* New York, NY: McKay.

Freud, S. (1961). *Studies on hysteria* (standard ed., 2, 1–17). London: Hogarth Press. (Original work published 1895)

Fromm-Reichmann, F. (1950). *Principles of intensive psychotherapy.* Chicago: University of Chicago Press.

Goldstone, S. E. (1999). *The ins and outs of gay sex.* New York, NY: Dell.

Gornick, V., & Moran, B. K. (Eds.). (1971). *Woman in sexist society: Studies in power and powerlessness.* New York, NY: Basic Books.

Hansell, J., & Damour, L. (2005). *Abnormal psychology.* Hoboken, NJ: Wiley.

Harkless, L. (2005). The construct of object orientation. *Psychoanalytic Psychology, 24*, 384–394.

Levant, R. F., Good, G. E., Cook, S., O'Neil, J., Smalley, K. B., Owen, K. A., et al. (2006). Validation of the Normative Male Alexithymia Scale: Measurement of a gender-linked syndrome. *Psychology of Men and Masculinity, 7*, 212–224.

Lowder, G., Hansell, J., & McWilliams, N. (2006). *The enduring significance of psychoanalytic theory and practice.* PowerPoint. http://www.division39.org. www.apsa.org

McWilliams, N (2004). *Psychoanalytic psychotherapy—A practitioner's guide.* New York, NY: Guilford Press.

Pope, K. S., Sonne, J. L., and B. Greene (2006). *What therapists don't talk about and why: Taboos that hurt us and our clients.* ABPP: American Psychological Association.

Reis, B., & Grossmark, R. (Eds.). (2009). *Heterosexual masculinities: Contemporary perspectives from psychoanalytic gender theory.* New York, NY: Routledge.

Shedler, J. (2010). The efficacy of psychodynamic psychotherapy. *American Psychologist, 65*(2), 98–109.

Stoller, R. J. (1968). *Sex and gender: On the development of masculinity and femininity,* New York, NY: Science House. London: Hogarth Press and Institute of Psychoanalysis.

The Ordinary Boys. (2004). Boys will be boys. On *Brassbound* [CD]. UK: Over the counter culture, B- Unique/Warner Music.

4

Ethical Considerations in Working With Men

MELBA J. T. VASQUEZ

INTRODUCTION: HELPING WOMEN AND MEN IN A TIME OF CRISIS

You have seen a heterosexual couple for two sessions. They are both in their early 30s, and both have professional jobs. Their presenting concern? They have been together 5 years, he had a one-night fling, and she discovered it. They both declare that they want their relationship to continue. He is contrite and has apologized. On the third session, the woman comes in alone. She reports that they had a huge fight when he accused her of having an affair—he had never accused her of this before. She says she has always been relatively independent, and she is bristling over the accusation, his increase in control, and his deviation from his initial postaffair posture of being contrite and nurturing of their relationship. What is more, she reports that in the second year of their relationship he became physically violent. He went to anger management sessions and has not been violent since. In their fight 2 days ago, while he did not hit her, she indicates that he smashed several possessions. She reports that she "is done" with him unless he goes to individual therapy or anger management again. She also wants him to return to his position of taking responsibility for the fling, rather than accuse her of potentially betraying him.

Consider the following questions as you decide how to proceed with this case. What do you feel? What do you think? What are the ethical and professional dilemmas you should be aware of? How do you proceed? What are your responsibilities to each of these clients? What would your approach be? Do you encourage her to urge him to return to therapy? Do you call him to return to therapy? Do you provide her with information about interpersonal violence concerns? Do you provide possible hypotheses about his behavior? What are the dynamics (both functional and dysfunctional) between them? How does your theoretical orientation figure into this? Now, consider that the female is biracial, and the male is African American. Does race/ethnicity affect your conceptualization of this case, and if so, how?

Much of my work in the ethics of psychotherapy has been about the duties and responsibilities of working with those clients who are different in some way from the mainstream population (Vasquez, 2007, 2009). An important aspect of this ethical issue is about working with those different from oneself, including those of us who are different from white straight men. Because white men's experience has often been the focus in mental health research design, we previously assumed that they were the norm, and that there was little more to know about working with men. However, since the 1990s, the increase in literature on the psychology of men has focused on the importance of understanding the social construction of gender and, to some extent, the biology of gender. The women's movement triggered the critical exploration of sex roles as a social construction. This includes looking critically at conceptions of masculinity, including power, social roles, and effects, both positive and negative, of the socialization process for men. Levant (1996), for example, described masculinity not as a normative construct but rather as a complex and problematic construct. Therefore, true ethical competence for female therapists working with male clients requires three skills in addition to core competence in the psychotherapeutic process: (a) a thorough knowledge and understanding of men and masculinity; (b) self-awareness of one's beliefs, biases, and experiences about one's identity as a woman; (c) how that awareness interacts with those you hold about men. An ethical approach to counseling men means that female therapists must understand how men in general are socialized about specific beliefs, attitudes, and behaviors. We also have to understand how those vary according to other factors, such as sexual orientation, race/ethnicity, ability status, socioeconomic status, and age. The intersection of these variables, for both the client/patient and the psychotherapist should be considered as part of the process.

It is important for all therapists, male and female, to be aware of the socialization and biological issues related to gender, race, sexual orientation, and other variables associated with identity, even if one is a member of those identity groups. Internalized sexism, racism, homophobia, and so on can be problematic unless we go through a process of gaining knowledge and understanding about our own identity groups. As female therapists, we have a special obligation to understand the world of men since we typically do not come from that world. We need also to understand how our own experiences as women may shape our attitudes toward our male clients.

PERSONAL JOURNEY

I was born to fairly traditional Mexican American parents in a small central Texas town in the early 1950s. I was the oldest grandchild to my mother's parents. My mother was the oldest in a family of nine children, and my father was the oldest in his family of eight children. I grew up in a large extended family with lots of contact with aunts, uncles, cousins, and siblings. When I look back on it, gender roles were fairly subscribed and structured. The women cooked and cleaned, and the men worked outside the house. However, when I was in elementary school, my mother began to work outside the house as well. Later, when I read about significant power differences among Latino men and women, I did not relate to the notion because of my own family dynamics. While men in my extended family indeed had formal power (e.g., they outwardly had the final word in decision making), the informal power of women in my family and in my observations of families in my community meant that women were very much listened to (e.g., in their influencing decision making). However, despite this fact, many of the traditional roles were alive and well. Women cooked and primarily attended to children; men were the primary breadwinners.

I am the oldest of five girls in my family and have two brothers, both younger than I am. Although my brothers are younger than I, they had more independence than my sisters and I did. When I was 2 years old, and my sister was born, I grew very attached to my father since my mother was focused with her new baby. I developed a strong identification with him during that period, and our relationship continued to build from that time.

I observed that my father and my uncles all had to work hard. I remember feeling pain and sadness if one of them reported struggles or disappointments at work. My mother had a protective attitude toward my father, her brothers, and her brothers-in-law, perhaps in part because of her awareness of injustice toward Mexican American men and other men of color as well. My parents were both active in various civic and religious organizations that promoted education and justice for members of the community, so I grew up with a strong sense of

the importance of justice and fairness. Yet, I also saw conflict between
my parents, often borne from power struggles in decision making. At
times, I sided with my father and thought that my mother was incredibly unfair and critical; other times, I thought that my father was too
patriarchal and insensitive.

I grew up in a socially segregated community and did not have close
White friends until my upper-class years in college. Issues around truly
trusting Whites were prevalent for me; I had significant negative experiences as a child related to my ethnic identity, including the realization
that we were somehow different from Whites in a "less-than" way. My
first "boyfriend" in second grade declared one day that he could no longer be my boyfriend because his mother said that I was Mexican. When
I went home and asked my mother what was wrong with being Mexican
and told her that my boyfriend broke up with me because of that, she
was furious. I do not remember her explanation, but I remember her
anger. On the bus, an older White male bullied my sister and me until
an older African American female confronted him and watched over us
from that time.

In high school, I was part of the movement in the mid- to late 1960s
to push minority representation among student leaders in high school. I
was one of a handful of Mexican American and Black students elected
to various leadership roles and positions of honor. But, those experiences were often isolating and lonely. Cheerleaders left me out of events
when they gathered, although I also had been elected by the student
body. When I was the only ethnic minority elected to the homecoming
royalty, not one of the White males wanted to have to be paired with me
to walk in the presentation ceremony. Shame, hurt, and anger became a
part of the social rejection I felt from that experience of prejudice and
discrimination. My identification as a girl and then as a young woman
was complicated by the intersection of ethnicity and gender (i.e., I was
not only Mexican American but also female), and the negative view of
my ethnicity in one segment of the community in which I developed.
However, my Latino/a community was a salient, powerful, and positive
influence. Leaders in the community hailed the success of many of us
in the schools and honored us with recognitions, scholarships, and personal positive messages.

Despite negative experiences, I also had many positive experiences
with White students and teachers in school. This helped create my
belief system that one had to discern between those who "bought into"
the separate lives we were required to live at the time and those who
were willing to reach across the divide to connect with me in some
ways. I remember my White civics teacher, who coincidently used to be
my bus driver when I was in elementary school. He nominated me for
the annual civic award for the Daughters of the American Revolution
(DAR). When I was elected, it was the first time that a Latina had been
named for that award, and he did not know if the DAR chapter members would respond positively. He therefore ensured that my mother

and I were honored with the annual tea that they held in honor of the awardee so that I would not be slighted. I was touched by the caretaking involved but also cognizant of the concern that there could be negative repercussions to my selection based on my ethnicity.

In college, I was introduced to feminism at the same time that I was exploring my racial/ethnic identity. This integration of various aspects of my identity continued in graduate school and as an early career professional, after I obtained my doctorate in counseling psychology. One key article I read and resonated with was Peggy McIntosh's 1988 essay *White Privilege: Unpacking the Invisible Knapsack*. This has been informative to me in my understanding of a racial/ethnic and gender-stratified culture. White privilege is the unearned advantages and benefits that accrue to White individuals and men by virtue of a system whose default assumption about human behavior is based on the experiences, values, and perceptions of the group in power who has traditionally been composed of White men. White privilege automatically subordinates groups of color and confers dominance to one group. There are many kinds of privilege. White women have White privilege; men of color have male privilege; first-borns may have privilege; attractive people have privilege. What issues are involved in psychotherapy when women psychotherapists (who theoretically have less privilege by virtue of their gender) provide psychotherapy treatment to men as clients (who theoretically have more privilege by virtue of their gender)? What are the ethical issues involved when the psychotherapist is a woman of color and the client/patient a White male?

The early feminist and multicultural movements to which I was exposed had elements of both anger and dichotomous thinking. I believed then (and believe now) that the development of awareness of one's oppressed role in society necessitates becoming angry to some degree to be motivated to push against restrictive expectations. I used to feel intimated by powerful men, both White and of color and would react angrily at times. Fortunately, I have come to understand that we are all "victims" of erroneous beliefs about others based on our experiences and exposure to biased messages. As psychotherapists, teachers, and supervisors, we have to develop compassion and understanding about those erroneous beliefs and attitudes that others may hold. I have learned over the years not only that men were basically good people but also that some men had not had the benefit of exposure to alternative ideas about equity and justice in gender and racial/ethnic roles, which would counter socially constructed gender role expectations. I came to realize that some men were challenged by the changes that feminism posed and resisted change. Others were open to understanding the importance of equity and justice in the distribution of power. Thus, the feelings of intimidation that I used to feel with powerful men have diminished substantially. This is important because if I felt intimidation, then I probably engaged in a self-protected distancing stance, not conducive to effective psychotherapy, in which the alliance between psychotherapist and client/patient is so vital to successful therapy outcome.

PROFESSIONAL JOURNEY

My professional growth included being a schoolteacher, a graduate student, and then a psychologist in two different university counseling centers. I went through periods of feeling that I could indeed move adequately in the "White world." At other times, I felt overwhelmed by feelings of rejection, isolation, shame, or confusion. Those feelings can still be awakened in me, but because I have spent a good deal of time exploring these feelings through therapy, supervision, and life experiences, they are rarely triggered now in the psychotherapy room with men.

As a schoolteacher, I developed new forms of relationships with my White colleagues; I was able to see, experience, and understand their sources of pain and sorrow as well as joys and successes in life. This more intimate view into the lives of individuals (whom, as a group, I had relegated to members of a group with power) began the process of my evolving view that we were "all in it together." That is, we were all more alike than different. I continued to change my views of those with White culture versus racial/ethnic minority culture, and men versus women as more complex, rather than viewing members of these groups in dichotomous ways.

In graduate school, I continued to learn more about the complexities of human behavior. I also continued the evolution of my own identity as someone who could indeed relate more closely to others whom I had put in the "other" categories of White men and White women. I continued to develop closer friendships with White men and women, which was still a new experience for me.

At times, I experienced instances of sexism and discrimination. For example, when I received an American Psychological Association (APA) Minority Fellowship, a White male graduate student angrily told me that had he been allowed to apply, he should have gotten the fellowship, rather than I, because his Graduate Record Exam (GRE) scores were higher than mine. That entitlement of "meritocracy," that his score on a test entitled him to more, was a painful message to hear. I felt shame and confusion. A few months later, when I spoke to the head of counseling psychology program at my university, I shared my concern that my GRE scores were lower than some of my peers. My professor indicated that he had conducted a study over several years in which he correlated GRE scores with the capacity to complete the doctoral program. He indicated that he actually found an "inverse relationship" among those with the highest scores and those who completed the program. He then told me that my scores were adequate for completing a graduate program at the University of Texas, and that my motivation and persistence were more important than the score itself. What a kind intervention he provided for me.

I was so glad that I took the risk to disclose my concern about my GRE scores. That level of kindness from a White male faculty administrator went far to help me dispel my categorization of White men as singularly entitled, competitive, and oppressive. I realize, in retrospect, that the development of positive friendships with other graduate students also helped me dispel negative stereotypes of oppressive White men and women. Indeed, the literature indicates that contact with people from diverse groups helps reduce discrimination and prejudice.

My first postdoctorate position was at a major university counseling center and came with an appointment in the counseling psychology doctoral program. Once I was licensed, I also began a small part-time independent practice. When I first started seeing White men in therapy, particularly powerful White men, I had to consult about and manage the feelings that were stirred up in me at times. Some male clients had difficulty being vulnerable, resisting responsibility and blaming others for their problems, which reinforced my concerns. However, gentle probing, empathy, compassion, and sharing of direct observations have helped most such clients open up to their core pain. Hearing firsthand about the heartfelt vulnerability, pain, and sorrow from these individuals helped me truly realize that all individuals have pain. My objectification of White men as powerful, privileged, and not in need of care and support came crashing down. I knew this intellectually, but learning this in an experiential, emotional manner was quite a different thing.

One elderly couple whom I saw for relationship psychotherapy, for example, involved a retiring former chief executive officer, who was finally able to hear his wife's wish for more care and intimacy in their relationships and for less-dismissive treatment of her. When he finally "got" that she simply wanted the same care and regard she had provided him for years, he began to provide it. When he experienced the joy of reciprocity, he wept with sorrow as he thought about the years of lost opportunity to be able to meet his wife's needs more thoroughly. I saw how his socialized way of being had robbed both him and his spouse of years of better quality in their relationship.

Over my years of clinical work with men, I have resonated more and more with the psychological science that has been evolving with respect to men and men's development. I do not ascribe to any particular model of gender conceptualization (e.g., essentialism, gender role strain theory, ecological systems, etc.). However, feminism, men's studies, and multicultural theories have deeply influenced my work. I, like many current therapists, work from an eclectic, integrated model of conceptualizing various identity groups. I strongly believe that in doing our work competently, we must have an appreciation for human cultural diversity, including the varied ways that society constructs our identity groups. We must know what these variations are among people, including when these are relevant and when they matter in the problem definition and resolution. We must also be careful not to automatically and perhaps erroneously stereotype men based on this knowledge (Beutler, 2009). One of my basic themes in this chapter is the ethical responsibility to recognize that men belong to a group with a special culture, and that diversity training must include attention to the area of men and masculinity.

This does not mean that men do not suffer from attitudes and behaviors that reflect inappropriate entitlement that is distancing and off-putting at times. Many men are socialized to cope with difficulty, pain, hurt, disappointment, losses, and challenges in destructive ways that are distancing, controlling, defensive, or violent. All therapists, including female therapists, have an ethical responsibility to recognize that men belong to a group with a special culture, and that diversity training must include attention to the area of men and masculinity. The alliance, a critical factor in positive therapeutic outcome, will be enhanced if boys' and men's experiences are better understood (Good & Brooks, 2005) by all psychotherapists, including women psychotherapists.

It means that I (and we all) can better help in the psychotherapy process when we understand the pain that usually underlies those problematic behaviors. My early understanding of equity issues transformed over the years into understanding that, although White men continue to benefit from White privilege, all men and women are oppressed by gender role restrictions, albeit in different ways. Men's oppression includes the unique restrictions and expectations about success and power, which often result in depression and anxiety. Much destructive, "bad" behavior comes as a result of inappropriate defenses to one's vulnerabilities, fears, and anxieties. A feminist model that attends to the varied but significant oppression that results from the traditional social constructions of gender for both men and women as well as for race and ethnicity and other dimensions of diversity is a much more inclusive one.

ETHICAL PRINCIPLES IN WORKING WITH MEN

Kitchener (1984) suggested that five ethical principles are the foundation for ethical decision making in psychology and may help guide us when faced with ethical decision making with all of our clients. These have been incorporated into the general principles of the *Ethical Principles of Psychologists and Code of Conduct* (Ethics Code) of the APA (2002, 2010) and are described next.

Principle 1: Beneficence and Nonmaleficence

The principle of beneficence and nonmaleficence means that psychologists strive to benefit those with whom they work and take care to do no harm, including inflicting intentional harm or engaging in actions that risk harming others. It is our responsibility to have knowledge about which behaviors have potential for harm. We are urged to safeguard the welfare and rights of those with whom we interact professionally. Understanding as much as possible about men is thus an important way to help and to prevent harm.

When conflicts among our obligations or concerns occur, we are encouraged to attempt to resolve these conflicts in a responsible fashion that avoids or minimizes harm. Because our judgments and actions may affect the lives of others, we have to be alert to and guard against all factors that might lead to misuse of our influence. We are encouraged to strive to be aware of the possible effect of our own physical and mental health on our ability to help those with whom we work (APA, 2010). This may take the form of getting counseling, supervision, or consulting when a male client stirs up unresolved issues in you. Another option is to refer if, as psychotherapist, you determine that it is not viable to manage those unresolved issues with that particular client/patient.

Principle 2: Fidelity and Responsibility

We have a unique obligation to establish relationships of trust with those with whom we work, including, of course, male clients. Fidelity involves questions of faithfulness, loyalty, and promise keeping. These are issues basic to trust, and fidelity is especially vital to all human relationships, especially the therapist-client relationship. This relationship is dependent on honest communication. The rule of maintenance of privacy and confidentiality is based partly on this moral principle: Men may be particularly cautious about opening up in therapy when they have been trained to be guarded. We must also be aware of our responsibilities to society and to the specific communities in which we work, including those based on gender, race/ethnicity, religion, and so on. We are encouraged to consult with, refer to, or cooperate with other professionals and institutions to the extent needed to serve the best interests of those with whom we work. This could include obtaining training in men's studies, taking continuing education workshops on the topic, or consulting with colleagues familiar with men's issues. Finally, we are encouraged to strive to contribute a portion of our professional time for little or no compensation (APA, 2010). This could include working with homeless men, for example, a population who often have deep psychological issues that are exacerbated by male norms of success and competence.

Principle 3: Integrity

The principle of integrity is designed to encourage us to promote accuracy, honesty, and truthfulness in the science, teaching, and practice of psychology. We are not to steal, cheat, or engage in fraud, subterfuge, or intentional misrepresentation of fact. We are encouraged to keep our promises and to avoid unwise or unclear commitments. When deception may be ethically justifiable to maximize benefits and minimize harm, we have a serious obligation to consider the need for, the possible consequences of, and the responsibility to correct any resulting mistrust or other harmful effects that arise from the use of those techniques (APA, 2010). This is important for women who do research in the area of men's studies.

Principle 4: Justice

Justice, in its broadest sense, means "fairness"; dealing with others as one would like to be dealt with oneself, behaving toward others in an impartial manner, and treating others equally. The general principle states, in part, that we are to recognize that fairness and justice entitle all persons to access to and benefit from the contributions of psychology and to equal quality in the processes, procedures, and services conducted by psychologists. Thus, in our work with all our clients (including our male clients) we must exercise reasonable judgment and take precautions to ensure that our potential biases, the boundaries of our competence, and the limitations of our expertise do not lead to or condone unjust practices.

Principle 5: Respect for People's Rights and Dignity

This principle states that we should strive to respect the dignity and worth of all people and the rights of individuals to privacy, confidentiality, and self-determination. Mutual respect, a basic element to the therapeutic bond for many of us, implies a relationship between autonomous individuals. Confidentiality, a cornerstone to trust in the relationship, stems in part from the principle of autonomy and respect for people's rights and dignity. The notion that clients/patients must consent to treatment and be informed of the implications of that, informed consent, also stems from this general principle. In working with men, some of whom may have difficulty simply being in the role of needing help, therapists may wish to be particularly cognizant of the need for confidentiality and the challenge for men to be vulnerable with another person.

We must be aware of and respect cultural, individual, and role differences, including those based on age, gender, gender identity, race, ethnicity, culture, national origin, religion, sexual orientation, disability, language, and socioeconomic status. We are urged to eliminate the effect on our work of biases and issues, including toward men, based on those factors. We do not knowingly participate in or condone activities of others based on such prejudices. This would include not "male bashing"; when challenging a client/patient or colleague about their inappropriate "sexist" behaviors, we must do so in a "hearable" way, designed to enhance effectiveness, appropriate to the situation.

There are also specific ethical standards for women working with men, including competence. Standard 2.01, "Boundaries of Competence," of the APA ethical code states that

(a) Psychologists provide services, teach, and conduct research with populations and in areas only within the boundaries of their competence, based on their education, training, supervised experience, consultation, study, or professional experience.

(b) Where scientific or professional knowledge in the discipline of psychology establishes an understanding of factors associated with age, gender, gender identity, race, ethnicity, culture, national origin, religion, sexual orientation, disability, language, or socioeconomic status is essential for effective implementation of their services or research, psychologists have or obtain the training, experience, consultation or supervision necessary to ensure the competence of their services, or they make appropriate referrals, except as provided in Standard 2.02, Providing Services in Emergencies. (APA, 2010, paragraphs 24 and 25)

A number of special guidelines have been developed by the APA to provide more specific guidance for providers who work with members of diverse populations. Guidelines for psychological practice with boys and men are in the process of development. Until this document is done, it is important for women therapists to be aware of the issues outlined next as they work with men.

Based on the increasing body of literature on men and masculinity, I think several key aspects of the male experiences are important to note for women therapists who work with men. Men and women are socialized to have a set of specific attitudes, beliefs, and behaviors based on societal views of gender. The following include those related to masculinity. The traditional male role emphasizes independence, control over one's destiny, physical prowess, and restriction of emotions (Levant, 1996). As women therapists, we have to assess to what degree this is true for each of our male clients and to what degree traditional male role values, attitudes, and beliefs are true or vary for men of color, gay men, men with disabilities, younger men, older men, rich men, poor men, and so on.

Society reinforces boys to be aggressive, dominant, competitive, emotionally restricted; anger has historically been the primary emotion allowed to men. They are also expected to be self-sufficient and to possess physical/sexual prowess (Pollack & Levant, 1998). Male clients therefore might show anger more easily than sadness, sexualize the intimacy of therapy with us, or never even show up in our offices. We must also understand positive aspects of masculinity and many of the desirable aspects of socialization of boys and men, such as generative fathering and the worker/provider role (Kiselica, Englar-Carlson, Horne, & Fisher, 2008). It is important to learn about and identify the noble aspects of masculinity to view men and help them understand themselves more complexly. Seeking and utilizing those male strengths can then be a part of the therapeutic process (Kiselica & Englar-Carlson, 2010).

Men receive a confusing combination of messages about the characteristics and skills they must have. Expectations for men include valuing achievement in areas such as work and school, but not necessarily valuing competency in intimate relationships, focusing on collaborative efforts in work settings, and so on. Men therefore often find that demonstrating traditional expectations is rewarding in some settings but can have maladaptive consequences in interpersonal and intrapersonal settings. This may end up being a focus in treatment for men who are struggling in their interpersonal relationships. Men who cannot meet gender role standards due to aging or discrimination (e.g., men of color and gay men) may struggle with feelings of low self-worth, which can lead to serious health consequences for them. For example, men of color have a shorter life span than White men (U.S. Department of Health and Human Services, 2001). This is at least partly because they experience the same expectations and pressure to demonstrate success and achievement, but because of discrimination and oppression, they experience chronic stress, which often affects their health and well-being and ability to achieve. Female therapists who work with men of color need to be aware of the impact that racism can have on self-esteem and achievement. Before the repeal of "don't ask, don't tell" for gays and lesbians in the armed forces, gay men similarly struggled with a violation of their identity.

In addition to being aware of male gender role strain (as presented in part in the examples just given), we must acknowledge the reality and importance of the men whose lives we affect by our professional actions. This means instilling in and reminding ourselves of a care perspective when we work with men. Caring for the humanity of those whose lives we influence is a cornerstone to our work. Ethical therapy involves the recognition of trust that male clients place in us; power we have over those clients; and truly caring about them. It is also important to be cognizant of the fact that many, if not most, men are reluctant to use psychological services, a reluctance tied to their conceptions of masculinity, which include being independent and not asking for help. Many who do enter treatment do so because they have been encouraged, coaxed, or mandated into treatment by loved ones, bosses, and physicians or by the justice system (Good & Brooks, 2005). Our humanity and caring must extend to consideration of that state of mind in which many male clients/patients enter psychotherapy. In addition, identifying, affirming, and building on aspects of their strengths and positive masculinity will help engage the reluctant male client.

We must understand the nature of the professional relationships and professional interventions as women therapists working with male clients. We must be sure that we are competent in our work and take responsibility for the knowledge about how our behaviors help or potentially hurt our male clients. We must particularly understand how to modify and adapt our basic approach to psychotherapy to serve men better.

Finally, we must affirm accountability for our behavior. Taking responsibility for the climate and structures we set is an important basic task for professional ethics. Learning to be open and nondefensive with male clients, especially when those clients trigger our own issues is a critical personal and professional skill. Alternatively, we may be overly solicitous with our male clients and risk ignoring important key issues: denial of more vulnerable feelings; tendency to blame others for problems or issues; or failure to acknowledge emotional needs.

ETHICAL DILEMMAS IN WORKING WITH MEN

Learning to practice ethically is an ongoing experience. With all our clients, we are often presented with situations that present a dilemma with respect to how to proceed in therapy. There are many ethical dilemmas in our professional world today. An *ethical dilemma* is a situation for which "no course of action seems satisfactory. The dilemma exists because there are good, but contradictory ethical reasons to take conflicting and incompatible courses of action" (Kitchener, 1984, p. 43). A dilemma is present when two moral principles give us contradictory advice about how to proceed in a situation. Knowing how to proceed competently when attending to the overlay of how society constructs various identity groups is a related ethical challenge.

A variety of guidelines have been developed by APA to help psychologists provide competent services and enhance quality of care to members of specific populations. Among others, those guidelines include: Guidelines for psychotherapy with lesbian, gay and bisexual clients (2003a); Guidelines on multicultural education, training, research, practice, and organizational change for psychologists (2003b); Guidelines for psychological practice with older adults (2004); Guidelines for psychological practice with girls and women (2007); Guidelines for assessment of and intervention with persons with disabilities (2011).

I have outlined some cases below that you might encounter in your work with men. As you go through these scenarios, ask yourself: How would I handle this differently if I was a male therapist or if my client were female? Better yet, work with a male colleague to see how he would handle these scenarios. The difference between his reactions and yours will help both of you explore how you view those who are different or similar to you in terms of identity groups.

Scenario 1: Raymond

Raymond is a Latino client/patient who is a quadriplegic. He lived in a South American country and holds dual citizenship in his parents' country and in the United States, where he was actually born. He was living in a South American country with his wife and children and working in a very successful job when he was injured in a car accident that occurred because a drunk driver ran a stop sign. Despite his severe injuries, he tried to continue his job but was not able to do so. His wife convinced him that they should move to the

United States to be nearer his family and to have more help. After living here for 6 months, his wife decided to return to South America with the children for a visit. She decided not to return to the United States. He entered therapy at the suggestion of his mother because he is trying to decide whether to file for divorce, return to the home country, or continue status quo. He is very angry about the accident but does not blame his wife for leaving; he says he feels he is not the man he used to be. He also reports that he has never cried about the changes in his life. He has developed independence and does not want to be a burden to anyone. He does not really know how coming to therapy will help, but he wants to appease his mother. He does ask that you help with a couple of minor logistics each time he arrives and leaves, so that he can otherwise drive himself to and from his sessions with you.

QUESTIONS TO CONSIDER

What do you feel as you work with this man?

What information do you need that would inform you about the direction to proceed in therapy with him?

What aspects of the traditional male sex role are interfering with his adjustment to his disability?

What may serve as obstacles to therapy?

What aspects of his positive masculine qualities can help the therapeutic process?

Do you agree to the requests to facilitate his ability to drive himself to your office?

Do you facilitate his anger (or shy away from it)?

What about working with his other feelings? Do you explore problem-solving and decision-making options with him?

How do you develop his trust and a good working alliance given the multiple differences that you may experience with this client in terms of gender and physical handicaps?

DISCUSSION

I felt tremendous sadness for Raymond's status as a quadriplegic, including the subsequent loss of job and potentially the loss of his wife and children by virtue of their returning to South America. He had, in effect, lost life as he knew it as a consequence of the accident, through no fault of his own. Like many men, having a job and being able to be physically independent and competent has always been an important part of his identity. I knew that he felt tremendous shame as a result of his disability, which has made him feel less than a man. It was important for me to reflect my understanding of the positive masculine values that he held which led him to take responsibility for his situation and to not "blame" his wife for no longer wanting to be with him. The development of the alliance depended partly on my ability to convey my understanding as well as my empathy and compassion for his situation. It was also important that I facilitated his ability to drive himself to my office and to help him use the wheelchair mechanism for him to enter my office, in a way that did not leave him feeling that he was a burden or unmasculine. He abhorred the idea of being a burden to anyone (which I think tied in with normative expectations for a "man" to be independent and self-reliant). Exploration of his feelings of sadness, pain, and loss, other than anger, took a very long time, and he was able to acknowledge those only briefly. I was patient with his slow process of accessing and expressing his feelings because I knew how difficult it was for many men, including Raymond, to confront internalized male norms of emotional restriction. As he requested, we did explore his options, including the option to delay filing for divorce. I am careful to honor a male client's requests if possible since it puts him more in the driver's seat and less dependent on me for the content of therapy. He acknowledged that his initial reaction to file for divorce immediately after his wife left was based on his hurt pride and as a way to deflect rejection by his wife. I truly admired Raymond for the fact that, despite his many losses, he did not settle into blame or depression but was interested in exploring and understanding the social construction of his role as an upper-class Latino male and how his disability interfered with his expectations about himself. He was also willing to consider that his long-term goals would include a major task of adjusting to his life as a person with disabilities, including future occupational and social relationship options. I think my genuine respect and compassion for him helped him begin to work with his limitations and not to lose sight of his masculinity along the way.

Scenario 2: Mike

Mike is a middle-aged White male who came into therapy for a variety of reasons, including difficulty in his marriage. A couple of months after beginning therapy, he came in, angry because he had not gotten a promotion that he expected to get. He was seriously disappointed, devastated, and humiliated. He had expected to get the promotion. Furthermore, he declared being "victimized" by the fact that a minority woman, whom he perceived to be less important or capable, got the position, probably due to "affirmative action." Being a good provider is a cultural expectation for men, and the failure to obtain a long-expected promotion robs him of his ability to live up to this expectation and its impact on his male psyche (Skovholt, 1990).

QUESTIONS TO CONSIDER

How do you feel?

What are the issues stirred up in you?

What are the options in responding to Mike?

How do you proceed in the therapy session?

What are the goals?

How would you address the socialized expectation that a male should be a good provider, and that he is feeling robbed of that opportunity?

When, if ever, do you process the racist/sexist attitudes in psychotherapy?

What are the variables to determine this?

DISCUSSION

In this case, which I described previously (Vasquez, 2006), I described the importance of attending to various ethical decision-making challenges, including the importance of managing my own issues and being empathic with his pain and fear as a result of the failure to achieve promotion and to improve his income level. Yet, I also knew that his blaming others was a maladaptive way to deal with a painful and disappointing event, which threatened his male psyche. I suspected that, while he had improved during the course of therapy in his capacity to take more responsibility, the trauma of the failure to obtain a promotion likely resulted in his "relapse" to old defenses of blaming others.

Perhaps one of the biggest challenges for most, if not all, psycho-therapists is being able to be attuned to clients well enough to know when to support and when to challenge, especially when the client is expressing what we perceive to be destructive or self-destructive sentiments, thoughts, and opinions. This is especially true when our own reactions (countertransference) and issues are triggered. When a male client/patient is perceived by the psychotherapist to be abusing his White privilege (McIntosh, 1988) and not practicing "healthy coping," what kinds of interventions are appropriate? What is the appropriate timing for such interventions? If, for example, one conceptualizes Mike was fragile in his ability to take respon-sibility for how he may have contributed to his lack of promotion but instead to blame "affirmative action," venting his emotions as he did may be what he needed to do in that moment. My job was not to scold him for his attitudes but to help him explore over time his feelings of disgrace, shame, and despair and, when he was ready, to help him acknowledge how he may have contributed to his lack of promotion and how he might do things differently in the future to help him meet goals that would result in a promotion.

Scenario 3: Older White Male

An older White male phones to explore the possibility of entering psychotherapy with you. He asks an extensive number of questions about your background, training, years of experience, and approach to treatment. He wants to know who you share your office with and how confidential the information you glean about him will be. This potential client/patient reports that he has a medical degree as well as a law degree, and that he has never been in therapy before. He got your name from a couple of sources and says he wants the very best but does not know exactly what he should be looking for in a psychotherapist. He wishes to deal with career and family issues. His manner is gruff and distant.

QUESTIONS TO CONSIDER

What do you feel?
What does this potential client's approach tell you about him?
How do you respond to his questions?
What do you need to know to consider taking him as a client/patient?

DISCUSSION

Often, people see me as a woman of color first and a professional second (or third or fourth). In the past, my automatic reaction to the client/patient described would have been to deal with the anxiety he evoked in me by pathologizing him as paranoid and obsessive-compulsive. I have learned that the healthier alternative is to compassionately acknowledge that this was his first time to consider psychotherapy, and that it was very difficult for him to be vulnerable and ask for help. O'Neil (2008) described the concept of success/power/competition from his gender role conflict model to explain the gruff manner in which men sometimes engage in interactions. I was able to conceptualize his "interrogation" simply as strategies he used to feel safer in embarking on a vulnerable endeavor. The usefulness of these strategies can eventually be explored in the psychotherapeutic process once the therapeutic alliance has been formed. Looking at their positive or negative consequences can help the client make choices about his behaviors that are more informed in the future when he feels vulnerable or threatened.

His privilege in assuming he should have "the very best" was incongruent for him, perhaps, with the fact that I was a woman of color. I am aware that as a Latina psychotherapist, many of my clients of color choose to come to see me because of my ethnic identity. Other people of color, with internalized racism, might choose to avoid seeing someone like me. I am also aware that many of my White clients have to go through some process of cognitive dissonance to assume my competency because if they grew up in this society, people from my ethnic background are not assumed to be competent. In addition, he was considering seeing a female therapist (not a male therapist), and internalized sexist attitudes toward the competency of women may have played a part in his concerns. Perhaps most of all, his manner may have hidden his fears and concerns about whether someone (regardless of race or gender) could really help him. If I imagined him as worried or fearful rather than sexist or racist, I would be better able to form a positive alliance with him. A basic task for ethical practice is to remember the humanity of those with whom we work (Pope & Vasquez, 2010). Green (2007) suggested that "keeping track of your humanity" involves being aware of someone else's vulnerability to injury or harm as a result of our actions. We must especially do this when what we are doing involves using the power at our disposal.

Comas-Diaz and Jacobsen (1995) addressed the interracial dyad involving a therapist of color and a White patient, and they provided a dynamic analysis of the contradictions, such as significance of power reversal and transferential and countertransferential reactions. They conceptualized this dyad as an opportunity for therapists of color to acquire a perspective from White patients and witness the reality experienced by their majority group patients. Alternatively, White patients can benefit from the contributions of the therapist of color, who has experience in overcoming the odds of achieving success. An analysis of an "intergender" dyad might result in the same dynamic, with the opportunity for women therapists to acquire a perspective from male patients and witness the reality experienced by male patients. Male patients can benefit from the contributions of the female therapist, and both can thus heal and become more empowered.

Scenario 4: A Good Man Caught in a Dilemma

A Latino, Dan, entered therapy because his wife, also Latina, insisted that he try to understand why he had an affair with a coworker (a White European). He came in after his wife was devastated to discover that he was still having interactions with this woman after he had committed to having no more contact. Dan was surprised that his wife wanted to remain in the relationship. After 2 weeks of anger and rage after initially discovering the affair, she indicated that she wanted the relationship to work. They had three adult children and had had no sexual or emotional intimacy (such as the kind he experienced with his coworker) for several years. Dan was committed to remain in the marriage and to discontinue all contact with his coworker/lover. After the first session, Dan reported that his former lover had contacted him due to a cancer diagnosis. He accepted her call and was confused about how to proceed. He wanted to commit to his wife's request that he have no contact whatsoever. Yet, he was alarmed and distressed about the diagnosis of cancer of someone with whom he had been so close just a few months previously and felt a strong pull to be supportive in some way.

QUESTIONS TO CONSIDER

How do you feel?
With whom do you feel empathy?
How do you proceed in your psychotherapeutic choices?
What role does his ethnicity play?

DISCUSSION

I felt empathy for the dilemma in which Dan found himself. He was responsible for maintaining his promise to his wife to discontinue any contact with his former lover. However, this person for whom he had cared so much just recently was in physical and emotional distress. He was caught in a dilemma in which he continued to be motivated to demonstrate male ways of caring and generative fathering (Kiselica & Englar-Carlson, 2010) for both the women in his life, in spite of his wife's accusations. We explored several options and potential consequences of each choice, including disclosing to his wife that, with her consent, he would like to be able to check about his friend's welfare. He did not feel that the latter action (which he recognized as perhaps the healthiest option) was something that he was ready to risk. Instead he continued to respect the boundary of having no contact but kept up information about the former lover by hearing indirectly about her from other coworkers. Dan's ethnicity as a male Latino may have played a role in his prioritization of family as the most important factor in all his choices. My role was to be supportive of where he felt he was at this point in time, given that we had explored a wide variety of options.

CONCLUSION

It is not enough to have good, solid psychotherapy skills to be competent in working with men. One of our ethical responsibilities is that we more thoroughly understand individuals partly through understanding the social construction of their identity groups. Family members, peers, and cultural models teach all of us a confusing combination of characteristics and skills, and we have to assess those for ourselves, and how those influence our professional behavior, as well as for each of our clients/patients and understand how those help or hinder their mental health and well-being. Men in particular have to overcome the negative stigma of psychotherapy. We have to convey our understanding of the values that are inherent as part of our client's identity groups, without judgment, even when those values lead to destructive behavior. We must maintain a stance of compassion, care, and respect in our work, even as we work through challenging dilemmas. As women psychotherapists working with men, we must help them identify destructive patterns in ways that help the client/patient experience our care, concern, and understanding. Remembering the humanity of those with whom we work is a key strategy in doing so. Sometimes it is a long process for a male client/patient to accept the offer of assistance and to become comfortable with identifying and discussing his emotions, especially the vulnerable ones. We have to monitor our own biases and discomfort with seeing a "weak and vulnerable" man who may suffer from depression, anxiety, fear, or grief to develop a healthy working alliance. As women psychotherapists, we are ethically bound to remain aware of the evolving scholarship and research about men and masculinity. The more we learn about the complex and changing aspects of client identity groups, the more effective we can be to empower our clients to make healthy and satisfying life choices, have relief from distressing symptoms, increase their quality of life, and have fully functioning lives.

REFERENCES

American Psychological Association. (2002). *Ethical principles of psychologists and code of conduct.* Washington, DC: Author. Retrieved from http://www.apa.org/ethics/code/index.aspx

American Psychological Association. (2010). *Ethical principles of psychologists and code of conduct* (as amended). Washington, DC: Author. Retrieved from http://www.apa.org

American Psychological Association. (2003a). *Guidelines for psychotherapy with lesbian, gay and bisexual clients.* Retrieved from http://www.apa.org/pi/lgbc/guidelines.html

American Psychological Association. (2003b). Guidelines on multicultural education, training, research, practice, and organizational change for psychologists. *American Psychologist, 58,* 377–402.

American Psychological Association (2004). Guidelines for psychological practice with older adults. *American Psychologist, 59,* 236–260.

American Psychological Association. (2007). *Guidelines for psychological practice with girls and women.* Retrieved from http://www.apa.org/practice/guidelines/girls-and-women.pdf

American Psychological Association. (2011). Guidelines for assessment of and intervention with persons with disabilities. Retrieved from http://www.apa.org/pi/disability/resources/assessment-disabilities.aspx

Beutler, L. E. (2009). Making science matter in clinical practice: Redefining psychotherapy. *Clinical Psychology: Science and Practice, 16,* 301–317.

Comas-Diaz, L., & Jacobsen, F. M. (1995). The psychotherapist of color and the White patient dyad: Contradictions and recognitions. *Cultural Diversity and Mental Health, 1,* 93–106.

Good, G. F., & Brooks, G. R. (2005). Introduction. In G. E. Good & G. R. Brooks (Eds.), *The new handbook of psychotherapy and counseling with men: A comprehensive guide to settings, problems, and treatment approaches* (pp. 1–13). San Francisco: Jossey-Bass/Wiley.

Green, B. (2007, January). *The complexity of diversity: Multiple identities and the denial of privilege (within marginalized groups).* Keynote address presented at the National Multicultural Conference and Summit, Seattle, WA.

Kiselica, M. S., & Englar-Carlson, M. (2010). Identifying, affirming, and building upon male strengths: The positive psychology/positive masculinity model of psychotherapy with boys and men. *Psychotherapy Theory, Research, Practice, Training, 47,* 276–287.

Kiselica, M. S., Englar-Carlson, M., Horne, A. M., & Fisher, M. (2008). A positive psychology perspective on helping boys. In M. S. Kiselica, M. Englar-Carlson, & A. M. Horne (Eds.), *Counseling troubled boys: A guidebook for practitioners* (pp. 31–48). New York, NY: Routledge.

Kitchener, K. S. (1984). Intuition, critical evaluation and ethical principles: The foundation for ethical decisions in counseling psychology. *The Counseling Psychologist, 12,* 43–55.

Levant, R. F. (1996). The new psychology of men. *Professional Psychology: Research and Practice, 27,* 259–265.

McIntosh, P. (1988). *White privilege: Unpacking the invisible knapsack* (Working Paper 189). Wellesley, MA: Wellesley College Center for Research on Women.

O'Neil, J. M. (2008). Summarizing 25 years of research on men's gender role conflict using the Gender Role Conflict Scale: New research paradigms and clinical implications. *The Counseling Psychologist, 36,* 358–445.

Pollack, W., & Levant, R. (1998). *New psychotherapy for men.* New York, NY: Wiley.

Pope, K. S., & Vasquez, M. J. T. (2011). *Ethics and psychotherapy in counseling: A practical guide* (4th edition). Hoboken, NJ: John Wiley.

Skovholt, T. (1990). Career themes in counseling and psychotherapy with men. In D. Moore & F. Leafgren (Eds.), *Men in conflict* (pp. 39–53). Alexandria, VA: American Association for Counseling and Development.

U.S. Department of Health and Human Services. (2001). *Mental health: Culture, race, and ethnicity—A supplement to mental health: A report of the Surgeon General.* Rockville, MD: U.S. Department of Health and Human Services, Public Health Service, Office of the Surgeon General.

Vasquez, M. J. T. (2006). Counseling men: Perspectives and experiences of a woman of color. In M. Englar-Carlson & M. Stevens (Eds.), *In the room with men: A casebook of therapeutic change* (pp. 241–256). Washington, DC: American Psychological Association.

Vasquez, M. J. T. (2007). Cultural difference and the therapeutic alliance: An evidence-based analysis. *American Psychologist, 62,* 878–886.

Vasquez, M. J. T. (2009). Ethics in multicultural counseling practice. In J. G. Ponterotto, J. M. Casas, L. A. Suzuki, & C. M. Alexander (Eds.), *Handbook of multicultural counseling* (3rd ed., pp. 127–145). Thousand Oaks, CA: Sage.

Different Modalities of Treatment

5

Couples Counseling

ROBERTA L. NUTT

INTRODUCTION

It was always clear to me, even as a child, that the relationship between my parents was complex. While on the surface it looked traditional in that my father was the breadwinner who worked as an industrial engineer at the local DuPont plant and my mother stayed home and fulfilled the role of the housewife in the 1950s, their attitudes about their roles did not seem traditional. For one thing, it was obvious that decision making in the household was shared. For another, while my mother had given up her job at the DuPont plant upon marriage, my father's attitude was that they were partners in marriage and therefore partners in his paycheck. In fact, he preferred that she manage the household finances and give him an allowance for his weekly expenses. This background provided me with an open lens for later work with couples in counseling from a variety of situations.

PERSONAL JOURNEY

Of course, my personal awareness of gender roles began early. Like all little girls growing up in the 1940s and 1950s, I was surrounded by them. As I described, my mother was a homemaker, and my father went to work outside the home every morning. The same was true for most families in our neighborhood, first in northern New Jersey and later in southeastern Texas after we were transferred. Mothers and daughters cooked and sewed, and fathers worked and did the yard work with their sons (although I also had to do yard work, and thought it was unfair, at the time). I described that my parents shared power in decision making, and that my father's respect for my mother was strong and evident. I even recall his telling me as a young child that she was smarter than he was—powerful encouragement for a young feminist.

My father and I spent a lot of time together as I was growing up. I was firstborn, and on Saturday mornings, Dad and I would go to hardware stores together, so I developed an appreciation for tools of all varieties. We also sang in the church choir together. He always encouraged my academic interests and achievements. I always knew he believed I could do anything I set my mind to do. Such experiences probably made us closer in many ways than he may have been to my brother, which also gave me insight into his humor and love of music.

Before I leave family influences, I must talk about my one sibling. I have a wonderful younger brother who is also a close friend. I have learned much about men from my brother, who is an excellent role model of a male who is both instrumental and expressive. He has been successful in business and successful at rearing two wonderful sons. I have seen him model traditional roles in his business success in his office as an architect, including admiring the fruits of his labors in the buildings he has constructed. I also know how seriously he has taken and enjoyed his family roles as father and now grandfather.

The stronger gender messages were external to the family—in the school system, the peer group, the media, and other venues. I remember most the messages that I felt were aimed to silence me because men/boys were viewed as more important. I did well in school and was encouraged academically by my family, but the larger culture (i.e., peer group, popular magazines, movies, etc.) told me to hide my academic success and interest. Popular girls' magazines of the time were filled with articles telling girls how to get boys to talk about themselves and how to flirt. At the same time, boys were being instructed to act tough and hide their feelings. The important boys on campus were the football players, so boys who did not meet that athletic prowess did not measure up.

Fairly early on, these peer group rules just did not make sense to me. Playing dumb just made me mad, and I could not do it. This stance allowed me to be myself. For this I paid a social price, such as fewer dating options. However, I could also connect better to some of my male peers as friends. Back then I could see we all suffered from disappointments and setbacks as plans changed and relationships faltered. I did have an interesting (shall we say corrective) experience regarding my high school stance in this regard. It happened at a high school reunion—a later one, after something like 23 years. One of the high school football players, who in Texas are certainly the "big men on campus," approached me at the reunion party with an apology. He said that he had recently remarried, and his new wife had been her high school valedictorian, as I had been. He now had some new insight into what my life had been like in high school. He wanted me to know from his perspective as one of the football players that "the guys" had thought I was really cute back then but that they were scared of me because I was too smart. What wonderful, thoughtful feedback many years later!

PROFESSIONAL JOURNEY

After high school, I attended Rice University for my first two years of college, where being smart was expected and therefore no longer a social issue. However, after I decided on a major in psychology, Rice did not seem the best place to continue as it had only recently transitioned from Rice Institute to Rice University and only had two psychology professors. I transferred to the University of Texas at Austin, which had a much stronger psychology program and many more faculty, and I assumed would give me a broader preparation for graduate school. I cannot clearly remember my process of deciding to major in psychology, but I do know that I made an early decision to go for a PhD, so I planned the necessary steps to get there.

I did take one detour between my undergraduate program and graduate school that had a major impact on both my learning about gender roles and cultures: I joined the Peace Corps. From 1966 to 1968, I taught high school mathematics in Malaysia. My friends were Malays, Indians, and Chinese, so I learned much about many cultures and their gender roles. Several of my friends at school were married, and their marital roles varied by their religion, be it Muslim, Buddhist, or Christian. I found some of the very traditional roles expected of women in Malaysia extremely confining, and we had long conversations about these roles in the teachers' hostel over tea in the afternoons. Some of the younger women were questioning expected roles as they planned their futures and like young women in many places wanted to talk.

On returning to the United States, I entered graduate school in the counseling psychology doctoral program at the University of Maryland after working for a while at the School of Public Health and Hygiene at Johns Hopkins University. My original career goals were to work in university counseling centers, and my first job was at the Counseling Center at the State University of New York, College at Fredonia. That was followed by a split appointment at Texas Woman's University between the Counseling Center and the Psychology Department and a transition after three years into full-time teaching. I realized the flexibility of academia was a better fit for me, and I opened a part-time practice in Dallas to continue my therapy work.

My interest in men's issues began in the 1970s when I was teaching graduate courses in the psychology of women. It became apparent to me

that I really could not effectively teach women's issues without also considering men's issues that interfaced with many of the topics we were
discussing in class. As classroom discussion grew, and I had both women
and men students in my classes, it became clear to all of us that while
men certainly had a number of public cultural advantages in U.S. society, gender role socialization definitely restricted the full development
of both women and men, just in very different ways. Sharing of personal
stories of men of color and gay men in my classroom gave us examples
of even further restrictions. At the time, the women's movement was
blossoming in full force, and there was a booming literature on the psychology of women. Unfortunately, there was much less available on the
psychology of men, at least not truly in terms of gender development.

While I was teaching in a feminist-oriented doctoral program at
Texas Woman's University, the men in the program (after having their
consciousness raised regarding women's issues) requested a parallel
course in men's issues. I developed such a course and wrote an associated article (Nutt, 1991), which provided a beginning outline of topics
that might be covered, including the hazards of male socialization, relationships with other men, career and success issues, war and violence,
sexuality, ethnicity, and counseling issues, some of which were just
beginning to be considered at the time.

As I began delving into the literature for my classes, I was, as always,
learning a tremendous amount from my clients and began a particularly rich journey with three friends. Realizing the strong passion we
shared for gender communication, Gary Brooks, Carol Philpot, Don-
David Lusterman, and I began to do a series of workshops and symposia
at professional conferences that resulted in our book *Bridging Separate
Gender Worlds: How Men and Women Clash and How Therapists Can
Bring Them Together* (Philpot, Brooks, Lusterman, & Nutt, 1997). The
book details our view of how men and women are socialized differently and how they can learn to understand and accept each other. Our
goal was to write the book in one voice, and that blending of our four
voices was a wonderful, growth-enhancing process. Although each of
us drafted chapters individually, we then edited each chapter until our
voices blended, and the book was a product of us all. One important
tool used in the book is the gender role inquiry; the therapist teaches
the couple to interview each other about the details of their gender role
socialization to create greater acceptance and mutual understanding,
thereby giving the clients the tools for their own future growth.

Through my interest in men's issues, I also became involved in the
Society for the Psychological Study of Men and Masculinity (Division
51) of the American Psychological Association (APA) during its earliest
days of formation in the early 1990s. I felt it was important for feminist
women to support this new division of APA because these were the men
who understood both men's and women's issues and were working for
the mental health of both genders. I explained to other feminist women
how the agendas of both Division 51 and Division 35 (The Psychology

of Women) were similar—both were working to transform traditional gender roles—and helped recruit members and gather signatures for the petition. As the new division was formed, I worked on the bylaws, served as the first fellows chair, and served as a member-at-large on the executive board. I still enjoy serving on the editorial board of the journal *Psychology of Men and Masculinity*.

DOING GENDER-AWARE COUPLES COUNSELING

In therapeutic work with male clients, it is first important to consider how difficult it often is for male clients to enter counseling/therapy (Addis & Mahalik, 2003; Nutt, 2007). Assuming your clients are a heterosexual couple, in many cases it may be the woman who most desires the counseling, and the man may be coming to your office with reluctance. In these cases, it is helpful to spend some extra time talking with the male partner about his expectations of counseling and his reluctance to be there. Recognizing and normalizing those feelings can be helpful at the beginning of the counseling process by helping him to feel understood. It is also important to recognize that in help-seeking situations, men ask fewer questions than women (Courtenay, 2000), so it is particularly important for the counselor to provide information.

In addition, it is generally important to recognize and make explicit the concern that many men may have entering couples therapy with a woman therapist that they may be "ganged up" on by the therapist and their female partner. It is helpful to talk about the therapy process and the necessity for the therapist to be as neutral as possible as you work on the couple's issues. Invite them to let you know if ever they feel like you are leaning toward siding with one of their perspectives to the detriment of the other. Bringing the issue out into the open at the beginning of the therapy seems to work best. In other cases, for individual or couples counseling, it may take a crisis to overcome the socialized resistance a man may feel to enter therapy. It is important to be sensitive to the probable overload of pain that may have brought this man to seek assistance at this time; therefore, initially spend time being sensitive to the effort it took to access this help-seeking process.

As a second important issue, recognize that men are less likely to be socialized to the therapeutic process of sharing and exploring feelings. Some men may even have difficulty being aware of such feelings—a difficulty that has been termed *alexithymia* by Levant (1992). They have also been socialized to minimize pain (Lisak, 2001). Hence, as with any client, it is important to meet the client where he is, matching him with both language and emotion. Timing is extremely important. Explaining the process of counseling and checking out the client's preconceived expectations to allay specific concerns may be helpful (Mahalik, Good, & Englar-Carlson, 2003). Specifically addressing the differences between the culture of counseling and masculine socialization may also be helpful

(Good, Thomson, & Brathwaite, 2005), as may framing seeking help as a brave and courageous act. Listening, talking his language, and accepting where he is will help create a safe environment in which it is more probable that the male client and female therapist can create a working relationship. Many men will consider entering new territory, such as exploring emotional issues, only if they are first accepted as who they are. Many male clients make less eye contact than female clients and often fiddle with an object like a pen or cup, so do not interrupt these activities or interpret them. It seems that these behaviors speak to a male way of "being" in the therapy room and seem to create some comfort. Other examples may be to talk about sports or other comfortable topics.

In addition, knowledge of male socialization is helpful in working with male clients. If such knowledge can help the therapist guess what the client is feeling and aid him in articulating it, that knowledge and ability has helped to move the therapy process along. It is almost like using the classic Gestalt technique of "May I feed you a sentence?" although much less formal. In this technique, the therapist, with the client's permission, guesses what the client is thinking and speaks for the client. It creates a bond in that the client feels understood, and it helps him to communicate his own feelings as well.

There is significant evidence that men are born with the same kind of basic needs and feelings that women are, and that it is socialization that changes the expression of these needs and feelings (Hyde, 2005; Pollack, 1998). After rapport is established, an analysis of gender role messages with both partners can begin, including those from the family of origin, peers, school, media, and religion; establishing his personal gender role journal may create an understanding of both personal struggles and relationship difficulties (Nutt, 2006; O'Neil & Egan, 1992; Philpot et al, 1997). Gender role analysis entails a process of gender role inquiry in which the counselor asks a number of questions about the client's developmental history. There are no right or wrong questions, no necessary questions. Any inquiry leads the client to explore gendered messages and expectations.

Such questions might include the following:

1. How would you describe your family (father, mother, siblings, grandparents, etc.)?
2. What were expectations of others about you as a boy (girl) regarding behavior, future, goals, and so on? Were there things you were expected to do or forbidden to do because you were a boy (girl)?
3. Did teachers in school encourage or discourage you in sports, science, art, social activities, academics, appearance, competitiveness?
4. What career choices were you expected to make by parents, peers, teachers, others?
5. Whom did you admire as a child? Adolescent? Adult?
6. With whom was your first romantic relationship and describe what it was like?
7. How are you like your mother, your father?

8. Whom do you consider you mentors/role models?
9. If you could live your childhood over again, what would you do differently?
10. What was your adolescence like?

In working with couples, the therapist can teach the couple to use gender inquiry to deepen their understanding of each other (Philpot et al., 1997). This then gives them a tool to take away from therapy. In essence, the therapist has taught the couple Interviewing Skills 101. Couples can learn to interview one another using open-ended questions and active listening skills to produce empathy and deepen their acceptance of each other. This deeper understanding can lead to a major cognitive-affective shift, which can reduce conflict and increase emotional intimacy (Nutt, 2005).

While gender inquiry has most often been used to untangle gender miscommunication within heterosexual couples, it also has utility for gay and lesbian couples. Two persons who have received similar gender role messages may still clash around gender role expectations, and clarifying those expectations and learning each other's socialization history can avert a multitude of relationship problems. For example, one partner can learn why the other has certain expectations for birthday celebrations or Valentine's Day based on how the partner's parents celebrated such holidays in their families of origin.

There are some limitations of this approach to couples counseling, which would include couples with violence present and the violence issues unresolved. Safety issues are paramount and must take precedence. Couples counseling is not recommended until violence issues are resolved. In addition, a certain level of healthy functioning is necessary for the strategies described to be useful. Serious mental illness, depression, substance abuse, or other problems may negate the utility of these interventions.

Couples Counseling: A Case Study

Mary Ann and George are a couple who have been married for 25 years and entered counseling with me reporting increasing tension in their relationship. George is 51 years old, and Mary Ann is 48. They have two children who are grown and married. In the past two years, Mary Ann has gone back to college to finish the degree she interrupted long ago to marry George and start their family. She is thoroughly enjoying school and learning and looking forward to career possibilities that her degree may provide. George is working in sales in a large computer company, reports being tired of his job, and is looking forward to retirement.

Both Mary Ann and George report in the first session that their fighting and bickering have increased during the two years that Mary Ann has been in school. Mary Ann complains that she would like George to help more around the house now that she is in school. George complains that Mary Ann is less attentive to his needs now that she is in school. George misses the old days when the kids were at home, and they were a "happy family." Mary Ann zings back, "How could he remember? He was always working and never home." I called for a time-out and asked the couple to reminisce and recall their dating years and decision to get married. How did they meet? What attracted them to each other? How did they decide to marry? It helps to cut through the current conflict to remember the bonding of the past and create a foundation for working through the conflict. In this case, it also put them on equal footing. I was obviously not taking sides but asked each of them to remember the positive aspects of earlier times.

Following those early dating recollections, I asked them to describe how they negotiated their understanding of what being married meant to each of them. How did they understand the role of the husband? The wife? To truly understand how they developed their roles usually requires going back to a gender inquiry into their family-of-origin histories. What kind of role models for husbands and wives did they have in their own families, and how did those expectations carry into their family of procreation? Was that transition smooth or rocky? How had they negotiated household chores, finances, and other responsibilities while they were rearing children? How were they renegotiating those responsibilities now that their children were grown? How did these responsibilities fit with their own gender role expectations?

My hunch listening to Mary Ann and George was that neither really understood the other's gender role socialization. They were busy arguing with each other and not listening to each other. Neither seemed to understand the other's point of view or the other's feelings. In asking George questions about his early career aspirations and his family's, particularly his father's, expectations for him, it became clear that George had been brought up to gain most of his identity via his role as breadwinner, a role from which he was not getting much enjoyment. Specifically, we did discover that George's father pushed him into his career path. As a young man, George had been passionate about music. His father had been strongly critical of George's involvement in a band as an adolescent and his desire to pursue a career as a musician. His father insisted that he pursue a major in business in college and get a "real man's job." George felt unappreciated for his sacrifice in working for all these years in a job that he really did not like, was looking forward to retirement, and could not understand Mary Ann's enthusiasm about working possibilities. On the other hand, in pursuing the messages that Mary Ann had received from family, peers, and teachers, she had been brought up to gain most of her identity via her role of wife and mother and was now very much enjoying her new-found freedom to explore the world for herself through education and a new career. She wanted

George to join her in these new, exciting possibilities and could not see how they might be threatening to him and his role in the family.

Gender inquiry is not only a good tool to help Mary Ann and George understand their own socialization processes, but also a tool to interview each other to deepen their understanding of each other. Mary Ann needs to understand George's insecurities and vulnerabilities and support him. George needs to understand and support Mary Ann's excitement as she starts a new career. In many ways, although similar in age, they are at different life stages and need each other's support. In this stage of therapy, the therapist becomes a coach or teacher. Teach Mary Ann how to ask George what it was like to have his father disapprove of his career choice and push him into business. Teach her how to listen with active listening skills. Teach George how to ask Mary Ann about her excitement about being in school and learning and the possibilities of using her new degree in a career, again with active listening skills. Teach them both how to validate the concerns, needs, and hopes of their partner and not react defensively to what their partner is saying. In some ways, it can be going back and becoming reacquainted in ways that couples do when they are first dating. The difference is that there is a focus on the gender socialization messages with the goal of freeing the partners from the burdens of fulfilling roles they no longer wish to carry. This process allows the couple to identify those roles, discuss them, understand them, and renegotiate them.

HELPFUL HINTS FOR FEMALE THERAPISTS WORKING WITH MEN IN HETEROSEXUAL COUPLES

Gender-aware couples counseling can be rewarding work for the therapist and the couple. Helping a couple understand each other's gender role journey provides particular benefit, in part, I think, because so many forces seem to support the idea that men and women cannot understand and accept each other. Seeing a couple move from fighting and conflict to empathic understanding is one of therapy's greatest satisfactions. Part of that success is knowing how to work with the male partner in such couples, summarized in five basic points below.

1. Recognize male reluctance to enter therapy and make it explicit, if evident.
2. Be aware of male concern of being "ganged up" on in a heterosexual couple with a female therapist and bring the topic into open discussion.
3. Be sensitive to male ways of expression, match him with both language and emotion, and accept him where he is.

4. Use knowledge of male socialization to aid therapeutic process.
5. Use and teach gender role inquiry.

REFERENCES

Addis, M. E., & Mahalik, J. R. (2003). Men, masculinity, and the contexts of help seeking. *American Psychologist, 58*, 5–14.

Courtenay, W. H. (2000). Constructions of masculinity and their influence on men's well-being: A theory of gender and health. *Social Science and Medicine, 50*, 1385–1401.

Good, G. E., Thomson, D. A., & Brathwaite, A. (2005). Men and therapy: Critical concepts, theoretical frameworks, and research recommendations. *Journal of Clinical Psychology, 61*, 699–711.

Hyde, J. S. (2005). The gender similarities hypothesis. *American Psychologist, 60*, 581–592.

Levant, R. F. (1992). Toward the reconstruction of masculinity. *Journal of Family Psychology, 5*, 379–402.

Lisak, D. (2001). Male survivors of trauma. In G. R. Brooks & G. E. Good (Eds.), *The new handbook of psychotherapy and counseling with men* (pp. 263–277). San Francisco: Jossey-Bass.

Mahalik, J. R., Good, G. E., & Englar-Carlson, M. (2003). Masculinity scripts, presenting concerns, and help seeking: Implications for practice and training. *Professional Psychology: Research and Practice, 34*, 123–131.

Nutt, R. L. (1991). Family therapy training issues of male students in a gender-sensitive doctoral program. In M. Bograd (Ed.), *Feminist approaches for men in family therapy* (pp. 261–279). New York, NY: Haworth Press.

Nutt, R. L. (2005). Feminist and contextual work. In M. Harway (Ed.), *The handbook of couples therapy* (pp. 228–249). Hoboken, NJ: Wiley.

Nutt, R. L. (2006). Adam and the pain of divorce. In M. Englar-Carlson & M. A. Stevens (Eds.), *In the room with men: A casebook of therapeutic change* (pp. 285–300). Washington, DC: American Psychological Association.

Nutt, R. L. (2007). Counseling men: Necessary knowledge. *Counseling and Spirituality: Men and Counseling, 26*, 53–80.

Philpot, C. L., Brooks, G. R., Lusterman, D.-D., & Nutt, R. L. (1997). *Bridging separate gender worlds: Why men and women clash and how therapists can bring them together.* Washington, DC: American Psychological Association.

Pollack, W. S. (1998). *Real boys: Rescuing our sons from the myths of boyhood.* New York, NY: Random House.

RECOMMENDED READING

Brooks, G. R. (2010). *Beyond the crisis of masculinity: A transtheoretical model for male-friendly therapy.* Washington, DC: American Psychological Association.

Brooks, G. R., & Good, G. E. (Eds.). (2001). *The new handbook of psychotherapy and counseling with men.* San Francisco: Jossey-Bass.

Englar-Carlson, M., & Stevens, M. A. (Eds.). (2006). *In the room with men: A casebook of therapeutic change.* Washington, DC: American Psychological Association.

Gottman, J., & Silver, N. (1999). *The seven principles for making marriage work.* New York, NY: Three Rivers Press.

Harway, M. (Ed.) (2005). *The handbook of couples therapy.* Hoboken, NJ: Wiley.

O'Neil, J. M., & Egan, J. (1992). Men's and women's gender role journeys: A metaphor for healing, transition, and transformation. In B. R. Wainrib (Ed.). *Gender issues across the life cycle* (pp. 107–123). New York, NY: Springer.

Philpot, C. L., Brooks, G. R., Lusterman, D.-D., & Nutt, R. L. (1997). *Bridging separate gender worlds: Why men and women clash and how therapists can bring them together.* Washington, DC: American Psychological Association.

Rabinowitz, F. E., & Cochran, S. V. (2002). *Deepening psychotherapy with men.* Washington, DC: American Psychological Association.

Shepard, D., & Harway, M. (Eds.). (2012). *Engaging men in couples therapy.* New York, NY: Routledge.

Tannen, D. (1990). *You just don't understand: Women and men in conversation.* New York, NY: Morrow.

6

Practicing Gender-Aware Therapy

A New Clinician's Perspective

TERRI MORSE

INTRODUCTION

I came to the field of counseling in my early 40s and believe that my feminist perspective, my interest and education in men's issues, and my life experience have a positive impact on my work as a therapist. We are told that practicing our skill with an empathic framework is paramount for our clients' progress. In the early stages of my education, when considering what it would actually be like to work with clients, I felt I had little to fear when imagining working with females. I had experience interacting with females throughout my life; I knew how to communicate with them, and I had firsthand experience at how they are socialized. But, when I thought about what it would be like working with males, I got nervous. How would my past experiences in interacting with males influence my work as a counselor? Could I be objective in my work with males? How would they perceive or interact with me as a female clinician? These were all questions rolling around inside my mind, and the journey to progress in my work with males is ongoing.

During the early stages of my education, I began to realize that my passion for *women's* equality may negatively influence my perspective when counseling males in my future career. Throughout those years, I learned about the stages of feminist identity development (Downing & Roush, 1985). I came to understand that if I did not move from the stage of *revelation*, when women's oppression is acknowledged and often results in anger or guilt (Chester & Bretherton, 2001), I may project that anger onto men when working with them as clients. In addition, if I failed to comprehend how sexism might harm men as well, I was only getting half of the story. I spent my master's degree on a mission to understand more about men's oppression. My eyes were opened to a world of empathy and understanding for men's experience that ran counter to much of my women's studies education. A professor in my program suggested that I begin my investigation with two books, Terrence Real's *I Don't Want to Talk About It: Overcoming the Secret Legacy of Male Depression* (1997) and *Bridging Separate Gender Worlds: Why Men and Women Clash and How Therapists Can Bring Them Together* (Philpot, Brooks, Lusterman, & Nutt, 1997). This started my study of gender role rigidity and its influence on the socialization of males.

Through reading books about the psychology of men and masculinity, I learned about the defense mechanisms that males use to deflect potential vulnerability. These books included *A New Psychology of Men* (Levant & Pollack, 1995) and *The New Handbook of Psychotherapy and Counseling With Men: A Comprehensive Guide to Settings, Problems, and Treatment Approaches* (Good & Brooks, 2005). I began attending the annual conference of the American Psychological Association (APA) and became involved with its Division 51 (Society for the Psychological Study of Men and Masculinity). I started observing men around me through an investigative, yet more empathic, lens. Through gaining an understanding of male oppression, I have often mourned for men and their losses because I imagined their liberation from the maladaptive, traditional male social construct is more difficult for them than it is for women. The strictness and rigidity of the social norm to which men must adhere seems less flexible; as a woman, society allows me to integrate and weave in and out of the social norms with greater privilege and freedom. As I continue to grow as a therapist, I use the knowledge I have gained through formal education to guide my work with male clients, but I also learned that my personal experiences have an impact on how I interact with them.

PERSONAL JOURNEY

I am the youngest of three girls and believe that my father had always wanted a boy. He never verbalized it per se, but I grew up spending time with my father doing "boy" stuff like fishing, building things, playing with Tonka™ trucks in the dirt, and helping my father fix things around the house. He was a mechanical engineer, and his problem-solving skills intrigued me. During my early childhood, because most other neighborhood children my age were boys, the majority of my playmates were male. From them, I learned about boyhood and what boys believed, how they acted, and how they thought. I learned that boys were rugged and did not play with girls' toys. Boys were rough and strong. They were discouraged from exhibiting traditionally feminine-type traits like crying or whining. They were allowed to tell "dirty" jokes or be smart-assed in humor. Boys got to curse; "little ladies" did not. Boys wore black ice skates, and girls wore white, and they would give up the opportunity to go ice skating if the only option was that they had to wear white skates.

Throughout my childhood, I identified more comfortably with males and was considered by most a tomboy. I only wore dresses to church on Sundays and even that accompanied an argument. I disliked the restrictiveness of being made to comply with feminine attire, and I resisted being "girlie." During lunch recess, I often played football and other rough-and-tumble games with the same group of chums. I was "one of the boys" in the early years of elementary school and was accepted into the boys' group.

As I reflect back to a time in second grade, one spring day left a lifelong impression that influences my work today as a counselor. That particular day, I came to school "out of uniform" for I was wearing not a T-shirt and jeans—my daily attire—but polyester pants and a patchwork, multicolored blazer. I remember being proud of the outfit and felt, well...pretty. During lunch recess, I quickly learned that my brand new outfit was *un*acceptable to my cohorts, and the events that unfolded had a greater impact on me than I realized at that time.

At recess, I headed outside toward the playground where we usually convened for lunchtime play. As I hurried to catch up with my friends, I cornered the school building and an eerie feeling came over me as I looked up to find six of my male friends lined up across the top of the hill as if they were waiting my arrival. My pace slowed, and I greeted them with a weak smile, for their overall demeanor seemed unfriendly and hostile. Without notice, one by one the boys ran down the hill and skidded into my legs to knock my feet out from under me. Down I went. Just as I scrambled to my feet, down came another boy who knocked me over. I could hardly right myself before another came on attack. I was so caught off guard by their actions that I screamed every curse word I knew, stringing long phrases together to combat their physical aggression with my verbal assault. Their laughter and my cursing rang in my ears for what seemed like many minutes. With tears streaming down my face and anger and confusion pumping through my veins, I continued to fight an obviously losing battle. I cut my losses and quickly turned back toward the safety of the basketball court. I looked down at my beautiful new outfit; it was ruined, with grass stains on the knees and elbows. From that point, I ceased the daily routine of lunch recess with the boys as I was unwilling to take the chance to meet a similar fate.

This was a defining moment for me in my relationship with the boys and my understanding of gender role compliance (although I did not actually acknowledge it as such then). I was utterly confused by their actions. Did their attack come because I ventured outside a masculine norm by wearing my prized new feminine outfit? I remember that strong overtones of sexual aggression accompanied the boys' attack, perhaps in a somewhat similar way to how a woman may feel when raped by someone she knows. I can only fathom what motivated their actions that day, but I remember it forever put a wedge between them and me.

From that moment, I slowly shed my tomboy-like persona and began to feminize myself into conformity over the next four years. Until that day on the playground, I did not think of males as the "other"; I knew there were differences between us, but through that event I learned that males were powerful and could turn violent without obvious provocation. I felt cast out and treated like an other, whereas I had once felt like one of them. Those years separated me from the close friendships I once had with those boys. While at times I was invited to play in their masculine games over the years, I found myself feeling like an outsider and not welcomed in their group. No longer did I feel I was allowed to consider boys as friends, but instead felt forced into becoming a female, a nonmale.

After graduating from high school, I was faced with the dilemma of the next phase of my life. Because I did not have a strong desire to enter into a specific career at that time, I decided to get a job instead of investing in higher education. My first job was in customer service for a graphic arts company. For over 20 years, I found myself working in various capacities for several different graphic arts companies.

Perhaps motivated by a need for financial security, I got married at the age of 23 to a man who was 15 years my senior. At that period of my life, I was looking for someone who could steer me into adulthood. I figured that marrying someone older would provide me with the guidance I missed out on during my developmental years. I expected my partner to "show me the way" and help me minimize marital mistakes. My parents divorced when I was eight years old, and throughout my childhood, I do not remember them as happy people—either as a couple or individually. I rarely, if ever, remember our family of five laughing together wholeheartedly at dinner, my parents sitting together on the couch sharing a tender moment, or having a sense of security that my parents loved one another. These life experiences left me ill-prepared for knowing what it took to build a healthy relationship on a strong foundation, and I was fearful that my marriage would eventually meet the same fate as did my parent's. I knew I lacked communication and conflict resolution skills or how to be comfortable with the vulnerability necessary for human connection. I thought if I married someone who was older (and therefore wiser), I would learn these valuable skills from him. As I waited for him to take the lead, I soon came to realize that his understanding of how husbands and wives interact was based on traditional gender role assignments. Following his lead, I assimilated to a traditional lifestyle, only to find myself miserable after 10 years.

When I took a feminist theory course during my undergraduate education, I began to realize how truly frustrated I had become. This was a turning point for me because it was the first time I encountered the concept of *gender role socialization.* I learned that because of traditional gender conventions, I felt *expected* to clean the house, cook the meals, do the laundry, and oversee holiday preparations because society prescribes it. I would come home from school ripping mad about the rigidity of the gender role constructs within my relationship. I wanted an egalitarian marriage, and I had to convince my husband that we would be happier if we designed one. Unfortunately, but perhaps not surprisingly, my partner was bewildered by my goal to create a collaborative "partnership" instead of a "marriage." The concept was foreign to him, and I was just beginning to learn about it myself.

Reluctantly and cautiously, he acquiesced to my request because he trusted that my vision for the relationship would benefit both of us. Utilizing my mentors within the women's studies courses and the accompanying reading material as a guide, we began laying the groundwork for a different way of relating. Initially, we amended our language. Words like *wife* or *husband* felt restrictive to me and smacked of traditional gender role assignment, so I suggested that we adopt phrases such as "my spouse" or "my partner." We worded questions differently, such as, "What are *we* cooking for dinner tonight?" or "The house needs to be cleaned, how are *we* going to tackle this project?" In addition, we took a look at how we distributed household tasks. My partner once believed that men and women should divide labor based on gender. Now, he realizes that if a woman works a full-time job and then has to take care of the household chores as traditionally prescribed, she is the one in the relationship who gets the raw deal. Today, we negotiate the division of labor and attempt to divide the work so that neither of us feels as though we are doing a lot more than our fair share.

In the early states of our marriage redesign, I took the lead in achieving the ideal partnership I envisioned because I was the one more dissatisfied. As we wrestled with new concepts and ways of relating, we each explored independently and as a couple what would make our marriage more fulfilling. Throughout this transformation, we grew to realize that each of us brought maladaptive behaviors and cognitions into the relationship that needed to be addressed. He came from a traditionalist background, and I came from a home in which divorce had occurred.

In the early stages, I primarily initiated conversations about the status of our relationship. I also suggested we access counseling so that we could work on changes I thought we needed to make. As he developed an appreciation for the improvements in our marriage, he courageously brought issues to my attention that *he* thought I needed to work through to promote a more healthy marriage. This was the collaborative negotiation I had sought, as he increasingly acknowledged the benefits of investing in nurturing the relationship.

During this time, we engaged in marriage counseling and have participated in follow-up treatment over the past decade. Interestingly, it took us three counselors to find one we both agreed could help us. We met with our first therapist for four sessions before we determined that she was unable to support our desire to create an egalitarian relationship. While my partner felt vindicated in the first few sessions because the therapist frequently sided with him and thought that I was being too hard on him, he actually got embarrassed because, according to him, "I knew I couldn't be right about everything." We ceased our relationship with that therapist and decided we would try a male therapist next. When the therapist asked what brought us to therapy, my response was, "We're here because I want us to build a relationship based on an egalitarian perspective . . . a partnership." The therapist stumbled somewhat and asked me to describe what I was looking for in more detail. Over the course of six months, he definitely helped us and was more supportive than the first therapist, but I never truly felt he understood what we were attempting to create. My partner was supportive of my decision to find a new therapist.

A few months later, we finally found someone we felt was a good match for our marriage and our quest. She did not outwardly state that she was a feminist, but she definitely agreed that developing a partnership marriage was beneficial to both female and male and attempted to help us work toward that goal. We found her easy to talk to, she did not take sides, she always made us feel that we were both part of the solution, and she understood our goal. We remained working with her for over nine years and at times continue to meet with her individually or as a couple to this day.

While every couple's relationship and goals for their marriage are different, what my partner and I traversed provided me with firsthand experience regarding the challenges of negotiating marital problems. I use some of the techniques that we used to improve on communication skills with clients. Educating clients on the importance of being vulnerable with one another has been valuable. Even in working individually with a female or a male who is suffering relationship woes, it is possible for me to draw on my own experience with marital redesign to assist them in learning how to join together rather than blaming their partner.

PROFESSIONAL JOURNEY

During my undergraduate education at Plattsburgh State University in New York (SUNY) in the late 1990s, I studied mathematics and wanted to be a high school math teacher. However, in the final semester of that degree, I determined that teaching high school students was not my thing. The following year, while pursuing a master's degree in liberal studies with an emphasis on administration and leadership at SUNY Plattsburgh in 1999, I was able to explore my increasing interest in women's roles in the workplace. My master's thesis was *Are We on the Cusp of the Second Wave of the Feminine Mystique?* (Morse, 2000). During that time, the U.S. economy was flourishing. Many of the women around me began exchanging their careers to stay home and raise their children. I wondered if women would lose ground if this happened. It reminded me of what women did in the 1950s after World War II, when they had contributed enormously to workforce production only to be shuttled back to their homebound roles when men returned from overseas. Much like the women described in Betty Friedan's best-selling book, *The Feminine Mystique* (1983), women may experience depression and boredom as a result of losing privileges that males enjoy in the workplace. As the 20th century came to a close, I was concerned that women would suffer a loss of equality in both home and work as a result of the choice to stay home.

Following the completion of my master's degree, I found myself with a similar plight as my precollege circumstance. At the age of 35, I now had formal education on my résumé but had little access to professional career opportunities in my region and *still* did not know quite what I wanted to do. So, I chose to defer to an old standby—the graphic arts business—but this time in the position as a sales executive. It was not what I dreamed of doing; it was a job, and I was open to discovering where it would lead. However, there was another career that I had felt compelled toward throughout my adulthood, and I began to get restless in my current occupation.

During my early 20s, I wanted to be a therapist because I thought I could help others develop an understanding of themselves. Fortunately, during that time, I worked with a retired psychologist who was at the same graphic arts company as me. One day, I shared my hopes of becoming a psychologist, and his response forever changed my life. He said, "Before you invest in education, it would be more important for you to invest at least six months in seeing a counselor yourself." When I asked him why, he replied, "Well, a lot of people go in to the field of psychology because they believe they want to learn how to help others when in all actuality, whom they want to learn about the most is themselves." I took his advice and was in counseling for many years.

In 2006, during a counseling session when I was complaining about the soul-wrenching emptiness I felt in my role as a salesperson, my therapist asked me what it was that I *really* wanted to do for a career. I looked at her and replied, "What you do." After many years of therapy, I realized I had recovered enough from my childhood difficulties and could be effective in helping others, hoping to improve their lives. I also believed that being a client provided me with an education in and of itself and would benefit me in being an effective counselor. I now utilize various techniques I learned as a client with my own clients. These techniques include watching videos, analyzing photographs from my childhood, reading books and discussing them with my therapist, journaling, and writing daily gratitudes.

In pursuit of my dream, I obtained my master's degree in clinical mental health counseling in 2008 from Union Institute and University at the Vermont College campus. Union's learner-centered approach, or "low-residency" program, assisted me in gaining the education that I sought with minimal disruption to my career and personal life. It is through this program that my focus toward men's issues was ignited. In my counseling degree program, it became important to me to focus my education on understanding the male socialization process to a greater depth so that I could openly and empathically work with both males and females.

WHAT IS GENDER-AWARE THERAPY?

During my undergraduate education, I had become familiar with feminism, its construct, its theories, and its principles. As feminism was popularly considered a concept associated exclusively with females, I wondered if there was such a process or a term associated with the liberation of males. I was relieved to find a journal article, "Gender-Aware Therapy: A Synthesis of Feminist Therapy and Knowledge About Gender" (Good, Gilbert, & Scher, 1990), which described an alternative approach to feminist therapy that was inclusive of both women and men. At that time, feminist therapy was a therapeutic approach that helped women to strengthen their self-esteem and self-value, to challenge the traditional social constructs for women, and to take an active role for political and social change (Feminist Therapy Institute, 2000; Mejia, 2005; Sharf, 2003). As researchers observed the benefits that women were experiencing through feminist therapy, some of them (e.g., Good et al., 1990; Levant & Pollack, 1995; O'Neil, 1981) recognized that many males were suffering from similar social structure conflicts. Over time, various supporters of feminist therapy advocated for its evolution to a female/male-sensitive model (Corey, Corey, & Callanan, 2007; Mejia, 2005).

The roots of gender-aware therapy lie in feminist therapy principles. However, it integrates current knowledge of female and male gender theories and research (Good et al., 1990):

> Gender-aware therapy supports the notion that particular behaviors, preferences, and attributes need not be categorized as falling into the domain of traditional or nontraditional, male or female, gender roles.

Rather, what gender-aware therapy advocates is simply choice, despite gender conceptions or political correctness. (p. 377)

My master's thesis (Morse, 2008) investigated how clinicians assist females in coping with their male partner's depression and supporting their partners while protecting themselves. The research pointed to the importance of exploring how gender role norms intersect as a system rather than as separate entities, specifically, male depression and women's response to it. If gender roles are a system, then clinicians need to be knowledgeable about how the genders' interactions affect each other and about each gender's socialization process. If the clinician could educate clients about this gender system, then males and females would have a greater chance to more successfully survive throughout males' depressive episodes.

In addition, if clinicians and researchers were willing to integrate the psychology of women with the psychology of men, they might be better equipped to assist their clients in achieving a greater sense of self and ultimately be unrestricted by socialized gender norms. When people are able to respond to their world as humans, rather than as males or as females, or by any other socialized role, greater psychological health may be actualized. This is the perspective from which I operate in my clinical work with both males and females and in my personal life, as well.

PRACTICING GENDER-AWARE THERAPY WITH MEN

I currently work at a rural county mental health service provider in New York State as a psychiatric social worker doing individual and group therapy. My caseload primarily consists of both adults and children whose financial means are limited. In addition, I work part time as a counselor at a substance abuse outpatient clinic. There, I primarily facilitate three mixed-gender groups per week on topics such as relapse prevention, codependency, and recovery issues. In the mental health clinic, my caseload consists of equal numbers of women and men. In the substance abuse clinic, I work with more men than women because men make up a higher percentage of admissions at the clinic.

Before I started working with actual clients, I imagined what my experiences in working with males might really be like. I believed that I would encounter multiple opportunities to educate men on the negative effects of how males are socialized in American society. I also thought that they would be hungry to know how the harmful aspects of their socialization process could adversely affect their psychological health, physical health, and interpersonal relationships with partners and children (Mahalik, 1999). I wondered if male clients would enter into power struggles with me and engage in games of matching wits. I was leery about how I would respond if a male client would hit on me or flirt, and based on my old behavior patterns, would I flirt back? I was excited to finally have the chance to put my men's psychology education into practice.

While I have only been in this new career for a few years, I have recognized that some of my prior ways of relating to men would require adjustment. I outline next the personal standards that guide me in my work with males; these are based on my education and my experiences with my male clients.

Personal Standard 1: Alliance—I Ally With Male Clients

I work on partnering with males and solving problems together with them. When male clients say things like, "I don't know; you tell me. You're the expert," I respond with statements such as, "Well, perhaps I have education in this field, but you are the expert on you, and it's my role to assist you at figuring out solutions *with* you." I try to emphasize a partnership relationship with the male client as a way of diminishing my previous manner of relating to males through intimidation. Before learning that men were not the oppressors and coming to understand society as the oppressor (Philpot et al., 1997), I would have probably intimidated male clients to combat socialized male privilege and power. For most men, simply entering the therapeutic setting can be intimidating in and of itself, so it is my job to make it initially nonthreatening to promote their engaging in counseling as a first step. I must keep my previous pattern of "fight power with power" in relating with males in check in my role as therapist.

Personal Standard 2: Acceptance—I Am Mindful of Being Accepting of Male Clients

Given that my career involves working with people who have criminal and/or addictions backgrounds, I am especially aware of the potential for fear to cloud my ability to present myself in an objective and accepting manner. I have a few male clients who have criminal backgrounds, including those who are registered sex offenders. As an example, I have worked with an African-American man who served time for having sexual relations with his young daughter for approximately a year. He desired counseling because he wanted to learn how to help his young son cope with his feelings of abandonment by his mother (the daughter and son have different mothers). As a result of the trauma, the boy (the identified client) was known to display his frustration in a disruptive manner when his mother did not follow through on promises to call or visit.

Before my first meeting with this client, I was concerned about my ability to be objective with him. I wondered if I would be able to balance the caution that someone in my profession needs to employ when working with individuals with a criminal background with the impartiality that the profession also promotes. I noticed the following facts in his record, which helped me limit the potential to prejudge him as a "predator":

- The father was open about his past incarceration—not the details of the offense, just that he had been in prison and for what reason.
- He expressed a strong desire to be an appropriate parent.
- Within the past year, the local child protective services division was actively involved with assisting him on any parenting issues that concerned him.
- The father returned phone calls and complied with all requests for prior records and conversations with other service providers.

I believe that trust begets trust, and I summoned what I could to minimize socialized feminine fearfulness that could distort the therapeutic objectivity I desired to utilize while working with this particular individual. I did not want to distrust him based solely on what I knew from previous reports or society's portrayals of male sex offenders. Also, I did not want to recriminalize him for I believed that if I did, the work he desired to accomplish regarding his son might be compromised.

Personal Standard 3: Knowing Men's Issues— I Strive to Understand How Traditional Male Gender Roles Can Hurt Men

As much as society would have us believe that men are supposed to be strong and self-assured, many of the clients I have worked with in the mental health clinic hold on to their fears of being emasculated by a female clinician. Males can also be hurting humans, and their struggle with emotional pain can appear more physically excruciating than what I have observed in females. It is striking how they struggle with their need to avoid appearing weak. They battle their desire to rid themselves of pain, which is observable by watching their faces contort as they work to hold back the tears. There are frequent occasions when I have witnessed a male cut himself off from expressions of painful emotions and then slip on his mask of male bravado. It is a painful phenomenon to witness. And, in the substance abuse field there exists a real challenge in males acknowledging their reliance on mood-altering substances, prescribed or nonprescribed, for the purpose of quelling emotional pain.

Because my one-on-one work with men at the county mental health clinic is more intimate in structure, as compared to the group settings at the substance abuse environment, I find that I am more aware of the intensity of the role I play in their therapeutic work. I am finding that there exists a fine balance between my being sensitive to the male experience (for example, understanding gender role conflict, the harmful effects of male socialization, and power differentials between men and women) and regarding the male as a human being. I attempt to operate primarily in the "see-the-male-as-human" domain and weave into it the "sensitive-to-the-male-experience" perspective on an as-needed basis. Interestingly, Gary Brooks, in *A New Psychotherapy for Traditional Men* (1998), noted that he has observed a similar phenomenon. Brooks observed that a female or male gender-aware therapist will increase a traditional male's therapeutic success and stated, "I have strong suspicions that in many situations, non-gender-sensitive therapists may actually be destructive" (p. 205).

I have observed that my experiences in working with men are aligned with the literature on the psychology of men. I have witnessed the maladaptive messages that form men's beliefs about what it means to be a man. At times, it appears their heavily weighted masculine perspective clouds their ability to open up to a new or different way of thinking. In working with men, I have learned that when I downplay my femininity, this allows men to more comfortably open themselves up to interact with me (and I hope with others) in a manner that is less emotionally restrictive. When I interact with males in a gender-aware manner both personally and professionally, I have witnessed an adjustment in the reduction of males' masculinity, which seems to allow the client more freedom to explore a more natural form of communication and relating.

Personal Standard 4: Working With Eroticism—I Strive to Minimize My Own Sexual Impact on Male Clients and to Understand Their Eroticism Toward Me

I have heard it said by various colleagues that it is impossible to keep erotic (i.e., sexually arousing) undertones out of the therapeutic space, especially in female/male dyads. While that may or may not be true, I do believe that it is possible to minimize or exacerbate erotic messages within the environment. Although the manner in which we all dress can influence eroticism greatly, it is only a small part of it. How we walk, how we speak, how we gesture, how we sit, and our personal perspective all participate in the way in which our sexiness it brought in or left out of the therapeutic room. In my work environments, most of my male clients consider women as sexual objects, especially in the substance abuse setting, and I believe that if I present myself in a sexual manner, in *any* way, my work as a gender-aware therapist is compromised.

Erotic behavior is something I have worked to address in myself since becoming a therapist. In my earlier years, and especially in my career as a salesperson, I often used sexiness as a tool to combat perceived male privilege. Or, I used it to attract males in a manipulative way to sell the product, attract attention, become popular, or have projects pushed through or favors granted. I am embarrassed now by the sexually exploitive behavior I used in the past to distract men in personal and professional settings—how I toyed with men to exploit their vulnerabilities to elevate my position over them. When I became aware that I was using my manner of dress as a form of manipulation, I altered my style toward a more masculine fashion—khaki pants, loafers, and Oxford-type blouses. Other than my hairstyle, breasts, and makeup, I looked like a male. I thought this was what I had to do to become more gender aware. Perhaps it was at the time. I have come to learn that it is not so much how I dress that makes me gender aware, but more in my perspective and my manner of interaction. I am gaining more comfort with my style of attire—more feminine than my uniform of khakis and Oxford shirts but less sexy or provocative.

On those occasions when a male has overtly sexualized me in a therapeutic setting (which happens with a comment on my appearance or a certain outfit), I do not react strongly in either a positive or a negative way. At most, I may respond in a positive manner with a half-smile because, in the males' way, they are attempting to pay a compliment, and it is not helpful to shame them. Having a confrontational conversation about their comment does not produce positive results, I have found. However, if the comments or looks become frequent or increase in intensity, I would address this with the client in a more psychodynamic manner. For example, "Help me understand. . . . What kind of reaction are you looking for when you say those things to me?" or "How do you want me to interpret your comment?" I find that a nonreactive or half-smile response is enough to send a message that this relationship is human to human and not man to woman.

Personal Standard 5: Humor

I have also found that using humor to approach sexist attitudes can promote effective change as compared to addressing sexist behavior in an admonishing way. For example, a male in his 30s (call him Tom) typically referred to his significant other as "the old lady." One day I asked him, with somewhat of a sly grin, "I'm confused. How old *is* your girlfriend?" With a perplexed look on his face, he replied, "Well, she's a little younger than me." To this I said, "Oh, well, you refer to her as 'the/your old lady,' and so I wasn't sure." About 20 minutes later, he made mention of his girlfriend and referred to her as "my girl," which may not have seemed *as* demeaning to him. As the group sessions progressed, he also reduced his derogatory comments, which previously ended with the phrase, "well, you know how women are." Whether he was only minding himself in a female clinician's presence is hard to know, but he did seem to be pondering the perspective more carefully as the group progressed.

Personal Standard 6: Being a Professional "Friend"—I Use More of a Friend's Approach With My Male Clients

Based on my own personal experiences, I believe that it is possible for males and females to be friends, and that a potential role for them to serve one another is as "friend." Over the years, I have often asked the males I have encountered if they can be "just friends" with women, and the majority of them tell me, "No, it is not possible," especially after puberty begins.

My role in therapeutic work with male clients is as "counselor" and not "friend," but the perspective of the relationship is more human to human as compared to counselor to client. As I shared, I once enjoyed my male friends as "friends," and I am comfortable in that form of relating. I attempt to adopt that same cooperation within the counseling relationship. The overt mannerisms that I may exhibit in this principle may come in the form of calling a man "buddy" or using more humor in communication. Granted, the pace at which I introduce this interaction is slow at first as the client needs time to feel comfortable being in a therapeutic setting.

In the groups at the addictions treatment center, I have asked male clients whether they could see themselves as friends, and friends only, with a female in the way that they are friends with males. The large majority of them say "no." And, while they believe that it is not possible for them individually, they do not believe that it is at all possible for any male to be friends only with a female unless the male is a homosexual, or so they say. Therefore, opening themselves to relating to a female counselor as human first and as female second may be challenging and something new for them to consider.

To know what are the benefit and risk to this principle, one would have to ask male clients how this perspective of a female clinician treating men from a friends' perspective works. From the few who have offered their unsolicited opinion about their work with me, they say, "You're different from previous counselors I have worked with," or "I'm more comfortable in working with you compared to other therapists." They have expressed their ability to open up about things they never felt they would be able to with other counselors. They shared that they feel I can understand them, and I challenge them in ways that previous counselors have not. Some have also expressed that they feel comfortable in working with a female counselor, which is a new experience for them. Perhaps through the consistency of a gender-aware interaction, the clients are able to move toward developing a mutual, friendly interaction with me as a member of the opposite sex that is based more on shared respect and allows for openness that they may have never experienced with a female—either inside or outside the therapeutic setting.

Personal Standard 7: Egalitarianism—I Take an Egalitarian Approach to My Work With Men

Because the underlying root of gender-aware therapy lies in feminist therapy, I work to create a relationship with all of my clients, both female and male, that reduces the power differential within the therapeutic work, an attribute of feminist therapy theory. By challenging my thinking about sex roles and actually following through on my thinking and doing, my hope is that men will learn to think of females as humans, and their interaction with females can be more collaborative and less restrictive. I perceive that this paradigm will promote individual freedom and broaden their social network and framework to a new form of relating with others. Certainly, the ultimate goal is to expose men to a new model for their life experience, but by no means do I force male clients to change to this way of thinking for that would fly in the face of the gender-aware perspective of "choice."

Personal Standard 8: Objectivity—I Work on Being Objective With My Male Clients in Terms of My Own Background and Perceived Power Differences With Men

In learning more about men's issues and from my experiences as a salesperson, I realized that in the past I used power against men through female sexuality, intimidation through trumping their level of education with mine, with logic or matching wits, or perhaps through blatantly attempting to intimidate them through use of body language, tone of voice, or facial expressions. In my early stages of feminist identity development, I once thought I had the right to use sexuality to combat male privilege until a professor during my undergraduate degree explained that if I wanted men to "lay down their weapon of privilege," I must be willing to lay down my "weapon of sexuality." This has been important when it comes to my work with male clients, and I attempt to check my sexuality and concern about power differences with men when I leave for work each morning.

Personal Standard 9: Patience—I Try to Let Men Do Their Own Work on Their Own Timetable

At the mental health clinic where I work, I have a male client in his 40s (call him Michael). Michael has had multiple hospitalizations for major depressive episodes with suicidal ideation and experiences anxiety. As his treatment progressed, at various times he would comment that he "was attracted to women he couldn't have and would attract women he didn't want." While I was curious if he was hinting about his being attracted to me, I did not take the bait—and I waited. When I discussed it with my supervisor, she stated that his disclosure will eventually emerge, and there was no reason to push it.

Approximately five months into his weekly therapy sessions, he spent the major part of a session trying to get the courage to tell me that he was attracted to me. His words were, "My sister says that I talk about you a lot and said that it seemed as though I was 'smitten' with you." Early in the session, I observed him struggling with something important that he wanted to share and suspected it had to do with how he felt about his relationship with me, but I did not speak for him or guess at what it was he was attempting to share for two reasons. First, what if I was wrong? That would be shaming. Second, so often women come to men's rescue and fill in the emotional space. His admission was something that Michael needed to struggle with on his own without a female coming to his emotional aid. This concept was emphasized by one of the clinicians who participated in my thesis project. The clinician stated that women tend to be the couple's "relationship managers." Because of this, "men tend to rely on women to fill in the communication and emotional gaps, thus missing out on [men's] opportunities to grow and share their own feelings." After 25 minutes of Michael's hemming and hawing, he finally spoke the words and was able to break that pattern for himself. Had I rescued him, the opportunity for his personal growth could have been jeopardized.

Personal Standard 10: Education—I Strive to Help Men Learn More About Male Issues But Only When They Are Ready

When I first started my counseling career, I thought males would benefit from knowing that I had education in the field of men's psychology or that I was aware of how difficult it is for men to live up to society's expectations. In my excitement about actually getting to put theory into practice, my overzealousness scared a few male clients away. I have learned that adopting a more subtle approach in informing clients of my education about men's psychology was necessary.

Occasionally, during therapy men will reveal an attribute of their male experience that the psychology of men's research has shown to be a trait of gender role conflict (O'Neil, 1981) (e.g., homophobia; restrictive emotionality; socialization control, power, and competition issues; restrictive sexual and affectionate behavior; obsession with achievement and success; and health care problems). I have not yet devised an effective method to address the harmful effects of male socialization with male clients directly and have yet to determine whether the difficulty arises out of my approach or my femaleness. In the thesis interviews conducted for my mental health counseling graduate degree, one clinical respondent talked about this very issue. The (male) interviewee stated that he "waits for hooks" expressed by the client before activating a psychoeducational approach about the (harmful) effects of the socialization of men. The clinician stated that he found waiting for these opportunities allowed for the client's ability to be open to hearing the message and understanding that the client's difficult experience was probably more an attribute of the male socialization experience and not necessarily a deficit of the male personality.

I have yet to effectively develop this skill with my male clients. On those occasions when attempting it, the male client's eyes have glazed over with a look that I have not been brave enough to ask about or explore further. I have assumed that the subject either was introduced too early or was introduced to a client who was not able to understand the subject on which I was attempting to education him. Or, perhaps the client was perplexed by a female therapist who speaks to the male client of the male experience for, I imagine them thinking, how could a female ever understand their experience as a male? I have typically abandoned further exploration for fear of alienating the client or adding to his confusion. I have attempted to approach the nonverbalized, or infrequently verbalized, question by sharing with the client my understanding of the harmful effects of socialization on women and how men experience similar damage; again, this effort has collapsed like a flimsy, plastic grocery bag overloaded with soup cans.

The substance abuse treatment center where I work offers a men's group, and I have been fortunate to facilitate the first session of the group's term on one occasion when the primary counselor was out ill (the primary counselor is also a female). Prior to this opportunity, various group members shared they did not understand how a female was allowed to, or *able* to, run a men-only group; I was prepared for the question. Most of the group members knew who I was for I had worked with them at various times throughout their treatment experience. We opened the initial session by talking about the curriculum covered during the group's term and engaged in a discussion about why the clinic would offer a men-only group. After we covered these points and the group had settled into a comfortable state, I asked the members their thoughts about having a woman as the group facilitator of a men's group. Most of the men looked from one to another, nervously laughed, and wriggled in their chairs, and some took a deep breath and sat up a little straighter. After a lengthy pause, one young man, the only college-educated member of the group, who has become the "interpreter of feelings" for many of the group members, spoke up and said, "Within a group setting it doesn't seem like it's a big deal. If there was something highly personal that I felt like I needed to discuss, I feel like I could do it in here [because there are other men in the group], but if I was in a mixed group or meeting with a female counselor for one-on-one sessions, I don't think I could discuss sensitive topics." He was asked what he meant by "sensitive topics," and he stated that it would probably be about sex issues, but he was unable to clearly elaborate on what he meant by "sensitive topics." The other group members agreed.

The group continued, and we engaged in a productive discussion about a video that many of the men had viewed on the subject of men in recovery. The video included a section on the maladaptive messages that men receive throughout their youth, such as "boys/men don't cry," "hide your feelings," "don't let people know how you're feeling because they'll take advantage of you," and so on and how these messages create harmful belief systems that affect their use of substances. They comfortably discussed topics relevant to the male experience, and my involvement in the discussion was minimal. I had come to learn that talking as if I could completely understand what it meant to be male in our society is awkward for men, so I held back on interjecting my psychoeducational impulse in this first session. Most likely, utilizing visual media or reading materials or facilitating open discussion would be the most effective means for helping males understand the impact male socialization has on their experience and may be more necessary when a female is facilitating the group. Perhaps my role is only to serve as a bridge to that awareness.

Personal Standard 11: Role Modeling—I Encourage Men to Explore a New Way of Relating to Females as Friends

I have educated myself on what society encourages or requires of females to "fit in" and the extent of the boundaries of society's standard of being female. When it comes to adhering to the boundaries, I do not, at least by what motivates me in how I act or think. I consider myself androgynous. I am comfortable with being "one of the guys"; that is, I can tolerate cursing, I can talk about sports, and when something heavy needs moving, I take care of it myself if physically capable.

In one-on-one therapy, the perspective of being one of the guys is not as apparent as it is in the substance abuse environment, which involves groups of males—typically highly traditionally masculine males. I have come to learn that the majority of males in substance abuse treatment, especially in a rural setting, strongly adhere to traditional gender roles, are predominantly homophobic, and lack an ability to fully express their feelings with words (alexithymia). Gaining their trust and helping them progress in treatment and in improving their emotional well-being is a major challenge.

I am mindful about how friendly I am when I interact with males. While I think it is impossible to avoid transference of this form, I have come to learn from Michael (discussed in the preceding section) that he has a belief that women and men *cannot* be friends in the way that two men can be friends. Perhaps his work in treatment will be to challenge that perspective for it is my belief that it is possible for women and men to interact with one another without sexual overtones interfering with their relations. Maybe my role in working with males is to assist them in altering their method of relating to females in stereotypical forms by projecting their desire for me to play the role of nurturing or caring mother; relationship-managing mate; compliant wife; the emasculating, domineering female; loving sister; innocent daughter; or the demure and sexy love object.

The bottom line is that I do not make a huge deal about the differences between masculinity and femininity. I work to lessen the gap and do so through leading by example. I do not change who I am, but allow the comfort I know in interacting with males to come forth; this is where the friendship with my childhood male friends comes shining through. This form of interacting has carried through in my marriage relationship—a mutual respect for another human being whom we do not restrict with societal gender role constructs. It is my belief that if I do not practice it in my personal life, then how am I going to role model it in my professional life?

CONCLUSION

Over the past 20 years as a client and student, I have worked at developing a gender-aware perspective in my relationship with others. More important, I believe that as a female therapist working with males and presenting myself in the therapeutic environment as a strong and capable *person*, I can better partner with the male client. I am enjoying my work with males, and I do find it challenging—and it is different, in general, to how I work with females in the therapeutic environment. The work, the interaction, the pace, the dance *are* unique.

As much as I believe I am knowledgeable, experienced, and mindful of my work with men as a female clinician, I am reminded that I have more to learn. While I was putting the finishing touches on the manuscript for this chapter, I encountered an interesting experience with one of the groups I facilitate at the substance abuse treatment center. The five males had been in this particular group for four months or more, and we had grown to interact with one another comfortably and casually. I believed that we had established a gender-aware approach to working with one another, or so I thought. One session, as the members were checking in, an individual conveyed that he was struggling with something but was reluctant to openly share his thoughts in the group. When pressed about the source of his hesitation, he said that he would be uncomfortable revealing his thoughts "in the presence of a lady." I assumed that he meant, "You can't handle what I have to say because you are a female." I jokingly looked from left to right and said, "I'm sorry, I'm not sure I see a lady here." He responded by stating that he was "an old-fashioned guy," and that it would be "improper to say what was on [his] mind." I realized that I had made an assumption based on my own feelings rather than what he may have intended. As much as I tried to promote an environment that would allow open disclosure, there in that moment, societal stereotypes about gender were alive and present. I was both saddened and angered by the situation. I was saddened that he was restricted by a traditional standard that limited him in working through something that was troubling him because he was in the presence of a female. I was angered that not only did he restrict himself, but also he restricted me. I quickly recognized my anger at my assumptions and kept it in check as I did not want him to experience shame. In addition, my anger was at society, not the client.

If it is important for my clients to achieve a greater sense of self, which includes being less restricted by socialized gender norms, then the first person who needs to understand and exemplify that experience is me. It is my hope that when people allow themselves to respond and interact in their world as humans first and foremost, rather than just as females or as males (or by any other socialized role), greater mental health may be actualized for oneself, and society as a whole will be better off. It is my belief that because males and females are not socialized the same, then the approach I take in working with men and women will be different. In addition, if I fail to understand the harmful effects of the socialization process for men, then I potentially ignore the messages and miss opportunities to promote their personal growth, or I may exacerbate the messages that could cause harm. Through my own education, analysis, networking, and mindfulness of my thoughts, behaviors, and beliefs, I am in a better position to be aware of who I am and how I work and to assist my male clients in achieving a greater sense of themselves as *whole* human beings.

REFERENCES

Brooks, G. R. (1998). *A new psychotherapy for traditional men.* San Francisco: Jossey-Bass.

Corey, G., Corey, M. S., & Callanan, P. (2007). *Issues and ethics in the helping professions* (7th ed.). Belmont, CA: Thomson Brooks/Cole.

Chester, A., & Bretherton, D. (2001). What makes feminist counseling feminist? *Feminism and Psychology, 11,* 527–545.

Downing, N. E., & Roush, K. L. (1985). From passive acceptance to active commitment: A model for feminist identity development for women. *The Counseling Psychologist, 13,* 695–709.

Feminist Therapy Institute. (2000). *Feminist therapy code of ethics.* Retrieved June 2, 2006, from http://www.feministtherapyinstitute.org/fit_code_of_ethics.pdf

Friedan, B. (1983). *The feminine mystique.* New York, NY: Dell.

Good, G. E., & Brooks, G. R. (Eds.). (2005). *The new handbook of psychotherapy and counseling with men: A comprehensive guide to settings, problems, and treatment approaches.* San Francisco: Jossey-Bass.

Good, G. E., Gilbert, L. A., & Scher, M. (1990). Gender aware therapy: A synthesis of feminist therapy and knowledge about gender. *Journal of Counseling and Development, 68,* 376–380.

Levant, R. F., & Pollack, W. S. (Eds.). (1995). *A new psychology of men.* New York, NY: Basic Books.

Mahalik, J. R. (1999). Interpersonal psychotherapy with men who experience gender role conflict. *Professional Psychology: Research and Practice, 30,* 5–13.

Mejia, X. E. (2005). Gender matters: Working with adult male survivors of trauma. *Journal of Counseling and Development, 83,* 29–40.

Morse, T. A. (2000). *Are we on the cusp of the second wave of the feminine mystique?* Unpublished master's thesis, Plattsburgh State University, Plattsburgh, NY.

Morse, T. A. (2008). *How gender-aware clinicians assist females in coping with their male partner's depression.* Unpublished master's thesis, Union Institute and University, Cincinnati, OH.

O'Neil, J. M. (1981). Patterns of gender role conflict and strain: Sexism and fear of femininity in men's lives. *The Personnel and Guidance Journal, 60,* 203–210.

Philpot, C. L., Brooks, G. R., Lusterman, D.-D., & Nutt, R. L. (1997). *Bridging separate gender worlds: Why men and women clash and how therapists can bring them together.* Washington, DC: American Psychological Association.

Real, T. (1997). *I don't want to talk about it: Overcoming the secret legacy of male depression.* New York, NY: Fireside.

Sharf, R. S. (2003). *Theories of psychotherapy and counseling: Concepts and cases* (3rd ed.). Belmont, CA: Brooks/Cole.

7

Coaching Men

CAROLYN STEIGMEIER

INTRODUCTION: COACHING THROUGH
THE PERFECT STORM

Just the other day, Larry (a coaching client of mine) said—once again—I was the only person he would talk to about the things we were discussing. The conversation he considered confidential did not include anything illegal or unethical. He is not involved in anything shocking or socially inappropriate. In fact, because I often work with men, I have heard it all before. It is "the perfect storm" of personal and professional issues flaring up concurrently to exacerbate his doubts, fears, anxiety, and perceived weaknesses, hindering his ability to "keep it all under wraps"—a skill men learn early in life and strive to perfect over their lifetime. More positively, the storm helped him see it was time to search for other ways to live, if not find solutions. Yet, had he not already known me, having worked together a few years ago on career goals, he might not have heeded his family's pressure to "call someone." Toward the end of our session, Larry specifically asked me what it is I do for *other men* that helps them. I have been thinking about the answer to that question ever since. As I sat down to write this chapter, I realized it was the crux of what coaching is about. What *do* I do that helps men? Which tools work? Why do they work? And how can I best explain my approach to assist others as they work with men?

PERSONAL JOURNEY: LEARNING FROM MY FAMILY

Each of us should consider how our past influences our understanding of and attitude toward men. My early background holds the key to my affinity toward men. Love for my dad and a desire to be connected to him led to opportunities to closely observe the "world of men," thus providing an ever-broadening understanding of men—including the challenges they face. Ultimately, it increased my ability to determine which coaching tools will work most effectively for individual men. So, how did a girl growing up in the Midwest during the 1950s and 1960s become the first female manager at three different companies in male-dominated industries, travel the world, and enjoy significant relationships with several men? Why did she return to school in her 40s to get a master's in human development and then create the men in a cultural vise model while obtaining a PhD in human and organizational systems? Finally, how did she subsequently build a consulting business focused on leadership development and coaching men?

Ironically, my journey into the world of men started with the divorce of my parents. Divorce was so uncommon in 1957 when my parents got divorced that my sisters and I were the only divorced kids in the whole grade school. It was even more unusual that a father would get custody. Their divorce and my father's custody of their children provided me with different views of men than most women receive and the beginning of genuinely liking and appreciating men. The reason my mother left her three young daughters with the maid—and a note to my father on the dresser telling him she was going away for a few days to pull her thoughts together—did not have a good explanation until 1963. Betty Friedan accurately identified my mother's predicament as the "problem that has no name" in her groundbreaking book *The Feminine Mystique* (Friedan, 1963). Today, my mother would have more options than to escape to a hotel for a few days to try to understand her frustration raising three children while her husband traveled during the workweek. But in the 1950s, after a couple of such episodes, my father, a down-to-earth engineer, hired himself an attorney and gained custody of his three little girls. Daddy (as we called him all his life) took us to Indianapolis to live with his parents and younger brother, who still lived at home. Daddy had a good job in St. Louis, so he continued to work there, which meant we only saw him on weekends until he remarried while I was in high school. Getting up on Saturday morning, we knew he would be there; Sunday afternoon as we stood on the porch, waving good-bye—sometimes crying—he would drive away.

Because his time with us was limited, it was always special. More significantly, his short weekends, which included about 10 hours of driving, were devoted to us. He was a kind man who never raised his voice and treated each of us girls as if we were special to him. Gifts were always made or chosen with meaning. He wisely assumed we were smart and capable: We were expected to work hard, be responsible, get good grades, learn to play an instrument, and go to college. I believe that his expectations were as high for his girls as they would have been for a son. One concrete outcome is that all three of us have successful careers. One of Daddy's favorite games was to ask us questions about how the world worked—after all, he was an engineer—for which we were told to *think* to be able to figure out the answer. It is possible that had he had a son, he might have played this game—and our challenging Ping-Pong and badminton "tournaments"—with him instead of us, but I doubt it. Like many men of his generation who were socialized to be stoic and independent, he remained somewhat emotionally remote. One could fault him for not moving to be with us. More significantly, however, his interest in our lives, combined with our hunger to be with him, contributed to our growing up liking and respecting men. Because we grew up without brothers (or any male cousins close to us in age), which deprived us of learning about boys on a daily basis, it also created a situation in which my sisters and I were always trying to find ways to be around boys. Boys seemed to have lots of energy and were fun to play with—kind of wild and bit goofy. We loved 'em!

We did have two weeks with Daddy every summer when we all drove to Minnesota to stay in a cabin and go fishing out of canoes. "Jack's girls," as we were called, knew quite a bit about fishing, not to mention rabbit hunting, searching for mushrooms in the spring, and catching bullfrogs at night. We learned all this from Daddy, Grandpa, and Uncle Clay on summer weekends in the country, where we still owned the family homestead. Many of the outdoor activities the men had been involved in since *they* were boys now involved three little girls. Although we were not considered tomboys—I was even labeled "Miss Priss"—we did want to be with Daddy whenever he was home. Anything he was doing seemed interesting, from electrical repairs to changing the car oil. (My sisters and I have impressed plenty of guys over the years with our knowledge of men's chores.) However, we were just as likely to be at Grandmother's side learning to can food from the garden, sew an Easter dress, or decorate a birthday cake. Per the norm, activities in our family were generally divided by gender: Grandmother and the aunts tended to do the household chores, and the men did the heavy lifting and outdoor activities. Yet, the divisions were not as rigid as might be expected. Our large extended family (other family members were often at our grandparents' homes) all cared deeply for one another and followed the code of helping each other any way they could.

My mother also played a significant role in establishing my interest in men. After the divorce, we seldom saw her until we were teenagers, but when we did she told exciting stories about the men she knew. After marrying a much younger tennis player, she moved to Florida, landing a top secretarial job at Kennedy Space Center, where she hung out with the astronauts and other leaders during the heyday of the space program. After getting divorced from her second husband, she dated many men.

Perhaps because she did not raise us, Mother has always been open with us about her life. She is willing to discuss both her achievements and disappointments rather objectively and share her personal understanding of men and relationships. After all these years, she still finds men a never-ending source of friendship, amusement, intrigue, and challenge.

The stage was set. Daddy implicitly taught me that men are caring people doing interesting things with whom I can hang out, and Mother taught me that brilliant, fascinating men are out there in droves. It seems natural that I would look at men a bit differently than many women. At times, I am astounded at the attitude or lack of understanding some of my female friends—even with advanced degrees—have toward men. They go so far as to talk privately about men having all the power and being jerks, an orientation that would seem to interfere with getting a man to trust them sufficiently to productively work together.

After high school, I lived at home for my first year of college. Daddy now had four girls to put through school (he and my stepmother had a baby daughter), so he wanted me to live at home to help keep the cost down. Yet, I wanted more freedom. During the summer, I learned to sell encyclopedias (making $1,000 in one week as the number one salesperson in the country) and continued to work at a part-time job I had had since high school. This allowed me to buy my own car and get an apartment near campus. I also began to substitute teach and found time to have a couple of boyfriends, all the while keeping my grades up. Exhausted by the middle of my junior year, I moved to Florida to live with my mom, who I hardly knew, but she welcomed me with open arms. I continued to work as a substitute teacher there, but mostly I lay on the beach. This is where during spring break the following year, I met a guy from Western Michigan University. I went back with him to finish my last three semesters of school the fastest way I could—by getting a home economics degree.

After graduation, we traveled throughout Europe for four months. On returning to the States and deciding not to get married since we were not ready for a long-term commitment, I visited family, moved around the country, and worked at whatever job seemed interesting at the time. My jobs ranged from salesclerk at a small Midwestern clothing store to bikini-clad hostess at a hot dog and beer bar on Cocoa Beach in Florida. Men with whom I became seriously involved included an ambitious young man who was getting his master's degree and then a Vietnam vet recovering from a broken jaw he got in a fight *after* returning home. When the vet and I began living together, he and his friends shared with me traumatic personal stories about their time in Vietnam. Many of the stories revolved around things they had done or seen that were terrible and could not be talked about in public for a wide variety of reasons. It was years before they were able to be open about the atrocities they witnessed during the Vietnam War and the scars those events created in the forms of depression, substance abuse, and post-traumatic stress disorder (PTSD). His sweetness and anger, fear and fearlessness, and truths and lies caused us both pain and confusion. Although somehow wise enough not to accept his burdens as my own for life, I have been forever grateful to him for the insight he gave me to a world most of us never have to know, not to mention the obvious appreciation for what he gave to, and gave up, for his country.

At 25, I married a man—three weeks after we met—who I had been hearing about for months from sailors when their ships were docked in Port Canaveral, Florida. Dave was a brilliant, exciting, and experienced guy who traveled the world on one of the U.S. missile-tracking ships. After getting married, we only had three months together in San Francisco while his ship was in dry dock before he went back to sea for several months. Two years later, we moved to Kwajalein Missile Range, a tiny atoll in the Pacific where life is like a tropical vacation, but everyone needs a security clearance. Although it was Dave's career in the defense industry that provided us the opportunity to live there, I was given training that allowed me to have a job with MIT Lincoln Laboratory as a documentation specialist. Women and children could live on the island on which we were based, but I flew to work on another island, where I worked with 10 women and a few hundred men. While I was there, I enrolled in a master's of science in systems management program offered through the University of Southern California. I was the only female and only nonengineer in the program studying sociotechnical systems. This was my first experience thinking of things in terms of systems. After a couple of years on Kwajalein, Dave and I moved back to the United States, and after a couple more years, I decided I wanted to get divorced. There was nothing seriously wrong with our marriage, but we had grown apart.

During the next decade—the booming 1980s—I worked as a product or marketing manager for products ranging from temperature controllers to printing presses, at companies ranging from Fortune 500s to startups, before incorporating my own industrial marketing company (Sterling Stars Inc.), in 1988. I lived in Boston; Washington, D.C.; New York; St. Louis; and Durango, Colorado; was active in industry associations; and traveled extensively. Another window into the lives of men opened when a man, 16 years older, and I fell in love. His age, plus his wisdom and generosity, allowed him to share with me much about life, and his senior position in a worldwide industry—almost exclusively male—allowed me to travel and learn even more about the world of men.

Looking back, I see how often I was deeply submerged in environments populated by and familiar to men that are not as accessible to women. Furthermore, the variety of men with whom I had close relationships gave me a better understanding of individual men. (I now suspect my comfort with men as a result of my upbringing also allowed *them* to be more comfortable with *me*.) Not every woman will stumble across the opportunities I did or choose to embrace them. Yet, I think it is useful for women to keep an adventurous spirit and cultivate different paths open to them.

PROFESSIONAL JOURNEY: BECOMING AWARE

I must confess that I became aware of—and accepted that there were—gender issues later in life than most women my age. Successfully immersed in male-dominated industries, with wonderful experiences in my intimate relationships, and without children, I was as oblivious to gender issues as the men were. Like the guys I worked with, it took me a while to even "buy the whole feminist thing." It just did not seem accurate in my world. I have often said that as a woman I may have experienced discrimination in these environments. However, since I was not predisposed to look for it, and worked as hard as I could right alongside my colleagues, I still do not know. Rather, there may have been times when I received opportunities or was "given a pass" for something I did not know or do *because* I was a woman.

I added another chapter to my learning about men in 1988 by marrying a widower with two teenage sons and welcoming into our family a 12-year-old boy from foster care. This was a fast learning curve into family life that involved scaling back my business adventures, in which I had been participating for almost 15 years. The turning point in my awareness began 6 years later when, not as busy on the family front, I had time to consider going back to school. Psychology was my first choice; I had started college as a psychology major until I realized I had to take statistics. Friends over the years had kidded me about having the world's largest self-help library. It was not that I had any particular malady or vice; I was merely intrigued by human behavior. A colleague suggested the psychology program at Fielding Graduate University, so I set up a meeting with a faculty member—although I was having doubts about my eventual career as a licensed psychologist. As I understood therapy, I was not sure that sitting in a room listening to someone without being able to openly express my thoughts would be a good fit for me. During the meeting, Dr. Keith Melville explained that Fielding also had a doctoral program in human and organizational systems that he described as one third psychology, one third social psychology, and one third organizational theories. It seemed the perfect fit, and it tied in beautifully with my business background. One evening around the same time, a friend who is a psychologist invited me to go with him to a local American Psychological Association (APA) meeting. The theme of the meeting was how a new approach to helping called coaching did not require a license, was likely going to encroach on the practice of psychotherapy, and how psychologists could market their business to compete.

Soon after I started graduate school in 1995, I started noticing that men around me seemed to be struggling in many ways. The fact that I was in my 40s positioned me around more midlife men than had been the case when I was younger. I observed and talked to men of every age everywhere I went, from volunteer organizations to golf courses. As word spread among fellow students that I was "sympathetic to men" and curious about what was happening to them, male students started approaching me to discuss my research. They were intrigued by a woman interested in studying men and often doubted that they were going to be given a "fair shake," until they had a chance to talk with me. Contrary to popular notions about men's reluctance to open up, they and other men—husbands of friends, colleagues, casual acquaintances—were willing to talk about their lives and began telling me their stories. Men worried about their careers, the security of their jobs, and their health. They talked about wanting a more loving relationship with their spouse; about realizing they did not know their own children or how to have a meaningful conversation with them. They seemed to be searching for something they could not articulate. I noted recurrent patterns in their lives that confirmed my belief that they were indeed struggling.

To better understand what was going on and address the needs of these men, I began researching and writing papers. I created a number of workshops, which I ran in a variety of settings, including:

- "Midlife Men and the Search for Meaning"
- "Key to Success: Understanding the Rules of Manhood"
- "Stress: Recognize It, Reduce It, Replace It"
- "Men Only: Getting Back to Normal After Serious Illness"
- "Male Midlife Crisis"
- "Men in Dialogue: Gathering Wisdom for the 21st Century"

From the feedback I received from the participants and from my own observation, the workshops not only helped men but also provided me with additional access to men. It is important to note that the men sharing these stories were not stereotypically dysfunctional men. In most cases, they were guys with good educations and jobs, were married, and with no major mental health issues I could see. I would ask, for example, why they hadn't told their wives what was going on or shared their concern with *anyone* all these years. They had not told their wife because they thought she was too busy, they did not want to scare and upset her, or they felt that she would not be able to handle it. As far as sharing secret fears or traumas these men may have carried for years, I came to realize that regardless of how embarrassing it was for them, what they were shouldering was often not unusual. Frequently, the missing piece in their life related to a lack of purpose or meaning. Invariably, however, each man believed he was the only one so inadequate that he was unable to handle his particular issues the way other men would. He would feel this way even in the face of horrendous war experiences, the horror of which many of us cannot fathom. As a result of men not expressing themselves more often, they are left believing other men are not experiencing what they are going through. One reason I believe men are willing to talk openly with me is that in spite of their reluctance to discuss "their stuff" with other people, they are almost desperate to know how other men are able to deal with *their* stuff. Once they find out I know a lot about men, they engage with me to learn about *other* men and what is normal.

In 1997, my research consultant at Fielding, Dr. Michèle Harway, suggested I attend the annual convention of APA. There I learned that clinicians and academics were describing, researching, and treating the very phenomenon that few people in general society seemed to recognize or acknowledge—and with which I was becoming obsessed—how men struggle. Getting involved with APA's Division 51 (Society for the Psychological Study of Men and Masculinity) was validating for me because it confirmed my firsthand experience of men's struggles. Statistics on men's problems, such as male depression, substance abuse, executive suicide, and death within 1 year of retirement reconfirmed my interest while increasing my desire to find a way to do meaningful work that could help men and have a positive impact on their lives. Given my background and interests, coaching seemed the obvious approach.

COACHING: AN OVERVIEW

Coaching was defined by the International Coach Federation (2011) "as partnering with clients in a thought-provoking and creative process that inspires them to maximize their personal and professional potential." Coaching that an individual chooses to undertake on his own is usually referred to as life, career, or personal coaching. Coaching provided by an employer is executive, business, corporate, or professional coaching. It is probably no coincidence that within the levels of management most often populated by men, the term *executive coach* is used. The words *executive* and *coach* are seen as more masculine words that refer to roles commonly filled by men. Perhaps further embedded in the language is meaning from a younger, more carefree time of physical prowess, championship teams, and beloved coaches. Coaches range from those with no specific training to those with doctoral degrees and years of experience. They may have expertise in the specific industry in which they work or a field such as change, work/life balance, stress, or communication and may be certified by one of the coaching associations.

Regardless of where one looks—from academic research, human resource professionals, *Harvard Business Review*, to popular magazines—coaching is recognized as an effective way to help individuals and organizations identify and meet goals. Major corporations provide coaching to their top executives and midlevel managers; succession planning and leadership development programs include coaching; and many successful people now hire their own coaches. The often-referenced data on men's reluctance to enter therapy also applied to business coaching early on. The inside joke was that human resources had to hire a coach to document that you were not salvageable before they could fire you. Employees tried to prevent anyone from knowing they were receiving coaching. Today, in many situations, although not all, it has become a status symbol to be provided with a professional coach. I think two factors are at play here. On the corporate side, it seems the continued use of coaching by leading corporations for their top executives and widespread use of coaching for all levels of management have validated the status of receiving coaching. On the public side, over a decade of promotion by coaches and coaching organizations has led to a better understanding of what coaching involves. Now, there is little if any stigma associated with deciding to be coached. Rather, coaching is seen as a proactive way to improve one's life.

Coaching and psychotherapy are different in many ways, depending on the type of therapy employed. Although several types of therapy, particularly cognitive-behavioral therapy (CBT), use techniques and approaches similar to coaching, several key distinctions remain. Therapy is "therapeutic treatment esp. of bodily, mental, or behavioral disorder" (*Merriam Webster's Collegiate Dictionary*, 1994). Therapists have specific degrees and must be licensed to call themselves social workers, psychologists, mental health counselors, or psychiatrists, whereas in today's market, coaching can be just about anything anyone wants it to be. Therapists are bound by rules of confidentiality; coaches are not. Therapists typically provide diagnoses to their "patients" and often bill insurance companies for their services under a medical model. In contrast, corporate coaching is usually provided to employees as training or development. Personal coaching is done on a self-pay basis. In most cases, therapy utilizes a 50-minute hour and occurs in the therapist's office on a weekly basis; coaching time frames and schedules vary considerably and can happen almost anywhere, sometimes by phone. Therapists do not typically see clients as friends either during or after therapy; coaches can have clients who they see socially.

The appreciative inquiry (AI) model (Hammond, 1996) is useful for shedding light on differences between traditional therapeutic approaches to providing help and the coaching approach. The traditional psychodynamic approach in psychotherapy has been to begin by looking for the problems by focusing on them to find out what is wrong or broken, how long it has been broken, and how it became broken. The AI model proposes that by paying attention to problems, we emphasize and amplify them. This model offers an invitation to *do more of what works*. I believe this is a far better approach for engaging men. It is hard enough for a man to face the fact he cannot "solve his own stuff." But to believe that therapy means he will have to go find someone to listen to his "sorry story" to tell him what is wrong with him, and then try to fix him, is an obvious clue to why men might want to avoid a therapist. McKelley and Rochlen (2007) pointed out that since "coaching is often success-oriented and competitive in nature, it may be a better approach for men with high needs of success, power, and competition where the culture of therapy may be in opposition to the culture associated with traditional masculine roles and values" (p. 57). I always ask men what is working well for them—similar to a sports coach who helps the athlete visualize the perfect performance—rather than tell him what *not* to do.

However, the boundary between what happens during therapy or coaching is often not concrete, especially for CBT therapists. Therapy from a social constructionist standpoint or cognitive-behavioral style offers a framework closer to that of coaching than that provided by the traditional therapeutic stance. Assuming the client is expert on his own world and self, the therapist engages in conversation to collaboratively design a future. Engaging in conversation to collaboratively design the client's future is certainly part of the coaching frame. Whether one is practicing psychotherapy or conducting professional coaching, the belief that an "all-knowing expert" can provide the solution to a problem—that in many cases the expert has identified and defined—is rarely followed today. Rather, the expert partners in some way to work *with* the client, both to determine the problem and to craft a solution.

Successful coaching (like therapy) can be an intimate journey with another person in which the focus of the session is on the client, not the coach (or therapist). In my coaching role, I think of myself as a "professional friend." The two words seem to capture the combination of qualities we would choose in our most dependable, honest, generous, and intimate *friend*, coupled with a *professional*, whose knowledge complements our own to help us be more than we could be on our own. I take enormous pride in believing that every person I have coached is now a friend (although we do not see each other socially).

COACHING MEN: DOING THE WORK

When I was working for companies back in the 1980s, I had a number of experiences and insights that now serve me daily in coaching, including the underpinning of my appreciation for practitioners. In corporate marketing circles, we believed that a professor of marketing would not last a week in a *real job*. We had little use for what we called "granolas," those touchy-feely human resource types with silly ideas. I never considered the fact that I was the only woman in most of these conversations and was thinking the way the guys did; we were just like-minded colleagues. Once grounded in the business world, I have always since put my scholarly work to the real-world test. Does it have any meaning "out there" for real people dealing with the pressure of deadlines and bottom lines? Does it actually do anybody any good? *Does it even work?*

Therapists who have never worked in the corporate world, female therapists in particular, may not have an adequate understanding of the intense, constant pressure many men face in their jobs. Men not only have work-related pressures to fulfill their job obligation but also have to deal with the culturally imposed rule of manhood always to advance in their career and provide ever more adequately for their family. It is easy to think we can appreciate this type of stress once we know about gender norms. But, it is not reality until one sits next to a colleague on a long flight, hearing the heart-wrenching dilemma he faces between spending time with his kids and his challenging job, how he lies awake at night for hours, and how he has been having chest pain for weeks that he does not want anyone to know about for fear it could have an impact on a promotion he is hoping to get to start a college fund. A phrase has stuck in my mind for years that was used by two different men—normal family guys—while talking about our lives. Both said they consider "driving into the embankment" on the way home from work. Whenever you are trying to relate to the pressure men feel, remember the phrase: drive into the embankment. When it seems appropriate, I use this story to start a coaching conversation. At the time, I did not yet realize a significant difference between men and women's tendency to talk openly since my conversations with women were equally candid.

How I start the coaching process depends on whether I am hired by an organization to coach an employee or an individual is looking for a personal coach. At this time in my career, both my corporate opportunities and requests by individuals for personal coaching usually come from knowledge of previous work I have done for their organization or with someone they know. Other consultants also bring me in when they have large contracts. For corporate clients, I usually meet with someone from human resources, the individual's vice president, or the person the individual reports to before I am introduced to the person to be coached. I tell the corporate contact up front that I will not sign the contract if the individual to be coached does not want to work with me, whether it is because he does not want coaching or because he decides not to work with me personally. With personal coaching clients, I also have us meet before we commit to work together. This allows them to decide if they think I am an appropriate coach for what they want to accomplish and for me to make sure that I can productively work with them. I do not require personal coaching clients to sign a contract, although we commit to work together for a specific number of hours to accomplish identified goals.

With corporate clients, a contract spells out either 1.5- or 2-hour face-to-face meetings spread over a specific number of months, from 3, to 6 or 12 months or more. With men, I find it productive to meet longer than an hour. This allows for an unhurried conversation more like two friends would have before moving on to less-tangible, sometimes more delicate, issues, such as how their attitude or behaviors resulted in helping create the identified problems. A longer time also provides them with the opportunity to better educate me about their business environment. I then have a bigger and more accurate picture from which to draw conclusions and design learning opportunities. When a corporation is hiring me, I have an obligation to keep representatives of the corporation informed of our progress. However, I explain to all parties that the coaching itself will be confidential, but that I would obviously breach the confidentiality if I felt there was an immediate danger to anyone. Although I generally follow APA confidentiality guidelines, I would have the freedom as a coach (not a therapist) to expose other serious issues, such as stealing by an employee.

Built into the cost of my corporate coaching are instruments and assessments, colleague interviews, shadowing (which is observing the client in meetings and other interactions), management updates, unlimited coaching by phone, and ongoing support once our contract has ended. No one yet has abused the "unlimited" phone coaching or expected inordinate support when the coaching ends. If anything, it is a healthy way for the client to transition from intense interaction to occasional contact. For myself, after being deeply involved in someone else's life, I love hearing how things are going. It also provides ongoing data about the success of my work.

Once we have agreed to work together, I discuss with both my corporate and my personal clients where they want to meet. Corporate clients and I often meet in their office or places related to their work (assuming others are aware that they are being coached), allowing me to see them in their environment. At other times, and with personal clients, we may meet for coffee, lunch, or dinner. Some personal clients and I meet at their home because it is convenient, or others do so because they do not want anyone to see us together. Larry and I often meet near his office after work; when a colleague recognized him, I was introduced as a friend of his sister. I have also been told by a man that if anyone he knew were to see us together, he would prefer them to assume he was having an affair rather than meeting with "a shrink."

To help men consider whether coaching will serve their interests, I have crafted a few questions. You can use these or similar questions to start a discussion. I find that not many men can answer a hearty "yes" when I ask the following: Is your work satisfying and your life rich in meaning? Do you savor your relationships and take good care of yourself? However, I almost always get at least two "yes" answers to the following four questions:

1. Do you face challenging business dilemmas?
2. Are you finding it difficult to balance your work and personal life?
3. Are you struggling with stress or frustration?
4. Do you wish you had greater meaning in your life?

To enable men to see that there are a variety of normal situations that might be improved by coaching, I offer them the following list of reasons men work with me. Being able to compile such a list indicates that *other* men are using coaching to productively improve and enrich *their* lives. I then have the client go through the list to check the ones that are most relevant to him and note those that he might want to explore.

• Feeling at an impasse or stuck

- Believing there is more to life than they are experiencing at the moment
- Feeling concerned about stress, health, or virility
- Considering a change or struggling with a transition
- Dealing with the illness or death of a loved one
- Facing a new challenge
- Feeling "in over my head"
- Experiencing fear about something
- Being lonely, "lonely at the top"
- Needing professional, objective feedback or opinion
- Having (or being told they have) poor communication skills
- Rethinking yesterday's dreams
- Getting ready for a new goal or goals in life
- Recovering from illness
- Seeking growth, self-development
- Seeing others benefit from coaching
- Having successfully worked with executive coach at work
- Receiving a suggestion or ultimatum from someone they work with or care about
- Being aware that their work and personal life are out of balance

Most corporate clients have goals that have already been identified by their managers, which is the main reason a coach is hired. These goals can be anything from positive goals such as succession planning expectations that the person "become more likely to be the next chief executive officer" to overcoming negative patterns, such as "needs to get along better with colleagues." Even if goals are already established, once the client and I make the decision to work together, we start developing an action-oriented coaching plan that addresses his own goals as well. Goals, with which men are comfortable at work and in sports, usually have a clear—if not bold—purpose. Men think in terms of accomplishing, solving, doing, winning, achieving—all action words, not behaviors such as sharing, feeling, whining, spilling your guts, being a crybaby, or letting your guard down, which do not adhere to the rules of manhood and are uncomfortable for many men to address. Men want to solve problems or, at the very least, tackle issues. Ironically, however, most of what the men and I do during coaching is talk. The *framing* is of action and solutions with a focus on the end goal, but the *process* is often closer to talk therapy. We share stories, explore matters close to their heart, and examine the fabric of their lives to achieve breakthroughs. I tell them flat out that I will be committed to their goals while I support and challenge them in their development and change. As a confidential talking partner, I act as a sounding board and feel free to question them. When I start to work with a man, I tell him that what he can expect to gain depends on his coaching goal and an appropriate commitment. I always aim to increase his awareness, help him have more choice, and work with him to improve his ability to act in ways to achieve his goals.

Invariably, I have found that we deepen his learning, improve his overall performance, and enhance his quality of life.

To achieve all this, I developed the Men in Action™ coaching process. I explain the process up front to the client to provide a framework for what we will be doing together: tackling real issues in real time by following a plan. This process is spelled out below.

The Men in Action Coaching Process

1. Establish our relationship and decide how to work together
   - Meet with each other
   - Discuss the coaching process
   - Begin to clarify what he wants to work on
   - Decide if we want to work together
   - Discuss what he expects from me
   - Determine how we want to work together
   - Discuss how we will know when the work is finished
   - Create a coaching agreement or contract
2. Plan and complete an assessment of his needs and goals
   - Determine the future he wants (if he can articulate at this time)
   - Explore how to increase his awareness
   - Move from a problem orientation (what is not working)
   - Move toward a positive, future orientation (what to build on)
   - Decide what information is needed and how to get it
   - Create a learning goals worksheet
   - Choose instruments, tools, interviews, or exercises
   - Collect relevant data and information
3. Construct change scenario and learning plan
   - Figure out how to use assessment information
   - Explore how to increase choices
   - Think about what has meaning
   - Decide what to build on and what to let go
   - Decide how to learn what still needs to be learned
   - Create learning/action plan
   - Build in feedback
   - Look at what might go wrong
   - Consider the impact of his change on others
   - Cultivate support from those around him
4. Act and continually evaluate results
   - Put plan into action by trying things out and learning from the results
   - Evaluate new behaviors
   - Refine ways to get feedback
   - Consider new ways to learn
   - Explore new coaching areas

How closely I follow these steps depends on many things, one of which is whether I have been hired by an organization or an individual. Larry is an example of an individual I have coached twice over the past several years. He first called me as a result of his sister suggesting he do so after she participated in a team-building workshop I designed and ran for her corporation. When she heard of my work with men and knew I was certified to provide different assessments, such as the Myers-Briggs Type Indicator (Myers & Briggs, 1996), she thought I might be able to help him. He wanted to discuss his career and whether to attend business school—plus what he felt was a lack of motivation. We discussed Men in Action at the beginning of our effort. As our work progressed, we referred to it occasionally but mostly focused in our biweekly sessions on proceeding toward his stated goals. Through our work together the first time around, his graduate school issue was resolved since he decided to go to school and has since graduated. What he considered a lack of motivation was more a wide range of interests without a compelling reason to continue focusing on school when he was already successfully employed. During each session, we would discuss what he had done since our last meeting, review how that worked out for him, and outline a new action item for the next session. After a few months, he decided to attend business school and felt he had achieved enough not to need coaching any further at that point.

Four years later, he called again, this time because his family had been pressuring him to do *something* to relieve his stress over the collapse of the financial world (where he worked), coupled with ongoing personal relationship challenges. Although we still address his career path because he has options that require significant life choices, we now spend at least as much time on his relationship with his girlfriend, other relationships, stress, work/life balance, and his future. Our work together has always been similar to talk therapy, except that over time I suspect our relationship has become more that of intimate friends than a professional therapist/client relationship with specific boundaries. We have met at his home. He has educated me about the business he is in; I guide him as he makes business and career decisions. How long we meet depends more on what we are addressing or how long the meal is taking than it does on the clock. Although our time together is definitely focused on him, when it makes sense I reference my own experiences and share my opinions—probably far more than a traditionally trained therapist would. What I learned from Larry is that coaching can happen at different times in a client's life. A client will meet with me for a particular issue that is resolved but may come back again for a second round of coaching for a different (although possibly related) problem.

In contrast, Rob is a corporate client with whom I worked using the Men in Action process. After being told I was the only person human resources and the senior vice president could think of who might want to work with him—and have a chance at success—I could not wait to meet him. Further whetting my appetite were descriptions such as the following: "makes you feel like an idiot," "must walk on eggshells around him," "feels like he has a finger in your chest," "very competitive," "only seen one person stand up to him." Peers and people who worked for him were often cowed or pissed at him, including one female who felt he was directly abusing her. So, you might ask, why not fire him? The fact that he handled major contracts, both saving and making the corporation millions every year, had a lot to do with it. Top executives believed that his in-depth knowledge of the industry, years of experience, and approach to "win at all costs" and "take no prisoners" approach were what got the job done. Twenty years ago Rob's behavior would have been tolerated. However, in this day and age, especially at progressive companies, his behavior would not be acceptable, so I was brought in to help.

The first time I saw Rob, I was ushered into his office while he was still on the phone. He barely glanced up, finishing his business conversation before even nodding to acknowledge me. Already, I could see how some people would be offended. Luckily, given my years of working with guys like him, I felt totally at home. One of the first things I said to him was that I wanted him to know that if he decided he did not want to be coached, or did not want to be coached by me, I would not consider proceeding with the contract—regardless of what management or human resources wanted. It is important to me that the individual decides on his own that I am the person he wants to work with. It also gives him some immediate control over the situation. I gave Rob a copy of Men in Action, and we skimmed over it. He seemed to like knowing what was involved in this "coaching thing." He defensively said he would *like* to have help dealing with all the illogical stuff going on. He explained that he did his job better than anyone before him, and that he was one of the best in the business at what he did. He stated that when he treats certain people negatively, they deserve his blunt answers or comments, delivered with impatience or scorn. He believes they bring on their own problems.

During my first meeting with someone, I stay alert for things we have in common, especially things not everyone else does. Rob and I remembered being in huge computer rooms when they were freezing and raised a couple feet off the ground; we both knew about a recent missile launch from Vandenberg Air Force Base. I asked if there were anything else he wanted to know about me or about how we would work together. I made sure he knew I had an obligation to the organization, but that our work was confidential. I asked what he wanted to gain from this opportunity—regardless of why it came about. When our time was up, he told me he "wouldn't want to miss the opportunity to work with a Midwestern girl." To which I replied, "Fair enough. We Midwestern girls can be as charming and tough as you can be." Someone else might have been offended—How dare he call me a *girl?* (Others might be convinced he was putting down someone from the Midwest.) Yet, I chose to believe he was coming from an okay place. He had spent the previous hour in a vulnerable position, yet he was actually giving me his stamp of approval. Besides, I was already enjoying the challenge and our banter.

Although management had assumed Rob would balk at having me talk to colleagues or sit in on meetings, the opposite was true. He was so confident he was not doing anything wrong that he wanted me to see for myself where the problems were. As for which, if any, assessments he would be willing to take, he was more than amenable to take any I suggested—data were something he respected. I used the Myers-Briggs Type Indicator to give him information about himself, as well as how he could productively and more wisely interact with others. In addition, I conducted a series of lengthy interviews with a dozen of his colleagues including bosses, peers, and supervisees, to provide feedback on how others saw him. The negative views of him were repeated; also mentioned were many more strengths than I anticipated hearing. Oddly, he was not *personally* disliked—it was more how he made others feel. The complaints were that he was not friendly and did not make any effort to support others. Even gripes like the fact that he "never leaves his office and even eats breakfast and lunch at his desk" were cited as reasons he made people feel he did not like them. My favorite, because we were able to use it in our work together, was: "Rob doesn't understand the [company] culture. We measure how one gets things done as much as getting it done. Style counts. He's not collegial."

One of the more difficult coaching challenges I face is when the person I am coaching in a corporate setting does not want anyone to see us together. I miss the opportunity to see his physical environment, the organizational culture, and his personal interactions. It also prevents me from talking to others to get another opinion about the culture and the person being coached. I am at a loss to know how traditional therapists, sitting in their office and hearing only the thoughts, opinions, and observations of the person they are working with, can garner the range of information to which I have access.

Two examples come to mind. The first I call the "water cooler incident." While I was walking down the hallway with Rob, we stopped by the water cooler for him to ask someone from another department if the person had the information he was waiting for. The guy said no; he was working on it. Rob's response, in both tone and language, was nasty and dismissive. I realized then he would never have behaved that way in front of me if he had any idea what he had just done, let alone how he made the guy feel. Back in his office, I told him what he just did was *completely unacceptable*—and reminded him of my promise to provide unvarnished feedback. He pushed back by saying the information was late. I asked if he honestly believed his approach would speed things along. He said that it better because a big contract depended on it, and that he—Rob—had his own reputation at stake. I told him he upset the guy, and that I would be hurt if someone treated me that way. This carried weight with him because he already respected me and knew I was no "crybaby." He finally confessed that he had no idea how to get the information he needed other than to beat up on the other person. By the end of the session, he was beginning to understand the impact of his position and tough behavior on people. Referencing the water cooler incident was from that point shorthand for him to recognize there was an opportunity for him to try another approach.

The second example was when I arrived for a coaching session and again was ushered into Rob's office while he was on the phone. This allowed me to hear him being as sweet and tender as anyone I know. When he hung up, I laughingly told him he was "busted—he blew his cover," and I now knew he was a softie who could be as kind as anyone in the office. He said he was talking to his wife of many years, the only relationship, in addition to his little grandson, in which he felt comfortable. During our time together that day, he shared that he was extraordinarily shy, so much so that it caused him a rough childhood. He admitted it was the reason he usually chose to be alone. From this point forward, we developed a plan to learn, act, and continually evaluate results. I treasure the card he sent me that Christmas, thanking me for everything and "above all for being a friend."

TIPS FOR WORKING WITH MEN

So, why would a man work with a woman? How does one get a man to open up? And, what can a woman coach or therapist do that really works *with* and *for* men? I have identified a few points that I think are relevant to this challenge so that others can spot opportunities to expand their own repertoire of skills and behaviors while recognizing ways in which they already do these things.

First and foremost, men need to feel comfortable with us. Probably as a result of my upbringing, coupled with my wide-ranging life experiences, men with whom I have worked have recognized our common ground and are not on guard. I suggest you plumb your own upbringing to find your early, deepest feelings about men. Good, bad, or indifferent, you need to recognize how these feelings influence you in your work with men. Think seriously about the personal and professional experiences you have had with men as you have matured. For example, your gut response to men's risk taking might vary, depending on whether a male stranger risked his life to save you from a burning building or risked his life speeding on a motorcycle and causing the accident that killed your relative.

I am reminded of something an older male psychologist did before a session at the annual convention of APA that had several female students outraged. He was standing in the doorway as we were all entering the room. Evidently he knew one of the young women, who happened to have a big ponytail; he gave a slight, playful tug on it as he smiled and said hello. My read of the situation was that it was nice she knew him and that he was friendly enough to be somewhat familiar with her. Her read, and that of her friends, was outrage. As we moved into the room, I overheard them beating up on him for demeaning her and treating her less than professionally. I am fully aware that there are different ways to interpret this. Were I coaching him, I would tell him that in 2011 it is not a sensitive behavior because it could be misread. However, I think it is more useful for women in general, but particularly female therapists and coaches, to strive to connect with men of varying ages rather than look through a lens that is set to spot negative behaviors by men.

Men are more likely to be comfortable with us if they think we have "heard it all before." This gives them license to tell us things. Because we will not be shocked, it relieves them of the burden of protecting us the way they try to do for the people in their lives they care about. Because they are aware we have heard the same or similar things from other men, they are less likely to believe they are the only ones with such deficiencies. This may seem like a challenge for someone early in her career. However, you can make a point to reference stories or situations that run the gamut of what other men have experienced and how you have addressed those types of issues. This will reassure men you can deal with anything they bring in to sessions with you.

Men want to think we know as much about men as anyone. Otherwise, why should they waste time working with us, especially on problems they have difficulty articulating, can barely accept, and *probably assume do not have a solution*? They want to know how other men cope, in part so they can compare their situation to see how serious it is. They want to be reassured that nothing is wrong with them—in spite of the fact that they are convinced something is dreadfully wrong with their abilities. Once men know you study and work with men, they will start to pick your brain in all kinds of settings. They are curious about the experiences of other men. Do other men have the same issues they do? Is the lack of meaning in their life normal? What about their fears? Their inadequacies? The women in their life? Stress? Future? Legacy? How do others solve these problems? They wonder if other men are more adept, more capable—more "manly"—at coping with things than they are. From here, it is a short step to wanting to know if I have the tools for us actually to fix their stuff.

There are numerous ways to become known as someone who studies men's issues and has a large tool box with which to help men. Make sure people know you are a member of Division 51. Write articles, give talks, and offer workshops on men's issues. Make sure everyone who knows you is aware of your interest in working with men. Word will spread, and as it does, opportunities to have conversations with men will multiply, increasing your knowledge of men while you expand your repertoire of experiences with them. You can also put yourself in male environments where you can pay attention to what men say and do. You can still be yourself—a woman does not have to be "one of the boys" to join some of their activities. You just have to fit in well enough that they are not consciously aware every moment that there is a woman in their midst.

As I have been writing, it has occurred to me that the most important signal you can give a man is that you like men—*actually, in all honesty, truly like men*. This obviously does not mean you flirt, act foolish, or act inappropriately. So many men are cautious around women today about what they say, and how they behave, that it is sometimes difficult to start or have a genuine conversation during which both people can be themselves. At times, men avoid women in ways they might not have in the past. Before you discount this observation, I can assure you that men share among themselves and with me stories that support this. I am not talking about bad guys who hate women or think women are inferior to men. Rather, they are men who face the realities, and at times the absurdities, of political correctness in our society and the workplace. In addition, they struggle with managing their evolving role in their relationships and within their families, where there may be changing expectations as well. They face changing societal and corporate rules they may not fully understand, accept, or know how to cope with. Knowing about these struggles and working as a coach to help men with them provides an opportunity for you to serve to advance all our goals for healthier relationships and better workplaces.

REFERENCES

Friedan, B. (1963). *The feminine mystique*. New York, NY: Norton.

Hammond, S. A. (1996). *The thin book of appreciative inquiry*. Plano, TX: CSS.

International Coach Federation. Retrieved March 21, 2011, from http://www.coachfederation.org/

McKelley, R. A., & Rochlen, A. B. (2007). The practice of coaching: Exploring alternatives to therapy for counseling-resistant men. *Psychology of Men and Masculinity, 8*(1), 53–65.

Merriam-Webster's collegiate dictionary (10th ed.). (1994). Springfield, MA: Merriam-Webster.

Myers, I. B., & Briggs, K. C. (1996). *MBTI Step II Expanded Profile*. Palo Alto, CA: Consulting Psychologist Press.

Steigmeier, C. (1998). *Men in a cultural vise: Foucauldian genealogical analysis of the social construction of men as resistant*. Unpublished dissertation. Fielding Graduate University, Santa Barbara, CA.

RECOMMENDED READING

Block, P. (1981). *Flawless consulting: A guide to getting your expertise used*. San Diego, CA: Learning Concepts.

Bridges, W. (1991). *Managing transitions: Making the most of change*. Reading, MA: Addison-Wesley.

Hudson, F. M. (1999). *The handbook of coaching: A comprehensive resource guide for managers, executives, consultants, and human resource professionals.* San Francisco: Jossey-Bass.

Hudson, F. M., & McLean, P. D. (1996). *Life launch: A passionate guide to the rest of your life.* Santa Barbara, CA: Hudson Institute Press.

Leonard, T. J. (1998). *The portable coach: 28 surefire strategies for business and personal success.* New York, NY: Scribner.

Singe, P. M., Kleiner, A., Roberts, C., Ross, R. B., & Smith, B. J. (1994). *The fifth discipline fieldbook: Strategies and tools for building a learning organization.* New York, NY: Currency Doubleday.

Working With Different Populations of Men

8

Working With Men in the Minority

Multiple Identities, Multiple Selves

CYNTHIA DE LAS FUENTES

INTRODUCTION: INTERSECTING IDENTITIES

The way we identify ourselves is becoming increasingly understood in psychology as "intersectionality," or the intersecting identities embedded in systems of power relations. Psychological research on ethnicity, gender, and sexual orientation, for example—which has most often focused on analysis of difference, within-group variability, and social roles along singular variables—has begun to incorporate this new understanding. In working with clients whose identities and social locations have traditionally been viewed as divergent from mine, whether they are male, wealthy, or White, I have drawn from identity theory, multiculturalism, feminism, and my own awareness as a situated self. In this chapter, I explore the origin of how my identities, through the transformative relationship with my father and experiences in contexts I refer to as "social locations," have had an impact on my sense of self and my understanding and appreciation of the lives of men. I then introduce intersectionality as a theory for how I have come to understand the various ways men can experience both privilege and oppression due to their specific identities and focus specifically on men of color and gay men of color. I then present two therapeutic relationships I believe exemplify the points made in prior sections.

In locating my identity and perspective, I write as a third-wave feminist, multiculturalist, and psychologist. I have been deeply involved in these areas and with social justice my entire career. As such, I am an integrationist. Epistemologically global, I write with a belief that with intersectionality, the sum is indeed greater than the parts. I believe that being a Latina is not merely a minority twice over, but something greater that changes depending on my positions. Am I primarily in a relatively empowered position because of my education and titles (professor and psychologist) or in a relatively disempowered position as a middle-aged Latina and a single mother attempting to secure a low-interest mortgage? It is from this background of multiple identities that I form the foundation of this chapter, that of an educated, middle-aged, single Latina mom working with *men in the minority*.

PERSONAL JOURNEY

My relationships to and with men and my interest in the psychology of men must, of course, begin with my father. His parents divorced when he was an infant, and he and his older sister were raised by their single mother and widowed grandmother. Neither of these women remarried, but his father, who returned to Mexico, married twice more. My father attended all-boys schools run by Catholic priests. He joined the U.S. Navy and went to college at the University of Kansas. After graduation, he and my mother married (their first unchaperoned date was a double date the night before their wedding); I was born 10 months later, my sister 11 months after that. My father's relationship with his own father began after my birth on the insistence of my mother, who realized how important it was to her having a relationship with her mother while becoming one herself. When the two men were reunited, his father had by then another wife, three daughters (two younger than I), and one son, all half siblings to my father. They had a respectful relationship and visited off and on over the years prior to the elder's premature death at the age of 52.

My first memory of my father was long distance via a reel-to-reel tape recording of him talking about his adventures in Antarctica (where he was stationed), having penguins as pets, and the unbelievably frigid weather. My sister and I were about 2 and 3 years old, respectively, and we would record stories about our playmates and about our life living with his mother and grandmother, while our mother attended nursing school eight hours away.

When my father returned from Antarctica, he moved us back to Southern California, the state of my birth. My mother continued nursing school, and my dad began a tour in Vietnam. On one of his furloughs, he and mom met in Hawaii, and 10 months later, my youngest sister was born. Dad lived with us during her pregnancy. When the baby was about 1, he returned to Vietnam. Following my father's last tour in Vietnam, he moved us to Puerto Rico and never talked to us about his experiences in Vietnam. I was 8, and our family did not live apart again until we children were grown and in college.

My Mexican American father, a fatherless man, raised in a household of women, schooled by priests in the company of other boys, and an officer in the Navy, did not have role models for how to be a father. He knew how to serve and protect, command, discipline, and punish. He was a harsh disciplinarian who did not spare the belt. In spite of his mother and grandmother's successful businesses, which put him and his sister through private schools that prepared them for university, his perceptions about gender roles were strict and traditional. He taught his daughters that boys and men were to be viewed with suspicion because they wanted one thing—that thing he would never say aloud, much less explain—and it had to be strictly protected.

One time, a fifth-grade classmate harassed me for weeks asking to see me naked. He was sitting on the library floor the last time he asked, and I intended to kick him on his bent knee when he lowered it. Momentum being what it was, I inadvertently broke his nose. Blood spurted everywhere, and I was sick with horror and embarrassment. When my father discovered the reason for my violent act, he was furious and told me next time that kind of thing happened I was to kick the boy "where it counts." I cried out saying, "I tried—but he moved his knee!"

In adolescence, that "one thing" that boys and men wanted was elaborated on to include, "Why should a man buy the cow when he can get the milk for free?" "The gift you have, you give to your husband on your wedding night." "A good girl goes from her father's house to her husband's." Aye, aye, aye! I grew up knowing I was the weaker sex. I was supposed to stay away from men because they were sexual aggressors, and that my sexuality was to be guarded until my wedding night. My father never discussed the necessary transformations of my identity from guarded virgin to willing wife and my belief about men from sexual maniacs to honorable husbands. (By the way, my first unchaperoned date was when I was in college.)

As a Latina, I was raised to be educated and successful and not to question his authority, but as Mexican *American* I was also not permitted to adopt the American cultural values of independence of thought and belief and progressive individuation. I could not enjoy the American adolescent experiences of my friends. My relationship with my father was tense because I felt oppressed by him; as a result, I was resentful and frequently acted out. We had intense arguments and I ended up grounded because I disrespectfully challenged his authority and would break his rules. I learned that the only way I could release his grip on me was either to get married or to continue my education. The former I never did, and the latter I embraced reluctantly because the interpersonal dynamic between my father and me bled over into that area of my life as well. For example, I was hardly better than a marginal student in high school. Yet, my SAT and ACT scores were well above the 90th percentile. My father's demands for an explanation regarding this discrepancy were met with my flippant retort, "Genetics or environment—you choose."

My father's final tour of duty was in Spain. He was part of an elite team of U.S. and Spanish military personnel responsible for developing combined plans to defend the Spanish Territory in the event of a general attack on Western Europe, in other words, to get Spain to join NATO. During our time there, he and his colleagues, who were targeted by terrorist groups opposed to their mission, survived car bombings, kidnappings, and coups. Indeed, the school my sisters and I attended was also targeted for bomb threats. Because my father had served over 20 years in the Navy and had two daughters heading to college and another in middle school, he and my mother decided that he should retire, at the age of 42, to pursue entrepreneurial ventures rather than expose himself and our family to more violence.

The journey from these formative experiences that left me feeling oppressed by patriarchal sexual hegemony circles back to my relationship with my primary male object—my father. Back in the United States, my father had little success in his two entrepreneurial endeavors: building supplies and wildcatting (speculative oil drilling). Texas in the 1980s was not conducive for either of these businesses. He would wryly say that at least he had not gone into the savings-and-loan business. The personal economic challenges were too much for his marriage, and my mom filed for a divorce near the end of the decade after 28 years of marriage. Probably due to the tremendous stress, the last year of the decade brought with it a disabling multiple sclerosis episode with depressive symptoms. In the span of seven years, my father, the proud and powerful high-ranking military commander I grew up with and learned to fear and resist, lost his career and command, launched his daughters but not his businesses, was divorced by his wife, became disabled and depressed, and lived out of his office. He lost nearly every way he knew himself—and because of it I was able to talk with him, for the first time, genuinely. He told me he loved me, for the first time I could recall, in 1990, and with each visit he began to offer hugs and kisses on the cheek when we reunited and before we separated. We gently began to work to create something more tender and supportive, and we sought out each other's company. Just recently, while at a sushi restaurant in north

Austin, I sent this text message to my sister: "Having a conversation w/ dad about Vietnam!" Up to that time, my dad had never spoken to us, his daughters, about his experiences in Vietnam. He was visiting me, working on my lawn and garage (which is another book on a Latina's experience of traditional masculine role behavior!), when we decided to go out to lunch. I do not know how the conversation began, but I do know this was the first time he was open to responding to "tell me a story about. . . ."

From 1989 to 2011, my father lived with his mother, taking care of her and her property, being her constant companion, and willingly sacrificing his own independence as he fulfilled his duty and obligations as a son. Because of this, I know, she lived healthily to nearly 100 years old. His love, devotion, and dedication to her was palpable, and for that the pieces of my life and heart designated his have grown immeasurably. It is in large part because of my transformed relationship and accompanying compassion for my father that I was able to gain a deeper understanding and compassion for men in general, enabling me to be more open to recognizing, understanding, empathizing, and working with their experiences of pain, marginalization, and discomfort in relation to themselves, others, and the communities and cultures in which they live.

PROFESSIONAL JOURNEY

I went to college because it was what was expected. Both of my parents had gone to college, and my paternal grandmother attended business school. Among my extended paternal family of aunts, uncles, and cousins, all of us have college degrees and beyond. These aunts, uncles, and cousins who live in Mexico, except my father's sister and her three living descendents, are all college educated and beyond and are professionals, such as teachers, engineers, physicians, and business owners. Although I developed interests in psychology during childhood and adolescence, my maternal grandfather was influential in my decision to pursue the field when he announced to the family that he would pay the college tuition of any of his grandchildren who majored in it.

Why would a Mexican American man with only an elementary school education make such a peculiar offer? Well, he was the founder of a "mind control" system that trains people to apply self-hypnosis to change their lives in ways to benefit themselves and others. A radio repairman for many years, he became interested in the mind when the first of his 10 children were in school. Some of his children struggled in school in general, others in specific subjects. In attempts to help his children, he taught them to "meditate" and "visualize" on the subject matter at hand (e.g., mathematics, science, literature), imagining understanding the material, having no test anxiety, excelling in their work, and enjoying the learning process. Based on the success of his children, other parents began to send their children to be trained in his "method." By the time I was born, my grandfather had begun a business that would later go all over the world and be taught by hundreds of instructors in dozens of languages. A poor man by birth, he created and led a multimillion-dollar business in his lifetime. The problem, according to him, and the reason for his offer, was that at that time he did not have much "science" to back up his success, and his method was thus relegated to the field of pseudoscience. His aim was to "home grow" his own scientists.

The problem I had with my grandfather was that, although he was loving and generous to his grandchildren, he was also patriarchal, macho, and nepotistic. He did not put his daughters in positions of authority in the family business even though none of his three sons graduated from high school and six of his seven daughters (one was born with mental retardation) did, and several of the daughters earned bachelor's and master's degrees. When I heard my grandfather's offer to pay for the college tuition of any grandchild of his who majored in psychology, I did not know that the offer was for his grand*sons*, exclusively. I learned this halfway through my undergraduate career and was terribly heartbroken. I could not grasp how that brilliant man, a man whom I loved and admired and who I know loved me, could discriminate against me. Fortunately, my career interests in psychology were not dependent on my grandfather's funding or approval, so I continued and graduated with a bachelor's degree in two years.

At the age of 20, with a BA in hand, I was impressed by a member of my church who was a lawyer and for a short time considered studying law over psychology. During the decision-making process, I consulted with a former psychology professor from my university who told me, "I do not believe in educating premenopausal Hispanic women because all they do is use their uteri"—no kidding. I was prepared for sexual harassment from peers from a young age, and I was burned by sexism at the hand of my own grandfather, but I was definitely not prepared for this confluence of *racism and sexism* by an educator, a professor in psychology no less. Still triggered by patriarchal hegemony, I decided to prove him wrong, and in an effort to bolster my credentials in preparation for my graduate school applications, I accepted the first research position I could find—on the other side of the planet—in Guam. Ironically, I studied the influence of meditation and visualization on third-graders' academic achievement.

As a graduate student in psychology, I took courses in the psychology of women and gender issues, helped create the first multicultural class in our department, and took many classes in other schools to supplement my interests in diversity, especially Latino psychology. Unfortunately, the ivory tower was not without its own form of misogyny. I had a classmate who sexually harassed some of us and was finally booted out of the program because he simulated a sex act with the female office manager; a beloved professor who referred to me as "little" Cynthia as opposed to a peer who was "big" Cynthia in reference to our breast sizes; another professor whose marriage ended because his advisee became pregnant with his child; and yet another who averred that the best thing about being a professor was having a large pool of young coeds to date and marry, both of which he did multiple times. To be honest, at that time, I was not that interested in the psychology of men and men's issues. Looking back, I think this was likely due to my own personal development and need to deeply understand the meaning of sexual oppression in my family, cultures, societies in general, and within the institutions in which I participated. I had one classmate whose research interests involved boys and men, but I paid no more than polite curiosity when the topic emerged.

Following the completion of my course work, but prior to dissertation and internship, I was awarded a prestigious congressional fellowship in women and public policy from the Women's Research and Education Institute. I studied and worked in the U.S. Congress and created legislation that included the omnibus bill Women's Health Equity Act of 1990, which established the Office of Research on Women's Health at the National Institute of Health. It was while I was there that my parents were separating and divorcing. It was a stressful time for us all, and I was on the phone with them nearly daily. I worried about my father because he considered himself the main cause for the end of their marriage due to his unsuccessful business ventures and inability to stop trying to make them work. My mother begged for him to retire gracefully and assured him they would be financially solvent because by then she was earning more than he ever had. When I look back, I can clearly see that, *at that time*, my father was strained because of his masculine gender role expectations: productivity equals financially compensated employment, such compensation must be greater than a wife's, and lack of it means the inability to adequately provide, dependency, disempowerment, and shame. Because of my need to be there for both of my parents, I decided to return home rather than accept job offers to stay in Washington, D.C.

I never intended to become an academic. However, a chance meeting with the chair of a psychology department that had just begun a doctoral program in psychology led me into a career path I greatly enjoyed. I focused my scholarship and courses in the areas of diversity, multiculturalism, ethics, and feminist psychology. Unfortunately, neither this environment nor my new status as a professor made me immune to sexual harassment. For example, a married administrator confessed to me that he had broken into my office to see what pictures I had up on my desk so he could see the kind of "competition" he faced when he declared he was going to pursue me romantically. When I rebuffed his advances, he told the chair of my department and the chair of the tenure and promotion committee that he and I had had an affair. As chair of the Academic Affairs Committee, I confronted a male colleague about his persistent devaluing of the content of my statements during meetings. Smiling, he told me he was imagining how I would look in lingerie, and that he liked

Hispanic women because we are "hot and submissive." A student told me during office hours that he had a hard time focusing on my lectures because when he looked at me all he saw was "sex on a stick." Another male colleague spread a rumor that the reason I was hired was because I slept with the chair of the department, a straight woman.

Despite these experiences, my male colleagues in professional associations and organizations provided me with curative experiences. They allowed me to chew on their ears and vent, and their responses of being aghast and stunned were validating and affirming. By the middle of my tenure as an academic, I had begun to actively embrace the field of the psychology of men and masculinity. I came to understand it as a form of diversity in its own right and as part of intersecting identities for men of color, gay men, men with disabilities, and so on. During this time, I had the opportunity to work with many men, including military veterans, gay men, men with disabilities, men undergoing sex reassignment, ethnic and racial minority men, poor men, conservative men, and straight White men in the classroom, university, and my practice. The perspective of intersecting identities helped me leave behind one-dimensional perspectives of men and develop a more comprehensive understanding about them in general and my father and our relationship in particular. For the first time, I was really able to see him as a man, with all that that meant, and I loved him for being whom he was, whether because of or in spite of all that life, cultures, and societies and their institutions had done to him and me. I caught myself when I stereotyped and "bashed" men, and I raised the awareness of others when they did the same. Through these experiences, I became a better psychologist, professor, aunt, friend, ally, daughter, partner, feminist, and person as a result.

MEN IN THE MINORITY: RESEARCH AND THEORY

Contemporary dominant theories about men and masculinity do not necessarily fit the lives of men in the minority. For example, normative masculinity in the United States is embodied at the socially constructed intersections of a specific race (White), class, sexuality (heterosexual), and ability. Stereotypically, this portrayal of masculinity includes men represented as lower to middle class, hyperheterosexual Whites in beer, cigarette, and sports commercials, while on the other end of the continuum, masculinity is represented by upper-class White "metrosexuals" as seen in GQ and *Maxim* magazines. The values and virtues represented in these characterizations of White men include independence, autonomy, competitiveness, and virility. For the lower-class men, some buffoonery, incompetence, and aggressiveness are also portrayed, while for the upper-class men, sophistication, accomplishment, and financial excess are emphasized. The women in these portrayals are usually ancillary to the main subjects (men), whether as purveyors of "Hungry Man" frozen dinners or scantily clad "arm candy."

These portrayals of masculinity exclude men in minority group memberships from accessing aspects of male privilege in terms of power and status (Pleck, 1981). For example, African American men are denied the presumptive male privilege of being intelligent and competent, Latinos are denied the same as well as industry and initiative, while gay men are denied the assumption they are psychologically and physically healthy. In other words, being a man of color, gay, working class, or differently abled creates various obstacles to accessing the full range of White male privilege that includes social, political, economic, and educational opportunities, attainment, and advancement. Therefore, men of color, gay men, men with visible disabilities, and so on encounter "glass ceilings and walls" when striving for status and power in social, political, economic, and educational institutions because they *cannot* "pass" as "regular" men. On the other hand, able-bodied, White, heterosexual men can and do pass because they more closely approximate the stereotypical ideal of a "real man," and can more easily access "male privilege," *if they choose to do so*, and leave themselves open to discrimination if they choose not to "pass."

Although adhering to traditional conceptions of masculinity provides material privileges to certain men, it is also associated with negative social and psychological consequences (hooks, 1992; Hurtado & Sinha, 2005; Messner, 1997; Pleck, 1981). The more strongly a man identifies with the "male ideal," a "man's man" if you will, the more his "privilege" has negative psychological consequences, including increased abuse of alcohol (Lemle & Mishkind, 1989), affective mood disorders (Good, Heppner, DeBord, & Fischer, 2004; Good & Wood, 1995; Mahalik & Rochlen, 2006), alexithymia (O'Neil 1981, 1998), and relational problems (DeFranc & Mahalik, 2002; Levant, 1992). Indeed, traditional masculine norms restrict all men (minority and majority) from engaging in certain behaviors (e.g., nurturing), activities (e.g., engaging in "domestic arts"), and careers (e.g., being a stay-at-home parent, day care provider, nurse, artist).

Notwithstanding the sometimes negative consequences to straight White men who embrace the male ideal, the negative effects to men in the minority of being denied this male privilege are grave. For example, when compared with straight men, gay and bisexual men are more likely to struggle with substance abuse (Drabble, Midanik, & Trocki, 2005) and have psychiatric disorders and attempt suicide (Cochran & Mays, 2000), largely due to the effects of stigma and discrimination (Meyer, 2003). These negative outcomes are found in racial minorities as well. Since 2000, a number of investigations have found that racism and discrimination experienced by African American men is causally linked to race-based physical health disparities affecting this population (Mays, Cochran, & Barnes, 2007). The research is not yet robust enough to make conclusions on morbidity and mortality outcomes in individuals with intersecting marginalized identities, such as those maintained by gay Black men. Are they three times at risk for problems because they are men, gay, and Black? Could not being a man be a "protective" variable because his access to male privilege might mitigate some of the negative effects of his race or sexual orientation?

The theories on intersectionality might be able to guide this exploration despite research lacking in this area. Unlike traditional theories of men and masculinities, intersectionality provides a paradigm that enables us to explore and understand how a gay man of color can experience privilege *and* discrimination depending on his social location (Zinn & Dill, 1996). Although male privilege has been argued by some (Liu, 2002) as not fully available to men in the minority (e.g., Asian men) to the extent that it is to straight White men, all men (when compared to women) benefit from it. For example, regardless of his sexual orientation, an Asian American man is likely to earn a higher wage than a woman. When walking to his car after a late-night class, he is less likely to fear sexual assault than a woman. He is more likely to see a male pastor at the pulpit in his church and feel validated through the male-dominated teachings as well. On the other hand, intersectionality can hold true the fact of male privilege in certain contexts while also understanding that this same Asian American man is more likely than other men to be viewed as effeminate (thereby reducing his masculinity), mistaken as a foreigner (reminding him he can never pass as a "normal" American), and if he is gay, be targeted for bullying and hate crimes because of his sexual orientation.

While understanding that all social identities are embedded in the context of power relations (Collins, 2000), intersectionality theories also eschew the polarity of discourses contained in more traditional models of identity that oppositionally place one demographic variable with another (e.g., sex vs. ethnicity) and groups of people against each other (e.g., White men vs. American Indian men). These theories maintain that a person's social identities are equally and concurrently valid. One identity is not more important than the other, and we cannot appreciate a single identity outside the context of the others for any given person. A gay African American man is that and more (e.g., husband, father, union craftsman), but to identify him solely on the basis of his race reduces him by devaluing his other identities and vice versa. All of his identities and experiences regarding them (e.g., racism, homophobia, fatherhood) collectively define who he is.

Intersectionality also provides us with a paradigm to understand that, depending on one's social location, one social identity may be more salient over another at any given moment. To illustrate, if the hypothetical man just discussed had his car vandalized with a homophobic slur sprayed on it, his identity as a gay man becomes more salient. Or, if his child became ill and had to be hospitalized, his identity as a father would be highlighted, but if he was denied power of medical decision making because his child's legal father is his husband, then both his identities as gay and father are more relevant *to that situation*. However, none of these situations can take away the fact that he is still a man, perhaps the most salient identity of all for him.

WORKING WITH MEN IN THE MINORITY: CASE STUDIES

Case Study 1: Albert: a Mexican American Male

Al, a 49-year-old Mexican American male, is a retired officer from the U.S. Army; he has been married 29 years and has four children, who are all "launched" adults. He arrived in therapy because his wife gave him an ultimatum: "Get a clue or I'm out!" He stated his presenting problem was his wife. They argued a lot, and he admitted that both of them felt unsupported and invalidated by each other. They were lonely in their marriage and had begun investing in relationships outside it as a result of their feeling hopeless in changing each other.

When Al retired, his children were in college, as was his wife, who was studying to be a medical social worker. On graduation she worked in local hospitals and developed new acquaintances and friendships with people unfamiliar to her husband. In addition, she began withholding a percentage of her salary for her own use. He "let" her have her friends, but complained, "She goes out too often [with single friends] and stays out too late. A married woman shouldn't do that." "Why did she have to go to college and go to work? She's telling me, isn't she, that I am not enough."

Al also perseverated on, and was dismayed by, their sex life. He wanted sex more than the twice weekly they were having it, and he wanted her to initiate and introduce more variety into their sexual routine. He complained about, and resisted, her pressure to eat healthier and exercise (he was about 30 pounds overweight); yet, he also knew that doing so was "like foreplay to her," and he resented it. Several weeks into therapy, he admitted to the "occasional" infidelity earlier in his marriage, "but she didn't find out—not a problem." "I was young, our kids came out bam, bam, bam, bam. My wife let herself go, and she stopped being interested in sex. I had needs. That's how we [men] are. If we don't get it at home, we need to get it somewhere else. Women aren't supposed to be like that . . . but do you think my wife is having an affair?"

We discussed Al's retirement fantasies: golf, travel, time with friends and his children. The reality, however, was that his friends were still working; because of his wife's job, they did not travel; and his children were busy with their own lives. His daily routine included waking up as his wife left for work, coffee and newspaper reading, and then not much else that was structured or routine until about an hour before his wife returned from work, when he would quickly put a load in the washing machine, make the bed, and get something frozen out for dinner. Some days, he would golf, but lately he resented the dress code at the club, so those days became fewer. Other days, he would go to the gym. With retirement, he lost his structure and identity because he went from "Al, active duty colonel" to "just Al." He felt unproductive, useless, and bored, bored, bored. I monitored his mood states throughout our work together, and I shared research reviews on the efficacy of sleep, diet, exercise, structure and routines, and generativity in the treatment of anxiety and depressive symptoms. He appeared interested when we discussed these articles, but he did not initially embrace the "work" of therapy.

We slowly began peeling back the layers of all those initial presenting problems and discovered a cognitive entrenchment I saw as symptom and origin of his distress. Once I called his gendered statements "biases and assumptions" and was met with Al's assertion that his gender role beliefs were culturally "normal." That first time I brought it up in a session, he was not open to viewing these beliefs as having been formed in the context of his family of origin within a lower-class barrio and reinforced in the military. He also protested that they were voluntary and modifiable. I tried to explain that his rigid adherence to them likely played a role in his marital discord as that system had dramatically changed in the four years since his retirement. "I haven't changed, she has!" Al exclaimed. I slowly, sympathetically, and kindly replied, "I know. That's part of the problem."

We were able to address these beliefs by way of first discussing the "other side of the story." If women have proscribed behaviors he believed in, then what were the rules for Hispanic men, and how did he learn them? What were they for his parents' and grandparents' generations? Did they change across the generations? Why and how are his grandfather and sons similar and different in their gender role beliefs?

The answers to these questions illuminated Al's belief that his roles within the family context, and indeed his intrinsic value as a husband and father, are defined as being a provider and head of the family. These roles changed when he retired and his wife pursued a career. At issue for him was that his retirement pay was 55% of his active duty base pay, and they had to rely on his wife's income to pay their debts and living expenses. Al's wife also began asserting herself more with regard to their financial decision making. He felt emasculated. In planning his retirement, he had not considered that he might later feel inadequate as a fiscal provider to his family. On further exploration, I learned that in the four years since his retirement, he had not taken on other paid work, and that the bulk of the marital debt was his wife's and their children's college student loans.

I inquired about his decision to remain out of the workforce and discovered that although Al's wife encouraged him to get a job for his own good, he said he was waiting for his wife to "go through her phase" so they could fulfill "their" retirement dream and travel. "She goes through phases with her hobbies," he reported. "If I just let her do her thing, she will let go of it faster than if I tried to make her stop." My initial reaction and response was one of confusion. ("Was he talking about her new career?" I wondered.) "I don't get it. You, your wife, and all of your children have earned college degrees, and aside from you at this time, they are all in the initiation and establishment phases of their careers. It is obvious you value higher education and professional careers; why do you belittle your wife's by referring to it as a 'hobby'?" Al replied sincerely by saying, "No disrespect, but my wife doesn't have to do it. We're fine. I made sure of it. She is doing this because she wants to, not because we need her to have a career that pays better than minimum wage." I pressed on by openly wondering about the relationship between his feelings of inadequacy and his belittlement of her career. I did not have to be more explicit. Al responded by saying, "Maybe . . . probably . . . okay, yes."

I pressed further and asked Al *how* (not *whether*) his resistance to getting a job was similar to his resistance to diet and exercise. That time, I had to illuminate the connection for him. (I did not mention my awareness of the parallel process of his "resistance" to *my* guided explorations.) I repeated what he told me: His income was reduced by half, they were paying off five student loans; as a result, they have to rely on his wife's income, he resents his wife's growing empowerment, he feels inadequate and emasculated, "and so you resist getting a job even when you know it will help financially, and it might help you personally and in your marriage as well?" After a few moments of silence, he said, "Yeah, okay, that's idiotic." I smiled warmly. "So, why don't I do it then?" he asked, and we explored that question for a few sessions. Weeks later, he chuckled as he reported that he had told his wife about this interaction saying that I had "busted his chops." She laughed and inquired if "tipping" me for my service was appropriate. We both laughed at his telling of it. (And again, I wondered to myself about a parallel process. "She's busting his chops. I'm busting his chops. Will he view me as withholding [sex, affection, mothering, merging] at some point as well?")

We later discussed their decision to pay for their children's student loans. He reported that he believed that being a Hispanic father means that his job does not end when the kids turn 18 and move out of the family home like "White people's families." We explored his "observations and conclusions" (not "biases and assumptions") about different family structures and father roles across racial and ethnic lines. Of course, his points of reference were mainly other military fathers, a skewed sample. This gave us an opportunity to explore his identity and how it has changed with his changing "social location." "There you were a full bird, in command, powerful, and virile. Now

you are retired, your wife makes you go to therapy, and you fear you
are losing your base of strength as a provider and head of the family."

I told Al that I was impressed by *their* generosity and sacrifice
and purposefully framed it as characteristic of being good providers (plural, as in *both* he and his wife). An obvious source of pride,
that opened the door to his sharing many stories about being a good
provider historically to his family and children—like his father had
been to him and his siblings. I was intending to go down a path that
I hoped would illuminate for me the decision-making process he
and his wife made to pay for their children's loans; however, I saw
a natural and perhaps more important opportunity to explore the
father–son relationship. "Tell me about your father" was the only
invitation I made. We spent the next few sessions talking about Al's
father and their relationship.

This part of our work was quite dynamic as Al recalled and
renewed his identification with his father—a blue-collar worker who
often held several jobs at a time to provide for his family. He had a
day job as a painter/carpenter and at night was a janitor at his kids'
private school. Al's memories of his father were touching and illu-
minating as he realized his military training and culture developed
a style in him that was decisive and authoritarian, whereas his father
was more collaborative. Al was proud and confident in his thoughts
and opinions; his father was humble and kept his opinions to himself.

Al recalled an early memory of his parents discussing money
and tight budgets; he was about eight years old, and he noticed his
parents were having a difficult conversation at the dining table. Al
joined them at the table only to have his father firmly tell him that
they were having a private conversation and asked him to leave.
Eavesdropping, he heard his mother complaining of sexual harassment at the hands of a restaurant manager in her workplace. He
heard his father insist, "Quit. Don't do it. They don't pay you enough
for that. We're fine. I can get another job." "What did she say?" I
inquired. Al could not recall. "Did she quit?" He did not know. "Can
you guess?" I pressed on. "I don't guess." Hmm. I murmured something about his father being a good and powerful role model in his
life, and that Al was shaped by him even while eavesdropping.

Some time later, Al reported that on a visit with his parents he
brought up this memory to his mother. She recalled that conversation and told him that she did not quit at first, "I couldn't do that
to him or the family; we needed the money" because he and his
younger siblings were in private school. "That must have killed him!"
Al replied. "He was mad, but I told him to trust me. I knew how to
take care of myself and knew what I was doing," she told him. She
later secured a better job, with benefits, at Levi Strauss, a job she
kept until her children were out of college and married. Because
of her employment, neither he nor his siblings had a debt load on

graduating from college. The similarities and differences between his parents' situation and his own were not lost on him.

"I am right, but my father did right," he once said. More gently this time, I revisited the idea that values and beliefs are voluntary and modifiable and added that although he and his father came from similar cultures of origin (albeit different generations) and they maintained the same values of providing and being the head of the family, the manner in which they manifested these values was different. Although the values did not change over time, the way they lived them did. He was open to hearing that there are ways of providing that are not financial and ways of being the head of the family that are not about commanding. We touched on these themes over many sessions.

A few months before we ended our work together, Al had secured a job with a private not-for-profit agency that created a clearinghouse of community services for military war veterans. Al's wife was a more-than-willing resource for him, and his salary alone was enough to make the monthly student loan payments. In addition, Al and his wife renegotiated the payment plan with their children: Once they earned $40,000, the portion of the monthly contributions the parents made would be reduced by one third, at $50,000 by two thirds, and at $60,000 the parents would turn over the payments entirely. Originally, Al had a higher base, beginning at $50,000, and his wife wanted it lower. He was able to hear her perspective with "two ears": one for the content, the other for the affect. He realized she was not challenging his authority but was worried about *their* finances and *their* retirement. He suggested that they consult with their children. She agreed. The children collaborated and mutually reached an agreement that naturally fell between their parents' parameters. Al was proud of them all (I was proud of him!). Indeed, two of their children began making contributions to their student loan debts at the conclusion of that family meeting.

In the last couple of sessions before we ended our treatment, we reviewed our work and our progress. Al reported that he initially resisted therapy because he liked who he was and did not think he was the one in need of change. Yet, through our work together he felt validated that he is a good man, father, and husband, and that essentially after months of therapy he remained the same man but was now able to see things differently (with "two eyes"), feel things differently (as a result of practicing not to jump to assumptions or to take things personally), and do things differently (like his father). "*We* didn't change you—*we* expanded you," I said, using the plural.

Case Study 2: Winston

Winston was a 24-year-old Japanese American man who originally presented with an anxiety disorder and academic problems. He was a second-semester student in an MBA program who had begun feeling a "sense of doom" that led to an intense stomach upset the night before classes. He had gone to the university health clinic hoping he had an ulcer but was told instead he had anxiety and was offered anti-anxiety medication and the number to a local psychotherapy referral service. That is how he found me.

Winston's family is from Houston. His father is a geologist who works in the gas-and-oil industry, and his mother is a recently retired magazine editor. She took an early retirement because her parents were getting older and she wanted to be more available to them. Winston and his sister (who is six years older) are yonsei, fourth-generation Japanese Americans, whose parents and grandparents were born in the United States. Neither he nor his sister speaks Japanese, and his parents also do not, although Winston's father understands it a little. I joked, saying that I was disappointed I was not going to hear Japanese spoken with a Texas drawl since his is rather pronounced, and he laughed.

As Winston explained his situation, he described a history of anxiety that waxed and waned back to his elementary school years. "Have you been able to figure out any patterns?" I asked. He took a deep breath and said that he thinks it is because he is gay and he hasn't come out to his family and most of his friends back home. "That would make me anxious, too," I said, normalizing this part of his stress.

When Winston was still in elementary school, he recalled wanting to marry Joey from the television show *Friends*. We discussed what he felt then: "I had the biggest crush on Joey and taped every episode!" he exclaimed. I wondered how he kept his secret back then. He said he did not at first, but then his sister and friends teased him and that felt very bad, so he denied his feelings. He even got into a few scuffles with his friends because they refused to stop teasing him. "That teasing must have hurt," I said. He admitted he felt betrayed by them.

We discussed Winston's decision-making around not coming out in the past and his thoughts about it now. He shared that the reactions of his friends shifted his awareness enough so that he became hypervigilant about peoples' attitudes and beliefs about homosexuality and gay people and "flew into the closet and nailed the door shut!"

Winston also disclosed that in high school, he and his best friend were inseparable; they even started to save money so they could buy a car together. One day while they were horsing around, Winston initiated a kiss with his friend, and it was met rather ardently. That surprised them both. Over the next two weeks, they could not stay away from each other, but then rather suddenly the friend transferred to another high school and stopped seeing him. When Winston asked for an explanation, his fear was realized when he heard his friend say, "It's because you're a fag, okay!?" Winston was devastated.

Over the next couple of months, Winston could not sleep or eat much. As a result, he lost 10% of his body weight, and his grades

slipped. I wondered aloud how his parents responded to him during this time. He said that his father was so concerned about his
grades he dedicated himself to ensuring his son's academic success
by sitting up with him at night and checking his homework, creating practice tests for him in preparation for the ones in his classes,
and coaching him on how to eliminate internal distractions while
he studied. Winston's mother, who was also concerned about the
grades, said, "Don't disappoint your father," and took him to a doctor who offered him Prozac, which he declined. She pushed him
to talk to her, but he withdrew. When I explored whether he ever
tried to hurt himself, Winston admitted to practicing using a belt as
a noose, but he said he could not follow through with it because of
how it would affect his family. (*"How?"* I wondered to myself.)

"How is this relevant to you now, Winston?" I asked. He admitted
that since he moved to town to go to graduate school, he had been
frequenting gay bars and had been promiscuous with multiple partners. He was drinking a lot on the weekends, and there were times
he would wake up in someone else's apartment and not remember
how he had gotten there. (I made a mental note to myself that in the
next session I would thoroughly discuss safety issues and safe sex,
recommend he get a comprehensive physical exam, and suggest he
investigate treatments, other than alcohol, to manage his anxiety as
a complement to our work.) "How do you feel about what is happening?" I inquired gently and indirectly so as not to provoke defensive-
ness because I needed to assess his mood, insight, and impulsivity.
After a moment, Winston replied, "It's okay," and shrugged sadly.
"It's okay," I echoed sadly. Then with a wry smile and solid eye contact, I said, "That's a pretty low bar, Winston. Do you think you can
hang out with me for a few sessions to see if we can raise it a bit?"
He matched my wry smile and said he would.

Early on, we created a metaphor of our work together that had
him giving me "beads" (e.g., his experiences and their meanings,
relationships, goals, etc.) while I "threaded" them. I frequently pantomimed taking a bead and stringing it to see how that bead looked
in the context of the others. "What do you think about this string?"
I would invite, as we collaborated on an interpretation, I guided his
awareness, or I offered an intervention based on what we had strung
together that day or month.

One of Winston's beads was his closeted gay identity, which was
partly due to his experiences with bigotry as a child. "I don't want to
have to deal with people's issues towards me when they don't even
know me!" "Is your sister 'people'?" I asked, remembering that she
had also teased him. Her behavior hurt badly because he idolized
her when he was younger and she was in high school. (She was a
National Merit Scholar and a national solo competition finalist in
viola.) More than that, he believed she was the closest he had to
getting a reading on how his parents would react if he disclosed

his sexual orientation to them. "Has she not changed since she was 14?" I asked. He had encapsulated himself so much that he had not noticed whether her views on homosexuality had changed.

When I asked Winston what his parents believed about homosexuality in general, he admitted he did not know directly but assumed that they would not be pleased because all his life he had heard multiple renditions of: "Respect your elders." "Be successful." "Work and study hard." "Behave appropriately." "Do not bring shame or embarrassment to the family." "If you draw attention to us, make sure it is because of your merits not because of trouble." ("Ah. Another bead," I thought and pretended to reach for one.) "That is so Japanese!" I said. "Really?" he asked. (Hmm. "He didn't know," I thought to myself while grabbing another bead.)

Over the next few sessions, we visited and revisited his ethnic identity, of which he was relatively unaware. Aside from Christmas gatherings where he would note that some of his cousins' spouses were "Anglos" (a term used in Texas to describe White Americans in general), he never gave it much thought. I asked, "Then, how do you know you are Japanese American?" He laughed and said, "Good question. I've been asked if I am Chinese, Korean, Vietnamese, and I always say, 'I'm Japanese American.' But how do I know? Because my parents told me so, I guess." I encouraged him to "put on his cultural anthropologist hat" and do a qualitative study of his family. Since spring break was around the corner, I suggested that might be a great opportunity to explore the question "How do you know you are Japanese?" with his sister, parents, and grandparents.

Since undertaking this exercise, Winston had become aware of surreal moments where he suddenly remembered 'I'm Japanese'! During these moments his perception shifted to include his awareness that "other people see me as Asian!" For the first time, he realized, "*I* am the 'diversity' among my friends! *I* am their 'Asian friend.'"

This was a fascinating time in our work together because he discovered that that single question opened the door to learning so much about his family. For example, he learned that when his grandparents were teenagers, they were interned in the Manzanar Relocation Center for over two years during World War II. They met and courted there. (Another bead, I pantomimed, and thought, "Keep your head down. Don't give White people a reason to think badly of us.") When he asked his sister, she shared that one of the ways she knew was that her "dating pool," which consisted mainly of Anglos, was constricted by having to encounter their stereotypes of her being "some version of a dragon lady" (which she interpreted to mean sexy, intelligent, devious, and power hungry). She also did not know about their grandparents' internment but was well aware of the expectations her parents had of their children's comportment.

Sometime later, Winston had the occasion to meet with some old friends. When they were trying to negotiate where to go out for dinner, one of them suggested a new sushi restaurant. Winston asked him if he made that suggestion because he is Japanese and thought he would like it. That friend replied by saying, "I don't think of you as a Jap, dude! I think of you as a normal dude!" "How did you hear that, Winston?" I asked. He said he was relieved because he knew his friend meant well. "How did you feel about him using the term *Jap*?" "Isn't it like saying Jew instead of Jewish," he asked. "Um, no. No, it isn't," I responded and explained. "What do you make of him thinking of you as a *normal* dude?" I asked, thinking that both of these statements would make an excellent entree to exploring racism and race constructions in the United States. What he said, though, was that he was relieved because he assumed normal *also* meant straight. ("That was totally unexpected," I thought as I grabbed and strung another imaginary bead.) Over the weeks that passed, we had many conversations about his cognitive distortion that his friend's response meant that he "passed" as straight instead of passing as a racial normal. And, we also explored the "normal dude" phrase as a way to hypothesize what his friend's automatic assumption was about normal in response to his question about ethnic identity. (Later, I would refer him to Harvard's Implicit Association Test Web site, https://implicit.harvard.edu/implicit/demo/.) I suggested that his gay and ethnic identity "beads" had positioned themselves next to each other along the way and wondered aloud if when he closeted his gay self, his ethnic self also got shoved in there.

Winston and I discovered a major source of his anxiety when we explored the conversations he had with his father that were prompted by the question, "Dad, how do you know you are Japanese?" His father's response struck me as interesting because it appeared to endorse the "model minority myth." His father knew he was Japanese because he was smart and worked hard and was rewarded by earning the highest marks in school and respectable promotions in the companies he worked for in the past and enjoyed a steady flow of lucrative contracts now that he was a consultant. He also knew he was Japanese because he took care of his parents in their old age and was a respectful and dutiful son who gave them no reason to hide their faces in public because he did all of this *and* he provided them with grandchildren. "Oh boy! That's a huge bead!" I exclaimed. "And heavy," Winston sighed.

During this discussion, I pretended to show Winston the string of beads we had been collecting of our work together because I wanted to know the relational proximity of each bead to the others. That week, the beads followed in this order: gay, son, homophobia, father, and Japanese. *Homophobia* came between *son* and *father*, and *father* was more influenced by *Japanese*; on the other end, *son* was more influenced by *gay*. (Other weeks, the beads changed positions depending on what was going on for him at the time. For example, the *student* bead was prominently positioned in between *son* and *father* at times when he was under academic strain or worried he would not make his father proud as a result.) For the remainder of the session, we explored the placement of those five beads that gave voice to his core anxiety that coming out would mean his father would reject him (homophobia) because it would mean that he failed in his obligations as the son because he was closer to *gay* than to *Japanese* like his father.

Over the next few months, we discussed what basically amounted to a model minority role strain because Winston's identities as a gay man and an acculturated Japanese American colluded to violate normative expectations in the various social "locations" in which he lived. While he often felt trapped between *gay* and *Japanese*, he longed to open the closet door because "not knowing my father's reaction is worse than knowing it, I think. If I knew, at least I could stop wondering." I decided then was a good time to share with Winston a pattern that I had been monitoring: the more intense the content and process of any given session, the less likely he would binge drink and the more studious and productive he would become. I pulled out our session notes from the past few months, and sure enough, one session would be intense and the next session he would report having had a good and productive week. Indeed, we noticed that lately he was having better weeks even without "the acute work of therapy." We explored the patterns and concluded (a) he was out to me; (b) I and the work we did gave him an affirming relationship ("location") in which to be his entire self; (c) he felt validated and connected; and (d) this allayed his anxiety.

"Our relationship is my medicine," he concluded. "Yes," I concurred, "anything else?" I asked encouragingly. While Winston knocked that around internally, I handed him the pretend string of beads. After a few more moments, he said that he was less anxious in a relational context where he can feel supported for being his whole self. "Besides me, is there someone else who you feel you can trust enough who might be able to give that to you?" The following week, he reported that he told his sister over the phone that he was gay. (He used the phone in case he needed to hang up.) "She says she had known all along," then added, "Then, doing her big bossy sister thing, she said, 'We'll tell mom first. No way dad can stand up to the three of us!'" My eyes grew wide, my jaw dropped, I clutched my chest, and he said, "Exactly! I nearly had a heart attack!" He told her he agreed with the plan, but that he wanted to keep it between the two of them for a while before taking the next step. She agreed to follow his lead.

CONCLUSION

Traditional theories of identity that espouse singular, hierarchal, and disconnected ways of viewing humans have unwittingly reinforced polarities that pit one identity or one group of people against another. It is not surprising then that there are tensions between people who identify as feminists and multiculturalists, men and women, prochoice and prolife, and in favor of traditional family and gay marriage, just to name a few. It is as if we are incapable of bridging the tenets and characteristics of both, *all*. Unfortunately, because of the imposition of contrived definitions of "opposite" and "otherness," exclusion is often a by-product. Oppression based on demographic and social identities deliberately and insidiously undermines the very fabric of how a person (and groups of people) understands and values his or her sense of self.

Because of the failings of traditional theories of identity, I have looked *in* at my own life and *at* the state of art to form a base where I join the men in my practice in collaborating on the creation of their own dynamic "personal theories." These theories embrace the totality of their unique lives, multiple identities, experiences, social locations, and power relations that define them. In telling the stories of my life experiences, I illustrated parts of my own evolution that informs my identity and my work. By sharing my work, my *relationships*, with my father, Al, and Winston, I hope that readers can examine their own experiences with men in the minority and find ways of being that affirm and expand how they know themselves and the lives of the men they touch.

By the way, my father has also grown considerably, as evidenced by his loosening grip on traditional female gender role stereotypes. You cannot imagine my surprise when, on declaring my intention to adopt a baby (my second adoption as a single parent; the first was a 9-year-old girl, a biological first cousin), he said, *"Porque no tienes uno tu misma?"* "What?" I asked, doubting that I heard correctly. He repeated himself in English, "Why not have one of your own?" ("He knows I'm not in a relationship, what is he implying?" I wondered.) I asked, *"Con quien?"* ("With who?") To which he replied, *"Que importa que con quien?"* ("What does it matter with who?") "WHAT?!" I exclaimed, and continued, "Who are you? Where is my old-school Mexican father? Did an alien abduct you and replace your brain?" His mother, who witnessed this interaction, started laughing, and we joined her.

REFERENCES

Cochran S. D., & Mays, V. M. (2000). Lifetime prevalence of suicide symptoms and affective disorders among men reporting same-sex sexual partners: Results from NHANES III. *American Journal of Public Health, 90*, 573–578.

Collins, P. H. (2000). *Black feminist thought: Knowledge, consciousness, and the politics of empowerment* (2nd edition). New York, NY: Routledge.

DeFranc, W., & Mahalik, J. R. (2002). Masculine gender role conflict and stress in relation to parental attachment and separation. *Psychology of Men and Masculinity, 3*, 51–60.

Drabble, L., Midanik, L. T., & Trocki, K. (2005). Reports of alcohol consumption and alcohol-related problems among homosexual, bisexual and heterosexual respondents: Results from the 2000 National Alcohol Survey. *Journal of Studies on Alcohol, 66*(1), 111–120.

Good, G. E., Heppner, P. P., DeBord, K. A., & Fischer, A. R. (2004). Understanding men's psychological distress: Contributions of problem-solving appraisal and masculine role conflict. *Psychology of Men and Masculinity, 5,* 168–177.

Good, G. E., & Wood, P. K. (1995). Male gender role conflict, depression, and help seeking: Do college men face double jeopardy? *Journal of Counseling and Development, 74,* 70–75.

hooks, b. (1992). *Black looks: Race and representation.* Boston: South End Press.

Hurtado, A. (1997). Understanding multiple group identities: Inserting women into cultural transformations. *Journal of Social Issues, 53,* 299–328.

Lemle, R., & Mishkind, M. E. (1989). Alcohol and masculinity. *Journal of Substance Abuse Treatment, 6,* 213–222.

Levant, R. (1992). Toward the reconstruction of masculinity. *Journal of Family Psychology, 5,* 379–402.

Liu, W. M. (2002, August). Perpetual foreigners: Asian American men's struggle for masculinity and nationality. In R. Levant (Chair), *Masculinities in multicultural perspective: Race, culture, nationality, and sexual orientation.* Symposium conducted at the 110th Annual Convention of the American Psychological Association, Chicago.

Mahalik, J. R., & Rochlen, A. B. (2006). Men's likely responses to clinical depression: What are they and do masculinity norms predict them? *Sex Roles, 55,* 659–667.

Mays, V. M., Cochran, S. D., and Barnes, N. W. (2007). Race, race-based discrimination, and health outcomes among African Americans. *Annual Review of Psychology, 58,* 201–225.

Messner, M. A. (1997). *Politics of masculinity: Men in movements.* Thousand Oaks, CA: Sage.

Meyer I. H. (2003). Prejudice, social stress, and mental health in lesbian, gay, and bisexual populations: Conceptual issues and research evidence. *Psychological Bulletin, 129,* 674–697.

O'Neil, J. M. (1981). Male sex role conflicts, sexism, and masculinity: Psychological implications for men, women, and the counseling psychologist. *Counseling Psychologist, 9,* 61–80.

O'Neil, J. M. (1998). Wade and Gelso's contribution to the new psychology of men: Male reference group identity dependence theory. *Counseling Psychologist, 26,* 413–421.

Pleck, J. (1981). *The myth of masculinity.* Cambridge, MA: MIT Press.

Zinn, M. B., & Dill, B. T. (1996). Theorizing difference from multiracial feminism. *Feminist Studies, 22,* 321–332.

Counseling Depressed Men

Making Darkness Visible

HOLLY BARLOW SWEET

INTRODUCTION: THE HIDDEN PROBLEM OF MALE DEPRESSION

A few years ago, I had an undergraduate advisee who was failing physics for the third time. He was homesick for his town in Nigeria, a country so different from the United States, and was questioning his faith in his newly adopted religion. He was the shining star of his small village, and the expectations for him were very high. I was worried about him (despite the fact that he said he was not depressed) and sent him to the college counseling center. Later that summer, I ran into him and asked how he was doing. He said he was fine, he would definitely finish physics this time around, and he did not need to see anyone anymore. I took him at his word. I did not see him around after that and assumed he was okay. Two months into the fall term, I got a call from a friend of his, who said simply "Nabelo killed himself yesterday." His funeral was the saddest I have ever attended. Although I was not responsible for him, I knew that I could have done something to help. Like many of his friends, advisors, and professors, we had not seen the warning signs. These included denial of any problems (despite circumstances that would be likely to bring on depression in anyone), resistance to getting help, and social withdrawal.

The other day, I picked up a newspaper and read about a man who had just been fired from his job. He went home, came back with a gun, and shot and killed some of his coworkers. He then turned the gun on himself and committed suicide. His boss said, "He seemed fine—I didn't see it coming." A few days later, I read about a man who was separated from his wife and killed her and their two children. The neighbors said, "He was a good father and family man—devoted to his wife and kids— we can't believe this has happened!" Were these men psychopaths? Or, were they, perhaps, psychologically unbalanced and unable to cope with loss of status and intimacy, in part because they may not have the tools to understand what they were feeling or may not have known how to get proper treatment for their problems? Closer to home, I have a male friend who has lost interest in work and stays home at night playing video games and drinking a lot. He has also stopped exercising; yet, when asked how he is doing, says, "I'm fine." Is he really fine, or is this the only way he knows how to handle what he is feeling—to drink, withdraw, and deny?

How many men suffer from untreated depression? Depression in boys and men often goes undiagnosed or misdiagnosed in our society because people do not understand or do not see how men experience and express depression. Every time I pick up a newspaper, I cannot help but wonder if the suicides and homicides that are committed by men have a great deal to do with undiagnosed and untreated depression. Several writers in the field of male psychology (Cochran & Rabinowitz, 2000; Lynch & Kilmartin, 1999; Rabinowitz, 2009; Wexler, 2006) discussed the problem of "masked" or "covert" depression—depression that is hidden from public view and, sometimes, hidden from the men themselves. They indicated that the consequences for our culture are potentially profound in terms of depressed males who are not getting the help they need and act out their depression through social withdrawal, workaholism, substance abuse, anger, and violent behavior toward self and others. It is possible that many of the problems we see that are more common in men than women (such as homicide, suicide, substance abuse, and earlier death rates) may be due in large part to poorly diagnosed depression or inadequate treatment.

As therapists, we are ethically bound to understand how depression presents in men and to learn effective ways to treat depressed males. As female therapists, we also have a special obligation to understand how our own socialization and training can help or hinder us in working with depressed men. If we have men in our culture who do not know they are depressed or are afraid to seek treatment for fear of being unmanly, we have a real problem on our hands. If they do seek treatment and are not properly diagnosed or are properly diagnosed but are not properly treated, then we have an ever bigger problem. It is my hope that this chapter will help prevent more tragedies like Nabelo's death in the future.

PERSONAL JOURNEY

I grew up in the 1950s and 1960s, the younger of two girls in a family with a traditional breadwinning male (my father was a professor at the University of Michigan) and a stay-at-home mother. My mother was a talented woman who graduated from Smith College in the late 1930s and became a fashion editor for *Glamour* magazine. However, after she met my father, she became his secretary and devoted herself to his needs and to her daughters. It was clear that my dad was in charge of the family (Mom called him "The Master"), but I thought she was really the one who was the emotional rock of the family, and it was to her that I turned when I was sick or needed help.

I was relatively happy as a kid, confident in my ability to make friends, do well in school, and have fun skiing and hiking on family vacations. However, I was supposed to have been a boy (being the second daughter in a family that valued boys more than girls), and my parents encouraged me in that direction. My sister was to be the pretty one; I was to be the smart one. She was social; I was athletic. She went to parties; I stayed home and watched football with my dad. I guess I really did not mind this distinction until I hit puberty, when being pretty and popular with the boys was suddenly important to all the girls in my school.

In adolescence, I began to become depressed and struggled hard with what it really meant to be a woman. I saw what my mother's life was about: being a full-time wife and mother. I did not want that kind of life because it seemed to mean losing my identity as my own person. I did not want to be an ornament on someone else's tree. I wanted to be my own tree, with my own roots. I did not have any role models for women who were both smart and desired by men, who were able to combine the best traits of femininity and masculinity. My mother was both smart and attractive, yet I did not see her as having power and control. My father felt that women were inferior to men, in terms of both their power in this society and their overall values, such as competition, intelligence, and assertiveness. Since I felt like I could not combine intelligence and femininity, I made a Faustian deal with myself: I would sell my feminine soul (which I felt was not valued) for my masculine persona (which I felt was, at least by my father). I was to be smart but not feminine.

I have always had male friends, starting in first grade and continuing through today. I was part of a crowd of guys and girls in high school who hung out together but did not date each other. We were all just friends, and that made it easy and safe for all of us. The guys were fun, funny, and interested in the things I was interested in (such as skiing, playing Monopoly and Risk, and singing). Instead of being members of the opposite sex to me, they were my friends. Looking back, I realize how fortunate I was to have had this opportunity because it created a foundation of trust in and acceptance of males in me at a formative age.

Starting in my senior year in high school, I had my first boyfriend. He was a "bad boy" who stole cars and was on day release to my high school from a local mental hospital. I thought he was a perfect fit for me since I wanted to break away from my good girl image. Others in my school began to see me in a new light: a smart girl who could also date. This was also the beginning of years when I was attracted to wounded males. In retrospect, I knew that my father, as successful as he was, was hurting on the inside. He never talked about it and always put on a positive face, but he was incredibly sensitive to criticism, rebuked anyone who challenged him intellectually, and drank many beers every night. I think my relationship with my dad left me in a tough spot in terms of being able to truly respect women (since he did not) as well as understand the pain of men (which he did not show openly). It would take me many years of life experience as well as therapy to heal this split.

When I entered college in the mid-1960s, I was fascinated with the connected fields of psychology and sociology. I wanted to study people, both individually and in groups. I was particularly interested in women's issues and, at the time, could only see how sexism had shortchanged women. I began to see that my own problem in liking being a woman was not just my personal dilemma, but that the personal was indeed the political. I began to take action. I joined women's consciousness-raising groups and went to feminist conferences and rallies. I also wore miniskirts and makeup and continued to get A's in college, in defiance of a world that had previously pushed me into one box or the other. I studied sociology, first at the University of Michigan and then at the University of Sussex in England. I enjoyed my time in England and grew into a young woman who enjoyed the attention of men. I was still able to have male friends but was also able to have a boyfriend with whom I shared many wonderful times.

After I graduated in 1971, I worked for a year in student activities in London. The job I had was fulfilling (placing students in volunteer opportunities in the community), but I missed my home country and my family, so I decided to move back to the United States. After drifting around for a while, I ended up in Boston. I had friends in the area and because of my years in England, it felt more like home to me than the Midwest. I worked for a year as a secretary in a college counseling center and decided that I wanted to become a counselor. I had seen some therapists during high school and college for problems related to my ongoing depression and thought that I would like to help others as they had helped me.

I started my master's degree in counseling at Northeastern University in 1973. There, I took my first women's studies class and helped start a women's center on campus. I began to read popular feminist writings, including *Sisterhood Is Powerful* (Morgan, 1970) and *Our Bodies, Ourselves* (Boston Women's Health Book Collective, 1973). After graduation, I continued my career in counseling by working at a youth outreach center. I focused almost exclusively on the problems of girls and women, helping them move away from chronic states of low self-esteem and passive behavior that seemed ubiquitous among women. However, my own personal life became a mess. I was living in a group household of strangers, I had taken a job I did not really like and for which I was ill suited, and my boyfriend was demanding and prone to fits of anger.

The turning point for me came when several of us were terminated from our jobs at the youth agency by a new boss looking to reorganize our program. I had just gotten over a terrible case of the flu, which left me depressed and defeated. I was also seeing a therapist, who was both ineffective and inappropriate. I called my sister for advice the night I got laid off. She asked me one question, which I have never forgotten: "What are the lessons you need to learn about your life that you haven't learned yet?" I know now that the lessons confronted stereotypes I had internalized about men and women, despite all my efforts to think and act beyond them. One stereotype was that women should be passive and just let things happen to them. "Women are victims" was a theme that seemed to be everywhere in the 1970s. Another stereotype is that you should not turn to men for help since they would not listen well and could not understand. The third stereotype is that a woman's self-image is dependent on what others thought of her. I decided then and there that I was tired of seeing myself as a victim and leaning too much on others. I took responsibility for my actions and started standing up for myself. I fired my therapist and stopped seeing my boyfriend. I moved into a new living situation and started dating a new guy, whom I eventually married. I got help from one of my male friends, who was kind and supportive. I found a job at a local university the next month that was much better suited to my interests and style. Like many things in life, what had appeared on the surface to be bad news became a door to a better future.

But it turns out I was not done with the ups and downs of my personal journey. I enjoyed my time with my husband, but something was missing. I was friends with him, and we did many things together, but I never felt like he really admired me as a woman but rather as a buddy. He, like my father, did not really respect women. Like my father, he was also somewhat depressed but never recognized it as such (nor did I for quite a while) and therefore never got help. When our marriage began to fall apart in the early 1990s, we went for couples counseling. While I expressed my sadness, he was silent. When I got angry, he remained silent. I became increasingly depressed. The therapist saw me as the identified patient and my husband as the together partner in the marriage, even telling me, "If you leave him, you'll hate yourself forever." In fact, we were both suffering, but neither of us was getting the help we needed. Our marriage eventually failed, and we parted as sad friends. In addition, my once-proud father had been reduced by Parkinson's disease to an old man with dementia sitting in a wheelchair in a nursing home, waiting to die. His death in 1992 and my divorce in 1993 were turning points in my life. My father's death taught me increased compassion for men who might appear severe, angry, and sexist yet were as vulnerable as the next person when it came to life's realities. My divorce taught me that I needed to be with a man who truly valued women and femininity, and that companionship alone was not enough to build a solid marriage. Most of all, I came to realize that men can look good on the surface (as did my spouse) yet suffer inside.

It was not until years later that I found a man with whom I am not only a buddy but also a woman, someone who himself has balanced his masculinity with a strong and healthy feminine side. I began to heal that lifelong split between being a female and being smart. In addition, I found a therapist who truly helped me get a handle on my depression through different modalities (including medication) and who believed in me. I sometimes reflect on my hard times, just to remind myself that dark clouds can truly have silver linings if we are willing to search for effective support and learn how to take action. I also think that because I have suffered, I may have more empathy for the sufferings of others and perhaps more patience with what can be a long and slow path to growth.

PROFESSIONAL JOURNEY

My professional journey began when I went to work at an experimental freshman program at the Massachusetts Institute of Technology (MIT) in 1977 where I did informal counseling and advising. The program encouraged me to pursue my budding interest in gender studies. I developed and started teaching a seminar called "Sex Roles and Androgyny." However, I was not as liberated as I thought. Even though the course was supposed to be balanced between men's issues and women's issues, I believed that such a course should mostly contain information about how women are socialized into roles that are harmful to them, with a smattering of material about painful aspects of the male sex role. I believed that men needed to learn more about women than women needed to learn about men, especially how women were damaged by sexism. My course reflected this bent and, not surprisingly, attracted mostly women. I was occasionally accused by the men in the class of "male bashing," a charge that provoked in me a defensive response that only contributed to a hardening of stances.

As I thought about my first experience teaching, I began to read the few books written at the time that addressed the downside of men's experience, including *The Hazards of Being Male* (Goldberg, 1977) and *The Forty-Nine Percent Majority* (David & Brannon, 1976). I started to see the value of addressing men's issues more frequently and more sympathetically in that class. Looking at how sexism hurt women without regard for how it entrapped and damaged men was misleading and ineffective for the growth and education of both genders. I also knew that my course needed a male colleague to help represent the male point of view. I was fortunate to meet a male graduate student at MIT who was knowledgeable about and committed to gender studies. I invited him to join me in teaching that term's seminar on sex roles. We decided to change the name (who knew what androgyny meant anyhow?). We knew that men might not be interested in becoming more like women (although I thought that would not be a bad idea!) but were convinced that most men really wanted to understand how they could improve relationships with women. We therefore decided to call our new course "Sex Roles and Relationships." We put together a new reading list and syllabus, which included more experiential work and a more gender-balanced approach to the course. Finally, we specifically recruited men by stating in our course description, "Men are invited to join this seminar to represent the male point of view."

The course immediately doubled in enrollment, with more men than women signing up for it. The seminar was warmly met by both genders. Comments by men such as, "This was the first time I felt safe expressing my opinions in a class about gender," were common. Women were positive about learning about men's restrictions. As one female student said, "This has really made me see how hard feelings are for men to show: I have a lot more empathy for men now." The course was team taught for another eight years and included a companion peer-training program we developed in gender relations that we called GenderWorks.

While working at MIT, I decided to pursue my PhD in counseling psychology with a focus on gender issues. My thesis was *Perceptions of Undergraduate Male Experiences in Heterosexual Romantic Relationships: A Sex Role Norms Analysis* (Sweet, 1995). One of the most important findings of my research was that women underestimated the degree to which men struggle with expressing their emotions because of fear of rejection, not knowing what they felt, or feeling unmanly if they showed their feelings to others. While finishing my doctorate, I cofounded a consulting company (Cambridge Center for Gender Relations), which focused on improving personal and professional relationships between women and men through experiential techniques designed to teach gender understanding and empathy. In consulting in academic, private practice and corporate settings, I found that, contrary to stereotypes, both men and women are eager to learn about how they can get along better as long as the information is presented in a gender-balanced and nonblaming way. I was excited to be able to work with men in this way in particular since they responded so positively to this approach and often said that previous trainings around gender issues had felt shaming and blaming to them as men.

While I was working on my PhD, I joined the American Psychological Association (APA) and attended my first workshop, "Teaching the Psychology of Women." There, I met Dr. Louise Silverstein, who was to become my first mentor in the area of men's studies. She introduced me to several colleagues in APA who were trying to start a new division of men's studies (Division 51). Since that time, I am proud to call Division 51 my professional home. I have met some truly wonderful and inspiring people who have helped me grow professionally. It is from my contact in this division that I have been able to run workshops, present papers at national conferences, and write articles and books on men's issues. Even after all these years of being immersed in gender studies, I am happy to say that I am still learning and growing as a therapist, consultant, and instructor.

DEPRESSION, MEN, AND THERAPY

The Difficulty of Diagnosis

Depression is one of the most debilitating of the mental illnesses: the frightening collapse of self, the crushing feelings of hopelessness and helplessness, and the dark void of despair into which one has fallen and the ongoing fear that one may never recover. William Styron, the famous American author, suffered from severe depression later in his life and wrote movingly about it in his book *Darkness Visible* (1990). He described it as "a dreadful and raging disease," "a gray drizzle of horror," "hell's black depths," and "a veritable howling tempest in the brain," accompanied by "immense and aching solitude" and "dreadful, pouncing seizures of anxiety." In an edited book on writers with depression (Casey, 2001), various authors talked about their depression in similarly evocative words. Casey described it as "a hidden shadowy terror of devouring misery," and Alvarez called it "a closed concentrated world, airless and without exits."

The formal diagnosis of major depression in the *Diagnostic and Statistical Manual of Mental Disorders, Fourth Edition, Text Revision* (*DSM-IV-TR*; American Psychiatric Association, 2000, p. 356) requires that a person experience five or more of the following symptoms during the same two-week period:

(1) Depressed mood most of the day, nearly every day, as indicated by subjective report (e.g., feels empty or sad) or by observation by others (appears tearful).
(2) Markedly diminished interest or pleasure in all, or almost all activities nearly every day (as indicated either by subjective account or observation made by others).

(3) Significant weight loss when not dieting, or weight gain...or decrease or increase in appetite nearly every day.

(4) Insomnia or hypersomnia nearly every day.

(5) Psychomotor agitation or retardation nearly every day (observable by other, not merely subjective feelings of gentleness or being slowed down).

(6) Fatigue or loss of energy every day.

(7) Feelings of worthlessness or excessive or inappropriate guilt.

(8) Diminished ability to think or concentrate, or indecisiveness (either by subjective account or as observed by others).

(9) Recurrent thoughts of death...recurrent suicidal ideation without a specific plan, or a specific plan for committing suicide.

The milder version of depression is called *dysthymia*—depression that does not incapacitate to the degree that major depression does, yet interferes with the normal pleasures and motivations in life. Major depression is unipolar, as is dysthymia. It should be carefully distinguished from bipolar disorder, type II, which can look like depression because the client is more often depressed than not, but includes episodes of hypomanic behavior. It is important to ask questions of your clients about episodes of hypomanic behavior to distinguish this from major depression or dysthymia since the treatment is somewhat different.

Depression has been called the "common cold" of mental illness because it is so frequently experienced by both men and women. *DSM-IV-TR* statistics (American Psychiatric Association, 2000) say that lifetime risk for major depression in men is 5–12% of the male population, and lifetime risk for women is 10–25% of the female population (p. 372). In contrast, the lifetime risk for bipolar-type I illness is equal for men and women—roughly 0.4% to 1.6% (p. 385). For schizophrenia, the lifetime incidence is 0.5% to 1.5% (p. 308), a figure that is slightly higher for men than women.

As clinicians, we rely on accurately diagnosing our clients through a combination of self-report from our clients, observation of their behavior (such as tearfulness), reports from others (such as primary care physicians and spouses), and relevant tests such as the Beck Depression Inventory (Beck et al., 1996). Most clinicians make diagnoses primarily based on self-report of clients and our own observations of their behavior since we do not typically have easy access to others who could observe our client's behavior.

Depression in men is often hard for a clinician to assess because men may be reluctant to show emotions and behaviors associated with depression that go against male norms of strength, independence, and being in control of their emotions. Although depression is typically viewed as more of a women's disease, some researchers believe that depression in men actually is underreported because depressed men may not act like the traditional model as presented in the *DSM-IV-TR* (American Psychiatric Association, 2000). In 2005, men committed suicide at four times the rate as women (suicide.org, 2005), and over twice as many men as women met the criteria for alcohol dependence in 2005 (National Survey on Drug Use and Health, 2007). These statistics suggest that depression may be more endemic in men than we realize, that it may be more severe when it appears, and that men may be self-medicating their depression rather than actively seeking help from a therapist.

Cochran and Rabinowitz, in their book *Men and Depression: Clinical and Empirical Perspectives* (2000), suggest that "since many depressed men may be missed in a quick or superficial questioning about their symptoms, a clinician must also carefully probe not only for the typical symptoms of depression but for other related symptoms and conditions" (p. 98). They say that these should include exploring the man's history for evidence of loss, trauma, and grief, as well as the gender-specific ways in which men may express depression, such as substance abuse, anger, interpersonal conflict, and self-destructive behaviors. Pollack (1998) indicates that the expression of depression in men might be different enough from that of women to warrant a new diagnosis. He calls this "depressive disorder—male type" and listed the following symptoms:

- Gets angry often
- Denies there is a problem
- Is irritable frequently
- Is physically aggressive toward others
- Works all the time
- Uses substances a lot
- Withdraws from others
- Acts out sexually
- Takes unnecessary risks
- Reports a number of physical ailments

One can see that these symptoms are more consistant with male norms and may also not be viewed in our culture as symptoms typical of depression. If men's gender role norms skew the way in which male clients experience and express depression, then clinicians will need to be on the lookout for symptoms of depression that might be more reflective of traditional male norms. In addition, if men are not open about their distress, then clinicians might misdiagnose them and therefore be less effective in treating them.

Impact of Male Norms on Depression

Cochran and Rabinowitz (2000) suggest that the origins of depression in men might differ from women, including normative loss across the life span, unresolved trauma, and unexpressed grief. Gender role norms for men in our culture may actually increase depression in men, particularly the following three norms:

1. **Restricted emotionality:** This norm identifies expressions of sadness, grief, or difficulty coping with one's life as unmanly or weak, which can cause men to be reluctant to express those feelings to others (or even themselves). These men are considered weak or effeminate and are often punished for not keeping their cool. That a man can be eliminated from a presidential race for showing his emotions is an example of how ingrained this attitude is. If men cannot grieve openly, then their grief cannot be worked through with the help of others. I have run an exercise in my gender empathy workshops called "Stiff Upper Lip." In this exercise, women pair off with each other and have to talk about something sad but with the instruction that they have to make light of it, not show any feelings, and resist all offers of sympathy or help. Women invariably say how difficult this exercise is for them. Many say they cannot (or will not) do it; others do it and talk about how empty they feel inside. This is the experience for too many men in our culture—a deadening of emotions that is the very definition of depression (literally to push under).

2. **Self-reliance:** One of the primary cures for depression is tapping into repressed feelings of sadness and grief in the presence of another person on whom one relies for emotional assistance. This approach is at odds with male norms of emotional restriction and self-reliance. The male norm glorifying self-reliance makes many men feel that they cannot talk to anyone about their feelings, that they have to bear everything by themselves. This can lead to loneliness and isolation, which are contributors to depression. How many men have confidants (beyond their partners) with whom they can open up and share their distress? In addition, self-reliance means that men are expected to be able to do things by themselves. If they cannot or do not want to, they may view themselves as weak, which can also lead to depression.

3. **Achievement:** This male gender role norm is reflected in the U.S. Army slogan, "Be all that you can be." Many boys start with aspirations of being a sports star, and most are told "you could even grow up to be president." Almost all men have to adjust to the fact that they will never achieve those goals. Even the few who do achieve them have to adjust to being unable to sustain that performance. No one can be at their best all of the time. Since virtually all men are "set up for failure," it is remarkable that many more men are not depressed (or maybe they are, and we do not know about it). Depressed men are also less likely to achieve, thereby making them likely to get more depressed, forming a vicious circle.

THERAPY WITH DEPRESSED MEN: A MULTIMODALITY APPROACH

Getting Started

Many of us have been trained to think of therapy with a certain set structure. It has a clear beginning, weekly sessions that rely primarily on a flow of talk and emotional expression, and a prepared ending that takes place over weeks (or sometimes months). In some ways, we could view therapy as a long and uninterrupted journey, with ourselves as the conductor and our clients as passengers. We set the schedule (50-minute sessions), the location (our offices), the fare (our fees), the itinerary (what happens in therapy), and the destination (removal of presenting problems). The client's job is to show up on time, hop on board, pay, and trust that we can get them to their destination safe and sound in the fastest way possible. This model seems to work reasonably well with depressed women but not so well with depressed men. They either do not show up, show up but jump off somewhere down the line, have a different itinerary than ours, or arrive at our destination but discover it is not theirs.

In the following section, I present a variety of ways of working with depressed men, based on both the literature on this subject and my own experience. If we can meet our male clients where they are and work with them in ways they can utilize and still feel manly, we can help them get to their destination without losing them on the way.

For many men, the idea of making an appointment to see any kind of therapist runs counter to norms of independence, taking care of one's problems by oneself, stoicism in the face of emotional difficulties, and being strong. This is particularly true for depressed men, who already may feel weak. Therapy to them may seem like an unpleasant experience for losers, so why would they want to do it? Many men come to therapy not through their own volition, but through doctors who see a need for it, spouses or bosses who are worried about them, or a court system that has mandated counseling. Therefore, we should reach out to other professionals (such as judges, lawyers, doctors, mediators, life coaches, employee assistance programs, etc.) to offer our services. This helps men suffering from depression find appropriate therapy and also help us establish connections with others in related fields. Once we begin therapy with depressed men, it is important to continue to consult with other health care professionals (including psychiatrists and primary care physicians) so that we know that our client's depression is not something that has a medical cause that can be treated (such as thyroid dysfunction) or could be alleviated by antidepressant medication. Depressed men often somatize their symptoms, so working closely with their doctors can benefit everyone.

We should offer our services in a package that looks more consistent with male values. For example, I advertise myself on health insurance

Web sites as a psychologist with a cognitive-behavioral approach and a specialty in relationships and gender issues. My business card states that, in addition to individual counseling, I run workshops and provide training on gender relations. Potential male clients see that I am an educator as well as a therapist, am likely to be action oriented, and have a specific plan of attack. My expertise in relationships suggests I can help them learn how to improve their relationships with their partners or spouses, often a primary concern. This can be a practical way of encouraging men to explore therapy in order to work through their issues without requiring them to acknowledge depression up front.

When a man shows up in your office for the first session, think about greeting him with a firm handshake and making some small talk before you start therapy. For many men, entering a therapist's office is like entering a foreign country where they do not speak the language. Help a new male client feel more at home by being friendly and down to earth. Tell him a bit about how the hour will be structured so he knows what to expect. Before the hour is up, make sure that you appreciate him openly for showing up. Depressed men probably already feel like failures, so it is particularly important that you validate the positive aspects of being a client. For those whose spouses referred them, acknowledge that they are showing that they care for their partners by taking the time to come in. If they indicate they are depressed, consider giving them some kind of assessment for depression such as the Beck Depressive Inventory and explain that tests like this can be helpful in figuring out the right plan. It also helps me do a quick assessment of the degree of depression as well as possible indications of suicidality.

Finally, finish your session by offering the two things that depressed male clients probably have need for: hope and control. You can give him control by asking what he would like to do in therapy and what he thinks of the session so far. You give him hope by saying that you can help him, that what he is experiencing is not uncommon, and that successful change is possible. Remember that hope springs not from pathology or the negative but a look into a better future.

Multimodality Therapies

Just as there are many roads to Rome, so there are many ways of helping men. Brooks (2010) suggests that a cognitive-behavioral approach might be the best fit for a variety of reasons, but that other approaches (such as psychodynamic therapy) can work well as long as they take into account the different ways in which men might approach and utilize therapy. I have outlined next some of the approaches and techniques that clinicians have found useful in working with depressed men. This is certainly not a comprehensive list but will give you some ideas about how to shape your own therapy style to work most effectively with depressed male clients. I have found that for me mixing and matching styles has worked best because it gives me a larger therapy tool box from which to work.

Client-Centered/Feminist Therapy

Rogerian therapy incorporates the principles of congruence, unconditional positive regard, and client-centered therapy. These work well with men in general since they give men more control and respect in the therapy process. Feminist therapy looks specifically at the social construction of a client's problem. It asks the following: How do the client's race, gender, and ethnicity have an impact on how others see the client as well as how the client sees himself or herself? Understanding the social construction of a man's depression and how it might be related to unhealthy male norms can help him understand that he may be part of a larger system that creates problems for other men as well. This reshapes the therapeutic frame as less pathologically focused and more educative. Feminist therapy also values therapist self-disclosure as a way to create a more egalitarian relationship between therapist and client. Being treated as an equal can help a depressed man feel less alone and more normal.

Strength-Based, Solution-Focused Therapy

A positive, strength-based psychology approach has become popular in the new millenium, with leading practitioners such as Seligman (2002) encouraging clinicians to be more positively focused in their work with clients. This approach is particular useful with male clients, who suffer from the double curse of not only being depressed but also feeling like a failure as a man because of that depression. A strength-based approach (Smith, 2006) includes the following tasks: (a) creating the therapeutic alliance; (b) identifying strengths; (c) assessing presenting problems; (d) encouraging and instilling hope; (e) framing solutions; (f) building strength and competence; (g) empowering; (h) changing/reframing; (i) building resilience; and (j) evaluating and terminating. Of these ten tasks, only one is specifically focused on problems. Interventions on your part could include reframing therapy as a game for winners and the client as heroic, acknowledging the strengths the man carries in with him, looking at goals as solutions, and giving him power through having some control over the therapy process. As therapy progresses, you can work on helping the man focus on the positive in the man's life, such as writing in a gratitude journal or developing a resource list for himself. I have found the book *1001 Solution-Focused Questions* (Bannik, 2006) a good source of ideas for questions that point the client in a positive and practical direction.

Gender-Aware Therapy

Gender-aware therapy focuses on how gender norms have played a part in the problem with which the client is dealing. In *Bridging Separate Gender Worlds* (Philpot, Brooks, Lusterman, & Nutt, 1997), the value of a doing a gender role inquiry is stressed. When taking a history of a depressed man, you might ask him about what messages he got about what it means to ask for help. You might also do some psychoeducational work with him about what male norms are and how they might contribute to depression, referring him to books on depressed men such as *The Pain Behind the Mask* (Lynch & Kilmartin, 1999) and *I Don't Want to Talk About It* (Real, 1997).

Psychodynamic Therapy

A psychodynamic approach explores how a client's personal history may have had an impact on his current depression, including triggers in today's environment that are related to old wounds. It also emphasizes the value of catharsis, the letting out of grief, anger, and sadness that can often lie at the root of depression. Freud discussed the importance of moving from melancholia (depression) to mourning (open expression of grief) many years ago. Most clinicians use some psychodynamic principles in their work with clients: Working with depressed men is no different. Understanding how the triggers for current depression may be related to unprocessed early memories and experiences, and allowing the man to express his feelings about these experiences in a safe and caring environment can have a profound positive impact on the client.

Cognitive-Behavioral Therapy

Cognitive-behavioral therapy (CBT) focuses more on the here and now, with less emphasis on exploration of feelings and more emphasis on teaching techniques that a client can use, both in therapy sessions and outside in his own life, to challenge his negative thinking and create new behavior patterns. Depressed men may feel stuck, mired down, or overwhelmed in their lives, so a solution-oriented, educational venture with clear goals may help confront some of those feelings in a practical way. In the first few sessions, clinicians typically take a brief history and develop a treatment plan. The treatment plan should have clear strategic goals (such as "write a new résumé" instead of "be more proactive"), an overall strategy for reaching those goals (i.e., weekly therapy, homework assignments), and an idea of when treatment would no longer be necessary. The plan should be collaborative and able to be modified. Concrete goals are useful for men, as well as knowing that there is an exit strategy for them. Dependency on anyone can be scary but especially for a depressed man who may have suffered interpersonal loss or not had much support in his life. In concert with the treatment plan, homework is typically assigned at the end of each session. It can be reading a book, watching a movie, taking a walk, or writing about his experiences, but is typically something that is tangible and doable by the next session. Cognitive therapists work primarily with client's cognitions, creating action plans and assigning homework such as mood logs or psychoeducational reading. Homework can include video therapy (suggesting films that illustrate points brought up in therapy) and bibliotherapy (recommending relevant books such as *I Don't Want to Talk About It: Overcoming the Secret Legacy of Male Depression* by Terrance Real, 1997). It can also include using a workbook such as *Overcoming Depression One Step at a Time* (Addis & Martell, 2004) that can be used at home as well as in a session. Clinicians help clients question irrational negative beliefs, using techniques such as cognitive reframing to help them see how they might be engaging in catastrophizing or "black-or-white" thinking. Pennebaker (1997) and Wong (2009) found that writing is a useful technique for men who need to proceed more slowly and privately in unveiling their painful feelings to themselves and to others.

Experiential and Expressive Therapy

Using experiential and expressive methods can be helpful for men who are not comfortable talking about feelings. Weiner, in his book *Beyond Talk Therapy* (1999), discusses different techniques, including expressive techniques in art, music, and psychodrama. EMDR (Shapiro, 2001) is useful for working with depressed male clients with a trauma history. Rabinowitz (2009) calls his work with depressed men "thawing frozen men" and reaches out to depressed men through Gestalt methods, such as the empty chair technique, locating feelings in the body, and using nonverbal means to express feelings. E. Golden (personal e-mail communication, 2010) also helps men access feelings through their body rather than through words and says:

> Words are where women tend to excel and sometimes men also but many men are much more apt to make an initial connection to their emotions through their bodies. I would suggest you try asking a man where in his body he feels his depression. I have asked this one over and over and the results are always good. The man pauses, gives me an incredulous look, and proceeds to point to the exact spot where he feels it. Once he has identified the spot it is a simple clinical exercise. Here's an example: I asked a man where in his body he felt his pain. He immediately pointed to his gut. I asked him what his gut felt like. He said "A black hole." We spent the session talking about that black hole and what it felt like to carry it, who knew about it, when it would arise, what made it disappear or reappear, etc. This conversation had a very easy flow. If I had asked that same man what he was feeling I am sure he would have looked at me and stumbled. Connecting into the body makes our job much easier. It

makes an initial connection that can then be used verbally. I think of it like a translator.

A Word About Words

Levant and Pollack (1995) write about the tendency of men to have difficulty putting their feelings into words (*alexythymia*). Men do not tend to say outright that they are depressed. Rather, a common phrase that depressed men might use is the generic phrase, "I'm not feeling right." Some other words they might use include down in the dumps, upset, bummed out, flat, stressed, burned out, dragging, not hitting on all cylinders, low energy, depleted, out of sorts, got the blues, and feeling crappy. Notice that many of these words refer to a physical sense of fatigue, often a lead indicator of depression in men. It is important to understand the words that depressed men might use to describe how they feel since they will not typically come out and say, "I'm depressed." I had a depressed male client once who refused to identify himself as depressed although he clearly was. We settled on the word *discouraged* instead because he felt it was a word with more personal agency than depressed, which felt to him like he was being pushed under (de-pressed) and had no power.

Couples and Group Therapy

For depressed men who have partners, it can be useful to invite the partner to a session as a consultant to you in working with your client. You can use that session to gain feedback about your client as well as help the partner learn how to better deal with the man's depression. Wexler, in his book *Is He Depressed or What?* (2006), makes a number of practical suggestions for partners of depressed men. For your female clients who have depressed partners, helping the women learn more about male-type depression can benefit both parties. Bringing in the depressed partner for one session can be helpful in getting his view on things, as well as allowing him to see what therapy looks like in action. Referring an individual client to a men's group can be an excellent addition to your individual work with a man. Andronico, in his book *Men in Groups* (1996), indicates that men's groups can give men support and bonding with other men that might provide protection for them from self-destructive behavior and alienation. For depressed men, support and connection with others is particularly important, as well as finding practical ways to deal with their depression.

Moving the Body

Yoga is coming into wider acceptance in therapy circles, because it is sometimes considered a stress management technique. Yoga classes can be helpful for a depressed male client, although yoga may seem a bit foreign to him. Exercise in general, especially walking, running, and riding a bike, is useful for depressed men because these activities are familiar to most men, nonverbal, in line with traditional masculine behavior, and readily available.

CASE STUDIES OF DEPRESSED MEN

Given how male norms inhibit men from understanding and treating their depression, it is likely that you have a depressed male somewhere in your personal life who has not gotten treated for it. As you read through these cases, see if you recognize anyone in them, not just your clients but perhaps your partners, fathers, sons, or colleagues. This chapter therefore may be of use to you not only as a clinician but also as a concerned partner, daughter, friend, or mother.

Tom—Dealing With Failure and Shame

Tom was referred to me by a psychodynamic therapist who found that psychodynamic therapy did not seem to be helping Tom's chronic depression. During our first session, I said to him, "Thanks for coming in; it must take some courage to get here—it also shows that you care enough about yourself and your family to try to get some help." This was a positive reframe on why he was there and part of the strengths-based approach that I think is particularly appealing to depressed men. I described how the hour would go and what to expect, then asked him some open-ended questions. This allowed him to understand more about what would happen in therapy with me, and that knowledge gave him some sense of control. Using a solution-focused approach, I also worked together with him to set his goals in therapy by using the miracle question ("If you woke up tomorrow and your life was just the way you wanted, what would be different?") and framing his goals in the positive. I asked him for his feedback on how the session had gone, which made it clear I was willing to work with him in a collegial fashion.

Tom was struggling with being laid off from his job as a computer programmer, a new baby boy in his family, and old issues of inferiority and feeling like a fraud that had plagued him for many years. He brought in with him a great deal of shame about his perceived failure as a "man," which contributed to his depression (and vice versa—shame fuels depression, and depression fuels shame). As I took a history on Tom, it became clear that a large part of Tom's depression came from never being able to please a critical and depressed mother. We explored that over many sessions, using a psychodynamic approach. As I listened and supported him, I gave him a chance to see older women as potentially nurturing figures. I also gave him space to be sad without judgment. In addition, we discussed what had not worked in the previous therapy (he said his therapist just sat and listened, and he did not feel he was getting anywhere). I said I would like to work with him in an active way; I would assign "homework" and work out specific treatment goals with him that we would create together. For a man who had suffered from feeling impotent in the world (as I believe many men do in one way or the other), this was a step in the direction of self-mastery.

Tom had scored very high on the Beck Depression Inventory that I gave in our initial session. I thereafter referred him to a psychiatrist for a medical evaluation. I had done a risk assessment at that time and felt the risk of harm to self or others to be very low and that he could benefit from medication. The psychiatrist prescribed Prozac, which Tom was reluctant to take saying "only really sick people take it." I made a self-disclosure that enabled him to reassess that opinion and get the medical help he needed. This is particularly true when the therapist is a woman, and the man is depressed because he already feels bad about himself and "less than." I am generally cautious about when and why I self-disclose, but if it is in the best interests of the client and I am comfortable with what I disclose, I will do it.

We dug into the origins of his depression and discussed what he could do in the here and now to make things better for him. I continued to express appreciation for what he was doing to help himself. I explored the gendered part of his depression (not feeling like a man) and gave him some reading about male gender role norms. I used a variety of stress management techniques to help Tom work through his depression, including meditation, muscle relaxation, and assertiveness training, using *The Relaxation and Stress Reduction Workbook* (David, Eshelman, & McKay, 2000). When he got stuck in his negative ruminations, I did some EMDR with him to help him get to the root of his memories, feelings, and cognitions associated with specific childhood experiences that had led to his continuing negative assessments in adulthood. I recommended that he get a copy of a workbook on depression (Addis & Martell, 2004) and that he join a yoga class (which he did and enjoyed a great deal). I also suggested he start walking regularly when the weather permitted.

I used self-disclosure with Tom on a number of occasions. One time, he was talking about himself, but in a detached way. I said something to the effect of, "I want to understand what's going on for you, but you're losing me." Because I knew about men's difficulty accessing their emotions, I was able to be honest with him. This helped him break through some of his defensive strategies that kept him apart from others and contributed to his depression. He said that my willingness to share my feelings with him made a difference for him because at least he knew I cared enough to connect with him.

Using humor with Tom helped alleviate the more painful parts of therapy for him. Humor was a bonding experience between us, as well as a chance for him to practice his "observing ego." This bonding is especially important for depressed men, for whom therapy can seem difficult and even unmanly. Starting and ending with some chitchat about areas of interest to him, such as our football teams, has also been helpful. The casual talk can serve as a comfortable transition between the real world and the therapy office and make therapy seem a little less threatening.

A few years ago, Tom said he did not think he needed regular therapy anymore but wanted to keep me as backup just in case he needed to come back. We did not do a standard termination since he made it clear he wanted the door left open. This past fall, he called to say he was struggling to get a project done at work and asked if we could meet occasionally to help him get going on his work. He has been coming in every few weeks, and I do more coaching with him than traditional talk therapy. I help him set goals, create action plans, give him feedback about his work, set timetables and look at 5-year plans for his work life. I know that, unlike his critical mother, I am a supportive female figure in his life who can help him with his current goals as well as past hurts. He also knows that he can set the pace for therapy, which helps counteract the dependence and lack of control he felt when he was a child. Like many of my male clients, he never quite "finishes" therapy but leaves treatment when he feels that he has done enough work and reenters when he needs some more help. This is valuable to a depressed male because he, in particular, needs to have a sense of efficacy, control, and growth in his personal life.

George—Intimacy Is Scary

George was a young man who was going through a difficult divorce and estrangement from his young children. He arrived at our appointment looking alternately frightened and hostile. Since I was a new clinician at a mental health clinic, I had been assigned the worst treatment room, a tiny space with no windows and a door that did not stay shut unless it was locked. I welcomed George in, locked the door, and sat down in the chair between him and the door, our knees almost touching. I started off by saying, "From your intake form, it looks like you are having a hard time right now in your marriage. Can you talk a little about it?" He looked around and said little. I tried again to establish some connection between us and said, "Well, if we are going to work together, it would be good to get to know each other a little," to which George replied "Why would I want to get to know you?" I took some notes along the way. At the end of the session, he said "What are you writing about me? Let me see your notes!" George left without paying for the session and never came for a second one.

Looking back, I do not blame him. I knew that he had a failing marriage and should have expected him to have some strong feelings about women at that point, such as anger, hurt, suspicion, and depression. His anger was what I noticed at first and what threw me during the session. My first job should have been to make him comfortable and to accept his hostility with curiosity, not resistance. I should have tried to see what he wanted from the session. For a female therapist, seeing a man who might have issues with intimacy in a small locked room probably was not a good idea. My experience with George and other male clients after that taught me that working with men was going to present different challenges for me than working with women. Given the average man's discomfort with the format of "talk therapy," I would have to create an atmosphere of comfort and safety on their terms, not mine. For most women, emotional expression and intimate connection are part and parcel of what it means to be female. But for male clients, trained to have a stiff upper lip and appear self-sufficient, the traditional model of therapy runs counter to much of what they have been taught about being a man.

John—Looking Good But Feeling Bad

I have been seeing Nancy, a woman in her mid-30s, for a year to help her work on her perfectionism and her insecurity about herself. She also said she was frustrated with her husband, John, whom she said was neither emotionally expressive nor interested in being sexual with her. On her urging, John had sought help. The counselor John saw said that he was fine overall and did not really need help. I suggested Nancy ask John to come in for a joint session with us. John agreed and came to our next session. He was an attractive, well-dressed man who appeared poised, answering my questions in a clear and articulate fashion. I asked if he thought he was depressed: "No," he said, "but I really don't know how I feel about much of anything." When I asked him to describe what that meant, Tom said that he had not felt passionate about his life for years, and that he did not really enjoy sex because it seemed like too much of an effort. I said, "It must be hard being a man who looks so good on the outside but feels shut down on the inside. I bet it's hard for others to understand your distress since men are supposed to be tough and not need help." John's eyes filled with tears, and he said, "Everyone thinks I'm fine because I can talk a good talk, but I know I'm not—do you think you can help me?" We discussed how he might be able to get the help he needed, including being more open with his own therapist about his depression. He did so, and his therapist was finally able to understand the degree to which John was depressed. Within the next few weeks, he got a referral for antidepressant medication and started exploring the real issues underlying his detachment. I also referred him to a weekend retreat that focused on cathartic emotional work. Six months later, Nancy reported that he was more sexual with her, enjoying a new class he was taking, and had that spark back that she remembered him having years ago.

WHEN DEPRESSION REACHES A CRISIS POINT

For clinicians, knowing when depression can be potentially lethal to our clients is a crucial skill. Most of us have been trained to do a risk assessment if we are concerned about our client's welfare and to be aware of the difference between suicidal ideation (with or without a plan) and suicidal intent (i.e., having a feasible plan). We know how to contract for safety and to hospitalize our clients when we think they are not safe. However, it may be harder for us to assess this risk in men because they may not present suicidality in the ways to which we are accustomed and may not show their distress or the degree to which they are decompensating. In addition, recent statistics (suicide.org, 2005) indicate that although women attempt suicide at three times the rate of men, actual suicide rates are four times higher for men than women (17.7 per 100,000 for men vs. 4.5 per 100,000 for women), due in part to more lethal means of killing oneself such as hanging, shooting, or jumping.

It would be good practice, therefore, to go through Pollack's checklist of "Depressive Disorder: Male Type" (Pollack. 1998) in working with men about whom you are concerned to make sure you do not miss symptoms that might indicate depression in men, such as social withdrawal, anger and irritability, and physical ailments, or circumstances such as recent loss or failure that might trigger feelings of shame or despair. If your male client expresses extreme states of anxiety, anger, or psychotic thinking and says he is feeling overwhelmed or has had recent loss, he may be feeling suicidal but not articulating his depression the same way a female might.

Recently, I learned of the suicides of two men. The men presented with extreme anxiety and mild paranoid ideation but did not express suicidal intent or say they were depressed. One had just seen a new clinician after being released from a mental hospital with new medication and no clear treatment plan (other than an intake scheduled for a therapy research study). The other man had been seen by a medical doctor for his extreme anxiety and was given several phone numbers of local therapists for him to contact. Both men had suffered recent loss and were in transition in the health care system. Sadly, they jumped in front of high-speed trains shortly after their last medical visits.

If you are in doubt about the degree of depression in a male client or his ability to withstand his anxiety and mental confusion, you do well to err on the side of caution. Ask him directly about the degree to which his anxiety, shame, or paranoia might make him feel suicidal and if so, if he has a plan. Work closely with his other providers and communicate your concern to his family or friends if you are alarmed about his safety. Increase the number of sessions you have with him and have between-session check-ins. Finally, do not be afraid to hospitalize him if necessary. Remember that women threaten and attempt suicide more often than men, but men are less likely to disclose how depressed they feel and more likely to successfully carry out a suicide plan.

CONCLUSION

Female clinicians can play a really important and positive role with depressed male clients. The therapy relationship can be a laboratory in which our clients can participate in a healthy relationship between a man and a woman. Men may be more comfortable sharing distress with a woman (who is seen as nurturing) versus a man (who may be seen as threatening). If depression is caused in part by lack of intimacy, we can provide a safe environment where men can open up to us and show sadness without being afraid of being seen as weak. We can provide hope in the face of hopelessness and offer techniques that give them a sense of efficacy in the world. We need to learn more about how depression is experienced and expressed by men, particularly how that expression may differ from traditional symptoms outlined in the *DSM-IV-TR* (American Psychiatric Association, 2000). We owe it to our male clients to be better educated about the psychology of men. We should consider different ways of working with them that might stretch our professional expertise, yet be more digestible to men. Done right, this is truly a win-win situation. Not only does our increased knowledge about men help our depressed male clients learn how to handle their depression more effectively, but also it can help us grow professionally and personally.

REFERENCES

Addis, M. E., & Martell, C. (2004). *Overcoming depression one step at a time: The new behavioral activation approach to getting your life back.* Oakland, CA: New Harbinger Publications.

American Psychiatric Association. (2000). *Diagnostic and statistical manual of mental disorders* (4th ed.). Washington, DC: Author.

Andronico, M. P. (1996). *Men in groups: Insights, interventions, psychoeducational work.* Washington, DC: American Psychological Association.

Bannik, F. (2006). *1001 solution-focused questions: Handbook for solution-focused interviewing.* New York, NY: Norton.

Beck, A. T., Steer, A. M., & Brown, G. K. (1996). *Beck Depression Inventory.* San Antonio, TX: Pearson Education.

Boston Women's Health Book Collective. (1973). *Our bodies, ourselves.* Boston: Touchstone.

Brooks, G. (2010). *Beyond the crisis of masculinity: A transtheoretical model for male-friendly therapy.* Washington, DC: APA.

Casey, N. (Ed.). (2001). *Unholy ghost: Writers on depression.* New York, NY: Perennial.

Cochran, S. V., & Rabinowitz, F. R. (2000). *Men and depression: Clinical and empirical perspectives.* San Diego, CA: Academic Press.

David, D., & Brannon, R. (Eds.). (1976). *The forty-nine percent majority: The male sex role.* Reading, MA: Addison-Wesley.

David, D., Eshelman, E., & McKay, M. (2000). *The relaxation and stress reduction workbook* (5th ed.). Oakland, CA: New Harbinger.

Goldberg, H. (1977). *The hazards of being male.* New York, NY: Signet.

Levant, R. F., & Pollack, W. (Eds.). (1995). *A new psychology of men.* New York, NY: Basic Books.

Lynch, J., & Kilmartin, C. (1999). *The pain behind the mask: Overcoming masculine depression.* New York, NY: Haworth Press.

Morgan, R. (1970). *Sisterhood is powerful: An anthology of writings from the women's liberation movement.* New York, NY: Vintage Books.

National Survey on Drug Use and Health. (2007). *Gender differences in alcohol use and alcohol dependence: 2004 and 2005.* Retrieved from http://oas. camhas.gov/2k/AlcGender.htm

Pennebaker, J. (1997). *Opening up: The healing power of expressing emotions.* New York, NY: Guilford Press.

Philpot, C., Brooks, G., Lusterman, D., & Nutt, R. (1997). *Bridging separate gender worlds.* Washington, DC: American Psychological Association.

Pollack, W. (1998). Mourning, melancolia, and masculinity: Recognizing and treating depression in men. In W. S. Pollack and R. F. Levant (Eds.). *A new psychotherapy for men* (pp. 147–166). New York, NY: Wiley.

Rabinowitz, F. E. (2009). Thawing the ice man: Coping with grief and loss. In M. Englar-Carlson & M. Stevens (Eds.), *In the room with men: A casebook of therapeutic change* (pp. 109–128). Washington, DC: American Psychological Association.

Rabinowitz, F. E., & Cochran, S. V. (2002*). Deepening psychotherapy with men.* Washington, DC: APA.

Real, T. (1997). *I don't want to talk about it: Overcoming the secret legacy of male depression.* New York, NY: Scribner.

Seligman, M. E. (2002). Authentic *happiness.* New York, NY: Free Press.

Shapiro, F. (2001). *Eye movement desensitization and reprocessing (EMDR): Basic principles, protocols, and procedures* (2nd ed.). New York, NY: Guilford Press.

Smith. E. J. (2006). The strength-based counseling model. *The Counseling Psychologist, 34*(1), 13–79.

Styron, W. (1990). *Darkness visible.* New York, NY: Random Books.

Suicide.org (2005). *Suicide statistics.* Retrieved from http://www.suicide.org

Sweet, H. (1995). *Perceptions of undergraduate experiences in heterosexual romantic relationships: A sex role norms analysis.* Unpublished doctoral dissertation. Boston College, Chestnut Hill, MA.

Weiner, D. (Ed.). (1999). *Beyond talk therapy: Using movement and expressive techniques in clinical practice.* Washington, DC: American Psychological Association.

Wexler, D. B. (2006). *Is he depressed or what: What to do when the man you love is irritable, moody, and withdrawn.* Oakland, CA: New Harbinger.

Wexler, D. B. (2009). *Men in therapy: New approaches for effective treatment.* New York, NY: Norton.

Wong, Y. J., & Rochlen, A. B. (2009). The potential benefits of expressive writing for male college students with varying degrees of restrictive emotionality. *Psychology of Men and Masculinity, 10,* 149–159.

RECOMMENDED READING

Erickson, B. (1993). *Helping men change: The role of the female therapist.* Newbury Park, CA: Sage.

Englar-Carlson, M., & Stevens, M. (Eds.). (2006). *In the room with men: A casebook of therapeutic change.* Washington, DC: APA.

Sweet, H. (2006). Finding the person behind the persona. In M. Englar-Carlson & M. Stevens (Eds.), *In the room with men: A casebook of therapeutic change* (pp. 69–90). Washington, DC: APA.

Sweet, H. (2010). Women treating men. *Psychotherapy Networker, 54,* 32–35.

10

Strength-Based Psychotherapy With Fathers

DORA CHASE OREN

INTRODUCTION: I'M A BAD DAD

"I was a bad dad," a new client said. His words triggered me, and I could feel the visceral response as my stomach tightened. I asked Dustin to say more about being a bad dad. He explained that he had not been involved with his daughter for the first several years of her life. He seemed embarrassed and ashamed as he recalled the many times that he would go to the sports bar near his house. He did not go there to drink, but to watch whatever game was on, preferring basketball. He expressed feeling guilty that he avoided being home with his wife and new baby. I noted his shame as a feeling that men commonly experience. It would likely be a recurring theme in his therapeutic journey. It was during the initial intake when Dustin described this disconnection from his family. He went on to express a quiet pride that being a bad dad was in his past but did not yet consider himself to be a good father.

Later, when I sat down to conceptualize the case, I wondered about the father piece of his story. How did a pattern of noninvolvement become part of Dustin's role as a father? How, when, where, and from

whom did he learn to be uninvolved? How would he describe his relationship with his own father? Was the lack of involvement primarily
a skill deficit on his part or something more? Did his disconnection
from his family serve to distance Dustin from his wife? How much was
the noninvolvement encouraged by her? More fundamentally, what did
it mean to him to be an involved father, a good dad? I was reminded
of how powerful, yet often unspoken, the messages are about what it
means to be a *father*. Dustin's presenting problem of depressed mood
was not explicitly linked to being a father but did seem related. The
restricted degree of his involvement with his children pointed to the
relevance of exploring experiences of nurturing and being nurtured,
intimacy, and family-of-origin relationships in our work together.

I also wondered how Dustin's choice to work with me, a female therapist, was linked to his style and patterns of emotionally connecting
with others. A man is likely to have transference with a female therapist based on his experience with significant women in his life, such
as his wife, mother, girlfriends, or female confidante. For many men,
sharing feelings with women can feel safer than sharing with men who
can be seen as less empathic, more intimidating, judging, or rejecting
under a gender-stereotyped view of men. When I asked Dustin why
he had selected a female therapist, he said, "It feels instinctually safer
and much more natural to talk about my private life with a woman. In
general, women have softer hearts and do not have the walls men have.
I don't have to worry about being judged or told what to do."

I have worked with fathers since 1999 both in group and individually.
Currently, my private practice includes young adults, primarily males in
their early 20s, and middle-aged and older men and women for individual psychotherapy. While the numbers fluctuate over time, about half of
my clients are men, and about half of those men are fathers. In this chapter, I highlight some of the literature related to U.S. fathers and their
experiences as well as my own personal and professional background that
led to some of my countertransference issues with fathers. In addition,
I address the usefulness of a strength-based approach to therapy with
fathers from the perspective of a female therapist.

PERSONAL JOURNEY

I was born into a traditional family in a middle-class Los Angeles suburb
in the mid-1960s. My mother and father adhered to more traditional
gender roles, and my mother took care of the children, the laundry, and
the cooking. My father was the financial provider and the handyman
when things needed fixing around the house. My parents had a close,
happy, and loving relationship throughout my childhood and to this day.
I remember a black-and-white photo of them together at their eighth-
grade prom. They are each other's first and only romantic relationship.

My two brothers and I are within four years of each other in age, and none of us, and no one we knew, went to preschool. We spent our early years playing and fighting with each other, my mother nearby, and my father at work. Every day, my father, an aerospace engineer, took the lunch my mom made him and headed to work. He was home every night for dinner, and then the children went to bed early. While we did not spend much time with him during the week, my father never felt far away. His presence was always felt in the house, whether it was my mom talking about him or the counter where we put our toys that needed repairs. I was secure in the knowledge that he would come lightning fast if there were a problem at home. All my mother had to do was call him. While I can recall a few times when an emergency actually happened, I grew up with a sense that my father was available to us.

As the only female child in the family, I played the games my brothers liked and was more comfortable playing with the boys than with the girls at school. Throughout my childhood and adolescence, I gravitated toward more traditional boys, sharing common interests in sports, music, competition, humor, and the underlying, unspoken agreement to avoid feelings. In high school, I was the girl who hung out with the boys, listening to music. I was a tomboy, proud to have once played on the boys' baseball team. I wore jeans and T-shirts and never thought twice about clothes or hair until many years later, when I discovered manicures and the like. As a girl, I remember being confused why I did not want or have the close friendships that other girls seemed to have with each other. As an adolescent, I steered clear of feelings or numbed them like many adolescents do, particularly boys, with risky and at times self-destructive behaviors.

My gender journey could be considered atypical because I embraced stereotyped views of men and women, yet adopted the norms of traditional masculinity. From a simplistic child's perspective, I saw men as powerful and women as weak. I wanted to emulate how I saw a "real man." Strong, tough, independent—the Marlboro man. I think I was particularly influenced by the media in its many forms: TV, books, magazines, movies. I accepted traditional stereotypes of what a real man was; what he did (action oriented, problem solver); how he felt (not very much other than anger); and what he wanted (power, sex, dominance). In my current clinical work, I am attuned to expressions of stereotypes based on my own experience and make time during a session to address the limiting and often-harmful consequences of them, not only for the fathers themselves, but also for their partners and children.

PROFESSIONAL JOURNEY

My journey to become a therapist has taken many turns, both personally and professionally. Ever since I was young, maybe eight years old, I knew that I wanted to be a psychologist. When I made this decision, I was not quite sure exactly what a psychologist was, but I liked the sound of it and the little I knew about it. I was curious why people acted the way they did. I wanted to know what made me and my brothers in some ways so alike but in other ways clearly different, beyond anatomy. The children in my family were expected to go to college, and right after high school I moved out of state for college. I briefly considered majoring in law or advertising, but always came back to psychology. When I learned that one needed a doctorate to be a psychologist, I was happy that pursuing this career meant that I could stay in school for a long time. I was comfortable in school and did not experience the stress that I commonly see in my work with undergraduate and graduate students and in the students I have taught.

In college, I was excited to find out more about psychology, this rather mysterious profession that covered such a broad range of topics. It was not until I took an undergraduate course about feminism in 1984 that I became aware of the concept of gender roles and broader social constructs that largely prescribed what the appropriate and expected behaviors were for men and women. I remember being stunned when I realized that much of what I grew up thinking about men and women, fathers and mothers, boys and girls, was through a restricted lens developed within my traditional family and portrayed by the media. I had naively embraced these rigid stereotypes. It was a hard pill to swallow when I recognized that I had also adopted some sexist perspectives. Through my own therapy and through my relationship with my husband, I began to make sense of my early years by making meaning of my early and strong alliance with boys and my simultaneous rejection of girls and self.

After graduating with a BA in psychology from Michigan State University in 1987, I married my boyfriend from college and moved to New York City. I started a master's program while he worked as a public defender in the Bronx. On a personal level, it had always felt important to me to be independent, yet I had a strong desire to be a mother. Our first child came less than a year after we were married, and our second one arrived two years later. I have a clear memory of holding my baby daughter in her car seat to register for classes. I scheduled school around my husband's work schedule so that one of us would be with our daughter. I took the subway into the city to go to school and then headed home to take care of my family.

After graduating in 1992 with an MA in developmental psychology from Teachers College, Columbia University, we moved to Los Angeles, close to my family and far from his. Years passed, filled with raising kids and experiencing a pleasant, yet distant, marriage. At 28, I was divorced and raising two amazing daughters. It was during this time when I finally got up enough courage to apply to a doctoral program in clinical psychology. My older daughters, now young women, still recount the sheer joy I had when I got the call offering admittance to the program.

Graduate school marked a busy time in my life. I had to compartmentalize school and home as each needed my full attention. I focused and learned as much as I could when I was on campus and then ran home to be with my girls. On days I did not have classes, I worked part time at a criminal defense law firm. As a single mom with an overcommitted schedule, I could not socialize after classes or on weekends as my cohorts did. I went out with friends when my daughters spent the occasional weekend with their father. My ex-husband and I are still close and talk to each other every month or so. Our running joke is that we make much better friends than spouses, and this was probably always true. I spent the years in the PhD program balancing family, school, and work.

I was fortunate to have had very different settings for my practicum and internship clinical placements. Most of the areas I studied, whether in school or clinically, were compelling to me in some way. The list of interests that I have includes development, linguistics, neuropsychology, addiction, traumatic brain injury, the Holocaust, adolescence, men and masculinity, and of course, fathers. My doctoral dissertation on Holocaust education was a far cry from the current interest in men's issues and fatherhood, but reflective of my wide-ranging professional interests. These broader interests have been surprisingly relevant at times in my clinical work. However, the exposure that I had to both inpatient and outpatient populations with a wide range of presenting problems has been foundational to treating clients.

I remarried two weeks after finishing the doctoral program in clinical psychology. Like the first time I had been married, I became pregnant almost immediately, and our son was born before our first wedding anniversary. My fourth and last child came shortly after. When my youngest one was old enough to go to preschool, I began working on the postdoctoral hours I needed to become licensed as a psychologist. I was fortunate to do my postdoctoral studies at a fine community college counseling center that gave me great training while allowing the flexibility I needed in my schedule so I could still be a full-time mom. I worked when my children were in school and picked them up when their days were over.

My current husband is a counseling psychologist with a specialty in men's issues and sports psychology. He has profoundly impacted and broadened my understanding of men and fathers. I remember an early conversation in which he challenged the myopic ideas I had held about men. Watching him interact with our children, family, and friends has continued to dispel my early simplistic views of men and fathers. It was a paradigm shift when I learned that fathers might want to be and could be involved in their children's lives.

I have worked alongside my husband on research and writing, accompanied him to symposia and lectures, and become immersed in the field of men and masculinity. I became interested in fathers and therapy through his involvement with Division 51 (Society for the Psychological Study of Men and Masculinity) of the American Psychological Association (APA).

I was intrigued when I was introduced to this division and its mission and was surprised and curious about research I saw in its APA journal.

In 2006, at the annual APA convention in New Orleans, my husband told me that he was approached by a recognized expert in the field of men and masculinity and asked to consider writing a book on counseling fathers. We weighed our other commitments and responsibilities and our collective areas of expertise and decided that we wanted to do this project together. A couple of years later, *Counseling Fathers* (Oren & Oren, 2009) was published. It is an edited book with theory, research, clinical interventions, and case examples integrated to inform the process of counseling a diverse range of fathers. One outgrowth of our work together on the book was a deepening awareness of my husband's importance both for the family and for him of being an involved father. To that end, we increased our focus on private practice and reduced other work commitments, allowing the flexibility we need so we can both parent and work.

THINKING ABOUT FATHERS: AN OVERVIEW

The majority of adult men in the United States have children in their homes (United States Census Bureau, 2006). As such, over the course of a career a therapist is likely to treat a fair number of male clients who are in the father role. Although attention has begun to focus within the field of childhood development on the role of fathers (Lamb, 2004), there is limited scholarly attention paid to the experiences of fathers and the clinical implications. Therapists often do not receive education or training in working with fathers outside a family context. This is unfortunate because in my work I have found that the exploration of fatherhood experiences often gives rise to core issues and can be a critical element of treatment independent of the presenting problem. Exploring the experiences of being a father can act as a springboard to deepen psychotherapy.

Generally, fathers are seen as important to family life. A father's significance to his growing child's development is widely acknowledged (Blankenhorn, 1995; Lamb, 2004). Children with involved fathers are more confident, are better able to deal with frustration, enjoy increased cognitive competence as seen in higher grade point averages, and are more likely to mature into compassionate adults (Lamb, 2004; U.S. Department of Health and Human Services, 2006). Children with absent fathers have problems in areas such as poor school achievement, early childbearing, difficulty with adjustment, aggression, and risk-taking behavior (Blankenhorn, 1995; Cabrera, Tamis-Lemonda, Bradley, Hofferth, & Lamb, 2000; Pope & Englar-Carlson, 2001). Less recognized is the significant positive impact that being involved can have on a father. Fatherhood and involvement are associated with the following benefits:

- A sense of accomplishment, well-being, and contentment
- Reduction of health risk behaviors, contributing to a longer life, fewer accidents, increased physical activity, and reduced risk of suicide
- Decreased psychological distress as emotional involvement with children acts as a buffer against work-related stress
- Less-frequent jobs changes
- A catalyst for men to reevaluate their priorities and become more caring human beings who are concerned about future generations
- Increased intergenerational, extended family, and other external social interactions
- Over time, increased marital stability

Due to the women's movement, shifts in family structure, and the loosening of gender roles, the responsibilities of today's fathers are not limited to being providers and disciplinarians. Within the last generation or so, the roles for fathers have expanded to include an expectation of involvement with his children, nurturance of both spouse and children, provision of moral and ethical guidelines, and involvement as educator and role model (Barrows, 2004; Coley, 2001; Jain, Belsky, & Crnic, 1996; Marsiglio, Day, & Lamb, 2000). Often at odds with the societal construction of what it means to be a man, the increased demands placed on fathers can leave fathers confused about their own experiences and roles. From the distant and absent provider, to the involved father, and to the more recent coparent (Pleck & Pleck, 1997), fathers may find themselves in blurred and often-contradictory roles with little training on how to manage these responsibilities. In a large Danish study, two thirds of fathers noted that they could not take anything from their own fathers to use when parenting their own children (Madsen, Lind, & Munck, 2002). The significant number of fatherless families in the United States (Blankenhorn, 1995) suggests a growing disconnect between children and their fathers and a shortage of positive fathering role models. Today's fathers may lack the skills and training that could help them fill their roles, and they often do not know where to turn for help.

Pleck (2010) revised his previous definition of father involvement and divided the concept into three primary components, often relevant in working with fathers: (a) positive engagement activities, (b) warmth and responsiveness, and (c) control. There are two auxiliary domains: (d) indirect care and (e) process responsibility. Pleck discussed *positive engagement* as more intensive interactions with the child that are likely to promote development. *Warmth and responsiveness* refer to the ability to respond to children's needs with warmth, such as praising, hugging, and the like. *Control* suggests paternal monitoring and knowledge of child and child whereabouts and the decisions that are related to the monitoring. *Indirect care* refers to activities undertaken for the child without interacting with the child, such as buying things or scheduling appointments. Finally, *process responsibility* refers to taking initiative instead of waiting for someone else, usually the mother, and monitoring what is needed for the children.

DOING CLINICAL WORK WITH FATHERS

I find it useful in my current work to help fathers broaden their ideas about the ways they can be involved with their families by identifying current areas of involvement and avenues for increasing involvement such as suggested by Pleck (2010) and outlined in the preceding section. Educating fathers about the different ways they can be (and often are) involved is an important intervention that increases motivation, sense of purpose, and overall positive fathering. It is also important to keep in mind the changes that fathers have throughout their life stages. I experienced my own father shifting his involvement from mostly control and indirect engagement to broader aspects of Pleck's revised concept with both his children and his grandchildren. It is common for fathers and grandfathers to become more nurturing and involved as they grow older.

As a female psychologist doing therapy with men in general and fathers in particular, I am aware that my personal history can give rise to specific countertransference issues. Common areas that arise for me when I work with a father tend to be in the areas of level of involvement with their families, difficult or distant marriages, authenticity, and attitudes about wife and children. I reflexively interpret problems in these areas as ones that need to be fixed. I remind myself not to become focused on finding solutions, something that is easy to do and welcomed by most men in therapy, but over time does little to increase fathers' understanding of underlying issues that can have a significant impact on their behavior.

Many men (especially men who follow traditional male norms such as being tough and not asking for help) hesitantly seek mental health services (Cusack, Deane, Wilson, & Ciarrochi, 2006; Fagan & Hawkins, 2001; Good, Dell, & Mintz, 1989). It is more acceptable for men to get help from a primary care physician than from a mental health provider (Hudson, Campbell-Grossman, Fleck, Elek, & Shipman, 2003). Having physical ailments does not contradict the male norm that discourages talking about problems as one would do in therapy. When men do seek counseling, it is often for a limited number of reasons: (a) for themselves as a last resort, (b) with their wives for marriage counseling, or (c) with their families for family therapy. In my own work with men, I have yet to have a man start therapy who said that being a father was the reason he sought treatment. What I have found is that including the father piece in individual psychotherapy can markedly deepen the work.

By considering the experiences of a father and his related history, including gender norms, therapists are uniquely positioned to bring a strength-based approach to their work with fathers. Strength-based perspectives are part of the emerging field of positive psychology (Smith, 2006). When I work with fathers from a strength-based approach, I focus first on the discovery and identification of overlooked, undervalued, or hidden positive qualities that are often conceptualized from a deficit perspective. For example, it is common to hear about men as workaholics, but less recognized are the qualities of persistence, dedication, and commitment that can be seen in the men who relentlessly provide for their families (Oren & Oren, 2009). In addition, many men suffer shame about what they have done or have failed to do, the bad dad syndrome, so it is particularly important to help them see the genuine strengths they bring to their families.

Case 1: Individual Work With a Father—Positive Reframing

Vincent, a father of two children in elementary school, came to me for individual therapy after his wife threatened to divorce him "if things didn't change." He described a tense household that he avoided by working late hours. Vincent did not want a divorce, did not understand that there was a real problem in his marriage, and became despondent when he thought about life without his son and daughter. One of his wife's nonnegotiable demands was that he go to therapy. Vincent reported that, "My wife thinks that my childhood has really messed me up." He resented being forced to see a psychologist and expressed a fair amount of skepticism about the usefulness of treatment. During the first session, he commented, "With all due respect, I don't believe in therapy." Instead of engaging in a discussion about the benefits of therapy, I commented on his obvious commitment to his wife and children that he had come to the appointment anyway. In this way, I framed his entry into therapy as behavior that reflected loyalty to his wife, dedication to his family, and courage to come for treatment in which he had little faith.

With early work focused on developing trust and establishing credibility, Vincent's resistance began to recede. He started to look at how he learned to be a husband and father. He recounted a memory from when he was four years old. One late night during a particularly heated fight, Vincent could hear his father kicking the walls and his mother screaming. He lay in bed terrified, and then he heard the front door slam. The next morning, he saw the holes in the wall, but his father was gone. It would be over a decade until Vincent spoke to him again. He grew up embarrassed and ashamed that his father left. Vincent saw his father as a failure and was embarrassed by him. Vincent promised himself that he would never be like his father.

As he grew up, Vincent and his younger brother were often home alone after school while their mother worked two jobs to support the family. When I asked Vincent about who nurtured him and who he nurtured, he talked about his mother. He saw her as sacrificing herself for him and his brother by working so hard. He remembered trying to be nurturing of her. Sometimes when his mother became sad, he tried to make her feel better by holding her shaking hands or patting her back and telling her not to worry, that everything would be okay. A turning point in treatment came when he acknowledged that he had not believed his own words. Vincent went on to realize that he had a deep fear of what would happen to his family with his father gone. It was within this context that Vincent had begun to fantasize about being a superhero who saved his family. He smiled as he remembered the Superman pajamas that he insisted on wearing long after he outgrew them. Vincent had identified with images of powerful and courageous men and wanted to be like them. Vincent believed that a father's most important job was to take care of his family. He frequently reminded himself that he would never be like his father, who had failed. Vincent dreamt of being a strong, silent, and invincible man.

Using a strength-based approach, I encouraged him to consider both the costs and the benefits of the restricted range of options he saw for himself as a father. Some of the costs of his single-minded focus of providing for his family could be seen in his troubled marriage, his chronic sense of agitation, and his dysthymia (a long-term, low-grade depression). The benefits of his approach were less obvious to him and took some work for him to discover. Vincent was surprised to realize that by carrying the weight of the provider role he had consistently displayed a deep sense of loyalty and commitment to family. He began to look more closely at his dreams for his children and wondered about his children's dreams. He also began to wonder about the legacy he would leave as a father. He did not want his children to remember a father who was distant and unavailable to them. He realized that he wanted to be more than just a paycheck.

As the therapy continued, Vincent expanded his ideas about what it meant for him to be a father. He began experimenting with ways that he could be involved with his children. He rearranged his work schedule so that he could take his children to school in the mornings. He reported spending more time at home and experiencing less tension between him and his wife. He tried out behaviors that he never thought possible for him, like crying in front of his family. He was surprised that his wife and children were supportive of him and was taken aback by their displays of concern for him. He began to connect his early nurturing of his mother with his family's current nurturing of him. He saw that his actions as a child toward his mother had been kind and loving. He became more accepting of himself and was able to experience his family as supportive of him. Vincent was surprised at how good he felt about the improved relationships he had with both his children and his wife. A strength-based approach allowed Vincent to capitalize on the qualities that made him an excellent provider, to recognize and integrate his positive qualities, and to reframe his old view of himself as a bad dad to a good father.

Part of working from a strength-based perspective is an attunement to the experience that fathers have. From the most basic level, I try to make my approach as male friendly as possible. For example, when my husband and I designed our offices, we were cognizant of the importance of creating male-friendly spaces for men to feel comfortable. The suite is furnished in warm and earthy colors, and the waiting room has magazines that may appeal to men and fathers. An early comment made by a client who is a father was that he felt relaxed in the office. This client, Manuel, had a fair amount of anxiety about seeking mental health services and worried that if he sought help it would mean that he was, as he put it, crazy. He was relieved when he did not feel intimidated by the office and viewed me as nonjudgmental. His ability to feel comfortable coming to therapy and being in the room laid the groundwork for some difficult self-exploration and several important realizations about his substance abuse.

Case 2: Group Therapy With Fathers—Getting Their Attention

When I was a brand new practicum student, I cofacilitated a parents' group designed to teach basic parenting skills. A typical class had folding chairs lining the room, filled by mothers and fathers court ordered to attend a 10-week parenting education group. One day, the cofacilitator of the group told me that I would be leading the group by myself at the next session. I remember being nervous and excited for this opportunity. The group convened, and the topic for the week was discipline. Previous leaders had relied on reading aloud the chapter of the week, but in my beginner's enthusiasm, I pictured something different.

I invited the group members to share their thoughts about disciplining their children. As the conversation gained momentum, it became clear that many members equated spanking with discipline. I asked the group what their reasons were for spanking. One father, George, explained that he spanked his daughter "to get her attention." Others in the room agreed. Soon after, I startled George by shouting his name. He quickly looked at me, a shocked expression on his face. I asked, "Did I get your attention?" There was silence in the group. Slowly, members began to speak about role models and messages they had received while growing up. We started to link current behaviors to previous experiences and to think of better alternatives to hitting, not only for their children but also for themselves. When George graduated from the class several weeks later, he proudly told the group that he did not spank his daughter anymore. He explained that his parents had often spanked him and his brothers. He thought that was how he was supposed to parent, but he had never felt good about hitting her. He seemed happy to discover that there were other ways that a father could interact with his children. The mothers and fathers in this group expressed a strong desire to be better parents and were eager to learn skills that they could put to use when they got home.

Leading the parenting group triggered a fair amount of countertransference in me in relation to the fathers ordered to take the class. Most were in the group because of abuse or neglect of their sons or daughters. I was aware of my strong desire to protect their children. At times, I felt nauseated and experienced a sense of dread when they recounted the reasons they had to take the class. I realized that part of my response stemmed from my own experiences of loneliness, pain, and confusion as a girl who aligned with the boys. I had tried to ward off these feelings for years. I understood that I wanted to shield the children from their own feelings of pain, confusion, and betrayal. Recognizing this countertransference and my urge to "help the children" was the necessary first step to becoming a less-reactive, more empathic, and more effective therapist.

A number of the topics talked about in the group reflected current areas in the literature and have clinical applications to working with fathers, such as the importance of role models, self-competency, the expanded role of father beyond provider and disciplinarian, and the father wound. The father wound (O'Neil & Lujan, 2009) encompasses unresolved issues with one's father and is an important concept to consider when working with fathers. An exploration of the father wound is applicable not only to the fathers we work with but also to every therapist, male or female, as we all have fathers, whether present in our lives or absent. Working with clients who are fathers on their relationship with their own fathers and its impact on their parenting is one application. Another aspect is for female therapists to consider their own father wound in the context of countertransference and unresolved issues they have with their own fathers that can influence the therapy and therapeutic relationship with clients who are fathers.

This early group experience and many more like it, when combined with my background in developmental psychology, formed the basis of my interest in working with fathers. Even though I have become aware of my internalization of gender norms and have worked on balancing my relationships with both genders, I frequently think about and monitor the impact of these experiences on my clinical work throughout my years working with fathers. I am aware that a female therapist who has spent early years feeling more comfortable with and better understanding of men can have identifiable countertransference to men and fathers. Via my personal gender role socialization, I understand some of the appeal of traditional masculinity. I encourage fathers to look more directly at the associated fears, hopes, and challenges they have as fathers and men in our society. I stay mindful not to overidentify with men and not to assume that I know their experience. I am also aware that when I do therapy with fathers that they also went through a gender journey as boys. I try to explore and help them make their own meaning of their early boyhood. With whom did they align? With whom did they share their thoughts and feelings? Did they feel loved by their father, and what did that love look like? And, how does their journey shape their current relationships with their children and partners?

One of my hot spots is fathers who emotionally reject their children. I come from a home where, although my father was often at work, when he was home he was never harsh or mean to us. He protected us when we needed it. I have a memory of him driving into my middle school in his little convertible and demanding that a perceived mistreatment I had told him about was remedied immediately. I have become aware that because of his reduced involvement yet hero status in my mind, I idealized him. I find that I am reactive to fathers who dismiss or diminish their importance to their children.

Case 3: Bob—Countertransference Takes Its Toll

Early in my practice, I had a client, Bob, 43 and married with three children, who came to therapy to work on his anxiety. The intake session seemed unusually flat, and there was not the normal energy associated with a new client. I asked exploratory questions about his experience as a father and about his children. I now see that his obvious distaste, which often bordered on disgust, for his overweight daughter triggered deep feelings in me. I found myself debating with him, even arguing with him from what at the time I considered a professional stance, but certainly not joining him or really hearing him. I lacked empathy for Bob, and he undoubtedly experienced it. Instead of helping him look deeper and recognizing the positive qualities that he brought to his role as a father, I had reinforced a deficit perspective with the implication that he was not being a good father and that something was wrong with him. He never called again, and that first session was our last.

ADVICE FOR FEMALE THERAPISTS

Over time and with a lot of trial and error, I have learned quite a bit about what works with fathers in therapy and what does not work as well. I would like to offer some specific techniques and approaches that have been useful in my work with fathers.

1. Being genuine and direct with fathers in particular helps establish an atmosphere of safety and trust. Fathers often have many voices in their lives, whether their bosses at work or their partners at home, telling them how to act and how they should approach situations. Letting fathers take the lead and allowing them to set the pace lay the foundation for deeper psychotherapy. Among the most important techniques for working with fathers is to acknowledge that they *are* fathers by asking father-related questions throughout the process. From assessment and intake to conceptualization and interventions, focusing on being a father helps to bring their thoughts, feelings, and behaviors about fatherhood into the room.

2. Using flexible instead of rigid time schedules when scheduling fathers seems to be helpful to them. Many of these clients have unpredictable work responsibilities or varied family commitments. I also avoid stacking sessions back to back, allowing for a session to run a little longer if needed. To be helpful and informative to frequently skeptical or hesitant fathers, I offer 30-minute consultations for potential clients.

3. During sessions with my male clients, I am mindful of using their language. I have found it helpful to stay abreast of what is going on in sports. For example, Dustin likes to begin sessions by talking about basketball, and I am also a big Lakers fan. We ease into our sessions with discussions about the pros and cons of three-point shots taken the night before or our team's prospects of making the playoffs.

4. Beginning therapists should read the literature on men and fathers as well as relevant literature on gender and gender development. In doing so, I encourage new female therapists to discover the impact of their own gender journeys. Within sessions, I encourage fathers to consider the impact of gender norms across relationships, including the ones they have with their children. Within your sessions, learn about a father's socialization process by asking about his experiences as a boy and adolescent and use these often-hidden influencers throughout different stages of therapy.

5. As with most men, it is useful to help fathers process emotional disclosures as they occur in therapy. I have asked questions such as, "What was it like to say what you just did aloud?" Fathers can feel embarrassment, shame, or relief by making disclosures, or they may be confused or unsettled. Further questions can look at how the disclosure had an impact on him. Did it shift the therapeutic relationship for him? After a particularly significant disclosure, clients often feel vulnerable. Educate fathers about obstacles in therapy and normalize the process, such as, "You may feel vulnerable and not sure about coming back after telling me what you did, but these

feelings are part of the process of therapy, and you will be able to learn from this experience and move through the discomfort."

6. Female therapists should use gender-sensitive interventions that explicitly include recognizing the gender differences in the room. Do not underestimate the significance to your male client that you are female. While we know that the thoughts, feelings, and behaviors of fathers are as varied as those of mothers, a recurrent theme that arises in my work is of gender differences, specifically that he is a man and I am a woman. Fathers will likely interact with their female therapists based on their past socialized experience. For example, fathers may see female therapists as individuals with whom they can share personal issues and obtain advice as they did with female friends in their teen years. Alternatively, fathers may see the intimate psychotherapy experience as a romantic or sexualized experience. In addition, we need to remind ourselves about the amount of countertransference that we may experience as a female working with a male. The exploration of gender differences in the room has consistently yielded meaningful and useful material.

In working with fathers, I have learned about strength, resilience, and true second (and third and fourth) chances. I have watched fathers dramatically turn around their relationships with their children and partners and discover hidden strengths that they bring to the different areas of their lives. I hope to bring an understanding of the roles and responsibilities the fathers can have and the associated pressures they face. Dustin, the father who started therapy by disclosing that he had been a bad father after his daughter was born, was in treatment for over six months. He realized that, "It's okay to have needs and have them met, instead of just feeling guilty that I do have needs." The buzzword of our sessions became *authenticity*. He made slow and steady progress toward becoming his genuine self, which included a deep desire to be a good father. Identifying and deconstructing gender role norms and stereotypes became an essential part of treatment with Dustin. Toward the end of treatment, he expressed that, "I am internally certain that I love my kids." When asked to elaborate, Dustin said that, "The thing that changed fundamentally is that I know I'm a good father." Dustin developed a clearer understanding of the relationships he had with his children, his wife, and himself. With significant relief, he acknowledged that he could be intimate within these relationships and expressed a growing respect for his own wants and needs. His depression had lifted as he became more physically active, improved his diet, and learned to set boundaries at work. Using a basketball analogy, he said, "It's a slam dunk with my kids. I'm 100% in the game." Dustin's transformation reminded me of the power of approaching men who are fathers from an angle that is usually not taught in school. I end this chapter with the best piece of advice I can give beginning therapists: When you are in the room with a father, talk to him about being a father.

REFERENCES

Barrows, P. (2004). Fathers and families: Locating the ghost in the nursery. *Infant Mental Health Journal, 25,* 408–423.

Blankenhorn, D. (1995). *Fatherless America: Confronting our most urgent social problem.* New York, NY: Basic Books.

Cabrera, N. J., Tamis-Lemonda, C. S., Bradley, R. H., Hofferth, S., & Lamb, M. E. (2000). Fatherhood in the twenty-first century. *Child Development, 71*(1), 127–136.

Coley, R. L. (2001). (In)visible men: Emerging research on low-income, unmarried, and minority fathers. *American Psychologist, 56,* 743–753.

Cusack, J., Deane, F. P., Wilson, C. J., & Ciarrochi, J. (2006). Emotional expression, perceptions of therapy, and help-seeking intentions in men attending therapy services. *Psychology of Men & Masculinity, 7*(2), 69–82.

Fagan, J., & Hawkins, A. J. (Eds.). (2001). *Clinical and educational interventions with fathers.* Binghamton, NY: Haworth.

Good, G. E., Dell, D. M., & Mintz, L. B. (1989). Male role and gender role conflict: relations to help seeking in men. *Journal of Counseling Psychology, 36,* 295–300.

Hudson, D. B., Campbell-Grossman, C., Fleck, M. O., Elek, S. M., & Shipman, A. (2003). Effects of the new fathers network on first-time fathers' parenting self-efficacy and parenting satisfaction during the transition to parenthood. *Issues in Comprehensive Pediatric Nursing, 26,* 217–229.

Jain, A., Belsky, J., & Crnic, K. (1996). Beyond fathering behaviors: Types of dads. *Journal of Family Psychology, 10,* 431–442.

Lamb, M. E. (Ed.). (2004). *The father's role in child development* (4th ed.). New York, NY: Wiley.

Madsen, S. A., Lind, D., & Munck, H. (2002). Fædres tilknytning til spædbørn [Fathers' attachment to infants]. Copenhagen: Hans Reitzels Forlag.

Marsigilo, W., Day, R. D., & Lamb, M. E. (2000). Exploring fatherhood diversity: Implications for conceptualizing father involvement. *Marriage and Family Review, 29,* 269–293.

O'Neil, J. M., & Lujan, M. L. (2009). An assessment paradigm for fathers and men in therapy using gender role conflict theory. In C. Z. Oren & D. C. Oren (Eds.), *Counseling fathers* (pp. 49–71). New York, NY: Routledge.

Oren, C. Z., & Oren, D. C. (2009). *Counseling fathers.* New York, NY: Routledge.

Pleck, E. H., & Pleck, J. H. (1997). Fatherhood ideals in the United States: Historical dimensions. In M. E. Lamb (Ed.), *The role of the father in child development* (3rd ed., (pp. 33–48). New York, NY: Wiley.

Pleck, J. H. (2010). Paternal involvement: Revised conceptualization and theoretical linkages with child outcomes. In M. E. Lamb (Ed.), *The role of the father in child development* (5th ed., pp. 58–93). Hoboken, NJ: Wiley.

Pope, M., & Englar-Carlson, M. (2001). Fathers and sons: The relationship between violence and masculinity. *The Family Journal: Counseling and Therapy for Couples and Families, 9*(4), 367–374.

Smith, E. J. (2006). The strength-based counseling model: A paradigm shift in psychology. *Counseling Psychologist, 34*(1), 13–79.

United States Census Bureau. (2006). Facts for features: Father's Day, June 18. Retrieved March 15, 2007 from http://www.census.gov/Pressrelease/www/releases/archives/factsforfeaturesspecialeditions/006794.html

U.S. Department of Health and Human Services. (2006). Promoting responsible fatherhood. Retrieved December 17, 2006, from http://fatherhood.hhs.gov/

RECOMMENDED READING

Coley, R. L. (2001). (In)visible men: Emerging research on low-income, unmarried, and minority fathers. *American Psychologist, 56,* 743–753.

Eggebeen, D. J., & Knoester, C. (2001). Does fatherhood matter for men? *Journal of Marriage and Family, 63,* 381–393.

Fagan, J., & Hawkins, A. J. (Eds.). (2001). *Clinical and educational interventions with fathers.* Binghamton, NY: Haworth.

Hawkins, A. J., & Dollahite, D. C. (Eds.). (1996). *Generative fathering: Beyond deficit perspectives.* Thousand Oaks, CA: Sage.

Lamb, M. E. (Ed.). (2004). *The father's role in child development* (4th ed.). New York, NY: Wiley.

Lamb, M. E., Pleck, J. H., Charnov, E. L., & Levine, J. A. (1985). Paternal behavior in humans. *American Psychologist, 25,* 883–894.

Marks, L., & Palkovitz, R. (2004). American fatherhood types: The good, the bad, and the uninterested. *Fathering, 3,* 113–129.

Marsigilo, W., Day, R. D., & Lamb, M. E. (2000). Exploring fatherhood diversity: Implications for conceptualizing father involvement. *Marriage and Family Review, 29,* 269–293.

Oren, C. Z., & Oren, D. C. (2009). *Counseling fathers.* New York, NY: Routledge.

Vann, N. (2007). Reflections on the development of fatherhood work. *Applied Developmental Science, 11,* 266–268.

11

Understanding Men's Issues

Assessing and Treating Men Who Are Abusive

MICHÈLE HARWAY

INTRODUCTION

My brother (at age 15) is sitting by the telephone. He is sweating profusely and muttering under his breath, rehearsing his lines: "Would you like to go to the movies on Saturday?" After taking a deep breath, he resolutely picks up the telephone and calls the girl. A few minutes later, looking devastated, he hangs up. She said no. My heart hurts for him. It did not seem fair then that as a boy he would have to take all of the risks (things have changed somewhat in this arena, but I still see inequities today).

Fast forward some 20 years. My son (then age 10), a precocious as well as physically attractive boy, effortlessly draws adults to him. With peers, it is a different story. He is skinny and not very athletic. He is smarter than all of them. He is emotionally aware and vulnerable. And, he is everything that a boy is not supposed to be. He is every girl's best friend, but he is every boy's punching bag. On that day, he has again been beaten at school. But as a survivor, he knows what to do. "Mom," he says, "I know you taught me to use my words, but I am getting killed on the playground, and I have to fight back." I instantly know that he is right, and I also become aware that his feminist mother has not prepared him well to face the world of boys.

There were messages from other sources (the media, teachers, etc.) that taught me about the separate gender worlds and gave me some hint of what it must be like to be a boy or a man in our society—it was not just the privileged world that I had learned about from my feminist readings, but it had a strong dark side as well.

PERSONAL JOURNEY

Growing up in the 1960s, just before the second feminist wave (during which women's rights were in the forefront of the news), it was not easy being a girl. I was ambitious and at an early age had intended to go to medical school. I was one of a handful of girls in my high school who took a heavy math and science curriculum. I had to fight with my school counselor, who strongly discouraged me from taking physics "Girls don't take physics," I was told. I took it anyway, 1 of 5 of about 600 girls in the high school to do so. Of course, the same counselor told me I would not get into the competitive colleges to which I had applied. Fortunately, he failed to derail me there.

But, one more anecdote about gender: It is my senior year in college. I have already applied to doctoral programs in psychology. My father, a very liberal man, who himself has been at the forefront of many political struggles, including the union movement and the civil rights movement, shocks me with his question: "So, what are you majoring in?" he asks. "Psychology," I reply. And then, the shocking words: "Don't you think you should get a teaching certification or something, in case you ever need to work?" Since I had taken it for granted that I would work and that I would pursue a doctoral degree, his reaction was unfathomable to me. In addition, that my father was so uninformed about me personally and what was happening in society to suggest that I should do something in case "I ever needed to work" was incomprehensible and bizarre. It made me wonder what other subtle messages I had incorporated from home about the limitations of being a woman. The fact that my father had been raised in a traditional household of immigrant parents contributed to his own traditional view of women and accounted for his misperception of me and my future.

Another factor in my professional trajectory was my marriage in 1969 to S., which I later came to realize was emotionally and psychologically abusive. He did his best to cut me off from family and friends (a strategy that most abusers use to obtain control over their partners, usually early in the relationship), but I refused to yield. He tried to undermine my self-confidence at every step, once even telling me that if I left him I would not even be able to balance my checkbook. As with most instances of emotional abuse, it was a little crazy making because I could not see the pattern: Sometimes my husband brought me flowers and treated me specially; other times he was awful. We consulted a therapist late in our marriage, by which time I was seething with anger (a fairly common presentation of abused women), and he behaved charmingly (as abusive men often do). The therapist never understood the dynamics of our relationship and, instead of helping, made things worse by empathizing with him (because he seemed so charming in sessions) and castigating me (because I was always so angry in sessions). As a result, S. was quick to point out that "even the therapist can see that you are the problem." A summer-long visit by my sister was the first validation of the craziness I lived with on a daily basis. After living with us a short while, my sister said, "I had *no* idea what you were living with!"

After two years of increasing misery, I was finally able to leave him because I realized that I wanted children, and I had intuitively avoided having them with him. The insight allowed me finally to leave the situation. I still remember the feeling of empowerment I felt when I closed the front door to my apartment and realized that I could do whatever I wanted, whenever I wanted. I was free. Although I did not initially make a connection between this first bad marriage and my interest in domestic violence, there is no doubt that they must be related.

PROFESSIONAL JOURNEY

After high school, I went off to Tufts University and enrolled in pre-med classes. They were challenging, and there was a lot of competition. There, also, my medical ambitions were constantly being challenged (few women enrolled in medical school then). I was told, "You'll fail organic chemistry. Women have a tough time with it." I did not fail for the simple reason that I became discouraged and switched to psychology. Here was a field that was scientific, that did not seem hostile to women, and at which nobody told me I could not succeed. Thirty plus years later, I can look back and see that it has been a good field for me. It has allowed me to do much of what I wanted to do with my career and my life. My initial intention was to be a research psychologist, and that was what I trained to do. My first few jobs were as a full-time researcher. I had several years of graduate assistantships where I did my own research on gender and women's development and collaborated with professors on their work. Courses in social psychology exposed me early on to issues of gender and feminism. This was one of the few areas of psychology at that time that had given any thought to gender, even though such an interest was not considered mainstream until many years later.

From my first day in graduate school, I had a sharply developed interest in gender. It was not clear to me what my fascination was, but I knew that gender issues were something I felt passionate about, unlike some of the drier laboratory social psychological research my professors were doing. We called it "psychology of women" then because we only looked at how women were being limited in our society. Psychology of women was not a discipline when I started my doctoral program, and we had to fight hard to get any exposure to this material. There were no courses on women or gender, not in our program and not in other departments at the University of Maryland. I chaired a committee of women on campus, and we put together the first brochure on women's studies. It encompassed any course that included even a lecture or two on the topic. We had to work hard to identify enough courses to fill even a slim brochure, but I believe it was the first of its kind in the country. I was pleased when some years later the National Women's Studies Association was formed and placed its first office on the University of Maryland campus.

It was not until three years after graduation that I began to think more seriously about obtaining further clinical training and developing that side of my professional life more. I began to realize that traditional social psychology was too constraining for me. During my years in graduate school, I was fortunate to be mentored by two extraordinary women. Helen (Lena) Astin had been my boss when I worked as a research assistant following my college graduation. She had written an important early book on professional women, *The Woman Doctorate in America* (Astin, 1969); was one of the first presidents of Division 35 (Society for the Psychology of Women) of the American Psychological Association (APA); and was the first chair of the Committee on Women. Lena was key in giving me the confidence to express my opinions and pursue my interests. She is still a good friend and an inspiration. The other woman was Nancy S. Anderson, a full professor in the psychology department at the University of Maryland. That in itself was an anomaly, as was the fact that we had three women faculty in a faculty of 35. Nan was a quantitative psychologist, and she coached me in how to be successful as a woman in the department. Among other things, she told me that I was not to laugh during my dissertation defense as women had been criticized for not being serious students, and laughter during such a solemn occasion might be interpreted incorrectly.

Nan also fiercely defended me when one of my thesis committee members wanted me thrown out of graduate school following completion of my master's degree. The thesis was on what was then called sex role stereotyping. One of the members of my committee said that every time he read my thesis, he would get angry. Some of his reaction was undoubtedly his own internalized sexism. It probably did not help that he was raised in Switzerland, which at the time did not even allow women to vote. This committee member also claimed that the statistics were wrong, but Nan, having been the architect of those same statistics, supported my point of view. A last minute negotiation ended with Nan and me at the Computer Center literally at 11 p.m. one night running an additional statistical analysis as a compromise.

Without Nan, I would not have gone on to do my dissertation, *Stereotyping: Some Effects on the Target Person* (Harway, 1975). I picked this topic because it involved a laboratory-based social psychological study that met the requirements of my program while it allowed me to pursue a topic that was linked to gender and of great interest to me. The study looked at the effects of being stereotyped on the perceived relationship between the target and the stereotyper. The stereotype was based on gender, and both men and women received an inaccurate attribution based on their gender. So, my professional interests have been on gender from the beginning. Most of my early publications were on this topic as well, to the great chagrin of some of my other graduate school professors, who thought I might be damaging my career by working in this area. This reflected the prevailing perception of that time, that research on women was not considered serious scholarship.

As a feminist psychologist, I have had a long-time commitment to working with and understanding women, both in the context of clinical work and in academic settings, as students and mentees. However, my feminism does not limit me to considering just the issues that women face in our society. From the beginning of my professional career and in particular in my work with clients, my focus has been on gender. This means that with psychotherapy clients I focus on the impact of institutional and societal sexism on women *and* men and focus many of my interventions on encouraging all to expand the range of behaviors and opportunities available to both men and women—something that might be construed as humanism.

Since the 1990s, I have shifted my focus to a study of men's issues. There are several reasons for this shift. First, looking at things from a systemic perspective has convinced me of the importance to women's well-being of understanding men's behavior, in both personal and professional arenas. Men's behaviors affect male/female relationships in myriad ways and are in turn reciprocally affected by women's behaviors. For example, we are all members of families (whether they are families of origin or families we have created), which typically include men as fathers, uncles, brothers, and, for some of us, life partners. Most of us are in workplaces where men are in positions of power over others. The faculty in our academic institutions remain largely male. Our legislators are mostly male. Because none of us operates in a vacuum, the behavior of those men in our lives has immediate consequences sometimes on how we fare.

UNDERSTANDING MEN WHO ARE ABUSIVE: AN OVERVIEW

My entry into professional work in domestic violence was almost accidental. My colleague, Marsali Hansen, and I were looking for an opportunity to do some research together. At that time, one of the big controversies in the family psychology literature was that family therapists often considered that women in relationships with an abuser were coresponsible for their own abuse. We decided to study that phenomenon. It was an interesting topic that became even more interesting as we conducted our research (Hansen, Harway, & Cervantes, 1991) and realized that most people in the field had little understanding of domestic violence and abuse and did not understand how widespread it really was. That shifted our interest and the focus of our research as well as what we did with it after the study. It was only after the fact that I wondered why I was even mildly interested when the topic first came up and looked at my own history with men.

My work in the area of domestic violence has convinced me of the necessity to understand men and men's issues to intervene appropriately with families affected by domestic violence. Much of my professional work has included publishing books on domestic violence (some of which are routinely used to train grassroots counselors in the field); working with individuals who have been affected by this kind of violence (the survivors, perpetrators, and children); and doing training seminars for mental health professionals on being able to identify violence in relationships. The situations described in this chapter include men as the perpetrators and women as the recipients of the violence. That is not to say that men are not also sometimes targeted to receive interpersonal violence, but rather that the gender distributions discussed are the more common situation.

The following vignettes describe a variety of individuals and families in which men have perpetrated emotional or physical violence in their interpersonal relationships, part of the 9 million incidents of partner abuse reported annually (Tjaden & Thoennes, 1998) and included in the 2 million injuries from intimate partner violence each year (Centers for Disease Control, 2008).

Vignette 1: Carol and James

Carol and James have been married 10 years. They have two children, Dana, 9, and Tracy, 7. James is employed as a foreman in a concrete-manufacturing plant. Carol is also employed. James is upset because on several occasions Carol did not return home from work until 2 or 3 o'clock in the morning and did not explain her whereabouts to him. He acknowledged privately to the therapist that the afternoon prior to the session he had seen her in a bar with a man. Carol tells the therapist privately that she has made efforts to dissolve the marriage and to seek a protection order against her husband because he has repeatedly been physically violent with her and the kids; the day prior, he grabbed her and threw her on the floor in a violent manner and then struck her. The family had made plans to go shopping, roller skating, and out to dinner after the session.

Carol, James, Dana, and Tracy were a real family. Only a few demographic details have been modified to camouflage their identity. Several years ago, my colleague Marsali Hansen and I found them described in a book on case law, and with the modified paragraph I just reported to you included them as a stimulus vignette in two studies we conducted in the late 1980s and early 1990s (Hansen et al., 1991; Harway, Hansen, & Cervantes, 1997). The facts of the case are that just prior to the family outing described in the vignette, during a violent episode, James beat Carol to death. He then went to jail, but only for 1 year because his attorney used the bitch-deserved-it defense. On release from prison, he sued the maternal grandparents for and got custody of his two children. Remember that this was a man who had repeatedly been violent toward this wife and his children. While it would be tempting to blame James's behavior on male norms and male socialization, interpersonal violence is widely recognized as a more complicated problem. While it is outside the purview of this chapter to review other evidence that may explain men's violence, refer to the work of Harway and O'Neil (1999) for a more complete description of related factors.

Vignette 2: Mildred and George

By contrast, Mildred, 68, and George, 71, have just celebrated their golden anniversary. George, a retired salesman, has been depressed since his retirement five years ago, and he has begun drinking substantially more than usual. George has no hobbies or outside interests, and he follows Mildred around the house as she goes about her daily chores. Mildred is a sociable woman who is active in her church group and with volunteer activities. She frequently suggests social engagements, trips, and outings, all of which George rejects with great anger. While for the most part their long relationship has been a good one, in the last few months George has been getting increasingly violent; last week, he savagely beat Mildred during an argument. She has become fearful of him but refuses to consider moving out of the home because she is afraid to leave him alone given his depressed mood. Although Mildred and George are a fictitious couple, they represent other older couples for whom the loss of traditional roles is problematic.

Vignette 3: Sari and Gabriel

On the other end of the life span, Sari, 16, and Gabriel, 17, have been going together for 11 months. Sari is president of the debate team, a member of the color guard, and an A student. Gabriel is on the water polo team, is a volunteer tutor, and is active in his church youth group. They are model teenagers. However, what this picture of perfection camouflages is the fact that Gabriel is extremely jealous of the time that Sari spends with her friends and family, and he controls her behavior by threatening to break up with her if she will not choose to spend time with him over other activities. Sari has always acquiesced, but she is becoming increasingly disenchanted with the relationship. Last week, when she refused to have sex with him behind the gym, he became enraged and forced himself on her, ripping her skirt and causing several ugly bruises to appear on her arms and legs. Sari and Gabriel are a composite of several dating couples for whom intimate partner violence has become a reality.

Vignette 4: Rhonda and Beau

Not all cases of domestic violence involve people who are in committed relationships: Rhonda is a vice president in a large advertising agency. Two years ago, she ended a long-standing relationship with Beau, another vice president and a married man. Since the breakup, Rhonda and Beau initially maintained a cordial work relationship. Over time, however, Rhonda has come to fear interacting with Beau at any level. When they are alone, Beau is often psychologically abusive, and he yells at her in a way that makes her afraid. With others around, he is more restrained, but he sometimes just gives her a look that chills her. Rhonda and Beau, also a composite couple, no longer have a personal relationship, but their history together has influenced their current interactions.

WORKING WITH MEN WHO ABUSE: SHIFTING GEARS

In my early career as a psychologist, my focus was exclusively on the women who had experienced violence in relationships and outside them. Carol and her children, Mildred, Sari, and Rhonda would have been my focus in my clinical work. I would have been interested in their state of mind, searched for information or services for them, been concerned about their safety—all important aspects of working with women (and children) in abusive relationships. Likewise, in my scholarly work, I would have been interested in documenting the impact of long-time abuse on women's development. I would have wanted to know what repeated exposure to domestic violence does to children. This is important work, and we must continue to provide services for survivors of abusive relationships and their children and to understand the impacts of living with abuse on women and children.

However, the reality is that focusing exclusively on women survivors is not enough. We must understand the psychological factors behind men's violent behaviors. The empirical and clinical literature is clear that men who are abusive do not spontaneously stop their abuse. They must be treated. Donald Dutton (1986), well known for his work on batterers, recognized that psychotherapy was a must for batterers to help them change their behavior. As a consequence, many jurisdictions now mandate long-term batterer intervention programs (52 weeks in California). Our science has always been behind grassroots efforts in this area, and the attempt to understand the biopsychosocial factors that may contribute to men's violence toward women and children is a relatively new phenomenon. A book I coedited a number of years ago about what causes men's violence against women (Harway & O'Neil, 1999) and the article that preceded it (O'Neil & Harway, 1997) were attempts to pull together what was then known about men's violence and to encourage further research into this area. While women who leave abusive relationships are likely later to enter healthy relationships, research also indicates that abusive men who are not treated simply cycle their victims. When one partner leaves an abusive male, he simply finds someone else to replace her.

Unfortunately, the statistics on the efficacy of batterer intervention are not impressive, probably because most have focused to a great extent on men's behaviors rather than their underlying psychology. Given that, we need to spend far more time than we have in understanding men's psychological development. We also need to develop interventions that are sophisticated enough to be effective in stemming abusive and violent behavior. Another benefit in understanding men's behavior in this area is that doing so may allow us to develop programs for young people aimed at preventing abusive relationships. Dating violence statistics show how widespread a problem is interpersonal violence: Approximately one in five female high school students report being physically or sexually abused by a dating partner (Silverman, Raj, Mucci, & Hathaway, 2001). The National Crime Victimization Survey (Bachman & Saltzman, 1996) reported that 16% of aggravated and simple assaults against women are perpetrated by boyfriends or ex-boyfriends, and other studies showed that 22% to 39% of college students experience dating violence (Sorensen & Bowie, 1994; White & Koss, 1991). Understanding violence in men, young men, and boys is important to prevent situations such as that of Sari and Gabriel. With preventive interventions, we may be able to decrease courtship violence as well as violence occurring with committed couples of any age. The bottom line is that when we work with the men who perpetrate the violence, we automatically improve the lot of the women and children who might otherwise be negatively impacted.

MEN AS ABUSE SURVIVORS

Rates of violence are reported to be similar in same-sex relationships as in heterosexual ones, although our understanding of interpersonal violence with gay men has not been subject to the same research scrutiny. In fact, there are few large-scale studies of domestic violence among gay men. Prevalence statistics (reporting that as many as 500,000 gay men are victims of domestic violence) are from Island and Letellier's (1991) projection of heterosexual figures.

Likewise, a controversial issue is whether females are as likely to be violent toward their male partners as men seem to be toward their female partners. Some studies suggested that both sexes are equally violent. However, Heyman, Feldbau-Kohn, Ehrensaft, Langhinrichsen-Rohling, and O'Leary (2001) indicated that "when only behavioral acts are measured, men and women appear to be equally aggressive. When the physical and psychological consequences of aggressive acts are included, women are far more likely to be victims than are men" (p. 335). A burgeoning literature is beginning to examine the causes of female-to-male interpersonal violence and suggests that self-defense may be a common rationale for women to be violent toward their male partners.

WORKING WITH MEN WHO ABUSE: CASE STUDIES

My approach to working with men from violent couples is the result of my own upbringing (of course), an adulthood built on empathy toward men and the limitations of their socialization, and what I have learned about domestic violence through my research, clinical work, and writing. I have learned that working in this area is unlike any other kind of clinical work in that the neutral stance of the therapist is challenged by the need to take an advocacy position to protect the client. Working with couples, many of whom might be violent, also requires me always to be on the lookout for domestic violence, even where it seems unlikely to exist. I have learned that the most unlikely couple relationship may hide a history of abuse and violence. This is why my focus is always on doing a thorough assessment with all couples (regardless of the issues with which they present) to rule out or uncover interpersonal violence. Often, the couple seeking marital therapy is secretly harboring relationship violence. There is evidence that couples who are violent rarely present the violence as an issue at intake. That is because they see the violence as infrequent, unstable, and not the main issue of concern. Thus, they almost never volunteer information about the violence. The result is that many therapists may be doing couples work and not know that their clients are in fact experiencing domestic violence. Holtzworth-Munroe et al. (1992), in searching for a nonviolent control group for their study of couples' violence, had great difficulty finding nonviolent couples who were in marital therapy. In five different samples of maritally distressed but supposedly nonviolent couples being treated at psychological and family therapy clinics, 55–56% of the men reported having at some time engaged in violent behavior toward their wives. Their therapists were unaware of the violence. This calls into question the importance of doing a thorough assessment at intake to identify interpersonal violence.

Case Study 1: James and Judith

I first met James when he and his wife, Judith, were referred to me for couples therapy. My referral source had indicated that they were having some serious communication problems but did not know the content of these problems or much more than that they were experiencing considerable distress. When Judith called to set up a first appointment, she also indicated that they were communicating with great difficulty, and that both were eager to get some help. As I usually do when a couple is seeking counseling, I described my intake session to the caller on the phone to set up the appropriate expectations right away.

I know that in some large percentage of cases, an innocuous referral such as that of James and Judith may hide an abusive relationship. I also know that if I do not do a thorough assessment at intake, ruling out the possibility of domestic violence, I may well end up treating a couple for a simple communication issue. As a consequence, I may not focus on the more dangerous and underlying issue of domestic violence. As I describe in the initial phone call, intakes with couples always consist of four parts: an initial brief segment with both members together, a few minutes spent alone with the woman, a similar time alone with the man, and then a final few minutes to make recommendations for the treatment. During the initial time together, I am looking for whether one partner appears to be afraid of the other or seems to be doing things to avoid angering the other. I examine whether I am feeling controlled by the client (usually the abuser). I listen for complaints of jealousy, especially those that seem exaggerated. I see whether one partner seems always to focus on what the other has done wrong (victims usually blame themselves). I assess whether the couple or one of the partners seem isolated from family and other social support. I evaluate whether one partner seems to want to be right at any cost. All of these would suggest that this may be an abusive relationship.

With this evidence, then, I ask to spend a few minutes alone with Judith. As the possibly abused one, she is more likely to disclose incidents of violence if they exist. Then, armed with that information I can speak with James, whom I hope will respond to my questioning with an admission that he has been violent. The specific procedure that I use entails asking a series of increasingly specific questions about how the couple handles disagreements (Harway & Hansen, 2004). I use what I call "the freeze-frame procedure": I ask Judith to describe in great detail how a disagreement has been handled. I ask her to describe what he said (or did) and then what she said (or did). I ask specific questions about a long list of physically violent behaviors (e.g., pushing, shoving, slapping, kicking—since there is evidence that some of those behaviors may not be construed as battering or even abuse if a more general question were asked). I also ask about whether Judith has ever felt afraid as fear is the single best indicator that abuse is a factor.

At the end of my time with Judith, I should have a fairly clear idea of whether violence is an issue in this relationship. If it is, I must provide Judith with information on the spot regarding how she can get some help. If Judith has clued me in to existing violence, I am better prepared to ask James similar questions. I will also be even more persistent with him than I might otherwise be. It will be important to have him own some aspect of the abuse, even if he underplays its significance or intensity. If he discloses that information, I can then make a recommendation for treatment of the domestic violence rather than focus on a couples' communication issue as this may not be the central issue at all. Although some would disagree, most clinicians would concur that doing couples therapy when domestic violence is a factor is not indicated. Most would recommend that the perpetrator be referred to some type of batterer's treatment group, and that the abuse recipient should get therapeutic support during this time.

During the final phase of my intake, I present the couple with the results of my inquiry. If violence has emerged during intake and I have been successful in getting James to admit to having used it, then I will usually say something like the following:

> James, you told me that when you and Judith had that disagreement last week, you got pretty upset and pushed her a little. Right? Given that and also the fact that you, Judith, told me about some of your issues which are impeding the progress of this marriage, I would like to recommend that we put off working on the issues that you have as a couple and first deal with these individual issues. So, James, I am going to refer you to a group that a colleague of mine does for men who have issues similar to yours.

(Note that I never mention abuse or battering by name.)

> And, Judith, you should probably consider individual counseling. I can provide you with some names of therapists. At the appropriate time, we may then want to take up the issue of couples counseling again.

In a great majority of cases, such referrals do not result in the couple getting the help they need, but they may instead leave my office with James muttering about my incompetence and determined to find a "better" couples therapist who may help with their communication issues. They are likely to find someone who will not assess for the violence and treat their communication problem instead. That is why we must ensure that all therapists are adequately trained in this area. Of course, in some number of cases violence does not seem to be an issue, and in those cases I can proceed with doing more standard couples work, focusing on their communication problems. With abusive couples, though, since group therapy is the treatment of choice, I am seldom in a position to work directly with the abusive man until issues of violence have been resolved.

Case Study 2: Tom

Occasionally, because of some extenuating circumstance, the man cannot attend group treatment and must be worked with individually. For example, I once had a client, Tom, who was a well-known television actor. His notoriety was such that it would have been impossible for him to attend group treatment without attracting the attention of paparazzi. It would also have been extremely difficult to find a compatible group of successful and sophisticated abusive men to which I could refer him.

I agreed to work with Tom, also explaining what the benefits of group treatment might have been: participating with a group of men, all of whom have had to confront their own abusive behavior. Because the denial system of abusive men is so great, it is easy for them to discount what a therapist might say about abuse, especially a female therapist. It is much more difficult to ignore a confrontation from another man who is only a few weeks removed from his enrollment in group treatment but who is beginning to understand the issues that must be addressed. Typically, in a group, there are men at all stages of treatment: some who have recently begun the work, others who are starting to grasp the problem, and still others who are well on their road to completing their treatment. The more "advanced" men thus serve to encourage, prod, and otherwise motivate the newly enrolled men.

With Tom, since group enrollment was not an option, it was my job to expose him to as much of the work that he needed to do as possible. I have been influenced in my thinking about abuse intervention by the work of Kendall Evans, a master clinician who specializes in group treatment of this population and who has conceptualized the underlying dynamics for most abusers as resulting from what he called the cycle of feeling avoidance (Segel-Evans, 1994; Harway & Evans, 1996). Essentially, the cycle is built around Lenore Walker's cycle of violence (Walker, 1979), which does a good job of ordering the experience that battered women have while being abused. This may be a good model for what happens to the victim in abusive relationships but does not seem to capture what is happening for the abuser. By contrast, the cycle of feeling avoidance captures the phenomenological experience of abusive men and provides a framework for clinical intervention.

Walker describes the cycle of violence as consisting of three phases: a tension-building phase, the battering itself, followed by a honeymoon period. Because it is a cycle, the honeymoon period is inevitably followed by tension building again, another incidence of battering, and so on. Evans has described the tension as more akin to stuffing of unresolved feelings from the past—guilt, shame, fear of abandonment—which men are particularly adept at defending against, such that they most often do not even experience the underlying feeling. The tension is stuffed through using either active or passive defenses. Passive defenses include behaviors that abusive men are particularly adept at using: rationalization, denial, manipulation, and projection. Active defenses involve a variety of acting out behaviors, including the use of substances, high-risk behavior of various kinds, and anger and controlling (including making the other person into an enemy and feeling like survival is at stake). This provides the context within which the battering occurs—it also is an active defense against the underlying and usually unidentified feelings, and it involves a willingness to hurt the other person in the service of his own feelings. Following the battering experience comes a feeling of relief (which is the honeymoon period in Walker's scheme), but inevitably tensions rise again because of internal or external factors and at least in part because of the problems caused by the most recent battering episode. This then feeds into the ongoing cycle of violence that Walker described.

The cycle of feeling avoidance provided the framework for my work with Tom. In the early phase of our work together, we focused primarily on crisis intervention, with the crisis precipitated by the identification of the abuse in the couple. My first goal was to educate Tom about violence and violence control. Sharing the cycle of feeling avoidance provided him with a feeling of being understood by me. He said:

> I've never felt that I could talk to anyone about this issue because for one, I didn't understand it, sometimes I didn't even remember that it had happened, and I am so used to being blamed for things from my childhood on that I just couldn't tell anyone it had happened or even admit that it had when my wife confronted me. Your model makes me feel hopeful that I can do something about this so I don't end up in jail or hurt my wife or children, which would make me feel terrible.

The model is also an entree into helping Tom learn how to identify feelings. Levant (2001) described normative male alexithymia to capture men's normative experience of not having words to describe feelings. Similarly, Tom (and other abusive men) not only do not know how to label feelings but also often are unaware that they are having a feeling. So, I asked Tom in the middle of a difficult discussion about a recent argument he had with his wife, Jerrilyn, "What are you aware of in your body right now?" In response to his blank look, I said, "For example, as I am sitting in this chair right now, I am aware of the back of the chair hitting up against my shoulder blades. I can feel my buttocks pressed against the seat bottom. What do you experience in your body?" By beginning to describe the normal kinesthetic experience of sitting in a chair, I directed Tom's attention to his bodily sensations. Repeated questioning about his awareness of his body eventually led to his saying something like, "My stomach is really upset right now. I feel lots of rumblings in my stomach, and I feel a little queasy." Eventually, we were able to tie those bodily sensations to what we had been talking about, and Tom learned that he could identify what he is experiencing through that mechanism.

Once Tom learned to identify feelings, then we could begin to examine how to channel those feelings in socially acceptable manners. Because Tom must keep his appearance up for his television work, additional workouts at the gym or jogging in the neighborhood provided the dual benefit of helping his physique while allowing him to divert his tension into this physical outlet. Finally, the last step in the crisis intervention phase of our work together was to help him develop a comprehensive danger management plan, something discussed all along about how he could keep himself from engaging in abusive behaviors that were dangerous for both himself and his partner. This plan included using appropriate time-outs, having a buddy to talk to, and having a structured exercise program.

After dealing with the immediate issues, my work with Tom began to explore how he might channel his power needs into socially acceptable channels. We next entered into an intense period in which we examined Tom's underlying feelings of shame and guilt, which resulted from childhood interactions with his abusive father and which he has learned to defend again. Dutton (1995) described shame as the basic underlying issue for abusive men and as such would be an important focus of our work together for quite some time. We explored Tom's feelings of abandonment (also from early experiences in his childhood home), which popped up in the most unexpected manner. One day, we explored why Tom was so infuriated when he returned late from long hours on the set to find that the dinner roast was overcooked. This resulted in a major abusive episode during which he stopped short of hitting Jerilynn (demonstrating some progress over what he might have done at an early stage of treatment). As we explored why the overcooking of the roast led to such an outburst on Tom's part, he told me (with a sad expression on his face), "Jerilynn spends hours on the phone with her friends. She knows that I am starving when I have been on a shoot, and you would think she would make this her top priority. That she instead was talking to her friend Marilyn and 'forgot' that the roast was cooking shows that she does not care about me." As we discussed alternative explanations for the overcooking of the roast, we also considered the reality of Tom's place in Jerilynn's life, which he acknowledged was considerable. This led to several sessions that considered Tom's abandonment issues.

As the final steps in our work together, Tom and I began to work on healing the abuse he experienced in his childhood home and considered the connection between those experiences and how he was behaving in his current relationship. In a group setting, we would also focus on developing better relational skills with other men and women. Abusive men are often awkward in social situations as well and need to be socialized—something that is easier to do in a group setting where other men can provide the material for developing such social skills. We talked about how he might develop new friends, and I gave him homework assignments designed to encourage him to relate to a greater variety of people in his life. We also spent quite a bit of time dealing with ways to improve his interactions with his wife.

At this point, Tom and I had been working together for 17 months, and there had been no violence in the couple's relationship, a fact that Jerilynn affirmed in a conjoint session I held toward the end of our work together. In fact, both Jerilynn and Tom described a much improved relationship overall, with moments of great intimacy. It was at this point that we discussed the possibility of the couple seeking some ongoing couples' therapy for the remaining issues in the relationship. When, unlike Tom, an abusive man has been referred to group treatment, this point might be one at which the couple returns to me for couples work.

WHAT WORKS WELL AND WHAT DOES NOT WORK WELL WHEN WOMEN COUNSEL VIOLENT MEN: COUNTERTRANSFERENTIAL ISSUES

Not every therapist can work effectively with this population. The gender of the therapist is only one factor in providing a good counseling fit, and not the most important factor at that. What is important is that the therapist be comfortable with parts of herself that can be aggressive or abusive. She must also understand what is at the root of the abusive behavior for most men and empathize with their pain. Without such awareness, the therapist may shame clients for behavior about which they feel ashamed already. Therapists working with such men need to be flexible and streetwise to avoid losing credibility with these clients.

Moreover, given that batterers are often charming, it is important that therapists be comfortable confronting a polished external demeanor to avoid being easily misled. A woman therapist must also be knowledge-able about the male client's experience. She also needs to understand her reaction (and that of other women) to women's experience of male violence and oppression. She must be able to simultaneously understand multiple perspectives: to understand how a man can feel controlled by his wife, who in turn is being terrorized by him, without losing a sense of objectivity about what is real and what dangers exist in the situation. She needs to be comfortable being nurturing, nonjudgmental, wise, and firmly in control of the therapy situation—in other words, she needs to be a "good parent."

Case Study 3: Steve

Steve entered individual therapy with me after 12 months in a court-mandated batterer treatment program. He had been officially dis-charged from the mandated treatment. He evidently had acquired sufficient awareness of his past behaviors and the inherent risks in not continuing to manage them that he chose to pursue additional therapy. Steve presented as a good-looking, well-dressed professional with a comfortable interpersonal style. He warmly welcomed me and assured me that he was there to work. Unsolicited, he described to me how he wanted the therapy to proceed (clearly he had not totally given up his controlling ways) and then described his current conflicts with his wife of eight years. His wife, Sue, was completing a nursing degree and then planning to work for the regional hospital where she had been offered a job. Although the couple had no chil-dren, Steve was convinced that Sue would do better if she remained the homemaker she had been since they first began living together. Steve told me that Sue is of a different opinion, and this has resulted in a number of difficult interactions between the spouses. While Steve denied any abuse, it was clear because of the way he described his interactions with Sue that Steve still wanted to control outcomes at home, and that this was stressing the marriage. My task, as his therapist, was to provide nurturance and acceptance to my client while also setting firm boundaries for him both in the therapy room and in his outside relationships, especially his marriage. Steve may have learned a great deal about his physically abusive relationship during his mandated treatment. However, like many men with a history of abuse, he had much more work to do to learn how to relate to others without trying to control or manipulate them. This is the kind of learning that may take substantially more time than is provided in most mandated treatment programs but will occur in groups that provide psychotherapy, not just psychoeducation. Depending on the kind of treatment he experienced, he may have learned how to stop the physical violence to "fly under the radar" of the authorities. Yet, he may not yet have given up his emotionally abusive ways. The challenge for me, as his therapist, would be to help him understand how to get his needs met in his relationships without abusing or controlling. A good starting place would be for me to set clear boundaries in the therapeutic relationship. At the same time, I may have some judgments about Steve and his behavior and will need to find a way to divest myself of such judgments. This is so that I do not shame someone whose abusive behaviors may well have started as a reaction to having been shamed in childhood.

WHAT I HAVE LEARNED FROM WORKING IN THIS AREA

One of the benefits of being a psychologist—a secret they do not tell you in graduate school—is how much you learn about yourself from clients and other aspects of the work you do (at least that has been my experience). I do not think I would have the perspective I do about men if I had not become a psychologist, especially if I had not begun to write about and work with male clients. It is hard to know how much of the personal stories I told in the early pages of this chapter would have been so clear to me today if I had not been in this field. I learned a lot about empathy for men in working with abusive men. Many of my students recoil when they think about working with abusive men, but I change their mind about those possibilities when we discuss the likely genesis of abusive behaviors. I am proud to be able to communicate to them a perspective about abusive men that allows them to develop an empathic approach to this population. I have also been blessed by being exposed to a stellar group of men, my male colleagues in APA's Division 51 (Society for the Psychological Study of Men and Masculinity). I have learned a great deal from the scholarship of these colleagues, but perhaps even more about the inherent value of good men from spending time with them. Sharing time, feelings, and scholarly work with female colleagues in the division has been a similarly enriching experience. Having good colleagues of both genders thus becomes critically important to the ability to do good work with our male (and our female) clients.

REFERENCES

Astin, H. S. (1969). *The woman doctorate in America.* New York, NY: Russell Sage Foundation.

Bachman, R., & Saltzman, L. E. (1996). *Violence against women: Estimates from the redesigned survey* (Bureau of Justice Statistics special report). Washington, DC: Bureau of Justice Statistics.

Centers for Disease Control. (2008). *Health, United States, 2008: U.S. Department of Health and Human Services, Centers of Disease Control and Prevention.* Washington, DC: National Center for Health Statistics.

Dutton, D. (1986). The outcome of court-mandated treatment for wife assault: A quasi-experimental evaluation. *Violence and Victims, 1,* 163–175.

Dutton, D. (1995). *The batterer: A psychological profile.* New York, NY: HarperCollins.

Hansen, M., Harway, M., & Cervantes, N. A. (1991). Therapists' perceptions of severity in cases of family violence. *Violence and Victims, 4,* 275–286.

Harway, M. (1975). Stereotyping. Some effects on the target person. *Personality and Psychology Bulletin, 1*(1), 290–292.

Harway, M., & Evans, K. (1996). Working in groups with men who batter. In M. Andronico (Ed.). *Men in groups: Insights, interventions, psychoeducational work* (pp. 357–375). Washington, DC: American Psychological Association.

Harway, M., & Hansen, M. (2004). *Spouse abuse: Assessing and treating battered women, batterers, and their children* (2nd ed.). Sarasota, FL: Professional Resource Press.

Harway, M., Hansen, M., & Cervantes, N. (1997). Therapist awareness of appropriate interventions in treatment of domestic violence: A review. *Journal of Aggression, Maltreatment and Trauma, 1*(1), 290–292.

Harway, M., & O'Neil, J. M. (Eds.). (1999). *What causes men's violence against women.* Newbury Park, CA: Sage.

Heyman, R. E., Feldbau-Kohn, S. R., Ehrensaft, M. K., Langhinrichsen-Rohling, J., & O'Leary, K. D. (2001). Can questionnaire reports correctly classify relationship distress and partner physical abuse? *Journal of Family Psychology, 15*(2), 334–346.

Holtzworth-Munroe, A., Waltz, J., Jacobson, N. S., Monaco, V., Fehrenback, P. A., & Gottman, J. M. (1992). Recruiting nonviolent men as control subjects for research on marital violence: How easily can it be done? *Violence and Victims, 7,* 79–88.

Island, D., & Letellier, P. (1991). *Men who beat the men who love them: Battered gay men and domestic violence.* New York, NY: Haworth Press.

Levant, R. (2001). Desperately seeking language: Understanding, assessing and treating normative male alexithymia. In G. R. Brooks & G. E. Good (Eds.), *The new handbook of psychotherapy and counseling for men: A comprehensive guide to settings, problems and treatment approaches* (pp. 424–443). San Francisco: Jossey-Bass.

O'Neil, J. M., & Harway, M. (1997) A multivariate model explaining men's violence toward women: Predisposing and triggering hypotheses (with J. M. O'Neil). *Violence Against Women, 3*(2), 182–203.

Segal-Evans, K. (1994, February). *Treatment issues for men who batter.* Paper presented at the Midwinter Convention of Divisions 29, 42 and 43 of the American Psychological Association, Scottsdale, AZ.

Silverman, J., Raj, A., Mucci, L. A., & Hathaway, J. E. (2001). Dating violence against adolescent girls and associated substance use, unhealthy weight control, sexual risk behavior, pregnancy, and suicidality. *Journal of the American Medical Association, 286,* 5.

Sorensen, S. B., & Bowie, P. (1994). Girls and young women. In L. D. Eron, J. H. Gentry, & P. Schlegel (Eds.), *Reason to hope: A psychosocial perspective on violence and youth* (pp. 167–176). Washington, DC: American Psychological Association.

Tjaden, P., & Thoennes, N. (1998, November). *Prevalence, incidence, and consequences of violence against women: Findings from the National Violence Against Women survey* [Special issue]. Washington, DC: National Institute of Justice and Centers for Disease Control and Prevention Research in Brief.

Walker, L. E. (1979). *The battered woman.* New York, NY: Harper & Row.

White, J. P., & Koss, M. P. (1991). Courtship violence: Incidence in a national sample of higher education students. *Violence and Victim, 6,* 247–256.

12

Working With Traditional Men in the Military

Dealing With Trauma

JERI NEWLIN

INTRODUCTION

Everyone I meet and talk to seems to be intrigued when I tell them that I am getting my doctorate in psychology. It is a fascinating topic, and it inevitably sparks conversation. When they hear that my area of concentration is the psychology of men and masculinity, they are even more interested and often surprised. "Men? Really?" "Didn't you say you were a feminist? So why would a feminist study man? That just seems odd." "Why would a woman choose to specialize in men's mental health issues and the study of masculinity?" These are just some of the questions and comments I hear. When I explain what the new psychology of men is all about, I inevitably get a mixed response. Explaining the ways the ideals of traditional masculinity can have a negative impact on both men and women is something that not everyone can understand. Regardless of whether they completely understand what I do, they always are able to see the passion I have for my chosen focus in psychology.

A passion for what I do might very well be an understatement. Perhaps that is because the path that led me to the study of masculinity could be considered a rather dramatic one. On the one hand, I am a single mother to a young adult male son. As he has grown and as I have tried to guide him, I have seen him shaped by social forces that attempt to mold him into an acceptable representation of American masculinity. The process of raising a son by myself has had its dramatic moments, but nothing that would catapult me into the study of men's psychology. However, when, in 2006, the love of my life took his own life, I was hit head on by the fact that I could never again look at male suicide as a statistic to be read about in psychology textbooks.

My grief process led me to try to understand why men who commit suicide seem to have a good grasp on their lives and who, on the outside, show no signs of suicidality. The more I read and the more I tried to understand why this happens, I was made aware of how trying to live up to the traditional male standards can affect our men in some highly negative ways. Moreover, I became angrier and angrier at the societal "rules" that dictate what a man can and cannot do when he is in psychic pain. It was this process that shaped my desire to work with men as much as I could in my clinical life to do whatever it was I could to help them lead happier and more authentic lives.

PERSONAL JOURNEY

Born in 1964, I was the youngest child of three, with one older brother and an older sister. I grew up in a relatively traditional home in which both parents came from working-class families in the Midwest. My father worked, and my mother stayed home to raise the kids and keep the home. My father moved from the blue-collar to the white-collar field when I was quite young; as a result, we moved around quite a bit as he was promoted and transferred within his company. Through this, my mother was the anchor in the home. She supported my father in all that he did and was a source of constancy as we changed homes every two to four years.

I do not recall much talk about what I wanted to be when I grew up. It was almost an unspoken given that we girls would work until we got married, but marriage was the ultimate goal. I did not dream of being a doctor, a lawyer, or a psychologist when I was a little girl. I did think about being a teacher and a mommy. That was the norm for me. It was not until I was older, in high school, that I really saw models other than the stay-at-home mom in regard to what I could be when I grew up. Of course, there were friends whose mothers worked and women who worked for my father in a traditional "man's field." But, that seemed so exotic to me, and probably not something I would do when I grew up. And when I thought about the type of husband I would have (because, of course, I would have a husband), I wanted him to be just like my father, the strong, stoic provider for his family—the quiet and dependable rock.

In hindsight, I can see how growing up in such a traditional household shaped the way I look at gender and gender roles. The man was the leader of the family, the law, and the provider, and his career dictated the family journey. Although the wife was a huge part of the family with a major contribution, it was not as overt a concept as that of the father's role. My father's traditional upbringing influenced the way in which our family was structured. He was born in the Great Depression, raised in post–World War II America, and grew up surrounded by traditional male role models as he learned what it meant to be a man. Football players, cowboys, John Wayne, the strong-and-silent type—these were the types of men my father admired. His father was a veteran of both World War II and the Korean War. Being the oldest child, my father was the man in charge when my grandfather was away. It was both the time when he grew up and the circumstances under which he became a man that shaped the way he viewed masculinity. At the same time, his mother was a strong woman who worked outside the home and was not afraid to let her opinion be known. Although she was traditional in the sense that she did all of the cooking, cleaning, and child rearing, she also was able to step out of the traditional role of a midcentury housewife and pursue interests outside the home.

I think that it is because of my father's experience in his family of origin that the gender lines were more fluid for my sister and myself than they were for my brother. We girls were allowed more flexible roles and behaviors than my brother. My father loved teaching me the rules of football and was thrilled that his girls were such big fans of sport. In fact, when I decided I wanted to major in sports broadcasting in college, my father was proud of me. He liked the idea and was proud of the fact that his girls were "strong" and "tough." His expectations for his son were much more restrictive. He wanted a son who was as success driven, competitive, and sports oriented as he was. However, my brother was the quiet one of the family and best described as an artistic loner. As a result, my father and brother have never been close. I think that by not fitting into the traditional masculine mold that my father was living in, my brother was a disappointment to him. Although never overtly stated, this remains a strong example to me of what is expected of boys as they grow into men in our culture.

My adult life continued to provide me with lessons about manhood in some interesting ways. I dropped out of college my sophomore year and returned home to live with my parents while I decided what to do with my life. Looking back, I can see that I was really not prepared either functionally or developmentally for the college experience. So, home I went. I thought that I would return one day when I figured out what I wanted to do with my life. Little did I know it would take as long as it did.

After dropping out of college and moving back home, I worked in different types of jobs and was quite content to be just kind of drifting along without a great deal of direction. I then met and began dating a young Marine named Bob. He was a fun, funny, and dynamic young man my parents really liked. After dating for two years, we got married. I can honestly say that at this point I did not give going back to college much thought. Now that I was married, I figured I finally got what I dreamed of growing up, and it just was not that important for me to get an education.

During the five years we were married, I was surrounded by traditional males. I think the Marine Corps might just be the epitome of traditional masculinity norms. Tough, stoic, prone to violence and displays of bravery and machismo, these men were the proud brotherhood of which my husband was a part. Unlike what many folks may hear about the Marine Corps, we did not get to see any exciting duty stations or go to any exotic locales. My husband actually got stationed in the middle of the desert not long after we were married, and it was difficult for me to find a satisfying job that was not an extremely long way from our home. The job that I did have consisted of long hours that were inconsistent with my husband's hours, making our time together limited. So, after several months of listening to my husband pitch the idea of me joining the Marine Corps, I became a part of that "brotherhood" by enlisting in July 1988. At the time, women only made up approximately 9% of the Marines Corps. From July 1988 until August 1992, I was one of them.

For 4 years, I developed close relationships with men who were the epitome of hypermasculinity. Their ideas of masculinity and femininity were restrictive, and many times I felt like an outsider in a sea of testosterone. On the one hand, I feel like I gained a lot of respect from my "brothers" during my enlistment. It is very much a family atmosphere, and because I was not afraid to work, I was taken seriously as a comrade. However, because I was not afraid to work, I was told I was one of the guys. This was meant to be a compliment. Although my colleagues meant well in instances such as that, misogyny was present almost everywhere you looked in the Marine Corps of my younger years. Unfortunately, I was often the unintentional victim of that sexist attitude and sometimes the intentional victim as well. Derogatory comments about women, jokes about women and what they are really useful for were commonly bandied about, with no regard for the fact that even though I was one of them, I was a woman as well. I felt as if I were undercover in the men's locker room and overhearing things they would never say in front of their girlfriends or wives.

In the midst of this education about and among men, my marriage was coming apart. My husband and I married very young, and while we were in love when we married, we simply were not at the right place in our lives to be married to one another. Almost immediately after finishing boot camp (and quite by surprise), I became pregnant with our son. Not long after I became pregnant, my husband was sent overseas on an unaccompanied tour. For reasons I may never know, he had an affair while he was away. While I know that it is never solely the fault of one partner when a marriage ends, the affair was something I was unable to get over, and we were divorced before our son turned two years old. My experiences with my husband and my colleagues were beginning to negatively affect the way I viewed men. I began to construct a one-dimensional view of most men as sexist, loud, obnoxious, self-centered, driven only by sex, and hard to trust.

The years passed, and I raised my son on my own. Subsequent relationships with men did little to change the ideas that I developed about them However, by the time I met Timm, I had been divorced for a long time and had gone back to school to finish my education. Timm was different from any man I had ever met; he was truly unique in my eyes. He really wanted to provide for me, yet he was not a man who seemed to have come from the same mold of the traditional men in my past. He was caring and loving and, from what I knew, extremely open in sharing himself and his feelings with the woman in his life. He appreciated me for who I was: a thinking, feeling woman, not simply a sex object. Here was a progressive man who broke the mold in terms of how I had viewed men up to this point in my life. He showed me that men are not all alike. They are not all concerned with being the big wheel, with winning at all costs, or with being so tough as to appear to have no emotions whatsoever. This was the most satisfying and trustful relationship I had ever had with a man.

When he tragically killed himself, I realized that even a man who seemed so progressive and nontraditional was still being ruled in some ways by traditional male norms. Although at times he said he was depressed (and, looking back, much more depressed than he ever let on to me), he would not seek help. He admitted to me that he had struggled with depression, that he was not happy in his profession, and that he was frustrated with the fact that he was unable to perform sexually from time to time. We had talks about things that happened in his childhood that left scars and caused him to search for happiness throughout his life. The times that he would become irritable over small things and the pressure he sometimes felt to be the perfect man for me would cause him to withdraw from me when he became stressed. But, no matter how much I suggested he try counseling or therapy again, he said he could "muscle through it," and that it was just a passing funk. In his final letter to me, he let me know that he felt that he was not man enough for me because of the problems he was trying to deal with in isolation. He felt he had failed in trying to live up to everyone's expectations of what a man should be. His solution to ending his pain was to end that pain in the most irreversible way possible.

PROFESSIONAL JOURNEY

My son was in middle school and I was working as an administrative assistant for a countywide school attendance improvement program when I made the decision to return to college. I had spent the years between dropping out of college and returning to college working as a secretary, a receptionist, a toy store manager, an elementary school secretary, a cellular phone customer service representative, and a Marine. Yet, in all of these jobs, I was never really happy in the work that I did. I enjoyed the people I worked with and most of the work environments I experienced, but I never really felt truly happy or fulfilled with the actual work I was doing. I knew I was capable of doing more and of finishing that degree I started long ago. I knew that this time around I would be going to school because I wanted to go. Although I was not sure what my major would be when I restarted my education, I knew I wanted to work with people. People fascinated me, and working with them was enjoyable to me.

Not long after I returned to school, my father suffered a stroke. As a family, we watched him and helped him work his way through all kinds of rehabilitation: speech therapy, occupational therapy, physical therapy. He worked incredibly hard and never gave up in his efforts to regain as many of the losses he suffered as he could. I was fascinated by the human potential to come back from something so devastating and life altering as a massive stroke. I was amazed by the power of the brain, the mind, and the human spirit to work together to heal themselves against so many odds. At the same time, I was taking several psychology courses to fulfill core course requirements and was leaning toward choosing psychology for my major. However, I was hesitant as I knew that if I truly wanted a career in psychology, I would have to go to graduate school.

After researching the options and career paths that I could take with psychology, I thought my best bet would be to get a master's degree in clinical psychology or marriage and family therapy and go from there. I knew I wanted to work with people, to help them in an applied or clinical context, and I felt that at my age, it would be best to take the shortest route to getting to do that kind of work. A master's degree seemed to make the most sense, not to mention the fact that a doctorate was intimidating to me at that time. However, a professor I worked for as an undergraduate talked to me about the advantages of getting a doctorate. She talked about increasing your options in terms of the things you can do with a doctorate, such as teaching, research, administrative work, and clinical work. She also assured me that there is no such thing as being too old to pursue a doctoral degree. I read more about what is involved in getting a doctorate and decided to follow that path and get my PhD in counseling psychology. I applied to and was accepted into the counseling psychology program at the University of Illinois in Urbana-Champaign and began my studies there in fall 2005.

Going into graduate school, I was not sure what kind of research I wanted to be my focus. I had originally considered bullying, but it was not something that really spoke to me. It was at the end of my first year of graduate school that my partner committed suicide. In trying to understand his suicide and his pain, I read a great deal of literature about men's mental health, masculine norms, and the new psychology of men. It was in reading the works of Michael Addis, Chris Kilmartin, Glenn Good, Jim O'Neil, Ron Levant, Sam Cochran, Fred Rabinowitz, and many others that I found my eyes opening up to the ways in which gender and societal expectations for men (and women) play a big part in shaping who we are and how we deal with events in our lives. I had many "aha" moments as I read and studied. I began to understand a bit more about why men are the way they are and how the disparate socialization of masculinity and femininity gets in the way of men and women truly understanding one another. Understanding our gendered culture helped me to better understand men and women and their unique needs in the context of psychotherapy.

As I began my practicum experiences, I was surprised to see that not many textbooks or courses discussed the culture of masculinity when teaching the process of counseling and psychotherapy. In learning to be competent multicultural therapists, we are taught to consider the unique needs or issues that may come up in the therapy room surrounding differences in sexuality, religion, race, ethnicity, and culture. We learn about the psychology of women in terms of their sociopolitical status and history or oppression. But, conspicuously absent was the discussion of the unique needs of male clients. The techniques that do and do not work with men, the different ways that rapport is established, the ways in which men utilize therapy, and the possible resistance of men to therapy do not appear to be addressed in the majority of clinical training settings.

TRADITIONAL MASCULINITY: AN OVERVIEW

What is traditional masculinity? There are four underlying principles or ideals that bound the masculine role (Addis & Mahalik, 2003; David & Brannon, 1976; Levant & Pollack, 1995; Pollack, 1998; Thompson & Pleck, 1986). First, *no sissy stuff* refers to the stigma associated with all feminine characteristics and traits, including emotional openness. It is necessary to avoid all things feminine as any behaviors that might be interpreted are not allowed if you want to be seen as masculine. As Tom Hanks succinctly said in *A League of Their Own*, "There's no crying in baseball!" Just look at the way boys are teased by their peers if they are caught crying. Second, *the big wheel* refers to the masculine ideal that men with status are looked on as better models of masculinity than lower-status men. This ideal teaches boys and men that there is an expectation that they should seek success and status throughout their lifetime, both in the professional world and in the sexual arena. The man with the best job, the best salary, the most girlfriends, and the most sexual conquests is looked on as a hero by other men. Third, *the sturdy oak* represents the ideal of stoicism, toughness and self-reliance. Men are pressured to be self-reliant, stoic, tough, and confident in all they do. Men are not allowed to show vulnerability or ask for help. "Real" men do not need instructions or ask for directions. Last, *give 'em hell!"* refers to the masculine nature of aggression, violence, and risk taking. This is the ideal that says men should be aggressive and if necessary turn to violence. Think of John Wayne or General Patton. Think of Tyler Durden and all the violence he promoted in *Fight Club*. The military is a perfect setting for all four components to be enacted by and taught to our men.

Other components have been added to this idea of the traditional male as the study of male psychology has grown since David and Brannon's (1976) definition of traditional masculinity. These components include homophobia and sexual dysfunction (Solomon, 1982), restrictive emotionality and restrictive affectionate behaviors between men (O'Neil, 1982), power over women, risk taking, primacy of work (Mahalik, Good, & Englar-Carlson, 2003), and nonrelational sexuality (Levant & Fischer, 1998; Brooks, 1998). All add to our knowledge of the societal norms that men feel the need to enact to be thought of as "real" men. Yet, these researchers and clinicians have found that the majority of men feel they fail to live up to these traditional ideas of what it means to be a man in today's world. Traditional norms guide the socialization of boys and can result in some negative consequences by the time they reach adulthood. Masculinity is not a set of intractable traits that are hard-wired into a man's person but a process of learning what to and what not to do to be seen as male. Through the observation of their fathers and other men around them, as well as being directly told how to be a man, boys internalize many of the traditional male norms described. This socialization of the male gender role encourages the suppression of vulnerable emotions, such as sadness, while encouraging instrumental behaviors as opposed to emotional processing and expression. This may result in a limited spectrum of emotional expression. Often, whatever emotion a man may be feeling will be expressed as anger or simply stuffed and held deep within. Not only do men have trouble expressing the full array of emotions, but also because of the many years of being told that emotions bring vulnerability, many men do not recognize the emotions they are experiencing and cannot put a name to them.

This learned emotional suppression can lead to intrapersonal and interpersonal difficulties, which often lead men into therapy. When some men come into the therapy room, they may be doing it for someone else. They may say they are there to save a relationship or to keep their job. They may be there because they are mandated by the courts or as a part of a military program. To many men, the idea of seeking counseling or psychotherapy is a sign of weakness or not being able to handle something on their own, and they may be highly resistant to the process. The simple fact that they are in therapy can mean to them that they have failed at truly being a man because they have openly acknowledged in some way that they need help.

Regardless of the catalyst that put them in the chair across from the therapist, many men can take quite a while to feel comfortable with the process of therapy. You may find yourself sitting across from the sturdy oak as the pressure that your male client feels to remain stoic and self-reliant can keep him from opening himself up to you. As therapists, we are in the business of expressing and exploring emotions. Yet, male gender norms emphasize restrictive emotionality. The socialization of suppressing emotions can result not only in men not being comfortable or able to express emotions, but also in their inability to even name what they are feeling. Men tend to tell you what they are thinking, not what they are feeling. The therapy process may be much slower with traditional men than with other clients, male or female.

Men are also socialized to strive for status and power. The traditional male client may come into a therapeutic relationship with a feeling of superiority over the therapist, especially a female therapist. He may treat the therapist in a sexist or sexual manner or may condescend to a female therapist as a way to defend against appearing vulnerable in front of a woman as this would break the principle of no sissy stuff. He may also appear angry or defensive due to his expectation of a one-up position of the therapist since he is the one asking for assistance.

In addition, it may be hard to help your traditional male client understand the process of therapy. Looking within, trying to gain insight, and understanding gender and the role it plays in creating some of his psychological issues may confound him at times. Because many men are socialized to be problem solvers, they may come to therapy with the attitude that they just need you to fix their problem or just tell them what to do to make things better. While some of life's problems can be approached in this manner, many issues that are brought to the therapy room are not that easy to fix.

Although the flavor of therapy with a traditional male client is most certainly different from what we think of when we imagine the way we work with our clients, it can be a highly rewarding endeavor for both therapist and client. Patience must be stressed. The building of rapport can take longer than one might expect, but the benefits for both are many.

WORKING WITH TRADITIONAL MEN: CASE STUDIES

At the beginning of my clinical practica, I did not think there would be any difference in the way I would treat my male clients and my female clients. There was no mention of what unique issues men might bring to therapy or how working with men and women would look and feel different. As I began, I approached my work with male and female clients in the same way. As rapport was built, I found that females would open up and discuss emotions and feelings and were good at using insight and seeing others' perspectives, depending on the situation and the reason they came to counseling.

In contrast, many of the men seemed clueless about what lay behind their discomfort or unhappiness. Instead, they wanted to know how long therapy would take to fix their problem. I would get frustrated when I would ask a client what his thoughts or feelings were regarding an issue he had brought to the session and be told, "I don't know." Many times, a session would end and I would feel like nothing had been accomplished, or that no progress (as I viewed progress) was being made with my male clients.

Working at a Veterans Affairs (VA) hospital, I had a chance to explore the way men utilize therapy in a much more traditionally masculine setting than in the college counseling centers in which I had previously worked. Although not a hard-and-fast rule, many of the male college students I encountered were more flexible in their attitudes toward traditional gender roles and more willing than the stereotypical traditional male to explore their thoughts and feelings. Within military institutions, men are indoctrinated into a culture of highly traditional masculinity and are not accepted if they show any sort of vulnerability. Vulnerability gets you killed. Vulnerability or any type of feminine emotion or characteristic is quickly quashed through shaming and even bullying. Toughness, stoicism, aggression, invulnerability, extreme self-reliance, and the ability to take anything and charge through it— these are the characteristics one needs to survive in the military and are rewarded via promotions, awards, and a sense of belonging to a brotherhood. These characteristics are not conducive to a deep and insightful therapy experience. This is especially true with a rookie female therapist who has not yet learned that therapy with men, especially combat-hardened veterans, looks much different from therapy with women and college students.

Case Study 1: Alex

Alex was one of the first veterans I worked with in my practicum at a VA hospital while I was in Tennessee. I was working in the post-traumatic stress disorder (PTSD) clinic and was excited to be working with fellow veterans. As I had not been sent to any combat situations while I was in the Marine Corps, I felt particularly proud to be able to help fellow veterans in their postcombat recovery. Alex first came to me about six months after he returned from a deployment to Iraq that was longer than twelve months during Operation Iraqi Freedom. He came in because he said he was having problems at home, and that his wife has expressed being fed up with their conflicts. He said she wanted him to get help to be more like "his old self." He was not particularly invested in getting therapy except to save his marriage. It is not uncommon for traditional male clients to see the problem lying in interpersonal relationships, not within themselves. Alex was in his late 20s and married with two children. He was raised on a farm in Tennessee and was living and working on a farm when he came to the VA. He was one of two boys raised by a traditional mother and father. When asked about his experiences growing up, he said that he had a relatively close family, but not one that was affectionate. His mother stayed at home and raised Alex and his brother, while his father farmed and taught the boys how to farm as well. He said he was taught to fish and hunt at an early age and did not remember crying while he was growing up. He said the men in his family did not even cry at funerals. When I asked why men did not cry, Alex responded, "Because they just don't."

Alex was not sure if he was suffering from PTSD, but wanted to find out if that was a possibility as everyone said he just was not the same old Alex since he returned from the war. After he relayed his combat experiences to me in our initial counseling sessions, I had no doubt he was suffering from PTSD. I suspected that this was what was affecting his relationships, his general mood, and his need to drink alcohol for the first time in his life. Alex said he was almost completely uninterested in playing with his children or in spending time with his family. He said he was totally distanced from everyone he had been friends with, would fly off the handle at the smallest provocation, and dreaded going out in public. He had lost his desire to have sex with his wife, lost his desire to go fishing (which he said consumed a majority of his free time before the war), and seemed only to want to sit out in his garage and drink beer from the time he got off work until the time he went to bed. What seemed to baffle him the most was that he never liked to drink alcohol prior to his deployment to Iraq. He had no idea why he was behaving this way and was having a difficult time connecting any of the changes he was experiencing to his time in Iraq. It seemed to me as though he was looking to me to tell him what was wrong and what to do to fix himself. However, my experience as a counseling student was that we were not supposed to "fix" our clients or tell them what was wrong but rather to listen to them and let them take the lead, so we might have been at cross purposes from the beginning of our work together.

We discussed the traumas Alex experienced in Iraq, including ambushes, improvised explosive devices, having comrades shot dead right next to him, and having to be on guard constantly, not knowing if the enemy was around the corner. I listened to him as he described a mortar attack on his company's compound. This resulted in having his best friend get blown off of his feet by the mortar and landing, dead, on top of him. As I listened to his experiences and his descriptions of what he heard, saw, and experienced, I was awash in thoughts and emotions of what it must be like to go through something so horrific. Yet, Alex told me about these things as if he were reading a newspaper account of something that happened to someone else. There was no emotion in Alex's voice; there was hardly any inflection in his manner of speech. I knew that the experience of combat can numb one to a lot of emotions, and that this is a "hallmark" of PTSD, but I do not think I was prepared for how matter-of-factly Alex would present himself to me.

After five sessions with Alex, I felt like there was still little (if any) rapport between myself and Alex. He still felt to me closed off to the idea of discussing emotions that he experienced in Iraq or the emotions he was experiencing now that he was back home. I felt stuck more often than not because I could not understand why sessions with Alex felt like pulling teeth when I was used to sharing emotions in nearly all of my past practicum counseling sessions with university students. The only emotion he seemed to recognize in himself was anger. When asked how he felt about his buddies dying right in front of him, he simply said, "I was surprised that I didn't die, too." When further probed, there was never a mention of guilt, sadness, loss, grief, or fear. However, Alex said he was truly fine and just wanted to know why he was angry, why he was disconnected from his family, and why he was drinking so much.

I have found that most of my clients are able to tap into some feelings surrounding their trauma via an exploration of their thoughts about the event (i.e., guilt, "It's my fault that this happened"; fear, "I can't get close to anyone now because I will lose them"; shame, "I should have died with my buddies"; etc.). However, Alex was not willing (or perhaps more accurately was not able) to discuss his thoughts about his traumas or process how the thoughts might be irrational. Looking back, I think that he was completely guided by the traditional masculine norms of self-reliance, not allowing himself to seem vulnerable or in need of help, and I was at the time unsure how to proceed with him.

At that time, I had never had any experience with men like this, nor had I been taught that traditional men will look and feel differently in the therapy room and may need to be approached in a different manner than most psychology or counseling programs have taught. I now realize that asking Alex to tell me about how he felt about his experiences in the war and expecting emotion from him was not meeting him where he was and only led to frustration on both our parts. I was asking Alex to relate to me and interact with me in a way that, while familiar to me as a therapist, was incongruent with the traditional male culture in which he was embedded. Asking a man who lives and breathes the norms of stoicism, self-reliance, and restrictive emotionality to talk to me about what he was feeling or to conduct deep self-reflection was akin to asking a member of the African Bushmen tribe to take an American driver's license exam.

After a little over two months, Alex lost his transportation and was unable to continue coming to sessions at the VA. I do not know if this was actually true or an excuse, but perhaps if I had been more savvy about how to work with him, he may have found a way to make our appointments. At the time, I did not know what continued therapy would have accomplished with Alex as I felt like I was so unsure of what to do with this man. I only hope that at some point he was able to find someone who could help him in a way that he could relate to and to help him confront and resolve his issues around the impact of PTSD on his life after combat.

Case Study 2: Robert

A little more than a year later, I was at a different practicum site when I began working with Robert. Robert was a veteran who was having symptoms of PTSD. In addition, he was a recovering addict who was feeling the urge to use drugs and alcohol after almost a year of sobriety. Robert was a combat veteran of the Vietnam War. He was in his mid-60s and described himself as a traditional man. He was proud of the fact that he had been self-reliant from a very young age. He was raised by a mother who stayed at home and raised her children while Robert's father worked long hours away from home. Robert said that he was married two times, and each time his wives took quite traditional feminine roles in the marriage. He said that he felt it was his responsibility as the man to provide financially for his family. He also stressed how important it had been to him never to allow his wife, his children, or his friends see him in any kind of emotional distress. When I asked Robert why this was, he simply told me that this was the way he was raised to believe a man should be.

Robert went on to discuss with me his experiences in Vietnam, how his company was attacked numerous times and how he was never sure if people who looked like civilians were actually going to attack him and his buddies. He recalled having dying allies and enemies screaming near him many times during his tour. He discussed how he was beginning to have flashbacks and memories of the war that he found disturbing and frightening. Robert said that prior to the last several months, he had been using drugs and alcohol to numb the feelings and erase the memories. He said he had been addicted to alcohol and heroin for over 20 years and had been abusing alcohol, marijuana, and other drugs since he returned from the war in 1970. He told me that he never told his wives, his children, or his friends about his experiences in Vietnam because he felt that he should just be able to deal with it himself. He also said that the few times he did try to tell someone, they would simply call him crazy and brush him off.

Robert was different from my first veteran client, Alex, in that I could see some emotion just below the surface of his stories. He was reluctant to admit to emotions or to explore emotions with me, but I still held out hope that the process of therapy would be more successful with Robert. Since my experience with Alex at the VA, I had spent more time reading the literature regarding how to work with men in therapy and what one might expect to see and hear from them. This included how gender norms can have an impact on the therapeutic relationship and the way men might approach therapy and counseling. I felt more comfortable with Robert and did not put as much pressure on myself to "fix" him and to uncover all of the emotions I was *sure* he must be feeling but unwilling to share. I worked much more slowly with Robert and was able to take my time building a rapport with him. It was much more like building a friendship with him than it was being his therapist. We talked about his favorite hobbies and how he passed his time when he was not working. Humor was a big part of our time together. He would often start or end a session with a joke he had heard. If we had common interests like movies or particular sports, we would spend some time talking about those things. He would tell me stories of camaraderie and fun with his buddies in the military. He talked about new ways he was devising to keep himself from using when he felt the urge to drink or find drugs. I was his partner in thinking of ways to keep himself busy when he was having trouble with boredom and loneliness so that he would be less vulnerable to the lure of drugs and alcohol.

The therapy with Robert felt more solution focused than any therapy I had previously done. Although I explored how he was doing and we talked about his history with relationships, mental health, and drugs and alcohol, I was careful not to push him to talk about emotional material unless I could sense his comfort and willingness to go there. As the rapport and bond grew between us, Robert was spending more time in session talking about his emotions and some of the pain he had experienced in life. He became increasingly open to more insight-focused interventions. I watched him grow more vulnerable in our sessions and be able to discuss feelings like guilt, shame, loneliness, fear, and sadness. We were never able to get to a point at which an entire session was focused on emotions. However, as we progressed, the balance of cognitive and analytical discussion, friendly chitchat, and emotionally oriented insight-focused processing was always shifting. I found that the rational component of rational emotive behavioral therapy (REBT) to be highly attractive to Robert. By assigning him this predominantly cognitive work, he was able to tap into the emotions behind the thoughts. Robert and I were now seeing real improvement in his well-being.

Robert did a lot of work and was able to help himself in a way that was most likely more meaningful to him than many other modes of therapy might have been. What started off feeling like a pleasant but ultimately unproductive relationship with a very kind and fascinating client turned into one of the most satisfying and fulfilling therapeutic relationships I have had. When we terminated therapy, Robert was no longer having flashbacks when he heard helicopters flying over his house and was feeling confident that he could trust the skills and tools that he had developed to help him remain sober.

ADVICE FOR FEMALE THERAPISTS

As I have journeyed through life, I have seen myself grow in my ideas of what gender is and what men and women can be, as opposed to what society says they should be. I have seen the gender roles for women become more fluid and less restrictive. Times are changing, and men are beginning to break free from many of the restrictions that dictate what is and is not masculine. However, there is still an overwhelming expectation from our culture, from their peers, from their fathers and mothers, and from themselves that men will remain self-sufficient, independent, stoic, unemotional, and successful. As women's gender roles change, men's roles are changing as well. But navigating these changes in a culture of restrictive norms can cause confusion and pain for the men in our lives. Being in relationships with women who want true partnerships, both instrumental and emotional, can lead to relational and intrapsychic stress when men feel they cannot balance both partner and societal expectations. How a man defines himself can be a difficult process in these times.

Working with men, especially with traditional men, has really opened my eyes to how important gender is when looking at our clients and conceptualizing what will work best with them. Yes, we are taught about gender in our training, but for many of us that means we are taught what feminist psychology is and what feminist therapy looks like. We learn about the effect of gender roles on women's psychological well-being, sense of self, and role in the world. However, this same gender effect is rarely taught in relation to men and what this means for how we do (or should do) therapy with men. Psychotherapy and counseling are based on an intimate sharing of thoughts and feelings and on a close intimate interpersonal bond that, frankly, are not part of the traditional male norm. Much of what we try to get our clients to engage in is in direct opposition of what they have been taught about being a man. Who would not feel resistance, barriers going up, even hostility when sitting across from someone who is trying as best as they can to get them to do exactly what they have no intention of doing, something that we feel will help them, but they feel will make them less of a man?

In situations such as this, no one is "at fault": We are both only doing what is natural to us. We are both doing what we have been taught to do. The culture of psychotherapy teaches us to get others to open up to release pain and discomfort, to develop meaningful interpersonal relationships, and to create corrective emotional experiences. The culture of traditional masculinity teaches men to keep things close to the vest, to remain self-reliant, and to remain stoic and invulnerable to fulfill their role as a "strong" man. These are good intentions at cross-purposes. Fortunately, female therapists and traditional men are potentially able to inform and teach the other how best to come together for the betterment of both. As a therapist, if you can take a multicultural view of traditional masculinity, you will find that you are better able to work with clients who endorse a more traditional masculinity ideology as you will learn how to view the world from the eyes, heart, and mind of a traditional man. This will allow you to meet the client where he is and remain aware of how his values, attitudes, and beliefs have shaped his experience in and outside the therapy room.

Be patient with yourself and your client. This may be something very different for both of you, and you may feel uncertain of what to do or where to go with him. Open communication is always helpful. Talk about how different this is and how strange it may feel. You might even tell him what therapy "usually" looks like, but that you have found a better way to make it more comfortable for him. Ask him to talk about his expectations and his needs as you work together. I always remind him that I work for him and am dedicated to making this comfortable and useful for him. I tell him that I will do my best to make sure he is getting what he needs from our time together.

In our training, we are always told to "meet the clients where they are." This is especially important in these situations. If your client needs to spend more time than you expect getting to know you (including asking about the process and seeking reassurance from you), work with him. Show him that he is under no pressure to be someone he is not when he is with you. One of the most beneficial things I have found in building a therapeutic relationship with my male clients is that by listening to them with an open mind and caring attitude and letting them know that I want to know about their experience of being a man, I not only help them to discover more about themselves but also am able to join with each client and help him to author his own change and healing. I hope that by working with men who feel bound by traditional male restrictions, we can help them to find out who it is they really are and what it is they really want from themselves and others.

REFERENCES

Addis, M., & Mahalik, J. (2003). Men, masculinity, and the contexts of help seeking. *American Psychologist, 58*(1), 5–14.

Brooks, G. R. (1998). *A new psychotherapy for traditional men.* San Francisco: Jossey-Bass.

David, D., & Brannon, R. (1976). *The forty-nine percent majority: The male sex role.* Reading, MA: Addison-Wesley.

Levant, R. F., & Fischer, J. (1998). The Male Role Norms Inventory. In C. M. Davis, W. H. Yarber, R. Bauserman, G. Schreer, & S. L. Davis (Eds.), *Sexuality-related measures: A compendium* (2nd ed., pp. 469–472). Newbury Park, CA: Sage.

Levant, R. F. (1995). Toward the reconstruction of masculinity. In R. F. Levant & W. S. Pollack (Eds.), *A new psychology of men* (pp. 229–251). New York, NY: Basic Books.

Mahalik, J. R., Good, G. E., & Englar-Carlson, M. (2003). Masculinity scripts, presenting concerns, and help seeking: Implications for practice and training. *Professional Psychology: Research and Practice, 34*(2), 123–131.

O'Neil, J. M. (1982). Gender role conflict and strain in men's lives: Implications for psychiatrists, psychologists, and other human service providers. In K. Solomon & N. B. Levy (Eds.), *Men in transition: Changing male roles, theory, and therapy* (pp. 5–44). New York, NY: Plenum.

Pollack, W. S. (1998). *Real boys: Rescuing our sons from the myths of boyhood.* New York, NY: Owl Books.

Solomon, K. (1982). The masculine gender role description. In K. Solomon & N. B. Levy (Eds.), *Men in translation: Theory and therapy* (pp. 45–76). New York, NY: Plenum Press.

Thompson, E. H., & Pleck, J. H. (1986). The structure of male norms. *American Behavioral Scientist, 29*, 531–543.

13

Psychotherapy With Older Men

KAREN M. WILBUR

INTRODUCTION

One especially bright man in his 80s often asks at the end of our session, "What have you learned today?" He captures the complexity of his age and stage with this question. He seems to be asking: How can I retain some sense of purpose? How do I understand what my role is as a man in late life? How does the retelling of my story help us understand my sadness and regret? What am I supposed to do now? Are you capable of helping me?

He triggers a range of responses in me. Have I been listening well enough? Have I given enough thought to formulating his problems and concerns? Do I feel like a student, or a daughter, instead of a seasoned clinician? Do I need more of a plan for helping? Can I trust the therapeutic process to bring us to a useful collaboration?

The examination of the current experience of female therapists and their older male patients offers an intimate view of our cultural attitudes toward gender and age. Men and women now in their 60s, 70s, and 80s have all experienced profound changes in gender roles over the course of their adult lives. The rules have changed. The prevailing narrative of men's domination and women's dependence, prominent after World War II, has slowly shifted toward one of shared influence and interdependence in the workplace and at home. Women are visible in all professions, and men have grown accustomed to sharing leadership roles.

PERSONAL JOURNEY

I grew up in a conventional suburban family in Rochester, New York. I was the oldest of four and the only girl. I had the freedom to roam the community on my bike, and I did. The public library was my favorite destination, and I loved to drop in on my former kindergarten teacher, later the superintendent of schools. (She was always gracious.) My mother was an active community volunteer, my father supported us, and we were all involved with the Presbyterian church that my parents had helped to organize. We were a typical 1950s family, including a dog and a cat.

Only one of the mothers in our neighborhood group worked outside the home. Gender roles were prescribed as soldiers returned from World War II and women made way for men in jobs of all kinds. My grandmother had run a factory and stepped aside, returning to community volunteer responsibilities even though my grandfather had died in the Pacific.

In 1964, at 17, I arrived at Mount Holyoke College. The oldest women's college in the country, Mount Holyoke offered an astonishing array of female role models. One half of the faculty were women, a rare proportion even now. It was still a time when an engagement ring was more desirable at graduation than a job, and most of us did not know that life would play out in so many distinct chapters. I graduated in 1968 with the country in disarray and started out on the path I had always planned: getting married, teaching school, and having children. For many years, my view of life was as simple as a timeline my daughter once made in elementary school from file cards and yarn.

The story of abandoned dreams is one commonly associated with women in middle and late life and with the consciousness raising of the late 1960s and early 1970s. The male version of the story is not as easy to see when it has been masked by cultural measures of success. My own father wanted to be an architect, like his grandfather, and was on his way to this goal when World War II intervened. When he returned from war, he was expected to start a family, and practicalities overrode his dream. Over the years, we saw glimpses of it still. He designed a house for a boss and later one for our family. But, we could see that he had been hoping for more.

My father's life was punctuated with loss. His father had died in the Pacific Theater during World War II, his only sister by suicide in her 30s, and our infant brother of multiple medical problems. He and my mother were a resilient pair. They had known each other all their lives. Their lives seemed predetermined by their place in the historical scheme of things, and they settled into them without complaint. They were devoted to one another and had many wonderful life-long friends. My Dad died at 72, after a brief illness, with grace and acceptance.

PROFESSIONAL JOURNEY

After college, I married and taught elementary school. I had always wanted to be a teacher, and this combination was just what my parents and I had hoped for. Many of my college classmates, however, had noticed that our women faculty were engaged in all kinds of academic pursuits. They thought beyond the expected roles commonly available to women in the 1960s and went straight to graduate school or set off on less-traditional paths. I stopped teaching when my first child was born, and before long, I began to ask, "What next?"

Along the way, with help from writers like Jane O'Reilly (1980) and her eye-opening book, *The Girl I Left Behind*, women in my generation figured out what we meant by equality, what was important about reproductive choice, what it meant to earn 60 cents on the dollar, and how to question assumptions about gender, ethnicity, and sexual orientation. We stopped listening to jokes that were sexist, racist, or homophobic. We tried to raise sons who could do the laundry and daughters who could cut the grass. Over time, we stopped assuming that a doctor would be male and a nurse female. We put a few cracks, at least, in the glass ceiling.

Our own life cycles overlap with those around us. My worldview is colored by my own history, my relationships, and my experience with loss and disappointment, with success and achievement. Even as I finished my PhD at 39, I did not fully understand that life would come in so many chapters. Patients like to know that mine has not been a linear path.

When I returned to graduate school in the early 1980s, psychoanalytic writers were beginning to ask about the effects of the women's movement on the practice of psychotherapy. Lisa Gornick's article (1986), "Developing a New Narrative: The Woman Therapist and the Male Patient," affected my professional development as profoundly as Jane O'Reilly's challenging book had affected my personal life. Psychotherapy is a relatively young profession. The earliest practitioners were mostly men and mostly medical doctors. Patients made assumptions about the effectiveness of their therapist that were rooted in the authority and respect given to men in general and physicians in particular. By the 1980s, women were well represented in all clinical disciplines, although not necessarily on the graduate school faculties. At the university student health center where I first worked, it was not possible to request a specific therapist, but a request to see a specific gender was always accommodated.

WORKING WITH OLDER MEN: AN OVERVIEW

What prompts a man, consciously and unconsciously, to seek a woman therapist? What is permissible for men to talk about with women? How does the authority assumed by a woman therapist affect the traditional male attributes of power and sexuality? Will men feel able to display feelings of weakness or dependence when they are culturally expected to be strong?

An intense maternal transference may be comfortable for the female therapist—accustomed as she is to the nurturing role assigned women by society—but frightening for a male patient. He may feel ashamed of his wish for comfort. His defense against a regressive dependence may be cast in sexual or aggressive ways. For the women therapist, an erotic or a hostile transference may trigger countertransferential feelings of arousal, powerlessness, or fear, which may inhibit the expression of these quite normal transferential wishes by her male patient. He may then feel ashamed of his feelings after noting the female therapist's response and refrain from expressing them.

Gornick (1986), Koo (2001), and Bernardez (2004) provided detailed psychoanalytic discussions of these specific mechanisms in the female therapist-male patient dyad. Bernardez (2004) warned that the emergence of the more extreme eroticized transference "may be one of the most clear indicators of childhood sexual abuse" (p. 244). She had long written about the cultural prohibitions against anger in women in this culture and wrote that the capacity of a female therapist to work well with men will depend on her own healthy relationships with men, including an understanding of the role of competition, aggression, and sexuality (p. 252).

Older patients often need evidence that I will be able to apprehend the complexity of their many decades. I may answer direct questions in a way I would not with a younger patient. It is essential to discuss developmental tasks in language a patient can understand. Older men have not grown up reading pop psych and often do not speak the relational or emotional language that is so familiar to younger men and women. They do not know that depression may have a biological base and is not a character flaw. They may not understand that they have been self-medicating with alcohol rather than endure the growing anxiety about the last chapters of life. But if they have arrived in the consulting room, they are trying to make sense of their age and stage and should welcome new ways to think about their experience.

There is freedom in letting go of old imperatives and assumptions, but older male patients need help with formulating meaningful activities based in the reality of a declining physical self. One older man still holds the ideals that motivated his younger self as evidence of his failure physically and intellectually. This keeps him from accepting what has been a fruitful and fully acceptable life. He denies himself a sense of well-being despite good health, an adequately attentive family, cultural stimulation, and material comfort because he expected so much more. He quietly helps others but does not let himself feel any gratification. As he worries about his debilitated wife, he silently wonders who will care for him. His generation no longer operates on the old assumption that wives will outlive husbands.

Our cultural definition of "old age" is also changing. Retirement at 65 may no longer be financially possible or emotionally desirable when life may last another 20 or 25 years. We are reconsidering the pace and stages of adult life, and we all know men and women who seem frail in their 60s and those who are hearty and vital into their 70s and 80s. Psychological variation can be just as pronounced. Those who have managed life with resilience and adaptability will likely face old age with the same flexibility and acceptance. But, for those who have been challenged repeatedly with loss or trauma, the later years may be especially challenging. A fear of dependency begins to have a basis in reality as the older patient begins to decline physically.

In the last stages of life, we must adjust to the gradual loss of mobility and autonomy. Gradual loss of hearing and visual acuity also make life more difficult as we age. Facing this inevitability seems especially hard for men in a culture that glorifies strength, performance, and autonomy. Stanley Cath (1997) wrote of "depletion anxiety" as an awareness of our loss of function in an increasingly disinterested world (p. 143). This age-specific anxiety will be added to the sum of earlier fears and worries, losses, and traumatic events, which may be unassimilated and unresolved and can be easily stimulated in the therapeutic relationship. What we might see as depression in a younger patient may well be a realistic anticipation of coming loss. Disengagement may be a logical preparation for the next stage, not a symptom of depression.

Erikson's famous grid of psychosocial development (1982) reminds us that at each developmental stage, we have the opportunity to revisit all the earlier tasks for refinement or repair. Development proceeds along two interwoven axes: the sense of self and the capacity for relationship. The degree to which older patients have been successful in forming important relationships will affect their ability to adapt to changes in existing relationships, with spouses and children for example, and to form new ones as they move into new living situations. Older male patients may well have put their energy into developing an autonomous, achieving self, often to the neglect of relationships along the way. A new need for dependence on caretakers may be distasteful to a formerly independent man.

A request for therapy may be seen as a way of maintaining connection or finding out if there is still a capacity for forming new relationships. A 73-year-old professional man, for example, wondered if he should get married for the first time. Cath (1997) noted that the "emotional support, guidance, and refueling" (p. 133) available in the therapeutic relationship may be more appropriate to older patients than our traditional neutral stance and well-chosen interpretations. In addition, building on the achievement in adolescence of an ability to see our strengths and weaknesses realistically, older patients may need help adapting goals to meet the physical reality and adjusting the sense of self to acknowledge new limitations, including the limitation of time. Erikson (1982) revisited the final tasks as he considered our increasing longevity. He saw wisdom, "informed and detached concern with life itself in the face of death itself" (p. 60), coming from the final developmental crisis, integrity versus despair.

The older men who present for therapy with a history of resilience and reasonably adequate resolution of previous challenges are able to redefine the meaningful parts of their contemporary lives and find new ways to contribute and maintain hope. Those who have struggled with self-doubt and self-deprecation over the years may well have a harder time with these final stages.

In addition to the usual diagnostic considerations, it is critical to take a developmental inventory. Erikson's model remains a useful tool for identifying disruptions that may have occurred across the life cycle. A thorough relationship history will give clues to resilience and a capacity for self-inquiry. An empathic understanding of how our older male patient sees himself will help to organize repair of a distorted self-image.

WORKING WITH OLDER MEN: CASE STUDIES

Three themes have been prominent in the presenting problems of older men I have seen for psychotherapy: trouble dealing with a recent loss, persistent discontent with the way life has gone, and the most tragic, the belief that life has no further meaning. Variations on these themes are as rich and complicated as each long life.

Case 1: Seeing No Point

Bruce was in his early 60s when we first met. He had worked his way up to a management position in a large steel company. He had gone to work after his tour in Vietnam, married, and raised a family. He did not report any problems with depression, anxiety, or posttraumatic stress during his working years and had no problems with alcohol or drugs after returning from the war. His early years were unremarkable, and he had grown up in an intact family. His mother was still alive.

Near retirement, Bruce was abruptly forced out of his managerial position by a young man he had mentored. The company changes were unexpected after so many years. He had assumed that his loyalty and seniority would protect him. Bruce was thrown into a profound depression and sought medical treatment. No one in the rural area where he lived thought to ask about his time in Vietnam. He had lived for many decades without thinking about that experience and had never revealed the details of his traumatic years as a young soldier. He was an 18-year-old infantryman and had seen the most horrific scenes imaginable. No therapy was suggested, and after a failed trial of antidepressants, he agreed to ECT (electroconvulsive shock therapy). He later acknowledged that this treatment had been an additional traumatic experience, one we discussed many times as therapy proceeded, and had not alleviated his depression. It may well have had long-term detrimental effects on his personality.

As they had planned to do on retirement, Bruce and his wife moved to another state to be closer to their adult children. His severe depression and prominent suicidal ideation persisted despite medication, which had caused an embarrassing tremor. And, for the first time, Bruce began to have flashbacks and nightmares of his Vietnam experience. His physician, also a woman, referred him to me for psychotherapy.

Bruce's adult life had been steady, predictable, and manageable. His children were grown and successful. He was in frequent contact with his brother and elderly mother. His marriage had endured, although it was not especially gratifying at this stage. Bruce seldom left the house. His wife tried to carry on without him, but she made her resentment clear.

Bruce had been holding two overwhelming sets of feelings at bay: his rage at having been forced out of his position and the terror and shame associated with his time in Vietnam. His memories of Vietnam had been locked away for decades. We came to understand that the intensity of his response to his forced retirement opened the door to his memories of Vietnam. No previous life experiences had challenged what we now saw as very brittle defenses, and his newly recovered memories made him feel despicable. He genuinely felt that his family would be better off without him. Bruce was unable to forgive himself for the things he had done as a young soldier. He was experiencing vivid, terrifying nightmares, as he relived his war experiences. He saw no hope for peace in his present or later life.

For Bruce, none of the "basic anchorages of life" (Cath, 1997, p. 140) seemed sufficient reasons to live when he was suffering so profoundly. Although he had some heart problems, he was essentially healthy. He was financially well-off after a lifetime of saving. His children were attentive, and his wife was trying hard to adapt to his severe personality changes. Bruce's severe depression, increasing anxiety, and PTSD (post-traumatic stress disorder) rendered him virtually housebound, except for his faithful attendance at our weekly sessions. Noisy restaurants could trigger flashbacks and rage. Feeling trapped in an interior theater seat or church pew triggered panic. Although he talked of yearning to return to the golf course, when the morning came to meet his friends, he could not get up and out the door.

However, he liked the quiet of my waiting room and came early, sometimes dozing as he waited.

As we started the slow work of dealing with his traumatic past, he sometimes could only stay for part of the session. After revealing a difficult memory, he would often feel the need to stop. The importance of empathic attunement was never clearer, and I always respected his wish to leave. His psychological development seemed to have halted in late adolescence, and most of his adult life had been spent playing a role. Bruce did not experience a continuity of sense of self from early to middle to late adulthood. Although he had negotiated the middle stages of adulthood competently, it would be necessary to identify with the traumatized young soldier before we could begin filling in the gaps. He had never talked about his Vietnam experience with his wife and children and assumed now that they would not be able to love him if they knew the details. Over time, he was able to tell them just that it had been terrifying and horrifying.

In the face of the suicidal wishes that were ever present, Bruce's young grandchild proved the only meaningful anchor and the only part of his world that seemed real. His delight in her was a surprise to him, but in her company, he could play and be himself. We were working together when each of my own grandchildren arrived and being able to connect around this wonderful stage of life seemed an important piece of our relationship.

Bruce's commitment to therapy and faithful attendance were interesting given the difficulty of the work and the limited nature of his other contemporary relationships. He did not question the need to continue and trusted my faith in the therapeutic process. He called me his best friend, although we rarely had contact outside the scheduled hour. He had always agreed he would call if he got to the point of considering suicide, and twice in five years he did so. I met several times with Bruce and his wife to help her understand the kinds of situations that might trigger his PTSD.

Through the years of therapy, I repeatedly suggested that the delight Bruce felt in seeing his grandchildren was evidence that contemporary and future relationships could make life worth living. I shared some of the events of my life, the arrival of grandchildren or worry about my mother's health, as a way of modeling a sense of continuity. None of his own historic anchors seemed real to Bruce. Although he seemed to live either in the traumatic past or in an empty present, his connection to me was evidence of a healthy early life. I continued to believe therapy would help him connect the developmental dots.

Returning to Erikson's grid, it seemed critical to revisit the need for a sense of generativity. Bruce needed to be persuaded that he had something to offer his children and grandchildren. He had not been able to integrate the achievements of parenthood and a successful career into his sense of self. Over time, the images of war faded, and he was less afraid of having his PTSD triggered, but I felt we had made little progress in establishing a basis for interest in the future.

When my relocation forced a premature ending to our therapeutic relationship, he was able to express his sadness as we worked through the termination. Bruce was able, without hesitation, to begin therapy with my officemate, a woman of my age. She was a familiar face, of course, and I invited him to contact me if ever he wanted to do so. His new therapist reports he is continuing to solidify gains, and from time to time tells her that he is going to call me. He never has. He has told his traumatic story again, however, and his own horror is subsiding. I think there is hope for making peace with his trauma and for crafting a sense of himself that will make the next years more gratifying.

Case 2: Is This All There Is?

Long-abandoned dreams may surface in later life. Discontent may be felt first in a long-standing relationship. Often, a sacrifice was made on behalf of the relationship, and if the marriage has not been gratifying, it may not survive the therapeutic examination in later life as resentment is allowed to surface. John was a semiretired corporate executive in his mid-60s hanging on to a consulting job for the health insurance it provided his slightly younger wife. Their marriage was increasingly unhappy, despite material wealth, good health, successful adult children, and many long-time friends. John had started his work life in an era when men were expected to be the providers. He had abandoned dreams of graduate school to provide for his wife and children. As his wife became accustomed to their lifestyle, John buried his own discontent in hard work and steady advancement. He traveled often, worked long hours, and moved up the corporate ladder. He later mourned the cost to his relationships with his children of being so driven. And in this late-life therapy, he set out to establish healthy, adult relationships with his children with good results.

John grew up knowing what was expected of him as a man and strived to conform to the norm of the day. He believed his parents' love and approval depended on it. Certainly, the expectations of his wife and the needs of his growing family left no room for experimentation. Over the years, as his life so successfully conformed to the American dream, it had not occurred to him there could be more.

John was moderately depressed when he decided to find a therapist. He was considering leaving his marriage of 35 years. It was many months before he could make the decision to do so. My support of his wish to compose a more meaningful life, even if it meant ending a long-term relationship, was a surprise to him. He may have assumed that, as a woman, I would not support a plan to leave his marriage. Our exploration of the possibilities of a whole new chapter for him challenged the assumptions he had been living with for so long. He was not required to sacrifice his own growth and development indefinitely.

John and his wife attempted some marital therapy as we continued our individual therapy. His wife's resistance to any changes was telling. It was all working quite well for her. In fact, she was hoping he would return to full-time work in the corporate world. Throughout the long divorce proceedings that ensued, it was clear that, just as John had expected to provide, his wife expected to be provided for.

When the legal battle was finally settled, John was left with a chance to reorganize his life and start again. He revisited the dreams he had entertained and abandoned as a young man. He enrolled in a paraprofessional program of study that, in concert with his career experience, led him to a gratifying new career. Before his divorce, he had been ready to settle into a long and premature retirement. Now, he was energized by a new business, which gave purpose and meaning to his life. His siblings were delighted for him and relished his renewed interest in his family of origin. His adult children were able to support both parents and found ways to relate to them as individuals. John is benefiting from our new definitions and, as a youthful older man, is enjoying this next chapter.

Case 3: One Loss Too Many

Joe was 83 when he made his first appointment at the suggestion of his son, who lived in another state and was concerned about his father. Joe's wife of 14 years had just announced she wanted to live separately and was preparing to move by herself to assisted living. She had been best friends with Joe's first wife, who had died of cancer in her mid 60s, and their families had grown up together. She cited stress as the reason for leaving and refused to come to therapy with Joe. When we spoke briefly by phone, she said they had tried counseling previously, and that life with Joe was very hard. She reported that she had tolerated too many years of his anger and had had enough. She had complex medical issues that she believed were exacerbated by life with Joe.

Joe had been a pilot in World War II and now spent his days playing golf and cards, singing with a local chorus, and running a part-time business. He downplayed his own bouts of serious illness over the years. He had also experienced the death of one son. He was obviously a resilient man but was devastated by this impending loss. He relished their life as a couple and their long history and could not understand her reasoning. Her decision was a blow to his idea of himself as a husband and support. Joe and Barbara had a large circle of friends, all of whom were stunned by the news.

A few months after her move, Barbara took a fall that landed her in a rehabilitation hospital. Joe started to believe she would need to come back home for continued care and became excited at any small request she would make of him. She did not return, however, and gave him few chances to help. Joe had some leverage. He had the health insurance she needed and would lose should they divorce. However, despite the financial struggle he was experiencing, he had no wish to punish her. He had stopped singing with his chorus, and temporary knee problems kept him from playing golf. He was increasingly immobilized by his sadness. In therapy, we tried to understand how Barbara had reached her decision. I pressed him to put himself in her place, to find some empathic sense of her life with him. He was truly at a loss.

After she recovered from her fall, Barbara periodically arranged to meet him for a meal, only to cancel at the last minute. Each time she agreed to get together, he became hopeful. At Thanksgiving, he prepared a meal for them after she agreed to come. He said he was "in seventh heaven." She did not show up. Joe began to consider moving closer to his children, but on Christmas Eve, Barbara died suddenly in her apartment. Instead of calling 911, she called Joe and died before anyone could get to her. Joe moved her furniture back into his home and seemed to be resuming his role as her husband, though widowed. He even struggled with one of her children about funeral arrangements, feeling it was still his place to make the decisions.

With encouragement, Joe was able to express his deep sadness. Tears did not come easily to a man of his generation, but he allowed them. He did not understand Barbara's insistence that the relationship had been abusive. No amount of exploration prompted memories that fit her version of their story. In session, he countered them with stories of their travel together and the way their children had celebrated their marriage. He was not defensive and seemed to consider honestly what her experience might have been. He was not accustomed to thinking about motivation and feelings. I posited that he might have been loud or overbearing at times, despite his love for her, and that he may have reflected the mores of the time by assuming the role as the man of the house, the boss. He considered this without it resonating.

His children by now had made it clear that they thought it best for him to stay put, although he was now many states away from his children and stepchildren. When Barbara first talked of moving out, his adult children made it clear that he was not welcome to stay with them during a trial separation. After her death, they did not encourage him to relocate. Joe seemed not to be able to understand the effect he had had on those close to him. While our meetings afforded Joe a place to express his grief and to feel some comfort, he did not yet seem able to consider the complexities of his relationships with Barbara or their adult children. I suspect that they would all be surprised to know how deeply he cared for them. Expression of such feelings are not commonly part of the repertoire of his, my father's, generation.

When I announced my own relocation about six months after Barbara's death, he did not want to see another therapist. He felt he could carry on. His resilience over the years suggests that he will. He had resumed singing with his chorus and playing golf with friends. Older widowers are prized in his community, and it is likely that he will be the object of plenty of attention. He does not have the inclination to consider the larger questions and likely would not have come for help without the urging of his son. He seems able now to accept things as they have come. Perhaps that is always a significant goal of therapy in later life.

WHAT WE HAVE LEARNED

Judith Viorst (1986) reminded us of Robert Peck's concept of ego transcendence. This is a way of assuring ourselves of a connection to a future we will not see by finding satisfaction in reflecting on those who will follow. This idea implies a capacity for enjoying the present and understanding that our participation, as an elder, in the present-day world makes a contribution to everyone's sense of continuity.

Our work with older men requires that we fully understand the impediments to achieving such transcendence. Older men are often tangled in the imperatives of their generation: be strong, be in charge, never give up, never give in, never cry. The older man in the consulting room of a woman, an age mate or not, will have to override the old narrative of superiority and dominance in order to work collaboratively toward a goal of peace and well-being in his later years. Some will have moved farther along on this path than others. At times, it is necessary for the woman therapist to establish some authority before the older male patient can trust the empathic connection offered. We can do this by articulating his concerns, by teaching him how therapy will work and how to be patient with the therapeutic process. For many older men, this will be their first experience in individual therapy.

Female therapists must be sure they have resolved their own issues around both gender and aging if they are to be helpful. Younger women may not have thought about what life will be like in later years and may need exposure to the issues via informal conversations with older friends or relatives. Fiction and film can provide insight as well. Jack Nicholson's film *About Schmidt* and Clint Eastwood's *Grand Torino* are two examples. And, for those who do not remember life in the 1960s and 1970s, Gail Collins's book *When Everything Changed* (2009) provides an accurate and readable account of the way the gender rules have changed over the past 50 years.

Of course, every patient's story is different from our own, but in working with older men, women may be forced to work harder to form an empathic connection. Women are accustomed to finding support in relationships with women, both personal and professional. Men do not often look for emotional support from male friends or relatives. The intimacy of the therapy relationship is difficult for older men, who may take many weeks to settle in. They may feel the need to entertain you with stories or to press you for a plan, for goals, for measures of progress. If we are unable to understand the main developmental tasks at hand for older male patients (affirming a contribution to the next generation and finding a peace and acceptance in the realities of the course of their life), we will not be able to identify ways to help them work through earlier developmental disruptions.

Older patients may not understand why we are interested in their early years or first relationships. They may be impatient for us to provide help for symptoms they experience presently. Men like action, and it is easy to get caught giving advice that is not needed or making suggestions that are obvious and superficial. After more than six months in therapy, one man in his 80s began, on his own, to list five positive things that happened each day. We laughed together at the resistance he would have felt had I suggested such a task myself. He had wanted my guidance and suggestions but would not have wanted to be told what to do. I had to reiterate my belief in the efficacy of psychodynamic psychotherapy many times and often repeated the psychoanalytic instruction to say whatever comes to mind. I tell him that it is our job together to connect the dots and to come to some sense of coherence, continuity, and contentment. We are still at work on this task. I understand that his sense of urgency is based in the reality that time may well be short. The principle challenge of all psychotherapy remains: to hold the trust in the psychotherapeutic process and to be patient while it unfolds.

REFERENCES

Bernardez, T. (2004). Studies in countertransference and gender: Female analyst/ male patient in two cases of childhood trauma. *Journal of the American Academy of Psychoanalysis and Dynamic Psychiatry, 32*(1), 231–254.

Cath, S. H. (1997). Loss and restitution in late life. In S. Akhtar & S. Kramer (Eds.), *The seasons of life* (pp. 129–156). New York, NY: Aronson.

Collins, G. (2009). *When everything changed: The amazing journey of American women from 1960 to the present.* New York, NY: Little & Brown.

Erikson, E. (1982). *The life cycle completed.* New York, NY: Norton.

Gornick, L. K. (1986). Developing a new narrative: The woman therapist and the male patient. *Psychoanalytic Psychology 3,* 299–325.

Koo, M. B. (2001). Eroticized transference in the male-patient female therapist
    dyad. *Journal of Psychotherapy Practice and Research, 10*(1), 28–36.
O'Reilly, J. (1980). *The girl I left behind.* New York, NY: Macmillan.
Viorst, J. (1986). *Necessary losses.* New York, NY: Simon and Schuster.

Sharing Our Experiences

14

Women's Voices Together

HOLLY BARLOW SWEET

SHARING OUR EXPERIENCES

For the final chapter, responses were collected about a series of questions not only for the authors of this book but also for other women who identify themselves as interested in men's issues and are members of a LISTSERV (women-spsmm@mit.edu) that focuses on women therapists working with men. The authors felt that, in their experience, female therapists are curious about how other female therapists work with men (and with women), especially for female clinicians who may not have learned a great deal about men's issues in their academic or professional training. Questions were based on what we thought new clinicians might want to know and on what had been asked of us in the past.

QUESTION 1: HOW DO PEOPLE REACT TO US WHEN WE SAY WE ARE INTERESTED IN MEN'S ISSUES?

De las Fuentes: The most common thing I notice is the initial slight knitting of the brows as if they are asking what their owner does not: "Huh?" I explain that the social construction of men and masculinity in the United States has unique variations depending on demographic differences (race, ethnicity, sexual orientation, class, ability, etc.). These constructions help define their group, subgroup, familial, and individual identities and their relationships to women, other men, and children in their various roles as father, brother, son, husband, colleague, boss, subordinate, and so on. That these constructions can be good or bad in that they can extend or constrict values, beliefs, and behaviors and impact men's relationships with themselves and others, sometimes taking them away from who and how they want to be. If the look I get from these colleagues remains unchanged, I sigh and simplify, "Men's issues are women's issues." Then they get it.

Farrell: Sometimes people are puzzled. I have a boys' project in schools, and this also causes some surprise.*

Harway: As a long-time member of Division 51, I am used to people's reactions to my telling them that I am interested in men's issues. Usually, there is some initial incredulity, followed by a question about why I, a feminist, am interested in men's issues. Of course, I explain that our relationships are systems, and that since most women relate to men in some capacity, as lovers, daughters, coworkers, or family members, we are all embedded in systems of relationships which require us to understand all stakeholders in the system, both men and women. And, as a result and as I describe in my chapter, I believe that women's fate is inexorably tied in with men's fate. It makes perfect sense that when we understand men and masculinity and help to bring about changes in their lives we also end up having an impact on the women in their lives. Therefore, I think that we all have a responsibility to study men's behavior and understand the factors that impinge on men's lives.

Logue: Positively and with curiosity and interest.

Morse: Most of my colleagues respond by saying something like, "What's the difference?" or "Why is that important?" Perhaps their response can be interpreted to mean that they may not see a need to educate themselves on the uniqueness of what it means to be a male in American society or acknowledge that men and women experience stimuli differently as their [socially constructed] filter is dissimilar. To assume that men and women are the same is perhaps as unethical as assuming that a native from China would be treated in the same manner as a client native to Africa—they are socialized differently, and therefore the techniques, approach, therapeutic alliance,

---

* Dr. Karen Farrell is director of training in psychology at Midwestern University and has taught "The Psychology of Gender," the "Psychology of Women," and "Diversity in Clinical Psychology." She currently runs a boys' project, StrongBoys, a psychoeducational program for middle school boys designed to keep the relational lives of boys open and assist them in expressing their feelings.

and so on would be adapted. Why would that principle be any different when working with females and males?

Newlin: Curiosity is the reaction I see the most when telling colleagues of my interest in men's issues. Although so many of us in this profession are cognizant of multicultural issues in counseling and psychotherapy, I have met colleagues who don't always think of men's issues as a separate area of multicultural knowledge. Colleagues who have been therapists for many more years than me have asked to have discussions with me about how best to work with men, how the issues they face are unique from women's issues, and where they can get more information about men as clients. It is always a pleasure and an honor for me to be asked to share what I know about something I am so passionate about.

Sweet: I have had nothing but interest from women I chat with on a personal basis about my involvement with men's issues and the importance of paying attention to men who have problems. Everyone seems a little disbelieving at first ("Men have problems? Really?") and then has a story to tell about some man in their lives who is struggling. Colleagues are also curious and often want to find out more. One book I have recommended time and time again is Terry Real's *I Don't Want to Talk About It*[*] because it seems so relevant to the men in the lives of women I have talked to. Men are also curious but in a sort of "what's a nice girl like you doing in a field like this?" way. I find that men really like to talk about all of this in a casual way (i.e., taking a rest after a doubles match in tennis) but are more guarded when it comes to anything more structured. As for colleagues, once they think about it for a while, they are generally very curious and want to pick my brain about their clients, students, and so on.

Weaver: I've gotten mixed reactions from both men and women. Some people think it's odd for a woman to be leading a men's group. However, some think that in the areas of relationships, communication, and parenting issues, men would seek assistance from a woman because they feel women are stronger in these areas. Some colleagues have also said that some men seek female therapists because they feel safer talking about their problems and feelings with a woman, who isn't competing with them or judging them.[†]

---

[*] Real, T. (1997). *I don't want to talk about it: Overcoming the secret legacy of male depression*. New York, NY: Scribner.

[†] Raelene S. Weaver is a licensed marriage and family therapist in San Jose, California. She works with men, women, couples, teens, and children in private practice and is currently in the process of forming a men's group.

QUESTION 2: IN WHAT WAYS, IF ANY, DOES OUR KNOWLEDGE OF MEN'S ISSUES AFFECT THE WAY WE WORK WITH FEMALE CLIENTS?

De las Fuentes: It is tremendously helpful to know how men's issues may contribute to feelings of disconnect many women feel in their relationships with men, regardless of their relational roles with them. Suggesting another way of thinking about a woman's interpretations of a man's behavior, motivations, beliefs, and so on (e.g., from "He loves his work more than the kids and me!" to "Perhaps one of the reasons he works so much is because part of his identity as a husband and father is to be a good provider") might help breach an impasse in their relationship.

Harway: Understanding men's issues has made me a better therapist to women clients. For instance, when I am working with a woman who is being abused by a man, my ability to understand the factors that underlie her partner's abusive behavior help me help her order a sequence of puzzling behaviors and interactions with the partner. Her understanding of the dynamics of abuse often allows her to feel more in control of her own life and better prepares her to protect herself against injury during a violent episode. Similarly, I think the authors of the chapters in this volume are most likely better prepared to help their women clients because most presentations in psychotherapy are the result of interactions with men.

Farrell: Wow! What a good question. I sometimes think that men's capacity to take some interpersonal events less personally is a wonderful skill that women, including myself, could do well to learn. I think putting relationships first without discrimination and sacrificing self-care breeds resentment in women.

Logue: I am much better able to help them understand, cope, and solve problems with men, in intimate, family, and work/professional relationships.

Morse: Interesting question! I thought I was pretty progressive thinking that I have an understanding of men's issues (as a female), and yet I've limited myself in considering how this knowledge could be progressed even further in my work with females. Ever since this question was posed, I've been listening to my female clients differently, but I will have to say that most of them are so angry with their male partners that advocating for men or educating females on the difficulties that men experience is going to be challenging. I'm not sure if I have to wait until their anger dissipates first or not. Also, I was watching an episode of the show *Heavy* a few nights ago, and it made me realize that women play a strong role in reinforcing society's messages in what it means to be a man. When the man arrived home after having spent 6 months at an eating disorders rehabilitation center, he was so overcome with emotion that he openly sobbed. His fiancée said to him, "Oh, don't cry." My heart went out to him, especially after she had come to the clinic within a month of his experience, sharing with the treatment facilitators that he was emotionally detached and she wanted to be closer to him and him to her. Maybe crying wasn't what she was asking for!? As female clinicians, it's important for us to understand men's socialization and get very comfortable with men stepping outside of the socialized norm lest we reinforce what we're trying to change.

Newlin: There are a couple of ways that my knowledge of men's issues affects the way I work with women. First, so many of the women that I see are in relationships with men, and these relationships inevitably get brought into the room when we are working together. My knowledge of men's issues helps me to hypothesize with women clients about what might be going on in that relationship from the men's point of view, especially if they are having relationship problems. Second, my interest in men's issues keeps me cognizant of gender roles and gender norms at all times when working with all of my clients, male or female. So I can't help but conceptualize all of my clients' issues and concerns by including how gender roles and norms have shaped who they are and the issues they bring to therapy.

Sweet: My knowledge of men's issues has had a huge impact on how I work with women. Because of my own personal and professional history in truly understanding the system of gender roles in which I grew up, I have found myself more liberated from enmeshed and negative thinking about "women as victims" and "men as perpetrators" and am eager to help my female clients gain more person power by knowledge.

Vasquez: Developing empathy and understanding for the experiences of both men and women allows us to intervene with our clients, both men and women, from a more complete context. Understanding and assessing the ways that society constructs gender, in both functional and dysfunctional ways, allows us to support men and women become the best that they can be as they work to improve functional and healthy behaviors, attitudes, ways of thinking, and rid themselves of those that are not healthy.

Weaver: I think because I do have such an affinity for male issues, when working with couples, the male feels less likely to be "ganged up on" by two females. I feel confident in feeling empathy and positive regard for both partners. I think a man feels more comfortable telling his side of the story. In working with female clients, looking at how they can make healthy choices, accept responsibility for their decisions, and not going into a relationship wanting to "change" their partner or "settle" for something they don't want, are areas that are likely to be covered.

QUESTION 3: ARE THERE ANY IMPORTANT DIFFERENCES IN THE WAY YOU WORK WITH FEMALE CLIENTS VERSUS MALE CLIENTS?

De las Fuentes: My first response was, "Not really," but on further reflection, I often find myself helping a man understand why his partner asks him to listen not fix, "do" not "help" (e.g., "He's another adult in the house, he needs to do his share, but I have to beg and when he does do it, he calls it 'helping'!" or "Why does he call it 'babysitting,' but when I do it I am being a mom?") and understand that tending and monitoring a relationship does not only mean whether and how frequently they have sex.

Farrell: I think I listen more acutely because I don't assume that I will understand. I also think I am careful about the affection which naturally develops in long, good therapeutic work. I do not want to be misunderstood.

Logue: Yes, although there are many exceptions. More typically, women want more empathy and listening instead of solution-focused brainstorming of options.

Morse: I don't think it's as easy as saying I work with [all] males this way and [all] females that way. Due to the fact that I'm female, I'm knowledgeable and experienced on how females [typically] converse and relate to one another. Working with men is at a much slower pace. As a female clinician, there are a certain percentage of males, usually traditional males, that are wary of working with a female—they either have poor attitudes about women, in general, they don't believe that a female could actually relate to them on their particular issues due to their maleness, or they're intimidated by females as they consider females as "the other." The work I do with men is to understand and to be patient with them as they gain comfort with considering me as something other than a bitch, the other, something to be objectified, manipulated, or conquered.

Newlin: Although I use humor, where appropriate, with all of my clients, I think that with my male clients my humor comes out much more often. I have found that humor is a wonderful tool in making my male clients more comfortable in an experience that can be unfamiliar and anxiety provoking for them. I have also learned to allow more time for the therapeutic alliance to develop. I'm more patient in my expectations regarding how quickly my male clients will be in opening up to me. Working from a cognitive stance before digging down to the emotions with my male clients seems to be more productive. Additionally, I see myself having to assist my male clients with naming their emotions more than I do with my female clients. If I can get them to see the emotions behind the thoughts, the work we do together is just as rich and profound as my work with female clients.

Sweet: I think that female clients tend to form more of a relationship with me in terms of ongoing and regular connection (i.e., weekly meetings, consistent openness, letting me into their emotional lives more openly). I also can resonate more with what they say, feel, and do—there's kind of an "us in this together" mentality that I don't usually feel with men. I also am more overtly demonstrative with women. I might give them a light touch on the shoulder or a hug when it seems appropriate. I almost never do this with a male client.

QUESTION 4: HAVE YOU HAD TO OVERCOME ANY STEREOTYPES ABOUT MEN IN WORKING WITH MALE CLIENTS?

De las Fuentes: Yes, of course. For example, for years I could not understand what men (especially able-bodied straight White men) could possibly want or need from me, beyond sex. I erroneously believed that men's issues with hegemony could only be worked through by them and them alone. As a result, I unfairly generalized my knowledge and experiences of a few and viewed most with skepticism. While I still harbor some stereotypic "expectations," I love it when a man blows them apart with what he says or does. For instance, recently, in couples therapy, a man complained that his wife is verbally aggressive with him, and as a result he becomes fatigued, weary, and wonders if their marriage is going to make it. I asked, "What happens to you, inside, when she does this?" He responded with, "I take a deep breath, move in closer, and open myself up more." WHAT?? "Wait a minute, say that again?" I asked, and he did. So cool!

Farrell: I have had to overcome many stereotypes (i.e., men can't talk about their feelings, men are not empathic, men are unaware of their feelings, and others). Sometimes this is true, but I have never (yet) treated a man who has been unable to make any gains at all voicing feelings, developing empathic abilities, or becoming more self-aware and self-reflective. Many men believe that women think/feel like they do; women make the same error.

Logue: Because in my childhood my experiences with men were so positive, I am fortunate that for the most part I generally have not had to overcome negative male stereotypes. In my experience, the ongoing challenge has been to encourage other clinicians to be aware of overcoming theirs. On the other hand, I believe that clinicians who do bring to the consulting room their own negative countertransferences to men—rooted in the past—are not doomed to failure. Just as I continually monitor my inclination to see the glass as half full, those who tend to see men through the lens of a painful or disappointing past must pay attention to their difficulty with trust or difficulty perceiving the positive. They will achieve better outcomes with their male patients if they do this.

Newlin: I think I have indeed overcome many of my stereotypes about men in working with them in the therapy room. I still have to be cognizant whenever I find myself thinking stereotypically about men and remind myself to not assume anything about a man until I have gotten to know him as an individual. The most dominant stereotype that I think I have been able to overcome is that men are unemotional, insensitive creatures who just can't "do" emotions. I've been privileged to see the very tender and vulnerable side of my male clients. With every client, I am reminded that men are not the bumbling, unfeeling characters we see portrayed every day in much of our culture's media.

Weaver: I think in American society, there is the thinking that "men always want sex." Although I loved the movie *When Harry Met Sally*, I have heard from some men that even though the instinct to "nail" that Victoria's Secret model exists, in reality, they'd "like to get to know her a little first." The stereotype that sharing feelings = vulnerability and crying = weakness is certainly strong for men, but in a safe environment, or in privacy, I think men are able to express sadness or grief with a little more acceptance these days. When I think of John Boehner, I wonder how far the comfort zone goes for crying, though.

QUESTION 5: WHAT HAS BEEN PARTICULARLY REWARDING OR CHALLENGING FOR YOU WHEN WORKING WITH MALE CLIENTS?

De las Fuentes: The most rewarding part of my work with men is to support them as they break the stereotypic "expectations" (i.e., values, beliefs, thoughts, behaviors, etc.) they have of themselves and others as well as those that others have of them so they can have and enjoy more authentic relationships and ways of being. Some men whose insight is so compromised by their strong adherence to stereotypic "expectations" that they oppress themselves and others are particularly challenging to me.

Farrell: The challenge has been to remember what I believe is some men's sense of shame for needing any help at all. I also remember not to "go after" feelings too hard early on. The rewards come when I "get it" about the particular way a man does experience something and how surprised we both are. In couples work, when I understand that this is a good man who is truly befuddled about why his partner is so upset and can interpret this to his partner, it is very rewarding. Recognition of the subtle "put-downs" both women and men do across genders has helped me recognize this in myself.

Logue: One of the personal challenges in working with male clients is my tendency to bring into the treatment room the positive countertransferences that are rooted in my childhood. While this is usually helpful, it can sometimes have a downside. A blind spot with regard to patients—or what is known as a *scotoma*—to negativity, anger, disappointment, sorrow, resentment, rage, and hostility is a highly undesirable factor that leads to unanalyzed negative transference or destructive character traits. A frequent result is that the patient unconsciously acts out conflicts in his or her life rather than analyzing and talking about them in therapy. In short, missing negative transferences can lead to unsuccessful and incomplete treatment outcomes.

Newlin: I have found that working with men in the psychotherapy room has given me a new understanding of the issues that men are dealing with in their lives and the ways they find to cope with those issues and concerns. It is so rewarding to me to help men gain insight into their distress and to help them understand themselves. Each male client I work with challenges me to adjust my expectations and preconceived notions about what our work together will look like. This in turn keeps me flexible in my approach with all of my clients.

Weaver: I think providing a safe place for men to express difficult feelings regarding romantic relationships has been very rewarding. I think being able to tell their side of the story is important. It can be challenging getting to a deeper level with male clients. I find for some, they like a little light bantering before getting to serious issues.

QUESTION 6: WHAT ARE IMPORTANT FACTORS TO CONSIDER FOR WOMEN WHO WANT TO WORK WITH MEN?

Farrell: Be self-aware of stereotypes. Sometimes what looks like "coldness" is really being frozen. Many men work their hearts out for their families and don't express their absolute loyalty and commitment in words but "love by doing."

Morse: Patience, patience, patience. Compassion, compassion, compassion.

Newlin: I think one of the most important things to remember is that no matter how much one works with male clients, or no matter how many books one reads about masculinity, men's issues, or how to work with male clients, one has to remember that every male client is an individual, and that everything we read may not apply to a particular male client. Each client is an individual, and you have to see each male client from his individual lens, not from a one-size-fits-all mind-set regarding masculinity and men's issues.

Wilbur: I continue to believe that men and women as individuals are more alike than different, and that the differences we observe and work to understand are often cultural artifacts. Developmental tasks may be tackled in different sequences but converge in later life when coming to a place of acceptance and peace is the essential task for all. I approach all my patients from a developmental perspective. What times in life were optimal? Where were the snags? What is the history of loss or trauma that had an impact on the growth and development? How about genetic or medical factors? What is causing the current suffering, and what are the roots of the distress? In this culture, men start out with a presumption of power. Personal strengths and talents often seem buried by disappointments and failures. Therapeutic excavation helps restore a steady base from which to proceed. Women, in contrast, are trained to accept a one-down position and need help questioning this assumption and articulating their personal strengths as assets. As I worked on this chapter, I looked hard for differences in my approach to men and women and for differences in male and female patients' responses to me. There is no doubt that as a woman I am able to identify more readily with the experiences of other women, and at times it seems that the empathic connection is easier to establish. Women get that I get it. Men seem surprised when I remember the details of their lives, particularly the emotional details, and may be less inclined to believe in the restorative power of relationships. They begin to feel better but don't know quite why. Always I come back to the dialectic between these two dynamics, our sense of self and our capacity for relationship. One informs the other, over time, across relationships, regardless of our gender.

LEARNING ABOUT OURSELVES
AND FROM EACH OTHER

The final question asked of the authors of this book was what they may have learned about themselves or others as a result of writing their chapters and participating in author retreats.

De las Fuentes: My chapter gave me an opportunity to reflect on my relationship with my father and understand how powerful he is to me beyond his "role" as father; he is the foundation of my understanding of men's psychology, empathy toward them, and relationships with all men.

Logue: I've learned a lot at the retreat in California about how different women clinicians focus and emphasize different aspects of gender-related therapy, and how factors such as age, experience, orientation, and type of practice appear to affect our perspective.

Morse: After reading Carolyn Steigmeier's chapter, I will use the term *therapeutic friendship* to describe the perspective I've found helpful to use in my work with males (Carolyn uses "professional friendship" to describe this phenomenon in her executive coaching work). That phrase works for me. Holly's chapter was so helpful in reminding me of the difficulties that men have expressing themselves, and it's wonderful to hear that every once in a while, lest I forget. The experience in writing the chapter helped remind me how important it is as a therapist to understand how our belief patterns of what it means to be male have influenced us as human beings and then as therapists. We need to pull back the curtain and look inside about how our ways of relating were established, enforced, or changed. If we fail to peel back the layers of our belief systems about men and masculinity, then we are doomed to reinforce, usually maladaptive belief systems, on our male clients . . . and our female clients.

Newlin: I've learned that I'm still learning! Every male (and female) client I see is a learning experience for me. As I wrote my chapter, I found myself recalling male clients I've seen in the past and thinking about the male clients I am currently seeing. I'm reminded that this passion I have for working with men is something that is constantly morphing and growing, and that each male client that comes through my door teaches me something new and continues to feed my interest in their unique concerns and issues.

Sweet: I have thoroughly enjoyed working with the book's authors, sharing stories, and finding like-minded women in the field of psychology who care about men's issues but stay true to their feminist roots. I am more convinced than ever that women who are educated about the psychology of men can be excellent therapists to men, despite backgrounds that might have predisposed them to not being able to feel as much compassion towards men as towards women. I was inspired by the personal and professional journeys of these women and have also learned more about myself as a result of writing my own chapters. Like Jeri Newlin, I too feel I am still learning, which makes my work in this field that much more enriching and exciting.

BEYOND THE ZERO-SUM GAME

In the last of the author retreats we held, we came up with the idea that we need to have a name for the kind of work we did with men, something that captured the idea that feminists (i.e., people like us who believe in equal rights and opportunities for women) could focus on women's issues but still have compassion for men. The old view is that paying attention to men's needs gets in the way of helping women (the zero-sum game approach). Our view is that women benefit when men are helped (the win-win approach). We thought about what this would be, and what we came up with is the idea of "fourth-wave feminism." We wanted to honor the roots of feminism since it has played such a vital role in so many of our lives, yet we wanted to acknowledge that feminism is not about being antimale or "just" profemale as is unfortunately sometimes believed today. Feminism for us is about acknowledging equal rights and opportunities for women and men. If women have been shortchanged in the areas of the workplace, academia, power, and respect by sexist attitudes, men have also been shortchanged by rigid gender role expectations that get in the way of leading productive and emotionally healthy lives. By exploring the impact of gender role norms on ourselves as well as our male clients, and by having compassion for the suffering of men, we will become not only better therapists but hopefully better people in our own lives.

Afterword

Understanding the Impact of Therapy With Men From a Male Perspective

FREDRIC E. RABINOWITZ

INTRODUCTION

It is a privilege to have my voice heard in this excellent and needed book for female therapists who work with men. Just reading about each woman's personal and professional experience gives me insight into why these women have gone into the field of psychotherapy with men. It takes a certain type of female therapist not only to relate well to guys but also to understand them on a deeper level. By enjoying the challenge of therapy and coaching with men, the authors of the book serve as strong role models for female therapists who see male clients in their work. While it is still true that many men are reluctant clients, there are specific therapeutic skills that can enhance the quality and depth of psychotherapy with men. These authors have outlined core themes that are significant for most male clients. These include the need not to be seen as weak or vulnerable, difficulty identifying and expressing emotion, and preference for taking action over just talking and accepting problems. By enjoying working with men as clients and seeing through their socialization as struggling human beings, these female therapists have a clear vision about how to help. Men may not want handholding, pity, or "over-the-top" empathy but rather want to be understood, appreciated for their strengths, and respected as problem solvers who have run into something that they cannot seem to master right now. Unlike many female clients who appreciate an opportunity to vent emotionally, male clients may have to learn first that the therapist can be trusted and only then will they be able to show how they think and feel.

MY EXPERIENCE AS A CLIENT WITH FEMALE THERAPISTS

As a clinician who has primarily worked with men in individual, couples, and group therapy over the past 30 years, I have relied on my therapeutic understanding of what it means to be a man from both the therapist and client side of the relationship. This inner knowledge has allowed me to be patient, empathic, and real with the men who have consulted me. My sensitivity to male shame and the need for a man to protect himself comes from both my own journey and thousands of hours of therapeutic work with all types of men. At different points in my life, I have consulted male and female therapists to get through impasses. At the time, I was not really attuned to the impact of gender, but through my own experience and analysis, I have come to understand how both the female and male therapists I encountered had an impact on me.

I share a short history of my personal counseling experiences as a man with female therapists with the hope of adding some true life support to the insightful perspectives shared in this book. My first encounter with a female therapist occurred when I was 21. I had just graduated from college and was now truly a "freshman" in life. As a successful student at Ithaca College with an enriched social life, I had separated from my parents in the supportive college town cocoon of Ithaca, New York. My homecoming trip to my parents' house in suburban Philadelphia the summer after graduation brought me in touch with who I was without the cocoon. It almost felt like the last 4 years had not happened. I felt young, almost back to being the adolescent I was before I went away. I wanted to run but did not know where. My girlfriend, who had been a year ahead of me, was in Washington, D.C. I applied to some clinical psychology master's programs and decided to head to Baltimore for graduate study. As someone interested in doing psychotherapy for a career, I rationalized that going to counseling myself would be an important experience. I knew I had issues, especially around dependence on my parents and my girlfriend. I desperately wanted to be strong and independent but felt scared and lost by myself.

As a poor graduate student, I qualified for a $5 sliding scale fee at the local mental health center. I was assigned to Emily, a social worker, who specialized in family therapy. As I sat in the waiting room, surrounded by children and adults, mainly from lower socioeconomic backgrounds, I got scared. As the minutes on the clock ticked, it took all my strength not to walk out. I looked around and saw some people with schizophrenia talking to themselves. I saw sad faces. I wondered if I was really that bad off. If Emily had not showed up right on the hour and called my name, I know I would have been out of there.

We walked into a small windowless room with a love seat and two chairs. I sat in one of the chairs. Emily seemed to be of Asian descent, in her mid-30s. She had kind eyes. Emily leaned forward, clipboard in her hand, and asked me what I wanted to work on. At that moment, I had no idea. I had forgotten why I had come in. I blurted something about being in a transition. I was starting to sweat. "Tell me about your family." That I could do, at least superficially. I first gave her the unblemished view of a tight, strong, Jewish upbringing with professional parents. Only when she said, "It must be hard to live up to those expectations," did I notice my body. I had butterflies in my stomach and a sensation of my throat being tight. I did not know what to say. She saved me in the moment. "It's not easy to be here, I know," she said. My stomach felt more relaxed. I had no vocabulary for my feelings, so it was all just sensations. "I thought we would just start by taking some history about your life growing up." That put it back on me. "Sure. What do you want to know?" "Just start when you were young and bring me up to date if you can." I spent the rest of that first session wandering around my childhood, talking about my brothers and going easy on my parents. I felt relieved to get out of there that day, but out of duty I had scheduled another appointment.

As I look back on the therapy I did with Emily, I am surprised at how frightened I was. I was terrified that I would be found out. Underneath my graduate student exterior was a frightened little boy who wanted to please. I wanted Emily to like me. I was more attentive the next times I was there and noted where she did her degree and enthusiastically explored my family dynamics from a Bowenian perspective. It was informative but often intellectual. I kept it from going too deep because I did not want to break down, and I wanted her to think that I was bright and insightful. I wanted to be her most "together" patient. Even though we never made the connection, I treated Emily the way I treated my mother. I was afraid that my mother would be angry and critical, so I did everything I could to be the "good boy." In retrospect, I was fortunate to have a female therapist like Emily to break the ice of my first counseling experience. She respected my boundaries and never pushed me too hard. She often said what I was feeling, so I did not have to struggle to come up with words I had not learned. As I took courses in psychotherapy in the program, I heightened my awareness of her techniques and perspective. Ironically, I got a job as a drug counselor in my second year and "didn't have time" anymore for therapy.

My next experience with a female therapist came a couple of years later when I was in my doctoral program in counseling psychology at the University of Missouri. One of the benefits of my previous therapy had been Emily's suggestion to keep a journal. While I had kept a drawing journal since my junior year in college, Emily had encouraged me to try to use words. Art had been my emotional language. Writing down my thoughts and feelings about my experiences had given me better ways to understand myself. My journals became rich sources of self-understanding, especially as I gained a vocabulary to describe my varying emotional reactions. Dr. Chiasson was a Jungian analyst who specialized in dream interpretation. She was in her late 60s and seemed very wise. I never knew much about her. I seemed to carry a positive grandmother-like transference with her. Our therapy consisted of us interpreting my dreams each week and connecting the "underground currents" of my inner self. At first, I was skeptical of this analysis, but within 6 months it became the most powerful type of therapy I had ever encountered. The story that the dreams told was of a boy who wanted to be a man. He had all kinds of frightening adventures that tested him. He was attacked and left alone. He experienced loss and feelings of being unacceptable. The boy wanted to please so much that he hurt. I had not cried in a long time, but I used to cry during our sessions. Analyzing the dreams was like watching a dark movie about my life. In her steady, calm, and grandmotherly way, Dr. Chiasson was able to ground me. I could get in touch with my shame and my incongruence between what I projected through my persona and what existed in my unconscious. I will never forget the breakthroughs of emotion that I thought I would never be able to feel or talk about.

My marriage to my college girlfriend, who was also a graduate student, deteriorated. I was certainly more in touch with my emotions, but this meant I felt the pain. I had only my dissertation left. She was in the doctoral program, a strong feminist, who had a way of talking about herself and our relationship that made me feel like I would never be good enough in her eyes. There was always something we should be working on, but I often had no idea what it was. I was still dependent on her opinions and found myself depressed when I could not please her. The "good boy" pleaser issue that I had struggled with in my female relationships was taking me down hard. Fortunately, my previous therapy and therapeutic training had given me more insight. I began to fight back rather than beat myself up all the time. It also meant the end of the marriage. As I stood up for myself, I was abandoned. My fear came true that if I was fully me in the relationship, I would be unacceptable. We briefly tried couples counseling, but the motivation for my wife to make our relationship work was outweighed by a new relationship she had already entered. I ended up scared and alone.

I was naked emotionally. I felt deep sadness and a sense of loss that left me teary at times. In the daytime, I coped by doing. I worked on my dissertation and took a job as a psychologist at the local psychiatric facility. This kept my mind busy and distracted me from the pain. On Halloween, my loneliness subsided. I met a woman who worshipped me. It was exactly what I needed: validation and lots of sex. At the end of my marriage, being sexually intimate had become so uncomfortable. I felt unattractive and undesirable. Like many men who have been wounded in their primary relationship, having a new partner want me sexually brought back some lost self-esteem. Unfortunately, the intensity of the relationship was like a hot flame that went from one extreme to the next. The rebound was painful. I felt out of control and scared that I would be trapped in this not very healthy relationship. This precipitated my consulting a female social worker, Dorothy. Dorothy was a realist. She confronted me on why I did not set boundaries or make my own decisions in the relationships. My good boy issue was now staring me in the face, and I needed to take action. Dorothy was all about action. She saw that I was intellectually aware of needing to set boundaries and take care of myself. For four straight weeks, she confronted me on why I was not acting on my awareness. Finally I did. It was hard, but it was empowering. I ended the wild relationship and initiated the divorce with my partner. Dorothy's action-oriented approach appealed to my internalized male socialization that said, "Take care of your business" and "Don't wallow in your pain." I did not linger in therapy. I felt my power and wanted to play it out, rather than talk about it.

I graduated with my doctorate, took a 1-year visiting faculty job in California at a small liberal arts school, and experienced my aloneness with vigor rather than sadness. I was so engaged with my temporary position that I was taken by surprise when I had to reapply for the tenure track job. I felt I had earned it. I was physically sick during my interview and teaching session. I did not prepare enough. I applied for other jobs. There was a long delay on letting me know if I got the tenure track position. Other schools were asking me to make a commitment. I really wanted to stay, but if my school did not tell me soon, I was going to have to leave for another position on the East Coast. I became anxious and depressed. Maybe they did not want me. I took the risk to decline my other offers, leaving me with the possibility that I would not have any job. They waited until the day before graduation in May to tell me. Although I was hired, I felt bad. I felt I had not done a good job, or they would have offered it to me sooner. While most of this was circumstantial, it touched off my issues of potential abandonment and loss.

I decided to spend a week at the Esalen Institute in Big Sur on the California coast that June in a Gestalt workshop led by Christine Price. This strong, intuitive, and attractive woman facilitated my next therapeutic experience. She used Gestalt techniques to have me connect to my internal contradictions. I spoke to the empty chair version of my mother and ex-wife. I had a top dog-underdog dialogue with my independent and dependent self. Finally, I encountered my loneliness in an image of a young boy abandoned emotionally. It was healing not only to work on my issues but also to be around others who were vulnerable in their struggles. This therapeutic experience also cemented my perspective about the importance of having witnesses to support and validate changes that occur in the group context. Within months of this experience, I approached another male therapist in my hometown and got a community men's therapy group off the ground that continues to flourish to this day.

When I look back at my counseling experiences with female therapists, I realize that I was less intimidated to approach them for help than a male, who I fantasized would be more critical of my inner world. For me, being with a female therapist really helped me look at my dynamics with significant women in my life. Inherent in the process, regardless of orientation, the female therapists helped me explore my emotional reactions to interpersonal situations. I often repeated the pattern of trying to caretake my mother in my relationships with women. I found that women challenged me to own and identify my caretaking dynamic and my desire to please. I projected onto each of the therapists an element of my dependency, and in each case, I was made to take responsibility for my actions. If I was to become autonomous, I needed to listen to myself, and each of these women reinforced that element. By identifying the pattern, I was able to trust myself more and embrace the process of learning about myself. My next choice of a life partner did not fit the mother-pleasing pattern. This was directly influenced by the work I did with female therapists.

WHEN A MALE THERAPIST MIGHT BE
KEY IN WORKING WITH MEN

While I am a strong advocate of the work that women clinicians do for men, I think it is important to consider when it might be beneficial for men to work with male therapists. In my own development, I noticed a difference in my therapy experiences with female and male therapists. There were some issues I did not talk to female therapists about. These included details about my sexuality, my mixed reactions to my father, my role as a man in my family and in the culture, my competitive nature, and my ambivalence about male friendship. It was easier to avoid these issues. As a client with a male therapist, I noticed fear of judgment but a paradoxical comfort level. I believe it is an unspoken acknowledgment of having the same body and socialization. Instead of having to explain myself, I feel like I am understood. There are fewer questions and more statements of empathy about the male journey. I have noticed that I easily projected a brother and father transference onto my male therapists. Most of my deeper work on understanding my complex and competitive relationship with my father came in my work with two significant male clinicians. It was not that I was unaware of these issues before with female therapists, but rather they were hard to bring up in our sessions.

In my own practice, I have noticed that in individual sessions and in the men's group, the issues of mixed feelings about father, male social-ization, competition, and sex are a good part of what we discuss. I notice that I can more easily use male metaphors and analogies with my male clients. Often, we talk about less-deep topics before diving into what is going on emotionally. It is not unusual to comment about sports, weather, or driving directions as we ease into more difficult material. Self-disclosure as a male therapist with a male client has been beneficial in breaking the ice and encouraging more openness from my male cli-ents. I have noticed that although there is a strong professional apprecia-tion of my therapeutic role from my clients, there is also a friendliness that permeates our work together. Regardless of sexual orientation or ethnicity, I find that we are fellow travelers in a world where we have been given male bodies and treated by others in a certain way because of our maleness. It is not that a female therapist cannot approach deeper male issues; it just has a different twist. The female therapist may really get what a man is saying, but because of our socialization, there is a little less trust that she can fully empathize with the male experience.

HOW FEMALE THERAPISTS CAN BEST HELP MALE CLIENTS

After reading the chapters in this book, I am even more convinced that female clinicians can work effectively with men. It is apparent that the authors like men and are able to convey this acceptance and care in a way in which men respond. Any signs of judgment or disapproval are likely to result in less sharing and less-productive therapeutic results. The female clinicians in this book are male friendly and willing to go to where the men actually are, rather than where the clinicians think the clients should be.

For me, it was initially safer to see a female therapist to talk about my emotions than it would have been a male therapist. I was used to see-ing women as understanding and being more expert on the emotional level. In retrospect, I was afraid that a male therapist would judge me as a "wimp" when I discussed my inner life. My father was a strong, traditional male who did not show much emotion. It has been my expe-rience as a psychologist that young men are a bit intimidated with older males. Older males have been in authority roles and thus are perceived as less understanding of vulnerability and inner doubt. In the men's group, younger men often project father and competitor images onto the older guys. In some ways, it is easier to talk to a woman, who takes on the mother, sister, or girlfriend projection. For many men, this is more comfortable and feels like it will be less judgmental. Ultimately, it is important to be aware of where a man is in his psychological development to know how to best approach him.

My sense is that if a woman clinician shows a deep understanding of a man's hesitancy to open up, she will become more aligned with him. By displaying sensitivity with how she uses language and with how powerful shame is in men's lives, the female therapist can make a huge difference for male clients. While cultural expectations make many men more comfortable opening up with women therapists, it takes a very special empathic response to have men talk about issues like sex, anger, and self-doubt. Many men want to please the women in their lives, so they are prone to speak in more muted and less-shameful tones about these significant issues.

When a man says, "I really shouldn't talk about this," it is an opportunity to say, "Try me out." When a man knows he can curse or say something that is not "politically correct," without judgment on your part, he begins to trust you. Often, men need to express anger at a particular woman or female behavior before working through their inner issues. It is important for you not to take it personally or to try to defend women when a man is feeling inadequate or challenged by a strong female in his life. By understanding his frustration, he will eventually own his projection. But, if you shame him or criticize him for his opinion, he will shut down and not talk about it. As many of the authors of this book state, to work effectively with men, one has to have worked through one's own psychological conflicts with men in one's life. Otherwise, it can be easier for a man to trigger an emotional reaction in female therapists around sexuality, rejection, pornography, and the objectification of women. By having empathy for his particular experience, the deeper underlying feelings of anger, hurt, and sadness can be better explored.

Finally, it is important to focus on strengths rather than weakness with men, at least initially. Men already feel inadequate coming to treatment. By understanding how a man copes with adversity and by supporting his attempts to do the right thing, a female therapist is likely to find that her male client will be more trusting and less afraid to show his inner emotions. By having an empathic understanding of a man's socialization and demonstrating it with language and metaphor, the female therapist is more likely to be successful and effective in working with male clients.

INDEX